Fundamentals of Islamic Finance and Banking

Fundamentals of Islamic Finance and Banking

SYEDA FAHMIDA HABIB

WILEY

This edition first published 2018
© 2018 Syeda Fahmida Habib

Registered office
John Wiley & Sons Ltd, The Atrium, Southern Gate, Chichester, West Sussex, PO19 8SQ, United Kingdom

For details of our global editorial offices, for customer services and for information about how to apply for permission to reuse the copyright material in this book please see our website at www.wiley.com.

Wiley publishes in a variety of print and electronic formats and by print-on-demand. Some material included with standard print versions of this book may not be included in e-books or in print-on-demand. If this book refers to media such as a CD or DVD that is not included in the version you purchased, you may download this material at http://booksupport.wiley.com. For more information about Wiley products, visit www.wiley.com.

Designations used by companies to distinguish their products are often claimed as trademarks. All brand names and product names used in this book are trade names, service marks, trademarks or registered trademarks of their respective owners. The publisher is not associated with any product or vendor mentioned in this book.

Limit of Liability/Disclaimer of Warranty: While the publisher and author have used their best efforts in preparing this book, they make no representations or warranties with respect to the accuracy or completeness of the contents of this book and specifically disclaim any implied warranties of merchantability or fitness for a particular purpose. It is sold on the understanding that the publisher is not engaged in rendering professional services and neither the publisher nor the author shall be liable for damages arising herefrom. If professional advice or other expert assistance is required, the services of a competent professional should be sought.

Library of Congress Cataloging-in-Publication Data

Names: Habib, Syeda Fahmida, author.
Title: Fundamentals of Islamic finance and banking / by Syeda Fahmida Habib.
Description: Chichester, West Sussex, United Kingdom : John Wiley & Sons, 2018. | Series: Wiley finance series | Includes bibliographical references and index. |
Identifiers: LCCN 2018014020 (print) | LCCN 2018014740 (ebook) | ISBN 9781119371045 (pdf) | ISBN 9781119371038 (epub) | ISBN 9781119371007 (pbk.)
Subjects: LCSH: Finance—Religious aspects—Islam. | Finance—Islamic countries. | Banks and banking—Religious aspects—Islam. | Banks and banking—Islamic countries.
Classification: LCC HG187.4 (ebook) | LCC HG187.4 .H33 2018 (print) | DDC 332.0917/67—dc23
LC record available at https://lccn.loc.gov/2018014020

Cover Design: Wiley
Cover Images: © Denis Burdin/Shutterstock; © Aun Photographer/Shutterstock; © Wang An Qi/Shutterstock; © Pichu/Shutterstock

Set in 10/12pt SabonLTStd by SPi Global, Chennai, India

Printed in Great Britain by TJ International Ltd, Padstow, Cornwall, UK

10 9 8 7 6 5 4 3 2 1

This book is dedicated to my parents, my friend and husband Anwar Habib, my daughter Anika and son Ishraq, my sister Fauzia and my many, many students, who have always inspired and motivated me. Thank you all for being my family and for being there for me always, with your love and trust in me.

Contents

CHAPTER 2

CHAPTER 3

CHAPTER 8
Salam 145

CHAPTER 9
Istisna 155

List of Figures

List of Tables

Acknowledgements

Writing a textbook on a still-developing subject is a lonely journey through a less traversed path that you chart for yourself. As I walked this path, I worked hard and long, and came across many interesting resource materials and people as I researched and they all shaped my learning with their work, their ideas and encouragement. They not only formed the references of this book, but helped complete the project.

I spent 22 years of my life in Dubai as the city worked towards playing a bigger role in the development of Islamic finance and banking. I spent a large part of this time teaching at the Higher Colleges of Technology, and there at some point I became the team leader to develop and lead courses related to Islamic finance and banking. I was encouraged to complete a diploma on the subject from the Institute of Islamic Banking and Insurance, London and certification from the Chartered Institute of Securities and Investment, UK. Islamic finance and banking was the topic of my doctoral thesis and all of this laid the path for me to write this book; as a long-time instructor in the areas of Islamic finance and banking, I felt the need for more structured textbooks designed for colleges and universities.

This was a journey that was often difficult, and often challenging, but towards the end became much more exciting than it was at the start. I found the motivation somewhere within myself, as I continued in this life-changing journey. Thank you to all who were part of my journey.

About the Author

SYEDA FAHMIDA HABIB

Dr Syeda Fahmida Habib is a passionate, student-centred educator with 23 years of teaching experience at universities and colleges. Her core teaching areas are finance and banking. Fahmida has also taught accounting, marketing and general management courses. She has been involved in textbook writing, curricula, course material and assessment development, as well as managing teaching teams. Fahmida completed her DBA from SMC University, Zürich and has a Masters in Applied Finance from Macquarie University, Sydney plus an MBA, majoring in marketing, from the Institute of Business Administration. Fahmida believes that learning happens when the material is adapted to the learner's abilities and interest. She has great rapport with her students and colleagues. She strives to instil in her students her own passion for lifelong learning, and learning beyond borders. Fahmida began her teaching career with Australia's Wollongong University and then spent 19 years with the Higher Colleges of Technology in the United Arab Emirates. Currently she teaches at the School of Continuing Studies, York University, Canada. Earlier in her academic career, Fahmida spent five valuable years in the industry, in multiple organizations gaining experience in business consultancies, feasibilities, planning and control.

This book is the culmination of the author's extensive teaching experience in finance and banking in general, and Islamic finance and banking specifically, as well as her research and interactions with industry participants in the Middle East and South-East Asia.

Preface

Modern Islamic finance and banking is a little more than half a century old compared with interest-based conventional banking that has been around since the 14th century, originating in Florence. Over these few decades, Islamic finance and banking has been able to make a place for itself in the global finance industry, showing considerable growth.

Islamic finance and banking is based on the rules and regulations arising from Shariah or Islamic law, which is an indispensable part of the Muslim faith. Its striking difference from the well-established conventional finance and banking lies in the prohibition of interest as a basis for financial intermediation, as well as other prohibitions on trading in financial risk, speculations, gambling, as well as any dealings with alcohol, pork, adult entertainment or immoral media, etc.

Religiously oriented Muslims constitute its major customers, though this niche alternative finance and banking sector has aroused the interest of non-Muslims as well, since Islamic banks profess to be more conservative and have ethical and social responsibility objectives. The oil boom and the establishment of OPEC brought affluence to many Muslim-majority countries, along with a renewed awareness of their need to conduct their financial dealings within the Shariah rules, and this served as a major catalyst for the establishment of Islamic financial institutions in Muslim-majority countries in the Middle East, South and South-East Asia and Africa.

The global Muslim population constitutes a quarter of the total world population, and some of them belong to the rich oil-producing nations. To meet their demands, several major players in the conventional finance industry have shown interest and entered the Islamic finance and banking sector in Europe, North America and Australia.

As Islamic finance and banking moves forward and aims to compete as a reliable alternative to the centuries-old conventional banking, its biggest challenge is the significant lack of knowledge about this unique banking system among stakeholders – customers, competitors, employees, regulators and the public. Customers, both Muslim and non-Muslim, do not fully understand Islamic banking: how it operates, what are its uniqueness and benefits, and how it differs from conventional banking.

From the Islamic finance and banking industry's perspective, a major hurdle is the shortage of manpower, both in respect of employees with Islamic banking as well as conventional banking skills and Shariah scholars with some knowledge of finance and banking. Educational initiatives and training opportunities are of the utmost importance to drive growth further. Major challenges in Islamic finance education and training are the lack of institutions offering specialized programmes and courses designed for Islamic finance and banking and the shortage of well-developed curricula, teaching resources and trained teachers with knowledge of the Arabic language and Shariah law. Modern textbooks geared towards tertiary education, as well as in-house training of finance professionals aiming to work in – or already working in – the Islamic finance and banking sector are also in short supply. The aim of this book is to meet this need. This book includes 12 chapters.

Chapter 1 lays down the foundation for learning about Islamic finance and banking by discussing Islamic finance and its features. It covers the core concepts of Islamic economics based on which the structure of Islamic finance and banking is developed. The chapter also discusses the evolution of Islamic finance from the birth of Islam to current times.

Chapter 2 is about the parts of Islamic Shariah law that design the products and processes of the Islamic finance and banking industry, highlighting the prohibitions and guiding principles. This chapter also elaborates the role of the Shariah scholars in ensuring the industry meets its religious requirements through the Shariah Supervisory Boards and Shariah governance.

After the first two chapters have laid down the basis of the subject, Chapter 3 moves towards the industry and discusses the Islamic banks in comparison with conventional banks and elaborates financial intermediation conducted by the Islamic banks and their sources and applications of funds, as well as the major challenges faced by Islamic banks. This chapter further covers the major international Islamic regulatory and standard setting bodies that are working to enhance the acceptability of the Islamic finance and banking industry in the global arena.

The next six chapters (Chapters 4–9) cover the six main Islamic banking products available in the industry: Murabaha, Mudaraba, Musharaka, Ijara, Salam and Istisna. Each chapter defines the instrument, discusses its key features and Shariah-compliance principles, the practical application of the products, problems faced in implementing them and their comparison to their conventional counterparts.

Chapter 10 is based on Takaful, the Islamic version of insurance, discussing the historical background of the product, its Shariah-compliance rules and general principles. This chapter also discusses the Takaful structure and models, compares Takaful with conventional commercial insurance as well as with mutual insurance, and finally touches on Retakaful, the Islamic alternative to reinsurance.

Chapter 11 covers Islamic investment products and markets, especially Sukuks, which are the Islamic substitutes for bonds. The chapter elaborates on Shariah-screened stocks, various Islamic investment funds, Islamic real estate investment trusts and compares them with their conventional counterparts. The chapter moves ahead with a discussion of Sukuks, their characteristics, the types of Sukuks, controversies related to Sukuks, their trading, rating and the comparison of Sukuks with traditional bonds.

Chapter 12 concludes the book with a discussion of Islamic finance and banking in comparison with conventional finance and banking and the global development of Islamic finance and banking amongst the Muslim community, in the Middle East, South and South-East Asia. The chapter also elaborates the opportunities, challenges and social responsibilities of this niche segment of the finance industry as it moves forward.

About the Website

This book is accompanied by a companion website:

www.habibislamicfinance.com

The website includes:

PowerPoint slides. The PowerPoint slides that accompany each chapter of the textbook can be used by instructors in class and by students to review the lessons.

Test bank. The test bank includes all questions from the End of Chapter Questions and Activities, with appropriate answers, to be utilized by instructors to prepare quizzes, tests and exams. The questions include multiple choice, true/false, discussion questions and calculation problems.

Fundamentals of Islamic Finance and Banking

CHAPTER 1

Introduction to Islamic Finance and Islamic Economics

Learning outcomes

Upon completion of this chapter, you should be able to:
  1. Define Islamic finance and explain the distinctive features of Islamic finance.
  2. Discuss the relationship between Islam and economics and the role of Islamic economics in social welfare.
  3. Describe the evolution of Islamic finance from the early days to the modern Islamic finance and banking industry.
  4. Identify the timeline of the development of contemporary Islamic finance and banking.

INTRODUCTION

The core concepts of Islamic finance are as old as Islam. Islam is not just a religion but a way of life. It provides guidance to its followers encompassing the social, religious, economic and political aspects of their lives. The Islamic law called Shariah law dictates specific dos and don'ts related to all aspects of a Muslim's life, including commercial and financial transactions. From the time of the Prophet Muhammad, peace be upon him (PBUH), specific financial instruments were used that were designed as per the requirements of the Shariah principles. Shariah law will be discussed in much more detail in Chapter 2 of this book.

The birth of modern Islamic finance and banking though happened in the second half of the twentieth century as an extension of Islamic economics, through the joint efforts of Shariah scholars and bankers. The global expansion of Islamic finance and banking was accelerated by the discovery of oil, rise in petrodollars and budget surpluses of the Gulf Cooperation Council (GCC) countries, with the concomitant increased demand among global Muslims to bank according to their religious beliefs (Natt, Al Habshi & Zainal, 2009). Initially Islamic banking experiments were private initiatives of individuals, but later governments in some Muslim countries significantly encouraged their growth, changing existing and developing new legislation and removing various handicaps in the predominantly interest-based environment (Ahmad, 1994).

For more than 200 years the finance and banking activities in the world have been operated on the conventional interest-based system. Individuals, businesses and governments have been completely adapted to conventional banks and an alternative to this system was unthinkable and seemed impossible. The concept of Islamic banking first emerged as an experimental Islamic bank was established in Mit Ghamr, Egypt in 1963, and the world's first commercial Islamic bank was set up in Dubai in 1975. Being new and different from the traditional conventional banking, there is a significant lack of awareness and knowledge about Islamic banking. Educational endeavours, trainings, seminars, conferences and the general spread of knowledge of the unique field of Islamic finance and banking are of utmost importance for its growth and acceptance in the global finance industry.

A major driving force that led to the revival of Islamic finance and banking in current times was the increasing awareness amongst the global Muslim population about the prohibition of interest in commercial transactions, mainly in banking and business operations, and their growing need to conduct their financial transactions as per their faith. This demand was predominant in the Muslim majority countries but began to grow amongst the Muslim population in non-Muslim countries also.

The operations of Islamic banks are quite similar to those of conventional banks, except that their transactions need to be free of interest and follow other Shariah law requirements. Although Islamic banking is still in its early days, starting from the feeble beginning of Mit Ghamr in 1963, it has been able to survive and grow at an unprecedented rate over the last five decades, something not seen in conventional finance, and is now viewed as an alternative form of finance and banking. It has attracted the attention of many investors and has the potential to attract new customers and grow further, earning market share.

CREATION OF MONEY AND CONVENTIONAL FINANCE AND BANKING

Before money was created, economic exchanges happened via the barter system. In the barter system one person exchanged a good or service with another person's good or service. This system had many inconveniences. Two people had to meet up where each owned something that the other wanted. The inconveniences of the barter system led to the emergence of money as a medium of exchange. Money separated buying and selling as two separate activities. Historically, many things have been used as mediums of exchange, like livestock (cows, camels, horses), grains (wheat, barley), precious metals (gold, silver) and finally coins and paper money.

The creation of money led to the development of financial institutions whose main purpose was to bring together those with surplus money and those with a shortage of money. Financial institutions have played important roles in the economies of all societies over time, collecting money from customers, providing them with safekeeping services and lending or investing these funds. This process is called financial intermediation and it is the core business of banks. Financial intermediation will be discussed in much greater detail in Chapter 3.

Western commercial banking started in around the 14th century in Florence and became more established in the 18th century with the advent of the Industrial Revolution. It was established by three groups of people and to this day conventional banking shows traces of its ancestors. These groups were:

1. **Rich and reputable merchants.** Like a merchant the bank finances foreign trade, issues bills of exchange and provides capital to new business ventures.
2. **Money lenders.** Like money lenders the bank pools the savings of the masses and lends it out to those with a shortage of finances and makes a profit by charging higher interest to the borrowers and paying lower interest to the savers.
3. **Goldsmiths.** Like a goldsmith the bank serves as a trustee of customers' valuables.

DEFINITION OF ISLAMIC FINANCE AND BANKING

Islamic finance and banking is a faith-based financial system and its foundation is laid down in Shariah law and the principles of Islamic economics. Islamic economics will be discussed further later in this chapter. Since the original knowledge of the system is derived from the divine source of Quran – the holy book of the Muslim faith – it supersedes scientific methods or human decisions. The guiding principles of Islamic finance and banking emphasize fairness, justice, empathy, cooperation, entrepreneurship, ethics and the general good of the environment and society, not just profit maximization. This unique religion-based financial system can be better defined and understood by elaborating its distinctive features as below.

Distinctive Features of Islamic Finance

1. **Religious basis.** Islamic finance is based on the rules and regulations derived from the Islamic faith and law, while conventional finance has no religious restrictions. All Islamic finance and banking contracts must be acceptable by Shariah law.
2. **Prohibition of interest.** At the core of Islamic finance is the prohibition of Riba – which is interest or usury, and means an addition to the loan amount with the passage of time. Earning money from money is not allowed. It is the time value of money which is prohibited in Islam. Islam identifies money as a medium of exchange but not having intrinsic value that can earn more money. In contrast, interest payment and interest charging are at the core of conventional finance. Riba and other prohibitions in Islamic finance will be discussed further in Chapter 2 of this book.
3. **Link to real assets.** To avoid money earning more money, all Islamic financial transactions are linked to a real asset and there is an exchange of goods and services, making them less risky.
4. **Bank as a partner.** Conventional banks borrow funds from depositors and lend the funds to borrowers/entrepreneurs, while Islamic banks act as a partner to both the depositors and the borrowers. Islamic banks also operate as a seller in certain financial transactions.
5. **Profit and loss sharing.** Conventional banks pay interest to the depositors and receive interest from the debtors to whom they lend funds. In contrast, predetermined

payments on loans are prohibited in Islamic finance; instead, the system operates on a profit and loss-sharing basis. An Islamic bank shares in the profit of the client to whom it provides financing and is also required to share in any loss incurred by the business. On the deposit side, the Islamic bank shares its profit and loss with the depositors, pro rata to their deposit amounts.

6. **More prudent selection.** Being a partner to the client, Islamic banks share in both the profit and loss of the borrower's enterprise and this encourages Islamic banks to be more prudent in selecting their clients and the projects they finance. Conventional banks charge fixed interest from their borrowers regardless of whether the client makes a profit or a loss, hence they are more concerned about the creditworthiness of the client and their ability to provide collateral rather than their business success. Islamic banks, on the other hand, give more emphasis to the feasibility of the project and the capabilities of the entrepreneur.

7. **Productive investment.** Islam encourages Muslims to invest in productive enterprises rather than hoarding their money, since idle money cannot earn any interest income. As such, Muslim depositors are encouraged to finance as partners, enjoying profit as well as bearing loss. This stimulates the economy and encourages entrepreneurs to put in their best efforts to succeed, which finally benefits the community also (Kettel, 2010).

8. **Unnecessary and excessive risk.** Islam prohibits any transactions that are based on excessive and unnecessary risk-taking leading to uncertainty. As such, speculative transactions are not allowed in Islamic finance.

ECONOMICS AND ISLAM

Economics in Ancient Times

Today we understand economics as the discipline that deals with the production, distribution and consumption of goods or services and wealth in general. Economic systems in societies from ancient times have been based either on religion or on capitalism. Faith-based systems promoted justice and fairness in economic activities and encouraged the rich to share their wealth with the poor. In contrast, capitalistic economic systems operated on the concepts of survival of the fittest, competition and profit maximization. During ancient times, economic activities like business and trade were mainly controlled by the rulers or by the religious leaders, and some rich and powerful merchants. Hence the profits generated were mostly consumed by the ruling elite, priests and rich merchants, and only small portions trickled down to the public.

During the 13th century, the below interlinked economic concepts began to appear and were the topic of significant discussions and debate.

Justice in economic exchange. The ancient Greek philosopher Aristotle considered the price of any good to be its intrinsic value, while according to the Romans the price of goods was decided by the factors of demand and supply and the contracting parties played a role in finalizing the price. On the other hand, Christian theologians believed that the intrinsic value meant the usefulness of the good and this would ultimately decide the price. Islam also recommends a just price for goods and services.

Private property. In their original form all three Abrahamic religions of Judaism, Christianity and Islam considered property to be ultimately owned by God with man serving only as its steward, and as such all property should benefit society. In Islam, the last of the Abrahamic religions, this view still holds and has a significant effect on Islamic economics and Islamic finance. The Church moved away from this view in around the 5th century and itself became the owner of substantial property and wealth. In the modern economy property is privately owned and is one of the factors of production.

Money, usury and prohibition of interest. In the early 4th century Aristotle opined that money was only a medium of exchange, without any intrinsic value of its own; hence money cannot earn money by itself. A complete ban on usury and the prohibition of interest was common to all three of the Abrahamic religions and not unique to Islam only. According to the Judaic belief, interest could not be charged from one's brother, and that was interpreted as another Jew, basically suggesting that interest could be charged from those of another faith. In the case of Christianity, 'brother' was considered as all human beings. Both the Old and the New Testament forbade earning from usury. Initially, Christian theologians applied a total ban on usury, which over time changed to the prohibition of excessive interest only. The ban on interest was repealed in France in 1789 and in the Vatican in 1838 (Schoon, 2016). Islam is the only religion in which a total ban on any form of usury or interest continues to date. Some of the factors that contributed to Western societies' gradual acceptance of interest in their economic life included the replacement of agriculture by the Industrial Revolution, the role of demand and supply in determining price, the acceptance of money as a factor of production and the separation of the Church from the State (Schoon, 2016).

Modern Economics

Adam Smith, the renowned economist whose works are the foundation of modern economic thought, with his seminal book *An Inquiry into the Nature and Causes of the Wealth of Nations* (1776), said during the beginning of the Industrial Revolution that money or capital was a factor of production, like land or labour. As such it had a cost, not based on usury but on the risk and opportunity cost associated with it. Adam Smith believed in the free market concept, competitive forces and prices determined by the demand–supply mechanism. A significant economic theory defined by him was the concept of economic scarcity. According to this concept people had unlimited wants, while the resources available to meet these wants were limited. This leads to the classic economic problem. Islamic economics differs fundamentally from Adam Smith's concept of economic scarcity, as will be discussed in the next subsection.

The modern economic system is described as a network of relationships between households, businesses and governments involved in the economic activities of production, distribution and consumption of goods and services in a manner that protects the rights of future generations and of the environment. Globally there are different economic models operating, and these differences are derived from the role of markets and governments and of morality and justice in these models. The four classic models, as discussed by Askari, Iqbal & Mirakhor (2015), are briefly defined below. The fifth model can be defined as Islamic economics, and this is covered in more detail in the next subsection.

Market economy. These economies are self-regulating, with no government intervention. Demand and supply determine prices. The disadvantages are that this system can cause polarization of wealth and can be detrimental to society – for example, the USA.

Mixed market economy. In these economies markets operate under the demand and supply mechanism but governments ensure that market rules beneficial to the country are not broken. Important economic sectors like public services, defence, infrastructure, etc. may be under governmental control – for example, Sweden, the UK, France.

Mixed socialist economy. In some market economies, to deal with income inequality, poverty and other social issues, some vital sectors are under governmental control, like banking, healthcare, education, energy, transportation, etc. – for example, China.

Command or planned economy. These economies are the opposite of the market economy. Government decides about production, distribution and consumption. Communist countries usually have this kind of economy – for example, Cuba, North Korea and the former Soviet Union.

Islamic Economics

Islamic economics, as a term, was first coined by Abul Ala Al Mawdudi, who sought to develop Islamic social science (Kuran, 2004). Since Islam is a way of life, it provides guidance for its followers in the material as well as the non-material aspects of their lives. According to Askari, Iqbal & Mirakhor (2015), Islamic economics involves studying rules provided in the Islamic holy book, the Quran, and the Sunnah (teachings of the Prophet Muhammad) pertaining to the economic concepts, comparing and contrasting these with contemporary economics, identifying the gaps and finding ways to bridge these gaps. Askari, Iqbal & Mirakhor (2015) further emphasized that social and economic justice is at the basis of Islamic economics, providing equal opportunity in the utilization of natural resources for all in society. It encourages cooperation and collaboration between individuals and society.

Islamic economics assists in the allocation and distribution of scarce resources, without curbing individual freedom, causing macroeconomic and ecological imbalances, or weakening family and social solidarity; it aims to find a balance between individual and social benefits related to private or public property ownership (Ginena & Hamid, 2015). Islamic economics encourages productive activities and the creation of wealth, considering it as an act of worship provided that these activities are compliant with Shariah rulings. Though on the flip side, Islam does not agree that material gain is the main reason for existence. Islamic economics discourages the hoarding of wealth.

History of Islamic Economic Thought

Mohammad Nejatullah Siddiqui, in his *History of Islamic Economic Thought* (2010), divided the development of Islamic economics into three periods. The first period began from the hijra (when the Prophet Muhammad migrated from Makkah to Medina, which is the first year in the Muslim calendar) to AH450, corresponding to AD1058. During this period the Prophet, his companions and other Islamic scholars concentrated on Shariah rulings relating to economic issues. The second period, spreading from AH450 to AH850, corresponding to AD1058 to AD1446, was a glorious period in the development of Islamic economics. This period focused on the following issues: individuals should satisfy their basic needs only and consider the needs of society; rulers must preserve justice and introduce accounting and fair pricing. The third period was from AH850 to AH1350, corresponding to AD1446 to AD1932, and it was a period of stagnation in intellectual and individual thinking. The economic concepts that were discussed and developed during the initial period of Islam included money as a medium of exchange, usury, taxation, market regulations, permissible economic behaviour, labour, wages, prices and ethical commercial behaviour (Askari, Iqbal & Mirakhor, 2015).

Principles of Islamic Economics

Some of the most important principles that guide the discipline of Islamic economics are detailed below.

1. Religion and economics are interrelated in Islam.
2. Economic and social fairness and justice is not forced on individuals, but they are encouraged to implement it.
3. Property and wealth is ultimately owned by the Creator, though man has control over it as trustee.
4. People are expected to be moderate in their expenses and avoid wastage and luxury.
5. Productive activities are encouraged, and all can pursue personal economic gain as long as they are Shariah-compliant and do not harm society or the environment.
6. All Halal trade and business, legitimate and permissible in Islam, is encouraged while all Haram trade and business, unlawful and prohibited in Islam, is to be avoided.
7. All human beings have the right to equal opportunity, and those who own wealth are responsible for sharing it with the community. To achieve this, Islamic economics dictates compulsory charity Zakat, which is a religious tax, designed to reduce the gap between the rich and the poor, as well as encouraging additional non-compulsory charity Sadaqah.

Islam's Solution to the Classic Economic Problem

According to conventional economics the classic economic problem is that of scarcity, since wants can be unlimited while resources are limited. Islamic economics has a two-pronged solution to this problem, as follows.

1. On the demand side, man should not have unlimited wants. They should concentrate on basic needs only, avoiding unnecessary luxury and wastage. As such, each would consume less of the available resources.
2. On the supply side, man should increase the resources Allah has provided by productive activity. Productive effort is a way of serving the Creator and thus increasing the available resources. Every capable individual should work for a living and the wealth they earn is not only to benefit them, but should also benefit society and the environment.

ISLAM AND THE WELFARE ECONOMY

Islam says that human beings are trustees only of the wealth they own, while the real owner is Allah. All Muslims are brothers and sisters and are responsible for each other's wellbeing. This establishes the welfare economy in Islam. Two important concepts encouraged by Islam and working towards the common good are **Al-Adl,** which means to be just and fair in dealings with others and **Al-Ihsan,** which encourages Muslims to go beyond the minimum obligation towards others and to show kindness. Other concepts in Islam that aim to achieve social welfare are Islam's special dictate related to property ownership and the charitable endeavours of Zakat and Sadaqah.

Property Ownership in Islamic Economics

In all practical senses, property ownership is allowed in Islam. The ultimate ownership of everything though vests in the Creator, and humans are only trustees of the property. As such, property should also be available for the benefit of the public and the environment. This identifies elements of both the capitalistic and the social systems. Islamic economics is not in conflict with the market economy. Demand and supply, competition, rights of contracting parties to determine price and earning profit from productive endeavours are all accepted concepts, provided fairness and justice are maintained.

In Islamic economics, the ownership rights of property are dealt with based on the below principles.

1. Allah is the ultimate owner of all property and He has allowed people to possess and use the property in trust, in such a manner that it is available to benefit society and future generations and causes no harm to the environment.
2. All human beings should have access to the natural resources bestowed by Allah.
3. Property can be acquired by people through their own productive activities or by diverse types of transfers like exchanges, contracts, gifts, donations or inheritance.
4. Islam limits the accumulation of wealth (thus socially harmful hoarding, which is prohibited) and dictates that all Muslims have a duty to share their income and wealth with the less fortunate, via Zakat, which is compulsory or Sadaqah, which is voluntary.
5. Islam recommends taking care of our property and discourages waste or destruction.

Zakat and Sadaqah

Every Muslim has specific economic obligations towards society – of which Zakat is compulsory charity and Sadaqah is voluntary charity.

Zakat is a compulsory levy imposed on Muslims who own above a certain minimum level of wealth. Zakat aims to take surplus money or wealth from the well-to-do members of Muslim society and give it to those in need. In the context of the economic system, Zakat is an obligation and can be defined as a duty or tax on a certain kind of wealth at the rate of 2.5% each lunar year. To motivate the practicing Muslim to participate in the process, the rewards of paying Zakat are identified in the Quran and Sunnah as increased prosperity in this world, purification of all assets and income, as well as the religious merit of purifying sins.

Zakat serves as the backbone of the Islamic economic system and encourages the rich to support the poor in the community. It was the first formal form of quantified taxation known to civilization, and is a form of social insurance. In Islamic countries it could be a source of income for the government treasury (which in Arabic is called the Bait-al-Maal) and used for public service expenses. Zakat is also a very important tool acting against the hoarding of wealth, since money utilized in productive endeavour is taxed only on its income while idle, unproductive money is taxed on the principal amount.

The Quran has identified certain categories of people who are most eligible to receive Zakat. These are the poor – who cannot feed or clothe themselves, the needy – who have income but not sufficient to meet all their needs, those who need financial help to integrate back into society, those who have high debt and need help to repay it, travellers, the disabled, the unemployed, orphans, slaves – to help buy their freedom, the Zakat collectors and general spending in the way of Allah.

In traditional Islamic society, the wealth subject to Zakat was gold and silver, including any jewellery of these metals, agricultural produce like dates, wheat, etc., all mineral assets, trading assets and productive animals like camels, sheep, etc. In modern Islamic society, the wealth subject to Zakat is determined by Islamic scholars as cash savings, gold, silver, other non-productive assets and the income of productive assets employed in a business. Any wealth that belongs to the government, or is for the benefit of the community or a charitable endowment or Waqf asset, is not subject to Zakat. For Zakat calculation the current market value of the asset is considered and for an individual or a company the net worth is calculated, which is assets minus liabilities.

Ban on Interest versus Cost of Capital in Islam

Islamic economics recognizes capital as one of the factors of production, and as such there is a cost to this capital. On the other hand, Islam considers money only as a medium of exchange and does not agree with money being treated as a commodity or having an intrinsic value (thus earning money from money). This is considered as Riba or interest, which is basically income against the time value of money or via exchange of goods in unequal quality or quantity. Riba will be discussed in further detail in Chapter 2. Islamic economics does not accept interest as the measure of investment efficiency, rather it believes that yields are determined by sharing in both profit and loss or by the negotiated prices of sales or lease transactions. All Islamic financial transactions need to be linked to an underlying real asset, or there should be an investment in a business and this investment of capital will earn a profit or make a loss as is the case with the underlying asset or business. To conclude, Islam allows for the cost of capital by allowing capital to share in the surplus but not without being part of the deficit also in any investment.

Conventional Economics versus Islamic Economics

Table 1.1 specifies the differences between conventional and Islamic economics.

TABLE 1.1   Differences between conventional and Islamic economics

Factors	Conventional Economics	Islamic Economics
Ownership of wealth and property	In capitalism individuals can be the absolute owners, while in socialism society collectively is the owner.	Absolute ownership is with God, man is only the trustee.
Wants and resources	Wants are unlimited while resources are limited, creating the scarcity problem.	Wants should be limited and sufficient resources have been provided by the Creator. Scarcity is created by improper distribution of resources, overconsumption, luxury and wastage.
Accumulation of wealth	Any amount of wealth can be accumulated, and the owner can use or waste it as they please.	Individuals can accumulate wealth if this is done in a Shariah-compliant manner, though the owner needs to share this wealth with the less privileged in society through the compulsory Zakat and voluntary Sadaqah. Islam says produce more than is needed and consume only what is needed.
Market economy	The market economy is the main determinant in capitalism, while in socialism demand and supply are not linked to prices, since supply is decided centrally.	The market economy applies, demand and supply determine prices, although all this needs to be done within a framework of social wellbeing.
Role of the State	In capitalism, markets play a more dominant role than the State, while in socialism, the State plays a dominant role.	The State ensures ethical activities, protects individuals' and society's interest and ensures efficient allocation of resources.
Law of inheritance	Individuals can pass on their wealth and property to anyone they please.	Islam has specific inheritance laws and does not allow giving away more than one-third of one's assets to anyone besides the legitimate heirs, thus ensuring fairness in the process of transfer of wealth and property.
Economic cycles	Economic cycles show significant ups and downs.	These ups and downs are reduced in Islamic economics through the moderation of consumption and the avoidance of luxury, wastage and unnecessary debts.
Reward for capital	Interest is accepted as the reward for capital.	Interest is completely forbidden, and an alternative profit and loss-sharing mechanism is applied as the reward for capital.
Social welfare	In capitalism, this is achieved by the free market and self-interest, while in socialism, the State achieves this by centralized production and distribution.	Islam encourages productivity at the individual level but through the moral requirements of sharing one's wealth aims to create social welfare.

EVOLUTION OF ISLAMIC FINANCE

Early Days

Islamic finance began with Islam in the early 7th century. The first Islamic financial institution established was the Bait al Maal or public treasury set up by Prophet Muhammad. Later, during the times of the Caliphs, various new issues and questions came to light, discussions were held amongst the companions of the Prophet and judgements were reached. This process is called Ijtihad, and many economic reforms were made through Ijtihad, but it was always important to maintain consistency with the Quran and Sunnah. Early in his Caliphate, the first Caliph Abu Bakr Al Siddique had to deal with a revolt against the paying of Zakat. Zakat was the main financial tool to ensure social welfare and justice in Islamic society, compelling the rich to share their wealth and income with the less privileged. The second Caliph Umar Ibn al-Khattab formalized the management of the Bait al Maal, which dealt with the revenue and expenses of the Islamic State. Later Umar identified Bait al Maal's main revenue sources to be Zakat, Sadaqah, a land tax called Kharaj, a tax on non-Muslims residing in Muslim States called Jizya, and other customs duties and toll income. The funds collected in the Bait al Maal were used for various governmental expenses and for public welfare activities, paying allowances to the needy, the elderly, the disabled, orphans, widows, etc.

The Islamic civilization flourished between the late 6th and the early 11th centuries. Muslim traders conducted financial transactions based on the Shariah rulings, using financial tools like Musharaka (joint venture) and Mudaraba (trust financing), Wakala (agency), Qard Hasan (benevolent loan), Salam (forward contracts) and Ijara (leasing). These products will be discussed in the later chapters of this book. Some evidence of the achievements of early Islamic financial activities is given below.

1. The Prophet acted as an agent for his wife's trading business and collected a commission as revenue.
2. Islamic financial systems encouraged trade and business contracts to be written and witnessed, reducing possibilities of conflict.
3. Trade and Islam arrived in Malaysia and Indonesia before the Europeans. Shipping business in the Indian Ocean used Mudaraba or trust financing as a form of financing. Besides the owners of the ship and cargo, the captain of the ship and each sailor was also a partner, not earning a salary but sharing in the profit along with the owners. As such, everyone had a stake. History shows that rarely did mutiny, deliberate drowning or damage of cargo on Muslim ships happen, compared with regular shipping.
4. Expansion of various forms of trade in the Islamic world led to the development of Islamic mercantile law in accordance with Islamic Shariah law. In comparison, Europe at this time was using a mediaeval form of business cooperation known as Commenda.

From the 12th century on to the middle of the 20th century, Islamic finance gradually disappeared. Some of the reasons for this were as follows.

1. The fall of the Ottoman Empire.
2. The dominance of Western countries and conventional financial institutions.
3. The onset of colonization around the Muslim world, with Shariah institutions consequently losing their capabilities under the colonial powers.
4. The continued growth of business and finance in Europe, developing larger enterprises, using the small savings of the masses to finance investment projects.
5. The application of any existing Islamic financial principles and tools went into inertia and disuse.
6. The differences between conventional finance and Shariah restrictions got blurred amongst most people, including the Muslim population.

Birth of Modern Islamic Finance

The concept of modern Islamic finance emerged in the mid-20th century with Asian and Arab Muslim-majority countries gaining independence from Western colonial powers, searching for their own identity and being inspired by Islamic economics distinct from both the Western capitalist and Eastern socialist models. Islamic finance and banking evolved from the concepts of Islamic economics, based on the profit and loss-sharing (PLS) system, and is considered more equitable and stable (Chapra, 2007; El-Gamal, 2006; Siddiqi, 2006). The idea of interest-free financing has existed since the birth of Islam, but its reintroduction into the world of finance is only a few decades old.

Modern Islamic banking is about 60 years old. The guiding principle of Islamic banks is the Shariah law, which prohibits the payment or receipt of interest and recommends the sharing of risk and of profit/loss between the bank and its customers. Islamic finance also emphasizes socio-economic justice and equitable distribution of wealth (Amin, Hamid, Lada & Baba, 2009). This is in stark contrast to conventional banks, which operate primarily on an interest basis and on a profit-maximization principle. Previously, the prohibition of interest made banking difficult for religiously oriented Muslims globally, and especially in the Gulf region – they either left their money in current accounts with no interest in conventional banks or stayed outside the formal banking system altogether, which hindered the free flow of capital between global financial markets and the GCC. The advent of affluence in the region, with the discovery of oil and the introduction of petrodollars, magnified the problem (Smith, 2006). The introduction of Islamic banking was a major solution, providing a distinctive means of financial intermediation. Islamic banking was conceptualized through the efforts of Islamic political activists, Muslim legal scholars, economists and businessmen, applying Shariah law to the modern economy and innovatively structuring traditional Islamic financial instruments to provide customers with most of the services associated with conventional banks, within Shariah restrictions (Smith, 2006). Today, Islamic banking has established its place globally.

Institutional Developments During the Revival of Modern Islamic Finance

During the early part of the 20th century, towards the end of the colonial era, several religious scholars in Egypt, India, Pakistan, Malaysia and Indonesia began to rethink the Shariah rulings relating to the financial aspects of the life of a Muslim and tried to reconcile the Shariah prohibition of interest or Riba with existing conventional banking. Significant academic research took place in these Muslim-majority countries during the 1940s and 1950s, which led to institutional experimentation in Islamic finance and banking. Some of the major developments during the following decades are set out below.

The Mit Ghamr Experiment

Dr Ahmad El-Najjar, an economist, first experimented with the idea of interest-free banking by setting up the Mit Ghamr savings project in Egypt in 1963. This was the world's first interest-free bank, set up through community effort and the pioneering endeavours of its founder Dr El-Najjar. The bank was modelled on the German cooperative savings bank, using the principles of rural banking. The Islamic cooperative savings bank had three types of accounts:

1. **Savings account.** This account was aimed at collecting the savings of depositors and allowed withdrawal on demand; the depositors, like the members of a cooperative, could also take small, short-term interest-free loans for productive purposes.
2. **Investment account.** This account allowed restrictive withdrawal, almost like the fixed deposits in conventional banks, and the funds in these accounts were invested in Shariah-compliant projects on a PLS basis shared between the bank and the investors; part of the profits/losses was passed on to the depositors, proportionate to their deposits.
3. **Zakat account.** This special account collected Zakat money from the members and redistributed the funds amongst the poor and needy as per the Quranic guidance of possible Zakat recipients.

The Mit Ghamr experiment had unexpected success and the savings deposits grew each year. However, the secular government in Egypt had reservations about the religious basis of this first Islamic bank and despite its success the project was abandoned for political reasons. The closing down of the Mit Ghamr experimental bank was not the end of Islamic banking, rather it was the beginning of this new and unique banking niche within the global banking industry. Within a few years Egypt had 9 Islamic banks and 9 years after the inception of the Mit Ghamr experiment, in 1972, it was integrated into the Nasr Social Bank.

Tabung Haji

Around the same time as the Mit Ghamr experiment was pioneered in Egypt, on the other side of the world in Malaysia the Tabung Haji institution was set up, also in 1963. The purpose of this institution was to manage the savings of Hajj pilgrims by investing them in a Shariah-compliant manner over a period of time and then the savings would be used towards their Hajj expenses. Hajj is the pilgrimage to Makkah that is compulsory for all able-bodied Muslims once in their lifetime provided they have the financial ability. The Tabung Haji institution is in operation to date, and it set up the platform for Malaysia to play a leading role in the global Islamic finance and banking industry. Malaysia's first fully fledged commercial Islamic bank, Bank Islam Malaysia, was set up two decades later in 1983.

Islamic Development Bank

The Islamic Development Bank (IDB) was established in 1975 to foster economic development and social progress amongst the member Muslim countries and to enhance the growth of the Islamic finance and banking industry. Its head office was set up in Jeddah, Kingdom of Saudi Arabia (KSA). Currently the bank has 57 countries enrolled as its members; a prerequisite for members is to be a member of the Organization of Islamic Cooperation (OIC). The core functions of the IDB include the following.

1. Participating in productive projects in member countries via equity participation or lending.
2. Providing financial assistance to member country governments.
3. Providing funds to Muslim communities in non-Muslim countries.
4. Promoting foreign trade amongst member countries.

Dubai Islamic Bank

The oil boom in the 1970s triggered a rapid growth of Islamic financial institutions in the Middle East and North Africa. The world's first fully fledged commercial Islamic bank was the Dubai Islamic Bank, set up in Dubai, United Arab Emirates (UAE) in 1975. It was established as a public limited company with a capital of AED50 million and the governments of Dubai and Kuwait owned 20% and 10% of its shares, respectively. The bank has grown, with both governmental and public support since its inception, and currently is the largest and most reputable Islamic bank in the country.

RAPID GROWTH OF THE ISLAMIC FINANCE AND BANKING INDUSTRY

Islamic finance concepts have been in existence and practiced for centuries, but have been institutionalized only in the last few decades, offering Shariah-compliant products and services. With the development of viable Islamic alternatives to conventional finance products, large numbers of Muslims are seeking Shariah-based solutions to their financial needs. Some non-Muslims also are Islamic bank customers, and some conventional banks are offering Islamic products on a limited scale via the Islamic windows within their regular distribution channel or by special branches or subsidiaries specifically established to offer Islamic banking products. Over the last five decades there has been rapid growth in Islamic finance institutions, instruments, regulations, educational and training facilities, publications and conferences and seminars on the topic (Hasan, 2014). The remarkable growth of an industry only a few decades old, with growing global interest, indicates the tremendous opportunities existing in this niche business for the participating banks.

Modern Islamic finance and banking, when first introduced, suffered from a lack of understanding by the existing industry as well as by potential customers. As such it was quite a while before significant success was achieved by this niche segment of the finance and banking industry. The industry developed through three periods. The first was a period of conceptualization (1950–1975), when Islamic scholars raised Muslim consciousness about the prohibition of interest, mostly from a religious aspect. The second was a period of experimentation (1975–1990), PLS Islamic banks were set up, Islamic financial instruments and institutions were established, Western financial institutions entered the market and the sector was accepted as an interest-free alternative to conventional banking. The third period (1990–present) is about earning recognition, confidence and credibility in domestic and international markets, the innovation of products and the standardization of products and procedures (Iqbal & Mirakhor, 1999).

The design of modern Islamic banking has mostly followed the structure of conventional banks, with the exclusion of interest-based transactions, replacing interest with a PLS system. Significant innovations in this unique banking system are yet to come, and so up to now the industry has mainly endeavoured to provide reasonably Shariah-compliant alternatives to the products and services offered by the more universally accepted conventional banks. Hence, some mismatch can be seen between the current structure of the Islamic finance and banking industry and its original objectives. The significant similarity of Islamic banking products and operations to conventional banking allowed the conventional banks to enter this niche segment of the industry with windows or subsidiaries. This also allowed Islamic banking to grow faster, as it was not viewed as isolated from the global financial infrastructure.

ISLAMIC FINANCE AND BANKING IN MUSLIM COMMUNITIES AND COUNTRIES

The revival of Islamic finance can clearly be linked to the religious movements in Muslim countries after they gained independence from the colonial powers to restore their Islamic values, including those related to financial and commercial dealings. Islamic banks provided Muslims with the opportunity to bank and invest in accordance with their religious beliefs and without interest, while previously they had to deal with interest if they wanted to participate in the banking system. The Muslim population numbers 1.8 billion, which is about a quarter of the estimated global population of 7.4 billion (Pew Research Institute, 2017). Moreover, Islam is the fastest growing religion and some Muslim countries are the richest in the world, like Qatar, Brunei, UAE, Saudi Arabia, etc. Most Muslim countries apply Shariah law to some extent in their social framework.

Starting from the Middle East, Islamic finance grew and expanded in South and South-East Asia. Bahrain and Malaysia have played pivotal roles in their respective regions to enhance research, innovation and development in the areas of Islamic finance. Bahrain was the first GCC country to contribute to the progress in this industry by setting up and supporting the development of several major international Islamic regulatory and standard setting bodies, like the Accounting and Auditing Organization for Islamic Financial Institutions (AAOIFI). Bahrain Central Bank has also provided a highly supportive role in the development of the Islamic finance industry. On the other side of the world, Malaysia, starting from Tabung Haji, is another major player and driving force in the internationalization of the sector. With the support of the Malaysian government, Bank Islam Malaysia was set up and the country has a well-designed dual banking system to meet the demands of a large Muslim population aspiring to Shariah-compliant banking. Today Malaysia is one of the most developed Islamic finance centres and the base for another major international Islamic regulatory and standard setting body, the International Financial Services Board (IFSB).

Pakistan, despite its decision to go completely Shariah-compliant in the financial sector, still operates on the dual banking system. The rapid growth experienced in the GCC countries over the last few decades has also served as a catalyst in the growth of Islamic finance and banking. KSA, UAE, Qatar and Kuwait have all formally set up regulatory structures to support Islamic finance and banking, and all of the GCC countries are using the dual banking system. Significant development in Islamic finance and banking is also evident in the rest of the Muslim nations in the Middle East, North and East Africa, as well as in South and South-East Asia – for example, Egypt, Jordan, Libya, Bangladesh and Indonesia.

ISLAMIC FINANCE AND BANKING IN NON-MUSLIM COUNTRIES

Islamic finance and banking has been spreading in some non-Muslim countries as well over the decades. Amanah Bank was set up in the Philippines in 1973. In Europe, Islamic banking first arrived in Luxembourg in 1978 and during the 1980s many other experimentations happened in Islamic finance and banking. In 1982 Faisal Finance House was set up in Geneva. Since 2002 the Bank of England and the Financial Services Authority in the UK have taken several measures to encourage and develop the sector and make London a major international hub of Islamic finance, and have licensed several Islamic banks. Dallah Albaraka Group established the first fully fledged Islamic bank in the UK in 2004, called the Islamic Bank of Britain. The bank was acquired by Masraf al Rayan of Qatar in 2014 and rebranded as Al Rayan Bank. In Europe, besides the UK, France, Germany, Italy, Luxembourg, Switzerland and the Netherlands are also trying to serve the minority Muslim population and take advantage of the opportunities in the fast-growing Islamic finance sector.

In Singapore, the first Islamic bank, Islamic Bank of Asia, was incorporated in 2007. Singapore currently plays a significant role in Islamic finance, especially due to its geographic and economic proximity to Kuala Lumpur, Malaysia, a major Islamic finance hub. Hong Kong is also participating in Islamic finance. In the USA Lariba, the American Finance House, has been operating since 1987. University Islamic Bank is another provider of Islamic finance in the USA. The major provider of Islamic finance in Canada since 1980 is Ansar Financial and Housing Cooperative, which plays a valuable role in providing Shariah-compliant home financing and other investment options. Similarly, Australia also offers some Shariah-compliant home financing.

SUB-SECTORS IN THE ISLAMIC FINANCE AND BANKING INDUSTRY

The Islamic finance and banking industry today comprises the following sub-sectors.

1. **Islamic banking.** This includes the deposit-taking banks that operate within Shariah guidance, like the Bahrain Islamic Bank. Conventional banks offering Shariah-compliant products may also participate via an Islamic window within their main operations or an independent subsidiary, like HSBC Amanah.
2. **Islamic insurance or Takaful.** These are the Shariah-compliant insurance companies, like the Qatar Takaful Company.

3. **Islamic capital markets.** These include Shariah-compliant shares, bonds, mutual and other investment funds and products, indices and the secondary markets.
4. **Islamic non-bank financial institutions.** Within this sub-sector are the variety of financial institutions that are not banks and operate within the Islamic financial principles. Some of these are Islamic finance companies, Islamic housing cooperatives, Islamic leasing and factoring companies, Islamic microfinance, charitable endowments (called Waqf in Arabic), private equity and venture capital firms, Hajj and Zakat management bodies, etc.

CURRENT STATUS OF MODERN ISLAMIC FINANCE AND BANKING

Islamic finance and banking, though still in its early days, has been able to provide a worthwhile alternative to conventional finance and banking. Some key issues and statistics related to the growth of the Islamic banking and finance industry, almost non-existent six decades ago, are discussed below (Abdullah, Sidek & Adnan, 2012; Benaissa, Nordin & Stockmeier, 2003; Duran & Garcia-Lopez, 2012; Hasan, 2014; Hassan, Kayed & Oseni, 2013; O'Sullivan, 2009; Pew Research Institute, 2017; PriceWaterhouseCooper Middle East, Financial Services, 2017; Rammal, 2010; Shamma & Maher, 2012; The Banker, 2010; World Islamic Banking Competitiveness Report, 2016).

Number of countries with Islamic finance and banking presence. Estimated to be around 75.

Number of Islamic finance and banking institutions globally. It is estimated that about 500 Islamic financial institutions, along with about a further 190 conventional institutions, offer Islamic finance products today. Many conventional financial institutions in Europe and North America, as well as in Asia, have opened Islamic banking windows or subsidiaries. Included within this group are global players such as Standard Chartered Bank, Citibank, HSBC, ABN AMRO and UBS. The global spread of Islamic finance products is also likely to happen in Latin America, Africa and the Commonwealth of Independent States (CIS) countries. The growth and expansion of the Islamic finance industry continued during the global financial crisis. Islamic commercial banking is experiencing a huge expansion in products and areas of influence across the world. This growth is expected to continue as legal and regulatory challenges are faced and dealt with and the emerging Islamic finance industry establishes itself as a potential alternative mode of finance.

Muslim population. The Muslim population is currently about 1.8 billion, a quarter of the world population of approximately 7.4 billion, and is expected to increase by 35%, twice the rate at which the non-Muslim population is growing, and reach 2.2 billion by 2030. The global Muslim population is growing faster than any other religious group. Simultaneous to the increase in numbers, Muslims are also increasingly interested in using Shariah-compliant financial instruments rather than conventional products.

Asset size and growth rate of the Islamic finance and banking industry. The industry crossed US$1.6 trillion by 2013 from only US$300 billion in 2007. This is still a very small percentage of the global finance and banking industry, standing currently at US$94.7 trillion. As per PriceWaterhouseCooper Middle East, Financial Services (2017), the Islamic finance and banking industry is expected to reach US$2.6 trillion by the end of 2017. The world's largest Islamic banks have outpaced average growth in conventional banks and are growing at approximately 15% annually.

Presence in the affluent GCC region. Some of the world's largest Islamic banks are located within the GCC countries and comprise about 20% of the GCC's banking assets (and expected to grow further), posing a serious challenge to the conventional banks. Oil-producing Middle Eastern economies, which are predominantly of Muslim faith, are booming with an increase in oil prices and this economic boom is expected to be a catalyst towards the growth of the Islamic finance industry.

Shift of economic power to Asia. Over the last decade a major shift of economic growth and development has been happening in Asia, including countries in South and South-East and Central Asia, several of which are Muslim-majority countries or with a large Muslim population, and is expected to assist in the expansion of Islamic finance.

Presence in the UK. The UK plays a pivotal role within the non-Muslim region of Islamic finance and banking operations. According to Schoon (2016), as of 2015 the UK had more than 25 organizations offering Islamic financial services and the Prudential Regulation Authority has regulated seven fully Sharia-compliant institutions, moving the UK towards its goal to be the largest Islamic financial centre outside the Muslim world.

TIMELINE OF DEVELOPMENT OF CONTEMPORARY ISLAMIC FINANCE AND BANKING

To understand the modern Islamic finance and banking industry it is important to walk through the timeline with the geographic positioning of the various events in the development of this emerging niche segment of the finance industry that may be the chosen finance method of more and more customers from the Muslim population, comprising a quarter of the world population, as well as winning some customers from the non-Muslim population. In the timeline below, individual years are placed in chronological order. Entire periods are highlighted in bold.

1890s	**Commercial banking in the Muslim world.** By the opening of Barclay's bank in Cairo, mainly to facilitate the construction of the Suez Canal, formal commercial banking first arrived in a Muslim-majority country. It was interest-based and brought about the first criticism from Islamic scholars.
1900–1950	**Discussions on the prohibition of Riba.** Islamic scholars and Islamic economists began discussing the prohibition of Riba in the Middle East and the Indian Subcontinent.
1951–1962	**Design of interest-free banking.** Shariah-compliant alternatives to interest-based products were researched in various parts of the Muslim world. Initial descriptions of interest-free banking based on two-tier Mudaraba, as well as the Wakala method, emerged. In Pakistan, a small experimental interest-free savings and loan society was established in a rural area to provide loans to poor landowners for agricultural purposes.

1963–1975	**Founding period.** The institutional foundation of the Islamic finance and banking industry was established during this period, from experimental efforts to moderate success.
1963	**Mit Ghamr savings association.** Established by Dr Ahmad El-Najjar. Followed the model of German savings banks. Interest-free and based on the PLS mechanism. Successful initially, but later ended for political reasons and due to lack of government support.
	Tabung Haji or Pilgrims Fund Corporation. A Shariah-compliant savings institution set up in Malaysia to enable Muslims to save gradually for their Hajj expenditures. Started with 1,281 registered members with RM46,000 in 1963 and by 2004 had 4 million depositors with more than US$2 billion invested. Tabung Haji is still operational and as such can be declared the oldest Islamic finance institution in the world.
	Few books on Islamic finance and banking and on the profit and loss mode instead of interest were published.
1972	**Nasr Social Bank** in Egypt integrated within itself the Mit Ghamr project and was established as a social bank and not as a profit-oriented institution, serving mainly those with low income and ignored by commercial banks.
	3rd Conference of Foreign Ministers of Islamic Countries. An important meeting where decisions were taken to establish Shariah-compliant and interest-free Islamic financial institutions.
1973	**Philippines Amanah Bank.** Established to serve the special banking needs of the Muslim community. It did not operate as a strictly Islamic bank, since interest-based operations co-existed with the Islamic products.
1975–1990	**Formative period.** Commercial and developmental Islamic finance and banking institutions established around the Muslim world. The products and services on offer are mainly replications of conventional finance, with some new purely Shariah-compliant products introduced.
1975	**The Islamic Development Bank.** Established as a multilateral bank and an inter-governmental institution to foster economic and social development amongst member countries, also bringing institutional recognition to the developing Islamic finance and banking industry.
	Dubai Islamic Bank. Established as the first major Islamic commercial bank, in Dubai, UAE, with full government support and some government shareholding.
1976	**First International Conference on Islamic Economics.** Held in Makkah, KSA.
1977	**Kuwait Finance House, Bahrain Islamic Bank, Faisal Islamic Bank of Sudan and Faisal Islamic Bank of Egypt.** Established as pioneering institutions in their respective countries.
1978	**Jordan Islamic Bank.** Launched formal Islamic banking in Jordan.
	Centre for Research in Islamic Economics. Established at the King Abdul Aziz University, Jeddah, KSA as the first specialized research institution for Islamic economics and finance.
	Islamic Finance House, Luxembourg. Established as the first for Islamic finance in Europe.
1979	**First Takaful Company.** Set up by the Faisal Islamic Bank of Sudan and called the Sudanese Islamic Insurance Company.

(Continued)

1980	**Pakistan** passes legislature to establish Shariah compliance across its entire financial system. The decision though was never fully implemented in the industry and despite the growth of Islamic banking, the country still operates on the dual banking system.
1981	**Islamic Research and Training Institute.** Set up by the IDB in Jeddah, KSA.
	Dar Al-Maal Al-Islami Trust. Provides Islamic banking, investment and insurance services to Muslim communities in the GCC, Switzerland, Luxembourg, Jersey, Bahrain, Egypt and Pakistan. Founded in 1981 in Cointrin, Switzerland.
1983	**Sudan** reforms its banking system on Shariah principles, applied in the North of the country while dual banking continued in the South.
	Bank Islam Malaysia Berhad. Founded as Malaysia's first fully fledged Islamic bank.
	Bank Islami Bangladesh. Established as this Muslim-majority country's first pure Islamic bank.
1984	**Iran** makes true its promise during the 1979 revolution and establishes interest-free banking in the entire country.
1987	**Al Rajhi** of KSA operated in Shariah-compliant finance and commerce since 1957 and was consolidated into one umbrella institution, Al Rajhi Trading and Exchange Corporation, in 1978. In 1987 it was formalized as the Al Rajhi Banking and Investment Saudi Joint Stock Company.
1990–now	**Development period.** This period is the new horizon for Islamic finance and banking, with the industry aiming not only to innovate and establish purely Shariah-compliant yet realistically applicable products but also to establish regulatory and standard setting institutes. Through this dual effort the Islamic finance and banking industry is working towards integrating with the global finance and banking industry and to earn its trust and confidence and be accepted as a reliable alternative to conventional finance.
1990	**Accounting and Auditing Organization for Islamic Financial Institutions.** Established in Bahrain.
1991	**Bank Muamalat.** Indonesia's first Islamic bank set up.
1990s	**Global expansion.** Islamic finance began spreading in Europe and the rest of the world. An Islamic Finance Forum was set up at Harvard University, Islamic indexes were developed by Dow Jones and the *Financial Times*.
2000s	**Entry of large conventional banks.** Many European and American conventional banks – like UBS, BNP Paribas, Credit Suisse, ABN Amro, Deutsche Bank, Citibank, Merrill Lynch, HSBC and Barclays – entered the industry operating via Islamic windows, which are partially separate operations within the same distribution channel of the bank.
	Several international Islamic regulatory bodies were also established during this decade – Islamic Financial Services Board, International Islamic Financial Market, Council for Islamic Banks & Financial Institutions, International Islamic Rating Agency, Liquidity Management Centre. These will be covered in more detail in Chapter 3.
2002	**UK and Singapore governments** extend support to the Islamic financial institutions via various tax-neutrality rulings.
2004	**Islamic Bank of Britain set up.** The European Union's first Shariah-compliant bank, today renamed the Al Rayan Bank.
2006	**Dubai financial market** announces restructuring to set up the world's first Islamic stock exchange.

KEY TERMS AND CONCEPTS

Classic economic problem	Islamic economics	Quran
Conventional banking	Islamic finance	Sadaqah
Cooperative savings bank	Islamic law	Scarcity of resources
economics	Islamic window	Shariah law
Hajj	Medium of exchange	Social welfare
Islamic banking	Money	Zakat

CHAPTER SUMMARY

Islam is a way of life and has influence on all aspects of a Muslim's life. The Islamic law, Shariah, prohibits any dealing with interest and over the last six decades the Muslims globally became interested in conducting their finance and banking in an interest-free manner. Before the emergence of modern Islamic finance and banking, conventional banking dominated the world, starting from the Florentine merchants and growing with the Industrial Revolution. Islamic finance and banking is religion-based and has unique features like being profit and loss-based rather than interest-based, real asset-linked, in partnership rather than a debtor–creditor relationship, with a prudent choice of projects and avoidance of speculation and excessive risk.

Economics in ancient times was linked to religion or capitalism. All three Abrahamic religions agreed on justice in economic exchange, that the ultimate owner of property was the Creator, while the prohibition of usury or interest had different interpretations. Modern economic thought, as laid out by Adam Smith, considered money or capital as part of the factor of production. A key issue in modern economics was the classic economic problem – unlimited wants and limited resources. Islamic economics is rooted in the Quran and Sunnah, and dictates that wants should be limited, production encouraged, waste and luxury discouraged. Thus solving the classic economic problem.

Islamic economics is closely tied to social welfare. The Islamic doctrine of property ownership dictates Allah as the ultimate owner and humans as the trustee, and as such the benefits of assets need to be shared via the modes of compulsory Zakat and voluntary Sadaqah. Islam totally bans interest, although it permits the cost of capital in the form of sharing in the profit, provided the losses are shared too. There are clear distinctions between conventional and Islamic economics related to ownership and accumulation of wealth, wants and resources, role of the State, economic cycles and market economy, rewards of capital, social welfare and inheritance law.

Islamic finance began with the advent of Islam and early Islamic finance concepts and tools developed during the times of the Prophet and the Caliphs with achievements in financing government treasury, social welfare, business and trade. From the 12th century to almost the middle of the 20th century was the period of decline and almost obliteration of Islamic finance due to the fall of the Ottomans, the dominance of Western economies and institutions, colonization and disuse. The revival of Islamic finance began from the middle of the 20th century, with discussions amongst scholars and experts leading to experimentations like Mit Ghamr savings bank, Tabung Haji and further institutional developments of the Islamic Development Bank and the Dubai Islamic Bank.

Muslims interested in living by their faith and following the Shariah rulings related to their financial and banking transactions were prohibited from dealing with interest and were unable to use conventional banking since most of their products are interest-based. To meet this demand from Muslims, Islamic finance and banking is growing and is now accepted and identified as a new, niche sector within the global finance industry. It has spread significantly in the Muslim-majority countries in the Middle East and North and East Africa, as well as South and South-East Asia, with Bahrain and Malaysia being major hubs. The sector is also gaining a significant foothold in the Western world, serving the Muslim population as well as taking advantage of the potential in this unique sector.

The Islamic finance and banking industry today is operating in about 75 countries, with almost 500 Islamic institutions and another 190 conventional financial institutions participating in Islamic finance. The rapid growth has been driven by an increase in the Muslim population and their desire to participate in Shariah-compliant finance and banking, affluence in the Middle East (especially in the GCC) and the economic rise of Asia.

END OF CHAPTER QUESTIONS AND ACTIVITIES

Discussion Questions

1. Briefly discuss the creation of money in the world.
2. Discuss the early establishment of commercial banking in Europe.
3. Which three groups of people established the original banking system in the Western world? What are their similarities to a modern bank?
4. Define Islamic finance.
5. Briefly discuss the distinctive features of Islamic finance.
6. Give a summary of economics in ancient times.
7. Who is Adam Smith and what is his role in modern economic thought?
8. Briefly describe the four classic economic models.
9. Describe Islamic economics.
10. Discuss the principles of Islamic economics.
11. What is Islam's solution to the classic economic problem?
12. How is property ownership dealt with in Islamic economics?
13. What is Sadaqah?
14. Discuss Zakat as a financial and social welfare tool in Islamic economics.
15. Why is Zakat an important feature of the Islamic welfare society? How is it different from a conventional tax?
16. Does Islamic economics agree to assign a cost to capital?
17. What are the core differences between conventional economics and Islamic economics?
18. Discuss some of the achievements of Islamic finance during the early days of the Islamic civilization.
19. Why is the period between the 12th century and the 20th century so meaningful for Islamic finance? What happened during this period and why?
20. Discuss the Mit Ghamr story.

21. What is Tabung Haji? Why is it important in the development of modern Islamic finance and banking?
22. What roles did the Islamic Development Bank and the Dubai Islamic Bank have in the progress of modern Islamic finance and banking?
23. Discuss the rapid growth of modern Islamic finance and banking amongst the Muslim-majority countries.
24. Discuss the spread of modern Islamic finance and banking in the non-Muslim countries of the world.
25. What are the main sub-sectors within the modern Islamic finance and banking industry?
26. Discuss the status of the modern Islamic finance and banking industry globally.
27. Walk through the timeline of the development of the modern Islamic finance and banking industry.

Multiple Choice Questions

Circle the letter next to the most accurate answer.

1. A key principle related to Islamic finance is:
   a. Encouragement to use Riba and loss
   b. Earning money from money
   c. Avoid hoarding
   d. Hoarding
2. Which one below is not forbidden in Islamic finance and banking:
   a. All kinds of risk
   b. Hoarding of goods
   c. Speculative behaviour
   d. Making money out of money
3. Which of the following statement(s) is/are correct about the early evolution of Islamic finance?
   a. Islamic finance was born in the early 7th century and continued to develop up to the 11th century
   b. Islamic finance contracts like Mudaraba and Musharaka were in use for trade and business
   c. Islamic traders and ships faced frequent events of mutiny while at sea
   d. Only a and b
4. Western conventional banking was established by three groups of people. Which group below is not one of them?
   a. Rich merchants
   b. Goldsmiths
   c. Money lenders
   d. Land owners
5. Islamic economics ensures:
   a. Socio-economic justice
   b. Harmony between the moral and material needs of society
   c. Shariah compliance in economic activities
   d. All of the above

6. Zakat is an important financial tool in Islam. Zakat application differs for money used in a productive manner or kept idle as cash. Which statement below best describes this goal of Zakat?
   a. To finance government expenses only
   b. To encourage holding cash
   c. To encourage productive activities
   d. To discourage acquisition of material goods
7. Islamic economics differs from conventional economics as it requires the benefit of society and the environment in addition to individual gain and business profit. Which statement below best describes this?
   a. To create public good
   b. To encourage profitable ventures
   c. To moderate profit through application of Zakat
   d. To control acquisition of material goods
8. The world's first Islamic banking experiment happened in:
   a. UK
   b. Malaysia
   c. Egypt
   d. Bahrain
9. The first commercial Islamic bank of the world was set up in:
   a. Egypt in 1963
   b. Dubai in 1975
   c. Saudi Arabia in 1960
   d. Malaysia in 1970
10. The world's first commercial Islamic bank was:
   a. Qatar Islamic Bank
   b. Dubai Islamic Bank
   c. May Bank Islamic
   d. Commercial Bank of Dubai

True/False Questions

Write T for true and F for false next to the statement.
1. Islam and trading arrived in Malaysia and Indonesia after the Europeans did.
2. Dubai Islamic Bank is the world's first commercially successful Islamic bank.
3. Islamic mercantile law for trading and partnership was already developed before European commercial law was developed.
4. London is an important centre for Islamic banking and insurance.
5. Islamic finance began from the time of the Prophet and continued growing uninterrupted to the present.
6. The main objective of Islamic banks is to make attractive returns for their shareholders.
7. The main objective of Islamic banks is to ensure Haram activities are not financed.
8. The main objective of Islamic banks is to provide an alternative to interest-based finance.
9. The main objective of Islamic banks is to finance the construction of masjids.
10. The goal of Islamic economics is to ensure socio-economic justice.

11. The goal of Islamic economics is to provide freely available financing for Muslims.
12. The goal of Islamic economics is to establish harmony between the moral and material needs of society.
13. Conventional banks base their lending criteria largely on creditworthiness and collateral.
14. Islamic banks base their lending criteria on investment potential and managerial capability of the borrower rather than on collateral only.
15. Hoarding of any goods is not allowed in Islamic finance.

Calculation Problems

1. Khalid has kept £2 million in his savings account with Al Rayan Bank. Last year he earned profit at an average rate of 6%. He did not take any money out of the account. Sara invested £2 million in a bakery business. She earned £150,000 last year and took £60,000 as her annual salary to manage the business. Calculate the Zakat applicable to both. What can we infer from this about Zakat as a financial tool?
2. Amna and her sister Mariam inherited (Arab Emirates dirham) AED1 million each from their father after he passed away. Amna has kept her AED1 million in her savings account with Abu Dhabi Islamic Bank. The bank shared profit with depositors last year at an average rate of 3%. The cash was in the account for the entire year. Mariam invested her AED1 million in a partnership with a friend to start and manage school uniform and other accessories production. As a start-up business they only earned AED70,000 in the first year. Mariam and her friend kept AED30,000 each as their annual management salary and split the rest as their profit. Calculate the Zakat applicable to both Amna and Mariam. From these calculations what do you learn about Zakat as an encouragement to participate in productive endeavours?

CHAPTER 2

Shariah Law and the Shariah Supervisory Board

Learning outcomes

Upon completion of this chapter, you should be able to:

1. Define Shariah law and explain the main sources of the Shariah law.
2. Explain Shariah prohibitions and principles and their impact on Islamic finance and banking.
3. Describe the Shariah Supervisory Board, its formation and functions.
4. Discuss the Shariah governance process.

INTRODUCTION TO THE ISLAMIC LAW – SHARIAH

The Arabic word 'Shariah' means path to the watering place. It is also called the Islamic law. Islam influences all aspects of a Muslim's life – as individuals, within the family, society, in relationships with the State and the community and in the manner business or commercial activities are conducted. Shariah law is a comprehensive code of conduct for the Muslim's life, given by the Creator – Allah. The global Muslim community, called the Ummah, serves as the trustee for upholding Shariah law. The Muslim population can derive rules from the Shariah law but cannot create the law. Islam is a democracy, so every capable Muslim has the right to interpret Shariah law and give an opinion. But when a clear command on any issue exists from Allah or his Prophet, no one, including a leader, court or scholar, or the entire Muslim community together, can change the Shariah law. The same Shariah law applies in all Muslim countries.

As discussed in Ginena & Hamid (2015), the Shariah rulings can be grouped into two types – obligatory rulings and declaratory rulings. There are five types of obligatory rulings. These are called Wajib – which need to be followed, like mutual consent in a contract; Mustahabb – which are recommended, like ensuring the contract is written;

Mubah – which are permissible and neither rewarded nor punished, like having two parties to a contract or having more than two; Makruh – which are discouraged, for example a poor person donating whatever they own rather than leaving it for their poor heir; Haram – which are forbidden, like taking interest on a loan contract. Declaratory rulings are those that make it easy to implement the obligatory rulings by describing causes, conditions and obstacles related to the obligatory rulings.

The best interest of the general public is called the Maslahah and is of utmost importance in the Shariah law. Maslahah has three categories. The first is Daruriyyat, the essential elements for a person, like their faith, their life, their intellect, wealth and the continuity of their family. The second category is Hajiyyat, the complementary elements, the lack of which will cause hardship but not disrupt life totally, like the availability of transportation or being involved in an economic activity. The third category is Tahsiniyyat, additional elements that make life nicer, customs and ways of behaviour, like being polite and pleasant in dealings with people.

The aim of Shariah law is to guide human beings towards that which is good and just, beneficial for them, builds a moral society and prevents them from that which is harmful to them and their community. Shariah or Islamic jurisprudence includes rulings related to man's relationship to his Creator, Allah, called Ibadat and rulings covering man's relationship to man, called Muamalat. A major part of the Muamalat involves economic activities and commercial dealings. Islamic finance and banking also falls within this. Shariah law thus includes the legal framework, statutes, norms, rules and ethics related to Islamic finance. The knowledge of Shariah is called Fiqh and those who are knowledgeable in Fiqh are the Fuqaha, Ulema, or Islamic jurists or scholars. Jurists are responsible for deliberating and debating any need for change in the Shariah rulings with changes in circumstances, and this is achieved through their abilities to reason and make deductions based on their extensive knowledge.

SOURCES OF SHARIAH

The first and primary source of Shariah law is the **Quran.** It is the word of Allah and was revealed only to the Prophet Muhammad. It was recorded in writing during his lifetime. It is universally accurate and is memorized by many and recited during prayers. The second primary source of Shariah law is the **Sunnah,** which is the sayings of the Prophet, his practices, his acts and conducts, whatever he approved. The Prophet discouraged writing down of the Sunnah during his lifetime to ensure it does not get confused with the Quran, which was written down. Mostly the Sunnah was retained in the memory of the Prophet's companions. Later the various Sunnah were selected, standardized and recorded and these records were called the Hadith.

As time passed and the Islamic society grew it was faced with new situations and to deal with them the Shariah rules derived from the Quran and the Sunnah were required to be expanded to match the needs of the time and circumstances. This responsibility lay with the jurists or scholars, the Fuqaha and Ulema. When jurists searched for solutions to various problems, the starting point was always required to be the Quran and the Sunnah, and rulings in the Quran had priority over those in the Sunnah. There are three ways of expanding or elaborating Shariah law. Firstly, **Ijtihad** – which meant independent interpretation by a scholar. Ijtihad was used to extend Shariah to situations not covered before by the use of human reasoning, and this is increasingly being used in Islamic finance. Secondly, **Ikhtiyar** – which meant choice, that is choosing from past views. This helped to connect the modern view with the views of the past. Thirdly, **Dururah** – meaning necessity, that is some relaxation in rules may be considered if it is a necessity. The expansion of Shariah rules leads to its secondary sources. All scholars agree to the secondary sources of Ijma and Qiyas.

The third most important source of the Shariah law is **Ijma.** The jurists were required to debate and provide opinions on Shariah issues not dealt with before from the very early days of Islam. Ijtihad is the process by which this is done. It began in the reign of the first two Caliphs of the Islamic State, Abu Bakr Al Siddique and Umar ibn Al Khattab. Collectively the jurists aimed to reach a consensus on their decisions. In case consensus was not reached, the Caliph would choose that opinion which was most beneficial for the public interest or Maslahah. The Muslim community at this time was small and lived within similar circumstances, so it was easy to reach consensus. After this period, Islam began to spread across places where people lived differently and in different circumstances, jurists began to differ in their opinions and decisions were made through the deliberations of Ijtihad. Differences in opinion often resulted from different interpretations of the Quran or Sunnah, disagreements on the strength of various Hadith, and political and cultural differences entering the Muslim communities. Today Islamic scholars debate issues not faced by the community in the early days of Islam, and seek a solution that will not contradict the Quran or Sunnah. The process starts from each scholar's personal analysis and opinion, and aims for a consensus of opinion. Once consensus is achieved, the opinion becomes an authority. Ijma is an important source in solving contemporary issues and is used extensively in Islamic finance and banking.

The fourth most important source of the Shariah law, **Qiyas** involves analogical deductions. It is the process by which any original ruling, or an existing case decision, is applied to a new matter with similar characteristics on the basis that the new case has the same effective cause as the former. Qiyas requires measuring or estimating one thing against another. The Shariah scholars would consider the use of Qiyas only if a legal ruling on the new issue could not be found in the Quran, Sunnah or Ijma. Use of Qiyas is also considerable in modern Islamic finance and banking to deal with the changing times and circumstances faced by the industry.

In addition to these four sources, Shariah scholars also consider two more things in elaborating rulings.

- **Istihsan** – which is the preference of a jurist; usually flexibility is granted in favour of matters of public interest, Masayil Al Maslahah, over strict Shariah rulings.
- **Istishab** – which is the presumption that a situation existing previously continues to exist unless proven otherwise.

SCHOOLS OF ISLAMIC JURISPRUDENCE

The two main divisions within the Muslim faith are the Sunni and the Shiite. Within each of these there are further divisions. The Shariah interpretations, especially those rulings related to Islamic finance and banking, amongst these divisions have many similarities but there are some differences. The schools of Islamic jurisprudence and Shariah interpretations and their geographic concentrations are given below.

Sunni Schools of Thought
- **Maliki.** Originated from Medina and has heavy reliance on the Sunnah. It is followed in large parts of the Middle East including UAE, Kuwait, parts of Saudi Arabia and of Egypt, North and West Africa.
- **Hambali.** Originated from Damascus, it is followed in most of Saudi Arabia, Qatar, Syria and parts of Iraq.
- **Shafi.** This is a more liberal school and countries in the Far East like Indonesia, Malaysia, Brunei, Philippines, Singapore, Thailand, parts of Egypt, Jordan, Palestine, Yemen and Somalia adhere to this school.
- **Hanafi.** Originated in Iraq and is followed in Turkey, Bangladesh, Pakistan, India, Afganistan, Levant, Central Asia, parts of Iraq and of Egypt.

Main Shiite School of Thought
- **Jaafari.** Followed in Iran and amongst the Shiite population in Iraq, Pakistan, India, Lebanon and Azerbaijan.

ETHICS IN SHARIAH-COMPLIANT BUSINESS AND FINANCE

Ethics involves the moral behaviour of a person and it is equally important in today's business and finance. Ethics in business includes social and environmental responsibilities and leads to sustainable business. Islamic Shariah-compliant commerce and finance is based on religious doctrines and thus is inherently ethical. Islamic business ethics outlines the permissible forms of business and Shariah-compliant products and transactions. Specific ethical rules in Islamic business, many of which are common to business ethics anywhere in the world, are as follows.

- **Honesty.** All parties should be truthful, fair and just to each other and fulfil their obligations.
- **Transparency.** All contracts should clearly specify the quality, quantity and price of the goods or services being transacted; they should also specify delivery details, and the rights and obligations of all parties.
- **Mutual consent.** All parties in the contract should have entered into it with mutual consent, without any coercion or exploitation.
- **Property.** No property can be appropriated wrongfully or unjustly.
- **Employees.** All employees of the business should be treated fairly.
- **Price stability.** Shariah prohibits hoarding or cheating, which achieves price stability.
- **Generosity and leniency.** Shariah encourages parties in the business transaction to be considerate of all other parties, and be generous whenever possible, sell or buy at a fair price and allow additional time to borrowers if they really need it.
- **Halal versus Haram.** Only Halal businesses, products and transactions should be dealt with and all Haram or prohibited items should be avoided.

MAJOR SHARIAH PROHIBITIONS AND PRINCIPLES AND THEIR IMPLICATIONS

Shariah law is a wide body of discipline. A part of it only deals with business and commercial transactions, and that includes the prohibitions and principles relating to the niche sector of Islamic finance and banking. The three main Shariah prohibitions that impact the Islamic finance and banking industry are the prohibitions of Riba, Gharar and Maysir. These prohibitions and other principles are discussed below.

Prohibition of Interest or Riba

As discussed in Chapter 1, in Islam money is only a medium of exchange and not a commodity which can earn on its own. Riba (or usury or interest) is the premium paid by the borrower to the lender along with the principal amount as a condition of the loan. It means the increase, addition, expansion or growth in the money that is owed. Hence Riba or interest means earning money from money. The characteristics of interest or Riba are that it is fixed and positive, the amount of Riba depends on the amount of the loan and for the period of the loan, and that it is guaranteed payment irrespective of the outcome of the purpose for which the amount was borrowed. Islam considers Riba to be unearned and undeserved income and prohibits all forms of it – small or large, simple or compound.

Islam is not the only religion to apply this prohibition. In their original forms, both Judaism and Christianity considered interest on borrowed funds to be unjust and unlawful, since the lender collected interest which was a fixed amount and had no link to the profit or loss of the economic activity for which money was borrowed. Later though both Judaism and Christianity accepted interest as the price for borrowed funds. The Church possessed significant wealth and was a major lender of funds from the Middle Ages to the 13th century, and to facilitate this the Christian charging of interest was legalized in Valencia in 1217 and in Florence in 1403. This formed the foundation for the conventional banking industry, which offered deposits and loans based on interest (Schoon, 2016).

There is no doubt about Shariah law's prohibition of interest or Riba. This prohibition continues in Islam and is the primary reason for the need to establish an interest-free system of Islamic finance and banking for people of Muslim faith. Islamic finance and banking replaced interest-based banking by the sharing of profit and loss by both the funds provider and the funds user or entrepreneur. In the conventional system a funds provider earns interest irrespective of the outcome of the funds usage, while in the Islamic system the funds provider shares in the profit at a pre-agreed ratio. In case of a loss, the conventional bank still needs to be paid the interest while the Islamic bank bears the loss and the entrepreneur loses their time, effort and any income they could have earned. As such, the conventional bank gives most emphasis to the creditworthiness of the borrower so that they are paid the interest and the principle; the Islamic bank focuses on the soundness of the project for which the funds are to be used and the abilities of the entrepreneur, because the higher the profit the project makes, the more the Islamic bank will earn.

Riba has been prohibited by Islamic Shariah law because of its harmful effect on the personal, social and economic life of people. Some of the criticisms directed towards Riba by Islamic jurists and Islamic economists are as follows.

1. The borrower pays interest to the lender irrespective of the profit or loss of the economic activity for which the money was borrowed. If the profit of the business is less than the interest payment, or if there is a loss, then the borrower still needs to pay the interest and may go out of business. This is harmful for the borrower and for the society and economy in which he operates.
2. The lender is paid a fixed interest amount. If the business does very well, the interest amount still stays the same, so the lender cannot benefit from the high profits.
3. Allocation of resources in the interest-based system is inefficient since it is linked to the creditworthiness of the borrower and any collateral the borrower can provide rather than the productivity of the economic activity or the skills of the borrower.

Riba is of two types.

- **Riba al Nasiah.** This is the main type of Riba, which is the interest paid on loans. It is the additional amount paid along with the principal and it is decided based on the principal amount of the loan and the period for which the loan is given. It is considered as an unjust increase in the amount of the loan, which is fixed in advance and has no connection to the economic activity for which the loan was taken.
- **Riba al Fadl.** This Riba happens when exchanging the same type of goods, a smaller amount of superior quality with a larger amount of inferior quality. Riba al Fadl is also applicable when money is exchanged for money but in different amounts, or when commodities that were used as money – like gold, silver, dates, wheat, barley and other homogenous goods – are exchanged against themselves in unequal proportions. In contemporary Islamic finance, foreign currency transactions are acceptable as long as they are concluded on the spot, hand to hand. In this case one currency is viewed as money while the other is considered as the commodity purchased.

Prohibition of Uncertain Dealings or Gharar

The second major prohibition in Islamic finance is Gharar. Gharar means taking excessive risk or having unnecessary uncertainty in a contract. Islam requires all aspects of the transaction or contract to be transparent and known to all parties, thus significantly reducing conflict. Some situations where Gharar could exist are as follows.

1. The sale of items which do not exist or whose characteristics are not certain. For example, the crop of a field that has not yet been cultivated. (Istisna and Salam are exceptions to the rule of an item not existing, though detailed specifications are provided. Istisna and Salam contracts will be discussed in Chapters 8 and 9 of this book.)
2. Goods that are impossible to deliver. For example, a fresh fruit during a season it does not grow.
3. A sale contract is executed without specifying the price.

4. When the payment terms and delivery schedule are not specified in a deferred sales contract.
5. A business or trade where there is no certainty about the results – speculative activities.
6. When all aspects of the contract are not known by all the parties, there is lack of transparency. For example, selling a car without revealing its specifications.

Prohibition of Gharar is like the regulatory protection provided by contemporary securities law, which requires that customers' funds are protected by providing clear specifications of the investments and by transparency of the contracts. In modern Islamic finance Gharar can be of two types: **Gharar Fahish,** which means a substantial amount of the objectionable characteristic and is prohibited and **Gharar Yasir,** which means a trivial amount of the objectionable characteristic and is tolerated by Shariah rulings.

Prohibition of Speculative Behaviour or Maysir

Maysir is the third major prohibition. Maysir includes all kinds of games of chance or dealings where one can gain significantly or lose all depending on which way the deal moves and is prohibited by Shariah law. It includes all kinds of gambling, where a party can suffer total loss based on mere chance or make a substantial gain without any effort. Maysir is prohibited in Islam because it leads to winning at the expense of others losing, so it is socially unacceptable. Maysir is different from risk in everyday life or in business, which is acceptable. It is risk taken to win without any productive activity involved and has the possibility of losing everything.

Other principles of Shariah law include the following.

1. **Encouragement to use profit and loss.** Contracting parties have the right to share in the returns as long as they share the risk also; this profit and loss system is encouraged as an alternative to interest-based conventional finance.
2. **Requirement for Shariah-compliant contracts.** The subject of the contract and the process of executing the contract should not include any element that is declared as Haram or not permissible in Islam – for example, alcohol, pork, adult entertainment, etc.
3. **Avoid hoarding.** Sellers are not allowed to hoard goods and services to force prices up, as this would cause hardship to those who need them, and are encouraged to sell at a reasonable price even if there is a shortage in the market.
4. **Avoid taking advantage of the seller.** If the buyer is aware that the seller is under duress and is forced to sell at a loss, Shariah requires that the buyer pay a reasonable price and not take advantage of the seller's difficulties.
5. **Freedom of contract.** All parties in the contract have mutually consented to be part of it.
6. **Original permissibility.** Everything is permissible unless there is a ruling in Shariah that makes it impermissible.
7. **Interests of society.** The best interests of society are more important than those of the individual.
8. **Relieving of hardship versus providing of benefits.** Both are important, but if one has to be chosen over the other then relieving of hardship would be given more importance.

9. **Small versus bigger.** To eliminate a small loss a bigger loss cannot be inflicted, and to keep a small benefit a bigger benefit cannot be given up.
10. **Removing extreme hardship.** When no other choice exists to remove extreme hardship even an unlawful thing is accepted, like eating pork when no other food is available and one could starve.

The main distinguishing feature of Shariah law from its Western counterpart is that it is completely religion-based, and its rulings derive from the Quran and the Sunnah. The early origins of most legal systems, including the Western conventional system, were also based on the norms of a specific religion, although these legal systems have since moved away from their religious basis and become independent bodies of knowledge. Meanwhile Shariah law still prescribes completely the rulings of Islam and has influence on all aspects of a Muslim's life – individual, social, economic and political, including allowable private and public behaviour, property ownership and family law. Another unique aspect of the Shariah law is that it is not country-specific, but applicable to Muslims in all countries. In Muslim-majority countries Shariah law (or parts of it) is applicable at State level, while in non-Muslim countries it would be applied informally to the Muslim population. The Western legal system shows significant uniformity globally, while Shariah law can be interpreted differently by the various schools of thought and this is a major challenge of Shariah law.

SHARIAH SUPERVISORY BOARD (SSB)

Introduction to the SSB

Islamic banks are set up in three different environments. Firstly, they could be established in a Muslim country where by State law all financial institutions are required to be Shariah-compliant. Secondly, they could be established in a Muslim or non-Muslim country where central bank and State regulations allow both conventional and Islamic banks to operate and often have some differences in the rulings for **Islamic financial institutions (IFIs)** in accordance with their different operational framework. This is called the **dual banking** environment. Thirdly, they could be set up in a non-Muslim country where central bank regulations do not provide any separate rulings or facilities for IFIs to operate. Basically, the IFI will operate within the conventional finance regulations. Countries that fall within the first category are Iran, Sudan and Pakistan. Pakistan initiated constitutional reform for a complete Shariah-based financial system from the late 1970s to the early 1980s, but today in reality it operates as a dual banking environment. Most other Muslim countries fall within the second category, where conventional and Islamic banks operate side by side and are formally recognized by the regulatory authorities, like the GCC countries, South Asia and South-East Asia and the Middle East and North African Muslim-majority countries. Most non-Muslim countries, like the UK, other European countries, the USA, Canada, Australia, etc., unlike the dual banking jurisdictions, do not have a separate set of regulations for IFIs and this can lead to some regulatory challenges. In the case of the first and second categories, the setting up of a **Shariah Supervisory Board** is mandatory, while in the third category it is optional for the IFI. Most IFIs that operate within the third category voluntarily set up an SSB to give confidence to their stakeholders rather than to satisfy the regulatory authorities of the jurisdiction they operate in.

Formation of the SSB

The SSB is a body set up with a group of **Islamic Shariah scholars** or jurists to assist the IFI to operate in accordance with Islamic Shariah law. The SSB is also sometimes called the Shariah Board, Shariah Committee, Shariah Advisory Committee, Shariah Council, Shariah Control Committee or simply the Religious Board. No matter what it is called, it is set up for the same reasons, to guide the IFI to develop its products, transactions, documents and all other operational activities in a Shariah-compliant manner by providing expert legal advice and recommendations. To achieve this objective the SSB regularly monitors the operations, transactions and product features to ensure Shariah rulings are followed and assists the IFI's management and **Board of Directors (BOD)** to meet the Shariah requirements within the jurisdictional and competitive challenges. The SSB is not only an advisory body but also has authority over the BOD, where Shariah permissibility or prohibitions are considered.

The AAOIFI, which is a major international Islamic finance regulatory and standard setting body and will be discussed further in Chapter 3, defines the SSB as an independent body of specialized Islamic jurists and it may include a member specialized in finance and banking, with expertise in business in general and in Islamic finance. The AAOIFI definition further elaborates that the SSB directs, reviews and supervises the IFI to ensure that it complies with the Shariah rulings and that SSB recommendations are binding on the IFI. Ginena & Hamid (2015) had two reservations about the AAOIFI definition. The first objection is to the term 'directing' rather than 'advising', as this could lead to issues with the management. The second objection was about the inclusion of a finance and banking expert who is not well versed in the Shariah law being involved in developing Islamic legal ruling. The finance expert's knowledge was considered useful in helping the Islamic jurists understand the financial industry and especially Islamic finance and the applicability of Shariah rulings to products and operations, but this person ideally should not be issuing Shariah rulings in the absence of specialized Shariah qualifications.

The SSB needs to be made up of scholars who are academically qualified to interpret the Shariah law and apply it to modern-day financial institutions and to the emerging issues in the Islamic finance and banking industry. They should also be able to research and develop Shariah rulings for the IFI and in general guide the IFI to achieve Shariah compliance. There is a lack of consensus in the industry related to the academic qualifications of the SSB members. Some recognized Islamic institutions globally are the Al Medina in Saudi Arabia, Al Azhar in Cairo, International Islamic University in Kuala Lumpur, Darul Uloom in Karachi and Darul Uloom in Deoband, India and others conducting Islamic Fiqh teachings which provide qualifications in Islamic jurisprudence, Islamic economics, Islamic banking and finance. General skills that would be useful for an SSB member in these modern times of globalization and technical advancement are time management, IT, communication and conflict resolution. Efforts are also being made to include in the SSBs qualified finance professionals with Shariah qualifications. Such scholars are very limited in number to date. Cross-training of finance professionals or Shariah scholars over time could solve this problem.

The **SSB Charter** is a document detailing the purpose, structure, responsibilities and accountabilities of the SSB. The number of members in the SSB is not fixed. AAOIFI suggests at least three, while the IFSB says not less than five. The shareholders, or the BOD on behalf of the shareholders, appoint the members of the SSB, while the SSB chairman is elected by the other members. The BOD and management set the strategic goals and objectives of the IFI, which need to be within the framework of Shariah compliance, so they need to work in close cooperation with the SSB. This dual authority within an Islamic bank and other IFIs may give rise to some conflicts. According to Ginena & Hamid (2015), the conflicts could be as follows.

- **Between SSB members** – which could be resolved through discussions, the process of majority choice or by the intervention of the chairman.
- **Between the BOD and the SSB** – this may happen if the BOD tries to influence or interfere with the SSB and its functions related to Shariah compliance, or if the BOD appoints an incompetent scholar for the SSB or wrongfully tries to remove a competent SSB member.
- **Between management and the SSB** – conflicts like those with the BOD can happen with management. If management interferes unnecessarily or tries to influence the SSB, or fails to follow through the recommendations of the SSB in the operations of the IFI, or fails to communicate effectively with the SSB on relevant issues.

Status of the SSB Within the Industry

The SSB positioning within the industry varies in different countries. IFIs in most Muslim-majority countries would have an in-house SSB. In some Islamic or dual banking environments, the central bank would also have an SSB which provides guidelines to the Islamic finance and banking industry and monitors the roles of the SSBs within individual IFIs. Countries like Malaysia, Pakistan, Indonesia and Sudan have such a system. In most non-Muslim countries there is no regulatory requirement to have an SSB, but the IFIs choose to have some form of Shariah supervisory body to meet industry practices and the market demands of the stakeholders. The aim of the global Islamic finance and banking industry is to reach standardization of the Shariah requirements on a global level which would significantly reduce the need to have in-house SSBs; rather Shariah consultants or advisors would be enough.

According to Abdul-Rahman (2014), Western regulators and central banks have some concerns about the SSBs. These are that in most Western countries there is a clear separation between the State and the Church. Thus, a financial institution operating under religious rulings, like the IFIs, is difficult to accept. Moreover, the existence of both the BOD and the SSB, where the SSB provides rulings that are mandatory on the BOD, could lead to conflict and this could affect sound management of the institution. The final concern is about most Shariah scholars on the SSB not having much knowledge or experience of banking and finance, and almost none about the regulations in the Western financial industry. An SSB, formed on a global platform, with well-qualified, globally acceptable Shariah scholars, who also have sufficient knowledge and expertise of the Islamic as well as the conventional finance and banking industry, and thus provide standardized and realistic rulings, would be a solution to such concerns and would be a major boost for the global Islamic finance and banking industry.

Functions of the SSB

The SSB's responsibilities are both internal and external. Internally it is responsible for guiding the IFI, its management, staff and the BOD towards proper application of Shariah rulings in its activities and externally it guarantees to shareholders, customers, depositors and investors the Shariah compliance of the IFI. SSB's responsibilities can also be categorized as academic and executive. The academic role primarily involves research and training, while the executive role is reviewing policies, products and transactions, recommending changes, issuing rulings and reports. SSB functions can also be grouped as supervisory and advisory or consulting.

The supervisory function is mainly to ensure Shariah compliance and is conducted over three stages. These stages and the jobs conducted by the SSB within these stages are set out below.

- **Set-up stage supervision.** This is the stage that takes place when the IFI is being set up. Jobs conducted under this stage would be:
  1. Setting up the SSB.
  2. Including the SSB position in the memorandum and articles of association of the institution.
  3. Developing the Shariah-compliance policies and procedures of the IFI.
  4. Reviewing the products and services planned for the IFI.
  5. Reviewing the IT structure and promotional material for Shariah compliance.
  6. Providing initial Shariah training to staff, management and members of the BOD.
- **Day-to-day ongoing supervision.** The jobs conducted by the SSB during the financial year are:
  1. Supervise the IFI's day-to-day activities for Shariah compliance.
  2. Review central bank regulations as received, seeking exemptions or suggesting alternatives if these conflict with Shariah.
  3. Review new products or services proposed by the management for Shariah compliance and suggest modifications if necessary.
  4. Review the IFI's investments and projects for Shariah compliance.
  5. Review documentation for Shariah compliance.
  6. Manage the IFI's charitable and social responsibilities, including provision of Qard Hasan to the poor and needy, collection and distribution of Zakat, and other social responsibilities of the IFI in case of any calamity.
- **Annual supervision.** The below jobs are conducted by the SSB at the end of each financial year:

  1. Complete the annual Shariah audit to ensure all transactions, calculations and payments of Zakat and distributions of Shariah non-compliant income to charity are conducted in a Shariah-compliant manner, thus ensuring all profits earned are permissible.
  2. Issue an annual Shariah compliance audit report and an annual compliance certificate for the benefit of all stakeholders, especially shareholders and depositors.
  3. Annual review of the Shariah governance process and manual.

The advisory or consulting jobs conducted by the SSB include the following:

1. Provide guidance and advice on Shariah issues related to operations on an ongoing basis to the IFI staff and management.
2. Advise the BOD and management on policies and procedures related to Shariah matters.
3. Conduct research and development, to innovate and design new Shariah-based and interest-free products.

4. Conduct seminars and trainings on Shariah for management and staff of the bank and customers, if required.
5. Maintain regular communication with Shariah scholars of other IFIs to promote consensus and develop common strategies.
6. Research and study previously issued religious rulings called Fatwa, assess their applicability in current times and develop their own rulings based on them.
7. Clarify the applicability of Shariah rulings on new economic issues as they arise.
8. Carefully document the process and all the religious bases and foundations utilized to arrive at a new ruling by the SSB.

CORPORATE AND SHARIAH GOVERNANCE

Corporate governance is a set of rules, laws, policies and processes by which a corporation is managed to safeguard the best interests of its stakeholders, including shareholders, creditors, customers, employees and government. According to Ginena & Hamid (2015), important elements of good corporate governance include an efficient BOD, disclosure, transparency and effective control of activities, commitment to corporate objectives, goals and shareholders' rights. Corporate governance has grown in importance globally since the 1990s, and in the finance and banking sector it is even more important as it is part of the Basel II banking supervision requirements. Lack of corporate governance is identified as the main reason for most bank failures, and it is even more important since the 2007 global financial crisis. In the finance and banking sector corporate governance provides protection for depositors, ensures strong internal control, risk management, transparency and regulatory compliance.

Shariah governance includes all the elements of corporate governance listed above, and goes beyond this since accountability is not only to the shareholders but also to religious requirements. Shariah governance requires independent oversight of Shariah compliance, issuance of Shariah rulings, application of those rulings and distribution of Shariah information. The risks faced by Islamic banks are the same as those for conventional banks, but in addition they have the Shariah-compliance risk, which could include incorrect, unclear or too complicated rulings; use of products, transactions, documents and promotions not approved by Shariah; insufficient training and resource allocation leading to communication and technological problems in Shariah matters.

SHARIAH GOVERNANCE PROCESS

The SSB is responsible for implementing Shariah governance in an IFI. To conclude this function effectively, the SSB needs to be independent of any pressure from the management or the BOD, needs to include members who have competent knowledge both in Shariah and in banking and finance, must be able to maintain confidentiality of the IFI's proprietary information and needs to achieve disclosure requirements related to procedures, decisions and rulings to maintain public confidence.

IFIs often face regulatory challenges in jurisdictions where the regulatory bodies do not formally recognize Islamic finance and banking; these challenges could be that regulators apply rulings on IFIs that may lead to Shariah violations, or that profit and loss sharing does not have tax benefits like interest payments, the uncertainty and inadequacy of the legal system to deal with Islamic banking products and transactions, restrictions on financial institutions being involved in sales contracts and ownership transfers.

The Shariah governance process as outlined by Hassan, Kayed & Oseni (2013) includes:

1. Appointment of the members of the SSB by the shareholders at the AGM or by the BOD on their behalf.
2. Coordination and interaction between the various members of the SSB and other bodies in the IFI to ensure complete Shariah compliance in operations, transactions and products.
3. Completion of internal and external Shariah audits. The internal audit identifies any shortfalls in compliance and leads to the external audit which provides additional confidence to stakeholders.
4. Reporting directly to the BOD and issuing an annual Shariah report and Shariah certificates. The annual report details the extent of compliance for the previous financial year. The report is published along with other financial reports for the sake of all stakeholders. The Shariah certificates certify the Shariah compliance of the operations and income of the IFI.

KEY TERMS AND CONCEPTS

Declaratory rulings	Maysir	Shariah scholars or Fuqaha or Ulema
Fiqh	Muamalat	
Fuqaha	Obligatory rulings	Shariah governance
Gharar	Qiyas	Shariah Supervisory Board
Ijma	Riba	

CHAPTER SUMMARY

Shariah or Islamic law has influence on every aspect of a Muslim person's life, including how they conduct commerce and deal with their finances. The Shariah rulings include both obligatory and declaratory rulings and the aim of these rulings is to guide the Muslim population towards a just and beneficial society. Shariah law is primarily derived from the Muslim holy book, the Quran and from the Sunnah, the teachings and sayings of the Prophet Muhammad. Ijma, the consensus of Shariah scholars and Qiyas, analogical deductions, are two additional sources of Shariah which are used to make Shariah rulings more applicable to current times without contradicting the Quran or Sunnah.

Shariah is an extensive body of law, of which a part only deals with commerce and financial dealings, and that is what this book is concerned with. The three main prohibitions listed in Shariah that impact the Islamic finance and banking industry are Riba (usury or interest), Gharar (uncertainty or unnecessary risk) and Maysir (games of chance). In addition to these major prohibitions, Shariah also encourages profit and loss-based financial transactions, creating mutually agreed contracts as per Shariah requirements, giving priority to societal interest, the removal of hardships, avoiding hoarding and undue advantage taking of any party in the contract.

All Islamic financial institutions require Shariah supervision and the body most commonly responsible for this is the Shariah Supervisory Board, formed by a group of Shariah scholars or Islamic jurists. The Shariah scholars usually have Shariah qualifications from acceptable institutions and some knowledge and expertise in the areas of finance and banking is useful. In the organizational structure of the IFI, the SSB has authority over the Board of Directors in matters related to Shariah compliance and the SSB may have conflicts with the BOD or management or there may be a lack of consensus within the members of the SSB. The aim of the Islamic finance and banking industry is to develop a global SSB that provides standardized rulings for institutions around the world to minimize conflicts.

The SSB has multiple functions revolving around the achievement of Shariah compliance in the products, processes and operations of IFIs and these functions can be grouped into supervisory and advisory roles. Shariah governance is to a large extent like corporate governance, ensuring that the organization is managed to uphold the best interests of all stakeholders; additionally, it guarantees that the IFI follows Shariah requirements and is in compliance. The Shariah governance process involves the internal and external Shariah audit and the production of the annual Shariah report and the Shariah certificates.

END OF CHAPTER QUESTIONS AND ACTIVITIES

Discussion Questions

1. Define Shariah.
2. What are the two types of Shariah rulings? Discuss both.
3. What does Maslahah mean in Shariah? What are the categories of Maslahah?
4. Categorize the primary and secondary sources of Shariah.
5. What are the three ways of expanding the Shariah law?
6. Briefly explain what Qiyas and Ijma mean.
7. Discuss the schools of Islamic jurisprudence.
8. How important is ethics in Shariah-compliant business and finance? Discuss.
9. What are the three main prohibitions in Islamic finance? Briefly explain each.
10. What are the two types of Riba transactions described in the Quran and the Sunnah? Describe each with an example. What are the main differences between them?
11. What are the criticism directed towards Riba by Islamic jurists and economists?
12. What is Gharar? Give two examples of Gharar in a financial contract.
13. What is Maysir? Why is it a prohibition in Shariah law? Give a contemporary example of something that constitutes Maysir.
14. Identify three sources of making gains that would not be permissible in Islamic finance.
15. Discuss any four principles of Shariah besides the three main prohibitions.
16. Briefly discuss the differences between Shariah law and Western contemporary law.

17. What is a Shariah Supervisory Board?
18. Discuss the formation of the Shariah Supervisory Board.
19. What is the status of the Shariah Supervisory Board within an Islamic financial institution?
20. What kind of conflicts can the Shariah Supervisory Board be involved in?
21. Define the supervisory and advisory role of the Shariah Supervisory Board.
22. Discuss in detail the supervisory function served by the Shariah Supervisory Board.
23. What kind of advisory functions does the Shariah Supervisory Board have?
24. What is corporate governance?
25. How similar or different is corporate governance from Shariah governance?
26. Briefly discuss the Shariah governance process.

Multiple Choice Questions

Circle the letter next to the most accurate answer.

1. Which one below is not correct about Shariah law?
   a. Sharia law is given by Allah
   b. Sharia law is updated every 30 years
   c. The same Sharia law applies to the entire Muslim population
   d. The Muslim population can derive rules but cannot create new law
2. Which one below is not a method of elaborating Shariah law?
   a. Ijtihad
   b. Qiyas
   c. Dururah
   d. Ikhtiyar
3. The three methods of elaborating Shariah law are:
   a. Quran, Sunnah and Ijtihad
   b. Ijtihad, Ikhtiyar and Dururah
   c. Ikhtiyar, Ijtihad and Qiyas
   d. Ijma, Qiyas and Dururah
4. Which one below is not a source of Shariah law?
   a. Quran
   b. Sunnah
   c. Ijma
   d. Shariah lawyer
5. The sources of Shariah are in the order:
   a. Quran, Sunnah, Qiyas, Qanoon
   b. Quran, Sunnah, Ijma, Qiyas
   c. Quran, Sunnah, Ijma, Ikhtiyar
   d. Quran, Sunnah, Qanoon, Ikhtiyar
6. Which principle listed below is not one of the key principles related to Islamic finance?
   a. Prohibition of Riba
   b. Prohibition of earning money from money
   c. Prohibition of profit
   d. Prohibition of Maysir

7. The Shariah rules expand over time through different methods. Which of the following means independent interpretation by an Islamic legal scholar?
   a. Ijma
   b. Ijtihad
   c. Qiyas
   d. Maysir

8. The Shariah rules expand over time through different methods. Which of the following is not one of these methods?
   a. Ijma
   b. Ijtihad
   c. Qiyas
   d. Murabaha

9. The Shariah rules expand over time through different methods. Which of the following means reasoning by analogy by a single Islamic scholar?
   a. Ijma
   b. Ijtihad
   c. Qiyas
   d. Maysir

10. The Shariah rules expand over time through different methods. Which of the following means consensus (agreement) by several Islamic scholars?
    a. Ijma
    b. Ijtihad
    c. Qiyas
    d. Maysir

11. Islamic finance prohibits the sale of undeliverable goods or goods without a specified price. This transparency in contracts is also known as prohibition of:
    a. Gharar
    b. Maysir
    c. Riba
    d. Ijara

12. Which principle listed below is one of the key principles related to Islamic finance and banking?
    a. Prohibition of profit
    b. Prohibition of Gharar
    c. Prohibition of Shariah Supervisory Board
    d. Prohibition of public good

13. Which of the following principles apply to Islamic banking and finance?
    a. Prohibition of speculative behaviour
    b. Only Shariah-approved activities are permissible
    c. Prohibition of all profit making
    d. Both a and b

14. One of the key principles related to Islamic finance is:
    a. To encourage the use of Riba and Gharar
    b. To earn money from money
    c. To avoid hoarding
    d. Hoarding

15. Unlawful earnings under the Shariah rulings involve:
    a. Excessive gains in business transactions and undue profits
    b. Excessive commissions and service charges by some banks and financial institutions
    c. Exploitation of a seller's distress while buying their property
    d. All of the above
16. What is the main challenge for Shariah Supervisory Boards as well as the main area for their future development?
    a. Increase competitiveness of Islamic banks against conventional banks by expanding Shariah rules
    b. Staff SBBs with scholars from recognized Islamic institutions who also have financial qualifications
    c. Promote Islamic banking to non-Muslim customers
    d. Ensure Shariah-compliant regulations from the central banks
17. The Shariah Supervisory Board is compulsory in all Islamic banks to:
    a. Ensure the bank is profitable
    b. Hire staff qualified in Islamic finance and banking
    c. Help the Islamic bank compete with conventional banks
    d. Ensure all bank transactions comply with Shariah
18. One of the functions of the Shariah Supervisory Board is to conduct an annual Shariah audit of transactions to ensure profits earned were permissible. Which statement below describes this function?
    a. SSB audits the final transactions of the bank for Shariah compliance, thus ensuring the bank's profit is permissible
    b. SSB audits all transactions of the bank for Shariah compliance, thus ensuring the bank's profit is permissible
    c. SSB audits all transactions of the bank to determine if they are Shariah compliant, so the bank's profit can be given to charity
    d. SSB audits only doubtful transactions to confirm if they are Shariah-compliant or not
19. As the Islamic finance and banking industry grows, the Shariah Supervisory Board needs to help develop new innovative and competitive products, so the role of the SSB in this regard would be to:
    a. Review new products and services proposed by management for Shariah compliance and suggest any modifications if necessary
    b. Review training and education materials about competitive financial instruments for the benefit of Shariah scholars
    c. Review the financial products and services to ensure conformity with the central bank's regulations
    d. Review the charitable and social obligations of the bank and its customers to collect and distribute Zakat
20. The Islamic banks must follow Shariah requirements and also follow the regulations of the central bank at the same time. Which statement below best describes the role of the Sharia Supervisory Board in this regard?
    a. SSB reviews regulations provided by the central bank and seeks exemptions or suggests alternatives if these regulations are contrary to Shariah

    b. SSB advises the central bank on Shariah-compliant regulations and ensures the central bank complies with Shariah

    c. SSB develops regulations together with the central bank to ensure that they are applicable to both Islamic and conventional banks

    d. SSB designs the regulations for Islamic banks, which are exempt from all regulations of the central bank

21. The most suitable scholar to be appointed to an SSB would be:

    a. A person who has both quantitative and qualitative skills

    b. A person who has extensive work experience in the finance and banking industry

    c. A person who has in-depth knowledge of Shariah and is also familiar with finance and banking

    d. A person who has worked as a Shariah lawyer

22. Which of the following is not one of the functions of the SSB?

    a. To ensure all products and services are Shariah-compliant

    b. To provide day-to-day consultations and advice to the IFI on Shariah issues

    c. To review investments made by the IFI

    d. To review the salaries and bonuses of the management of the IFI

23. Which one below is not a problem related to the Shariah Supervisory Board?

    a. Different Shariah scholars have different views

    b. Scholars with both Shariah knowledge and knowledge of banking and finance are very limited

    c. Shariah scholars use various sources like the Quran, Sunnah, Ijma and Qiyas

    d. A globally accepted Shariah Supervisory Board has not been formed yet

24. Which of the below is a major responsibility of the Shariah Supervisory Board?

    a. To ensure that the profits earned by banks do not exceed a certain limit

    b. To ensure that the bank's products and services comply with Shariah principles

    c. To limit the salaries paid to SSB members

    d. To decide the profit-sharing ratio between the Islamic bank and its clients

25. The Shariah Supervisory Board:

    a. Consists of scholars from finance and banking disciplines at prestigious universities

    b. Consists of scholars qualified from recognized Shariah institutions

    c. Is a department within the conventional bank

    d. Is a department within the central bank

True/False Questions

Write T for true and F for false next to the statement.

1. Under central bank supervision an Islamic bank can operate without a Sharia Supervisory Board.

2. Riba or interest is not prohibited when it is small and simple, but only when it is large and compound.

3. Riba is the increase, addition, expansion or growth of the loan amount.

4. Riba is any uncertainty or ambiguity.

5. Gharar is uncertainty or ambiguity.

6. Gharar is the sale of items whose existence or characteristics are certain.

7. Gharar is the sale of undeliverable goods, or those without a specified price.

8. Gharar is all parties in the contract knowing all conditions.
9. Gharar Fahish is tolerated and Gharar Yasir is prohibited in Islamic finance.
10. A lottery ticket is an example of Maysir.
11. Maysir is the sale of probable items whose existence or characteristics are not certain.
12. Maysir is the premium paid by the borrower to the lender along with the principal amount for the loan or for its extension.
13. Maysir is all kinds of gambling or games of chance.
14. Maysir is a risk taken to win without any productive activity involved and has the possibility of losing.
15. The Shariah Supervisory Board ensures compliance of transactions to Shariah law.
16. The Shariah Supervisory Board makes sure that the bank chooses the most profitable investments.

CHAPTER 3

Islamic Banking versus Conventional Banking

Learning outcomes

Upon completion of this chapter, you should be able to:

1. Discuss Islamic banking visàvis conventional banking, identifying similarities and differences.
2. Explain the banks' relationship to the central banks as well as the generic and specific risks faced by Islamic banks.
3. Define financial intermediation, and compare conventional and Islamic financial intermediation.
4. Describe the sources and applications of funds for an Islamic bank, including Shariah-compliant contracts and common retail and corporate products offered by Islamic banks.
5. Discuss the accounting challenges faced by Islamic banks and their status during the financial crisis.
6. Describe the international Islamic regulatory and standard setting bodies.

INTRODUCTION TO ISLAMIC BANKING

Banks are institutions licensed by the central bank and allowed to take deposits from people. They also provide a host of other products and services including giving loans, collecting cheques, drafts, transferring money, providing guarantees, dealing in foreign exchange and assisting the client to invest. From the economic viewpoint, Islamic banks have a similar role to that of conventional banks. Banks use the funds collected as deposits to provide financing to other clients and invest their own and customer deposits.

The uniqueness of the Islamic bank comes from the fact that all transactions need to be in accordance with the Islamic Shariah principles. The Islamic bank provides all common commercial banking services within the Shariah framework, mainly incorporating the prohibition of interest or Riba, which is a fundamental difference from the conventional banks. As discussed already in Chapters 1 and 2, in Islam money is only a medium of exchange and is a factor of production used for business activities. In contrast, conventional finance considers money as a commodity, with intrinsic value, allowing money to earn more money, which is interest or Riba. Riba is the increase in the principal amount of a loan, calculated based on the amount of loan and the period for which it was lent. In Islam, all forms of interest are prohibited, small or large, simple or compound.

The central problem to be solved in the process of developing modern Islamic banking was to identify a suitable alternative to the interest-based mechanism. This was achieved by replacing Riba or interest with a profit and loss-sharing mechanism in Islamic banking, and this will be discussed further later in this chapter. Shariah also requires the lender or investor or finance provider to link the funding to real assets or investments, thus the income would either be based on profit and loss sharing in equity-like transactions or profit from a cost-plus-sales contract or from the rentals of a lease transaction. These mechanisms will be focused on later in the book. Owing to their emphasis on the real asset and sharing in the profit and loss of the business activity that is funded, Islamic banks give more emphasis to the productivity of the business and the managerial skills of the borrower, rather than just the credit rating of the borrower and any collateral provided.

Modern Islamic banks, like the conventional banks, aim to provide an efficient financial system through the process of financial intermediation, reliable payment systems, effective links to the money and capital markets and standardization and globalization of the industry. All financial arrangements in the Islamic banks are linked to assets in the real sector, thus providing value addition to the real economy and sharing the risk and return. Islamic banking allows Muslim depositors to become partners in businesses rather than being creditors, where both the provider and the user of funds share in the risks and returns of the business. In conventional banking both the depositor and the bank earn fixed interest, while the risk of loss belongs only to the borrower or entrepreneur. In contrast, in the case of Islamic banking depositors, bank and borrower or entrepreneur all share in the risks and returns of the business.

The core objectives of an Islamic bank are:

1. To offer Shariah-compliant financial services.
2. To avoid all Haram activities and be involved in Halal activities only. Examples of Haram activities are those involving alcohol, pork, adult entertainment, gambling, interest-based businesses, etc.
3. To develop transactions that are free of Riba, Gharar and Maysir.
4. To refrain from using money as a commodity and earning more money from it, and rather backing every financial transaction with real assets.
5. To give more value to human efforts in the business venture, rather than the money only; money becomes capital only after it is invested in the business.
6. To allocate resources efficiently and distribute income equitably.
7. To aim for economic development by identifying efficient business opportunities, emphasizing productivity rather than creditworthiness of the borrower only.
8. To encourage savers to invest rather than keep their money idle, stimulating the economy and encouraging entrepreneurs to maximum efficiency.
9. To act in a manner that is ethical and socially, morally and environmentally responsible.

ISLAMIC BANKING VERSUS CONVENTIONAL BANKING

Despite the many differences of Islamic banking in contrast to conventional banking, the two systems appear to be more compatible than conflicting. At the onset of Islamic banking, conventional banks did not consider the interest-free system to be sustainable. Over time, as Islamic banking grew globally, the two types of banks – out of necessity – began to cooperate with each other. Both types of banks are working parallel to each other in domestic as well as international financial operations; cooperating in correspondence services – confirming, advising and negotiating LCs; depositing funds and receiving funds to and from conventional banks without interest; also exchanging information or working together as partners related to retail and corporate clients, as well as in various projects.

Similarities Between Conventional and Islamic Banks

According to the CISI (2015) workbook *Fundamentals of Islamic Banking and Finance*, the similarities between conventional and Islamic banks are as follows.

1. Both are commercial entities licensed by the central bank, involved in collecting deposits from the surplus units in society and applying the funds to borrowers, entrepreneurs or deficit units.
2. Both types of banks offer current accounts for the safekeeping of funds, payment facilities, cheque books, debit cards and without any interest or profit.
3. In fixed deposits of conventional banks and investment accounts of Islamic banks the customers agree to deposit their funds for a fixed period, though the return with conventional banks is a fixed interest while for Islamic banks it is a pro-rata share in the profit.
4. Both types of banks use the interbank market for liquidity management.

Differences Between Conventional and Islamic Banking

Table 3.1 lists the differences between conventional and Islamic banking.

TABLE 3.1 Differences between conventional and Islamic banking

	Factors	Conventional banking	Islamic banking
1	Risk taking	Operates based on risk transfer from the depositors and the bank to the borrowers or entrepreneurs.	Operates based on risk sharing between the depositors, bank and borrowers or entrepreneurs.
2	Economic versus social focus	Concentrates on economic wellbeing and profit-maximization principles.	Community oriented, encouraging entrepreneurship, promoting justness and fairness in society, grounded on ethical, social and moral framework.
3	Price of money	Time value of money, as in interest, is the price of money.	Money is not a commodity and has no price.

(Continued)

TABLE 3.1   (*Continued*)

	Factors	Conventional banking	Islamic banking
4	Fixed income versus profit and loss sharing	Depositors receive a fixed interest and deposits are considered as liability.	Depositors of investment accounts are partners of the bank and share in the profit and loss; these accounts have characteristics of both debt and equity.
5	Deposit guarantee	All deposits are guaranteed.	Deposits placed in current accounts are guaranteed only.
6	Income	The primary income of the bank is the fixed interest earned from the debt financing it provides, separated from the real economy.	The financing is linked to the real sector and the return of the financial transactions arise from the real economy.
7	Asset link	Transactions can be purely financial, with no compulsion to link to real assets.	All financial transactions need to be either asset based or asset backed, with an exchange of goods and services, making the system more stable.
8	Size of banks	Many of the global conventional banks are of very large size.	Most Islamic banks are small or medium sized.
9	Bank–client relationship	The bank–client relationship is that of creditor and debtor.	Depends on the type of contract, could be of partners, principal and agent, investor and manager, buyer and seller, lessor and lessee.
10	Default payment	Default to repay is penalized by compounding interest.	No penalty can be charged in case of default, except cost for recovery of repayments, any additional penalty if charged needs to be donated to charity.
11	Restrictions	No restrictions on the investments of funds or projects financed.	Only Shariah-compliant investments and projects can be financed.

Relationship with the Central Banks

For both conventional and Islamic banks, the central bank plays the important roles of supervisor in case of applying monetary policy, clearing house and lender of last resort. Central banks are required to balance the impact of the public's preference to save or to spend. Public demand for cash leads to a cash shortage in banks, and banks try to borrow at the interbank market. In case the interbank market is not able to meet the needs completely, the central bank acts as the lender of last resort and lends funds to the banks. In the case of conventional banks this loan is interest based, but in the case of Islamic banks the central banks need to provide an alternative profit and loss-based financing, like Mudaraba or Musharaka. Such special Shariah-compliant alternatives are usually only available from central banks in Muslim-majority countries with dual banking environments, or where the banking system is totally Shariah compliant. Central banks also provide cheque clearing services to both conventional and Islamic banks. Moreover, central banks need to deal with Islamic banks differently, due to the differences in their products and operations. Statutory cash reserves for both kinds of banks would be the same for their current accounts but are required to be different for fixed deposits compared to investment accounts, since the investment account holders – unlike the fixed deposit holders – accept some risk. The liquidity ratios, insurance schemes, credit ceilings, etc. also require differing treatment. Central banks have similar controls on permissions for new branches, minimum capital requirements, appointment of BOD members and auditors, regulations of foreign exchange and submission of financial reports for both conventional and Islamic banks.

RISKS OF BANKS – GENERIC AND SPECIFIC TO ISLAMIC BANKS

All banks, including conventional and Islamic banks, face some risks inherent to the industry. These are the generic risks of all banks. There are also some risks specific to the Islamic banks arising from their unique structure and operations.

Generic Risks

Liquidity or funding risk. This is the risk of a bank not being able to meet its obligations when they fall due, either because the bank does not have sufficient cash and/or liquid assets or because it is unable to raise the cash from external sources.

Banks are originally set up with shareholders' capital, which also provides for the banks' infrastructure and operational reserves. The financing business of the bank mainly uses depositors' money. When depositors want to withdraw their deposit, banks need to honour this obligation, or a panic will be created which may lead to a run on the bank. There are two types of deposits in a conventional bank – current (or demand) deposits and time deposits – with the savings account falling between these two. The demand deposits are payable on demand. Though technically banks do not have to pay out time deposits or savings account deposits on demand, they usually prefer to do so. Hence, withdrawal from these accounts can further deplete banks' cash. Often banks pay withdrawing depositors from funds placed by new depositors, but this is not a stable solution. Rather, banks should source the funds externally by selling commercial papers or borrowing from external sources. Similarly, an Islamic bank also holds current and savings accounts and instead of time deposits it holds investment accounts. In practical terms, an Islamic bank would honour withdrawal from any of these accounts too. The process of funds management to meet the withdrawals demand is also the same, either by using funds from new deposits or by external Shariah-compliant sourcing.

The conventional as well as the Islamic banks manage their depositors' cash withdrawals by holding cash and liquid assets, holding their own reserves and via the reserves held at the central bank. However there are some Shariah restrictions related to Islamic banks holding part of the deposits as reserve instead of applying them to profit-generating activities. Islamic banks deal with the liquidity needs best by raising deposits of varying maturities. Central banks that recognize Islamic banking also deal with their reserve requirements against their partnership deposits differently from conventional banks.

Risk of holding excess liquidity. When banks hold cash and other liquid assets, mainly to meet the withdrawal demands as discussed above, they are not investing this money and are losing income. Both conventional and Islamic banks need to balance the risk of holding too little in liquid assets and failing to meet withdrawal demands against holding too much in liquid assets and giving up on income. A conventional bank invests its liquid funds in the interbank or highly liquid money markets. While Islamic banks cannot avail of the common interest-based interbank or money markets, they rather deal with excess liquidity by investing in Shariah-compliant divisible and tradable instruments like Shariah-compliant certificates of deposit, short-term Sukuks (Islamic bonds, to be covered in Chapter 11), etc.

Credit risk of the client. This risk is when the bank client defaults on their obligations to repay. Some measures the bank can take to reduce this risk are to select creditworthy clients only, take security or collateral to recover payments in case of default, properly match the financial instrument to the client's need and abilities to repay and, especially in the case of Islamic banking, supervise and monitor the client's operations to ensure that they were managed efficiently and that any profit earned was shared with the bank.

Settlement or payment risk. This risk comes from interbank payments. A bank may not have sufficient funds to repay an interbank obligation or may not receive its dues on time from the other bank to which funds were loaned.

Interest rate risk. This is a major risk category in conventional banking, arising from interest rate mismatches in both volume and maturity. Islamic banks do not have this risk.

Market price risk. If the bank is exposed to equity market price changes, then any negative movement is a risk. The Islamic bank, especially, may be exposed to market price risk when it underprices its financing. To avoid this the Islamic bank needs to better forecast the market demand and supply; moreover, Islamic securities are affected by the volatility of market prices more, since they are linked to real assets.

Currency risk. Any adverse exchange rate fluctuations can affect both the bank's own and its clients' funds held in foreign currency. Conventional banks use foreign exchange options or futures to reduce this risk. These hedging products are not Shariah compliant and hence Islamic banks cannot use them.

Operating risk. This risk originates from the bank's operations. Some examples are unexpected expenses, fraud or involvement in litigation. The solution lies in prudent banking operations, minimizing fraud and ensuring legal issues are avoided as far as possible.

Risks Specific to Islamic Banks

Since Islamic banks tend to be partners to their depositors on the liability side and to their borrowers or entrepreneurs on the asset side of their businesses, and because they share in the profit and loss of the activity or enterprise financed by them instead of charging a fixed interest rate, there is inherent risk in Islamic banking. As discussed by Kettel (2010), a major source of risk is asymmetric information, which is known to one party only. Asymmetric information has an impact on the equity market where, since none of the returns are known, investors expect premium income from good stocks to compensate for less than expected return on weak stocks. Asymmetric information also affects the debt market, since the borrower or entrepreneur has more information about the project than the lender. Two of the major risks faced by an Islamic bank because of asymmetric information are:

- **Adverse selection risk.** This problem is faced before the transaction has happened. Since borrowers or entrepreneurs have more information than lenders about the project, the bank could make an error in the selection of projects. Risky borrowers are often keen to borrow and may get selected. As such, Islamic banks need to be very vigilant in selecting borrowers, concentrating more on the profitability of the project and the managerial skills of the borrower rather than their creditworthiness.
- **Moral hazard risk.** This problem is faced after the transaction has happened. Only the borrower or entrepreneur has full information on the running of the business, and may engage in activities that are harmful for the business, hence affecting the profit earned. Conventional banks charge the borrower fixed interest in addition to the principal repayment, irrespective of the profit or loss scenario of the business, and would be concerned only if the cashflow of the business is not sufficient to make the fixed repayments. In contrast, the Islamic bank shares in the profit or loss, thus a high profit of the business is beneficial for the bank while a loss would mean a loss for the bank, since as capital provider it bears the loss pro-rata. Islamic banks are therefore required to engage in thorough and careful monitoring of the business to ensure that all operations are in the best interests of the enterprise.

Other related risks faced by an Islamic bank are:

- **Equity investment risk.** Islamic banks in many contracts take partnership roles, as in Mudaraba and Musharaka; the bank and the borrower or entrepreneur mutually decide on a suitable profit-sharing ratio. The loss sharing, though, is as per the capital contribution. Usually the bank is the major contributor of capital and is exposed to significant risk. Moreover, in Islamic banking a collateral or guarantee cannot be taken against regular business risk, hence if the business fails, the bank can lose significantly.
- **Default risk.** If the borrower delays payment or fails to repay, conventional banks charge interest on interest. Islamic banks cannot do so and if they do impose a penalty, the bank cannot benefit from it but is required to donate it to charity.
- **Higher costs.** Islamic banks are concerned more about the profitability of the business than the creditworthiness of the borrower, leading to more conservative decisions, so less financing is achieved incurring higher costs. Moreover, due to the profit and loss-sharing relationship, Islamic banks need to monitor clients more extensively, incurring additional costs.
- **Shariah compliance risk.** Conventional banks match their operations to economic and business requirements only, while Islamic bank operations also need to follow the principles of the Islamic economics and the Shariah. Any Shariah non-compliance can affect their reputation and lower the loyalty of their customers.
- **Rate of return risk.** Conventional depositors earn fixed interest and are protected by bank regulations and deposit insurance. In contrast, Islamic bank depositors share in the profit and loss of the bank, which in turn shares in the profit and loss of its financing clients. Thus, the PLS system involves variability of returns both for the bank and in turn for its depositors.

FINANCIAL INTERMEDIATION

The Definition of Financial Intermediation

The core business of banks is financial intermediation. In other words, banks exist because of the need for financial intermediation. Financial intermediation is the process by which banks match savers with borrowers. The income and expenditure streams of the different economic entities are not always synchronized. As such, some have excess cash that they want to save or lend to others and some have a shortage of cash and want to borrow from others. Banks play the role of connecting these two groups. On the demand side, households may need money for general consumption or the purchase of items, businesses may need money for short or long-term expenses, while governments may need money to complete various projects. Conversely, on the supply side, households may save for the future, businesses for future expansion or replacement of assets and governments for future expenses. Through financial intermediation banks play the role of the trusted intermediary for all parties. Banks collect all information related to savers and borrowers, efficiently allocate resources collected from savers to borrowers, ensure safety of savers' money, and take the responsibility of recovering repayments from borrowers and returning savers' funds with additional income. Banks also assist the government in achieving its economic policies by channelling financial resources to priority sectors. Banks are profit-oriented businesses and they earn their margin from the difference between what they pay savers and what they charge borrowers.

Conventional Financial Intermediation

A conventional bank collects deposits from customers, mostly in the short term, pays them a fixed interest rate and then lends this money to other customers who are borrowers, usually in the medium or long term, and charges them an interest rate which is usually higher than that paid to depositors. This difference between interest charged and interest paid is the bank's spread or profit. In the process of financial intermediation banks are taking liquidity risk, since they are responsible for returning depositors' funds when they demand, while they cannot recall the loans they give before maturity. They also take credit risks, the risk of borrowers defaulting on repayments. The profit made by the bank is considered as income for taking these risks.

Islamic Financial Intermediation

Financial intermediation in Islamic banks has a fundamental difference from that in conventional banks. As discussed earlier, in Islam money is a medium of exchange and not a commodity, so money cannot be earned from money. As such, the conventional financial intermediation process of transforming deposits into loans and earning interest or Riba from them is prohibited and the justification for bearing credit and liquidity risk to earn the interest margin is not sufficient. In Islamic financial intermediation interest is replaced with profit and loss sharing. Instead of the debit–credit framework Islamic banks use the Mudaraba concept. In Mudaraba the capital is completely provided by one party, the Rab al Maal, while the business is managed by the other party, the Mudarib. Mudaraba will be discussed further in Chapter 5. In Islamic financial intermediation, the Islamic bank executes a Mudaraba contract with the depositors, where the depositors are the Rab al Maal while the bank acts as Mudarib or entrepreneur. On the other hand, the Islamic bank enters a second Mudaraba contract with the users of the funds, the borrowers or entrepreneurs. In this Mudaraba the bank acts as the Rab al Maal and the fund user is the Mudarib. This is called the two-tier Mudaraba of Islamic financial intermediation. In both tiers of the Mudaraba contract, profit is shared in a pre-agreed ratio, while the financial loss is borne solely by the Rab al Maal; the Mudarib is liable only to lose their time and effort. In case of profit calculation in Islamic financial intermediation, all operational expenses are deducted from the bank income to derive the net income or profit. From this the Mudarib, or bank's, profit share is deducted, and the balance amount is distributed on a pro-rata basis amongst the depositors. Islamic banks usually apply different profit-sharing ratios to different types of deposits.

As per Shariah requirements, the money lent by Islamic banks needs to be applied to real assets, usufruct or services. Productivity and entrepreneurship as measures to grow the economy are emphasized in Islam. Islamic banks provide financing in two ways. Firstly, as asset-backed financing, where all transactions have an underlying asset, enterprise or service and these are sales, trading, lease, investment or fee-based contracts. Secondly, as participation finance, where the bank becomes a partner in the contract and shares in the risk and return. This can be done as a Mudaraba contract, one party providing the entire capital and the other providing effort and skill. It can also be executed as a Musharaka contract, where all parties contribute to the capital and all or some are involved in managing the business with their effort and skills. Musharaka will be considered in more detail in Chapter 6. In both contracts, profit is shared in a pre-agreed ratio while losses as per the capital contribution. In Islamic banking the focus is more on the trustworthiness and abilities of the borrower rather than the creditworthiness or financial worth of the borrower and the collateral provided. Islamic banks need to be prudent in selecting projects to finance and are required to supervise and monitor much more closely, since they do not charge a fixed interest but rather share in the profit and loss of these projects.

The Mudaraba concept is used to structure both demand deposits (current and savings accounts) and time or fixed deposits. Demand deposits can be withdrawn on demand and the profit for them is calculated based on the balance maintained in the account at regular intervals, often every quarter. Time deposits, which are called investment accounts in Islamic banks, require the commitment of the deposit for specified periods (e.g. 3, 6, 9, 12 months). If the deposit is withdrawn early, the principal is returned, but no profit or only part of the profit is paid. There are two types of investment accounts: general investment account, where the depositor gives the bank complete responsibility to invest their funds as the bank sees fit and agrees to a standard profit-sharing ratio; specific investment account, where the customer specifies some conditions related to where their deposit can be invested and accepts a negotiated profit-sharing ratio. The deposited amount in the investment account does not have a capital guarantee from the bank and theoretically, in case of loss, depositors may lose their deposit. The rate of return is not fixed in advance, rather the historical rates of return are given as an indication. At the end of the investment period the actual rate of return is calculated and distributed; this rate may or may not differ from the indicative rate. The deposits of customers in Islamic banks, therefore, are not risk free, and as such they have equity-like characteristics.

For the benefit of the depositors and to stay competitive, Islamic banks take some measures to smooth the income provided to depositors. During periods of high profit, banks keep aside a portion of the profit in a reserve fund and during periods of low profit, they add to the profit from the reserve fund. There are problems related to such income smoothing and reserve funds. The investment account holders may not be aware of, or have any influence over, the income smoothing process and may have distrust related to it. To deal with such issues, investment account holders should be informed about the income-smoothing process and their consent should be taken. Moreover, the adjustment method should be very transparent and apply standard guidelines as specified by the supervisory authority of the jurisdiction. The Islamic standard setting body, AAOIFI, to be discussed in more detail later in this chapter, allows the Islamic banks to have two kinds of reserves.

1. **Profit equalization reserve (PER).** During years of high profit a specified amount is moved to the reserve to compensate for years of low profit. This amount is moved from the profit before any profit is distributed to the unrestricted investment account holders or shareholders.
2. **Investment risk reserve (IRR).** An amount is moved to this reserve after the bank has taken out its income as Mudarib, the balance of the profit being distributed to the unrestricted investment account holder.

In Mudaraba-based Islamic financial intermediation the Rab al Maal has no capital guarantee and may lose their capital in the event of a loss. Even though Islamic banks cannot directly provide any guarantee to the investment account holders as Rab al Maal, it is common for investment accounts to have a third-party indirect guarantee either from the government via the central bank or from a deposit insurance or Takaful scheme. This form of indirect guarantee is a topic of debate. Arguments against such guarantees are that Mudaraba represents risk capital and should have equity-like characteristics, and such guarantees are not Shariah compliant and may make the profit like Riba. Also, when such guarantees are provided on the bank's liability side with no such guarantee on the bank's asset side, it may create a mismatch in the risk profile affecting the design of the two-tier Mudaraba. Supporters of such guarantees highlight the comfort of investment account holders and the minimization of social costs in case of big losses at the bank and to encourage depositors to accept Mudaraba-based investment accounts instead of interest-based fixed deposits. Additionally, the capital adequacy requirements of the Islamic banks provide an indirect guarantee and sometimes the banks as Mudarib provide a quasi-guarantee for depositors' funds.

Islamic Financial Intermediation Models

As discussed by Askari, Iqbal & Mirakhor (2015), Islamic financial intermediation has three different models. These are discussed below.

Two-Tier Mudaraba   This model includes two tiers of Mudaraba. The first tier is on the liability side of the bank's balance sheet. Depositors and investors enter into a

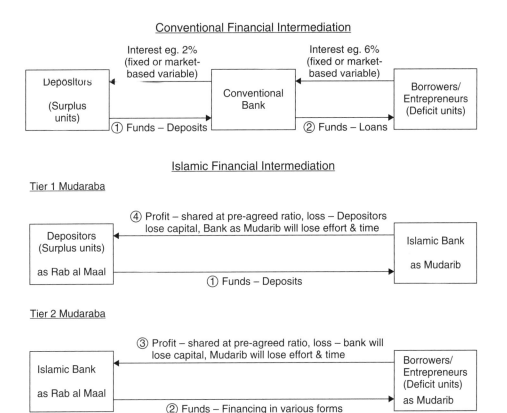

Conventional Financial Intermediation

Islamic Financial Intermediation

Tier 1 Mudaraba

Tier 2 Mudaraba

FIGURE 3.1 Islamic financial intermediation in comparison with conventional financial intermediation

Mudaraba contract with the bank, providing funds as Rab al Maal, and the bank is the Mudarib managing the use of these funds. The depositors share in the profit earned by the bank at a predetermined ratio. If there are any financial losses, depositors bear it as capital providers, the bank only loses its effort.

The second tier is on the asset side of the bank's balance sheet. In this Mudaraba the bank acts as the supplier of funds, Rab al Maal, to entrepreneurs or borrowers, who are the Mudarib. The profits are shared at a pre-agreed ratio. Any financial losses are borne by the bank, while the Mudarib lose their effort. Banks pool all the deposit, and provide funding to various projects. The income or losses from these variety of enterprises are also pooled together, and the combined profit is shared between depositors and the bank at the pre-agreed ratio.

The asset and liability sides of the bank are fully integrated, which reduces the need for active asset liability management, making the model stable and able to deal with economic shocks. This model does not include a specific reserve requirement on either side of the balance sheet.

Two-Windows Model   This model is almost the same as the two-tier model, the only difference being that it has a reserve requirement. The model divides the liability side of the bank's balance sheet into two windows, one for demand deposits and the other for investment deposits. It requires 100% reserve for demand deposits as these are placed with the bank as Amanah for safekeeping only. The bank may charge a service fee for these accounts. No reserve is required for investment deposits as these are placed for investment purposes and bear the risk of loss.

Wakala Model   In this model the bank acts as an agent or Wakil, responsible for managing depositors' funds and charging them a fixed fee. Other terms and conditions of the Wakala contract are mutually agreed between the bank and the depositors.

DISTRIBUTION OF ISLAMIC BANKING PRODUCTS

As discussed earlier, Islamic banks operate in three types of jurisdictions – those where the entire financial system is Shariah compliant, like Iran and Sudan; those where both Islamic and conventional banks operate side by side with central bank recognition, called the dual banking system, like most Muslim-majority countries (e.g. Malaysia, UAE, Egypt, Pakistan); and those of most non-Muslim countries where Islamic banks or other Islamic financial institutions may be allowed to operate under certain conditions but no separate central bank regulations exist for them, like the USA, Canada and Australia.

In most dual banking environments, there are fully fledged Islamic banks and some conventional banks that offer Islamic financial services. Some countries (like Kuwait, Lebanon and to some extent Qatar) do not allow conventional banks to offer Islamic products. Whether offered by Islamic or conventional banks, Islamic financial products need to be Shariah compliant with respect to Riba, Gharar and Maysir and need to be regulated by a Shariah Supervisory Board or similar body and receive Shariah compliance approval from them. When conventional banks participate in Islamic banking, they bring the benefits of their size, banking experience and specialized knowledge. Conventional banks offer Islamic financial services in the following organizational set-ups:

- **Windows.** They offer Islamic products within their existing distribution channel, via separate windows which often have separate operations and accounting – for example Lloyds TSB.
- **Branches.** They operate their Islamic banking activities via dedicated branches – for example Standard Chartered in Pakistan or HSBC Amanah in various countries.
- **Subsidiaries.** They provide Islamic banking services via a separate legal entity specifically set up. The subsidiary may have its own dedicated distribution channel or use that of the parent company. The subsidiary has independent management policies and strategies – for example Citi Islamic Investment Bank in Bahrain, a subsidiary of Citigroup and Badr al-Islami, a subsidiary of Mashreq Bank in the UAE.

CONVENTIONAL VERSUS ISLAMIC FINANCIAL INTERMEDIATION

Table 3.2 lists the differences between conventional and Islamic financial intermediation.

TABLE 3.2   Differences between conventional and Islamic financial intermediation

Factors	Conventional	Islamic
Religious requirements	No religious restrictions are imposed.	Islamic banks' products and operations need to be compliant with the Islamic law or Shariah.
Social, ethical and environmental responsibility	No such restrictions exist.	Islamic banks cannot finance any project that is harmful to society or the environment.
Fiduciary responsibility	Conventional banks have a debtor–creditor relationship with their depositors and provide guaranteed interest.	Islamic banks act as partner, agent, trustee in various asset-linked projects, earn profit on their asset side and share this in a pre-agreed ratio with the depositors or investors.
Project selection	Conventional banks as creditor emphasize the creditworthiness of the borrower and any collateral provided.	Owing to the profit and loss relationship with the borrowers and investors, Islamic banks select projects considering their soundness, plus the business acumen and managerial competence of the entrepreneur.
Terms of financing	Conventional banks as lenders adjust their interest rates as per the maturity of the financing project.	The profit and loss relationship with borrowers and investors makes long-term projects preferable to Islamic banks.
Monitoring of funded projects	Conventional banks are concerned mainly about the borrowers' cashflows to avoid default.	Islamic banks monitor projects extensively to ensure they stay profitable (since they share in the profit), causing the banks to incur higher costs.
Leverage versus risk sharing	Conventional banks finance via loans and thus encourage leverage; they earn interest irrespective of the profitability of the project.	Islamic banks promote risk sharing between providers of funds and users of funds and they earn only when a project succeeds and makes a profit.

BALANCE SHEET OF AN ISLAMIC BANK – SOURCES AND USES OF FUNDS BY AN ISLAMIC BANK

Sources of Funds

The sources of funds for an Islamic bank are the cash inflows and comprise the liability side of the bank. Islamic banks' liabilities or common sources of funds include current, savings and investment accounts.

   Current accounts. These accounts are opened by individuals and businesses and the funds are deposited as cash, cheques and bills. Current accounts are used by clients to pay and receive funds. Depositors can withdraw their money anytime. Islamic banks accept the funds in these accounts as Amanah (trust) or Wadia (deposit), which involves safe-keeping. Legally, Wadia authorizes the Islamic bank to keep the customer's funds in safe custody on explicit or implicit terms. In contemporary Islamic banking, the Wadia contract is combined with the contract of guarantee or Dhaman, to provide the same functionality as conventional current and savings accounts. In this case, the bank provides a guarantee of the deposited amount. The funds in these accounts are not usually applied to any risk-bearing venture. If the funds are applied to any venture, then it is at the risk of the Islamic bank itself not the depositors. Depositors are not entitled to any profits in this account. The bank may charge a fee for the safekeeping. Overdrafts are usually not allowed and if the account accidentally goes overdrawn a charge may be applied, but it will not be a proportion of the overdraft amount, rather it will be the cost of collecting and processing the items for which there was insufficient funds in the account.

Savings accounts. The Islamic bank accepts the savings account funds based on Wadia (safekeeping), Wakala (agency), Mudaraba (trust financing) or Musharaka (equity financing). The bank uses the funds in these accounts to finance borrowers and entrepreneurs. These accounts bear some risk and provide the depositors with some profit from the profit earned by the bank in a pre-agreed ratio. The calculation of profit and loss is made based on the minimum available balance left in the account during a calendar month.

Investment accounts. These are the most important sources of funds for Islamic banks. The funds are accepted on the Mudaraba basis, where the customer and the bank enter into a joint-venture agreement. The funds are applied to profit and loss-based ventures and bear the risk of capital loss. The investment accounts of an Islamic bank are in the true sense not liability but non-voting equity, where depositors are the principal providers of funds in the Mudaraba contracts, the bank being the Mudarib and sharing in the profit at a pre-agreed ratio while bearing the total financial loss.

Conventional banks guarantee the principal and fixed interest rate for their depositors; in contrast, Islamic banks can neither guarantee the principal amount nor a fixed return. Islamic banks take efforts to reduce this risk by providing efficient management, supervision, minimal risk taking, selection and monitoring of the projects with utmost care and investing in a portfolio of projects. Islamic banks also build a reserve fund by setting aside part of the profit in years of above-expectation profits to compensate for years when low or no profits are made and thus aim to provide a competitive return. Moreover, Islamic banks also hold a significant amount of capital on their liability side.

Since Islam prohibits interest and speculation, transactions that involve either of these will not be accepted in Islamic banking. When a conventional bank also offers Islamic banking via an Islamic finance window or through a separate branch or subsidiary, there is concern about the possible mixing of funds sourced from non-Shariah-compliant sources with the funds of the Islamic banking operations. On this issue, Qatar Central Bank asked all Islamic finance windows in the country to close in 2011.

Application of Funds

The Islamic bank applies the funds it raises from depositors as well as its own funds to various financing transactions with the aim of earning profit. The risk of loss is also there. The application of funds of an Islamic bank comprises its assets and includes a variety of products. For short-term, limited-risk investment they use Murabaha and Salam contracts which are used for trading, working capital, etc. Medium-term financing uses asset-based instruments like Ijara and Istisna. Both these instruments can have a fixed or floating rate feature, as required. Longer-term financing can be done using Mudaraba and Musharaka contracts, which act like private equity or venture capital.

Islamic banks, unlike conventional banks, do not deal in pure money lending. They act more like merchant banks. All liabilities and assets on an Islamic bank balance sheet are risk capital. The most common form of funds application is deferred exchange contracts with fixed income. There are four products in this category: Murabaha, Ijara, Istisna and Salam are all debt-like financing contracts, though each has an underlying asset. Murabaha or cost-plus sale, Ijara or lease, Salam or forward sale and Istisna or project finance. Mudaraba and Musharaka are equity-based products. The Islamic banks and the regulators prefer fixed-income products as their income is predictable, while scholars prefer the equity-like profit-sharing methods of Mudaraba and Musharaka. In conventional banks, the bulk of funds applied is in the form of fixed-interest lending.

CONTRACTS IN SHARIAH LAW

Contracts are the basis of all transactions in Islam. All aspects of Islamic commercial transactions are covered by the Islamic jurisprudence called the Fiqh al-Muamalat. Shariah-compliant contracts are like any valid conventional contract, with the addition of certain Shariah rulings.

Shariah-compliant valid financial contracts have the following requirements:

1. Two or more independent parties, with their mutual consent and for their mutual benefit.
2. All contracting parties should be adults under Shariah and be mentally sound.
3. The subject matter of the contract should be acceptable in Shariah.
4. The item of exchange should exist, be owned and be in physical or constructive possession of the seller.
5. The contract should be devoid of Riba, Gharar and Maysir.
6. The contract should be linked to a real asset or enterprise.
7. There should be an offer and an acceptance related to the product and price.
8. Transfer of ownership should follow the exchange of the asset and the payment.

Some examples of unilateral contracts in Shariah-compliant commerce are the following.

- **Wad.** A unilateral promise made by one party to another, binding only on the promisor not on the promisee. According to the Islamic Fiqh Academy, promises in commercial transactions are binding even if they are one-sided and if they cause the promisee to incur some liabilities.
- **Hiba.** A gift that can be revoked before it has been handed over.
- **Qard Hasan.** A benevolent loan, where the borrower is required to return only the amount of the original loan.

- **Wassiyyat.** This means the Will, by which a person dictates how to distribute their assets amongst their beneficiaries.
- **Waqf.** A charitable endowment under Shariah law, which involves donating an asset for the common good of Muslim society or for religious purposes, with no intention of reclaiming the asset.

Some examples of bilateral contracts in Shariah-compliant commerce are the following.

- **Muawadat.** Contracts of exchange.
- **Shirkah.** Contracts of partnership.
- **Dhamanah.** Contracts of security provided by one party to another.
- **Wakala.** Agency contracts for a specific work to be done by one party on behalf of another. Examples of Wakala contracts include brokerage services, funds management, insurance underwriting, etc.
- **Wadia.** Contracts of safe custody provided by one party for the assets of another.

CONTRACTS OF EXCHANGE IN SHARIAH-COMPLIANT COMMERCE AND FINANCE

The simplest contract in Shariah law is the contract of exchange or the contract of sale. It involves transfer of ownership of specific items from one party to another, which can be as a barter, exchanging one item with another or exchanging an item with money or exchanging money for money. All valid conditions of a contract would apply to a sales contract in Islamic finance. The most common sales contracts used in contemporary Islamic finance and banking are as follows.

- **Murabaha.** In this contract, an item is sold at a cost plus a markup price which would be paid in the future. The original price, markup and payment schedule are known to both parties. Murabaha will be covered in detail in Chapter 4.
- **Salam.** This is a trade contract rather than a loan, usually providing short-term production finance. In this contract the full price of the asset is paid in advance while delivery happens in the future. Salam will be discussed in Chapter 8.
- **Istisna.** This contract is used to finance long-term projects to build or manufacture capital items, which are sold before they are manufactured, while payments are made in instalments or as lump sums during construction or manufacture or at/after delivery. Istisna is the topic of Chapter 9.
- **Sarf.** This is a form of exchange, where one currency is sold for an equivalent amount of another currency. Here one currency is the asset while the other is the payment. Shariah requires the currencies to be exchanged on the spot. Similarly, metals originally used as currency (gold, silver, etc.) can only be exchanged with each other on the spot. Future trading of either currency, or the metals used originally as currency, is not permitted by Shariah law.
- **Musawama.** This sale involves a purchase when the customer does not know the cost of the product, but is aware of the price and decides to buy or not at that price. The customer may also negotiate with the seller and arrive at a mutually agreed price. This includes all the purchases made at shops, where customers are aware only of the price and not the cost.

- **Arbun.** This is a non-refundable downpayment made by the buyer against the purchase price of an item in a sale contract. If the buyer finally buys the item, the downpayment would be part of the purchase price but if the buyer does not fulfil the purchase obligation, the downpayment would be lost.
- **Hawala.** This exchange involves transfer of an amount from one person to another via an intermediary. The intermediary may charge a fee, but as per Shariah ruling this cannot be a percentage of the transfer amount and the transfer should happen at the earliest without any increase to the principal amount.
- **Kafala.** This is a third-party guarantee provided by a borrower against some obligation. If the borrower fails to meet their obligations, the creditor or bank can recover their dues from the guarantor. Shariah requires the guarantee to be provided without any charges, but the necessity of competition and commercialization has made most scholars allow guarantors to charge an administrative fee, which is not proportional to the amount guaranteed.
- **Rahn.** This is the security or collateral that is provided as a pledge or mortgage on an asset owned by the borrower. If the borrower is unable to repay, the financier can sell the asset and recover their claims from funds generated, though if any surplus remains from the sale value it will be returned to the borrower.

COMMON ISLAMIC BANKING PRODUCTS

According to Dr Sharifah Faigah Syed Alwi (Hasan, 2014), Shariah-compliant products are developed based on an existing conventional product and expect to meet similar needs, and the features are reworked to meet Shariah requirements; on the other hand, Shariah-based products are completely new products designed by Islamic bankers or Islamic scholars. These two types of Islamic finance products are not alternatives to each other. Both are required depending on the need, the competitive environment, the sophistication of the product and the difficulty of realistically applying Shariah rulings. Today's modern Islamic banks serve individuals, businesses and governments.

Retail Islamic Banking Products

The most common Islamic banking products offered for the retail segment, serving individuals and households, are discussed below.

- **Current, savings and investment accounts.** These three very important products have already been discussed in detail in the Sources of Funds section earlier in this chapter.
- **Credit cards.** Islamic banks offer credit cards but instead of charging interest like conventional banks, they have a variety of ways of charging for their cards. As discussed in Schoon (2016), these methods are:
  1. **Periodic service charge.** Monthly or annual fixed fee.
  2. **Deferred payment sale.** Here the cardholder uses the card to pay for goods or services, the card issuer becomes the owner of the good or service by paying the merchant, then sells the good or service to the cardholder at the original price plus markup to be paid at the end of the period or in instalments over a period.

3. **Lease purchase agreement.** The card issuer is the owner of the good or service till the cardholder makes the final payment and becomes the owner. During this period, the cardholder pays a rental on the good or service to the card issuer.
4. **Prepaid credit card.** The cardholder deposits an amount on the card and uses it to purchase goods or services.

- **Home financing.** This is provided using Murabaha (Chapter 4), diminishing Musharaka (Chapter 6) and lease financing or Ijara contracts (Chapter 7).
- **Personal loan.** Personal loans are offered most commonly by Islamic banks as:
  1. **Lease and hire purchase.** The bank buys and leases to the client. The client pays, over a period, repayment of the price of the asset plus rent.
  2. **Murabaha or deferred payment sale.** The bank buys the asset and sells to the client at a markup. The client repays over an agreed period in instalments.

Corporate Islamic Banking Products

Islamic banks provide products and services for most needs of corporates, like assisting in equity or Sukuk issue, financing joint ventures, financing acquisitions and management buyouts, working capital financing, trade and project financing, etc. Some of the most common Islamic banking products and services offered for the corporate segment and for governments are discussed below.

Trade finance. Murabaha and Ijara contracts are used to provide export and import financing. The importance of trade financing comes from the problems in trade – which are that there is a lack of geographical proximity between exporters and importers and both are concerned that the other party may not meet their obligations. Owing to these problems, hand-to-hand or spot trading is not possible, instead deferred payment and deferred delivery are essential features of import and export transactions. As such, exporters and importers both need reliable third parties as intermediaries and banks provide this intermediation. Shipping companies and insurance companies facilitate trading. Common trade finance services offered by banks are as listed below.

1. **Letter of credit.** Operates like a conventional letter of credit – an undertaking by a bank to make payment to a certain party on presentation of required documents. Often used with trade-related Murabaha and Salam. Depending on the type of client, the letter of credit ensures goods are delivered before payment is made or insures against non-payment for goods where the risk is transferred to the bank. Islamic banks charge an administration fee for this job, which cannot be proportional to the amount of the contract since that would be the same as interest. The letter of credit provides security to both exporter and importer.
2. **Bill of exchange.** Written by the exporter against the importer stating the exporter's payment claim, time of payment or tenor and any other payment terms. If the importer pays at the time of receiving the bill of lading, the tenor is 'at sight', otherwise it is when the importer is obliged to pay as per agreement.
3. **Banker's acceptance.** Exporters can receive a banker's acceptance on their payment claims against the importer, which they can sell to raise funds earlier if required.
4. **Bank guarantees.** The exporter may directly, or via its bank, ask for a bank guarantee for payment from the importer's bank.

Project finance. Islamic banks provide project financing to corporates based on the build, own, operate, transfer, lease and rent options. The most common is BOT: build, operate and transfer.

Syndication. When the financing required by the borrower or entrepreneur is very large or very risky, it may go beyond the capabilities of one financial institution. In this case more than one Islamic bank come together to provide the financing. This is called syndication. Not all banks play an equal role in the syndication. One of the banks usually takes the lead and has the most involvement. This bank is called the lead bank. The lead bank's role is to negotiate and prepare the documents and memorandum, communicate with all relevant parties and resolve all matters related to the syndication. The benefits of syndication are that the risk of the project is diversified amongst the banks, income is shared, the client relationship is managed – even though the funding is of a large size, each of the syndicate banks bring their own comparative advantage and reputation into the financing.

FINANCIAL ACCOUNTING IN ISLAMIC BANKING

Islam is a way of life and requires accountability in all activity. Moreover, the requirements of transparency and fairness in business dealings and in financial transactions in Islam emphasize the importance of accountability further. Conventional accounting principles are independent of any religious rulings but that is not the case for Islamic financial institutions, and with the growth in the Islamic finance and banking industry, there appears to be a need for the development of Islamic accounting as a sub-discipline within the subject of accounting.

Financial accounting is the process by which the activities and operations of a business and their financial implications are identified, measured and recorded for the use of decision-makers. The decision-makers internally are the management, and externally the creditors, investors, customers, regulators and the government. Islamic accounting, like financial accounting in general, is the process that identifies, measures and records all business financial activities but also continuously evaluates and ensures that these activities are being conducted within the rulings of the Shariah and are meeting with the Shariah focus of socio-economic, ethical and environmental responsibilities.

With the emergence of global companies and global investors, it has become very important to have financial statements of companies that are transparent, consistent and comparable. In the conventional system the International Financial Reporting Standards (IFRS) aim to achieve this. The IFRS was not developed with the Shariah-compliant finance industry's unique characteristics in mind. Yet in many non-Muslim jurisdictions the IFRS, the countries' GAAP rulings and corporate law apply to the IFIs also, creating various complications. The IFRS was developed for conventional forms of business.

For example, in an Islamic investment account the clients give the bank the right to reinvest their funds and co-mingle them with the funds of other clients, as well as those of the Islamic bank, into Shariah-compliant activities; they receive proportional profits as per a pre-agreed ratio and they also bear all risk of losses. As such, the capital is not guaranteed. The IFRS does not have any parallel for Islamic investment accounts and financial reporting, especially in non-Muslim jurisdictions, is a major challenge.

To deal with the Islamic investment account under IFRS, one of the following treatments is applied:

1. Considered as liability as in conventional deposit accounts, since under competitive pressure Islamic banks provide a capital guarantee using reserves.
2. Considered as equity since the returns are based on the income generated by the underlying assets.
3. Also considered as off-balance sheet item, since these accounts are managed as investment funds.

The Islamic banks' transactions, reporting standards and disclosures are different, and the need to develop an alternative set of accounting and financial reporting standards became increasingly evident. This led to the establishment of the AAOIFI in Bahrain in 1991. The main objective of the AAOIFI was to complement the IFRS's standards with its own standards that met the specific needs of the IFIs. AAOIFI started with a core set of accounting standards which were expanded to include auditing and corporate governance standards. AAOIFI has set up standards in financial accounting statements for the growing Islamic finance and banking industry, in conformation with the rules of the International Organization of Securities Commissions (IOSCO), International Accounting Standards Board (IASB) and Bank of International Settlements (BIS).

Competent and relevant financial accounting of Islamic banks is useful to the banks' shareholders, all depositors, current and future investors and creditors, management, employees, the Shariah Supervisory Board, government and regulatory bodies, business partners and suppliers of the bank, all Zakat-related bodies and the public.

Objectives of Islamic Financial Accounting

It is crucial to develop reliable and globally acceptable Islamic financial accounting standards and procedures because:

1. Existing conventional financial reporting standards are not adequate for the IFIs.
2. Commercial as well as the unique religious and social features of the IFIs need to be considered.
3. An accurate and fair system to recognize, measure and record financial information is required.
4. Transparent and equitable valuation and disclosure of financial information is important.
5. Growth of the Islamic finance and banking sector demands a competent and internationally relevant financial reporting framework.
6. Provision of standard information, understandable to all stakeholders and comparable with other companies, locally and globally, is important for the future of Islamic financial institutions
7. Shariah compliance of transactions needs to be ensured.

Features of Islamic Financial Accounting

1. Islamic financial accounting follows the same general framework as conventional financial accounting, with modifications made to ensure Shariah compliance is met.
2. A standard double-entry method of recording is used.
3. Shariah compliance principles and rules are clearly applied in the accounting procedures.

4. Unique Islamic finance products like Murabaha, Mudaraba, Musharaka, Ijara, Salam and Istisna are recognized and applied in the procedures.
5. Financial accounting information is generated in a manner that is useful for both internal and external users.
6. Islamic financial accounting includes the calculation and distribution information of applicable Zakat.

CHALLENGES FACED BY ISLAMIC BANKS

Islamic banks operate on an interest-free and profit and loss-based mechanism, significantly different from the conventional banks the world and its population are accustomed to. As the niche segment of Islamic finance develops on the global platform, it faces various challenges and some of these are briefly discussed below.

1. **Profit and loss system.** The financial markets all over the world operate on an interest-based system, while the Islamic banks operate via a profit and loss-sharing system; this unique operational mechanism is not well accepted or understood, either by the industry or the customers.
2. **Regulatory issues.** Most government and regulatory bodies globally are designed for the interest-based finance industry and do not cater to the unique characteristics of Islamic banking.
3. **Default penalty.** When payments are delayed or defaulted, conventional banks charge interest on interest while Shariah does not permit Islamic banks to increase their profit ratio. Although they can charge a penalty, they cannot benefit from it and are required to donate it to charity.
4. **Skilled employees.** The lack of knowledge and awareness, as well as the overall lack of Islamic finance and banking training and educational facilities, leads to lack of skilled and experienced employees for the industry.
5. **Shariah scholar confusion.** The Shariah scholars responsible for supporting the Islamic finance and banking industry to ensure Shariah compliance, as well as guide the banks to design innovative products and serve the needs of customers, often suffer from a lack of consensus and confusion. Their interpretations of Shariah rulings and products could be different, causing a lack of standardization.
6. **Shortage of multi-skilled Shariah scholars.** The total number of qualified Shariah scholars globally is not significant, moreover those with some expertise in finance and banking are even fewer.
7. **Partnership ventures.** Since Islamic banks often act as partners, sharing in the profit and loss of the venture they finance, they need a longer period to recover their investments.
8. **Tax considerations.** In most non-Muslim jurisdictions profit paid to an Islamic bank by the borrower or entrepreneur is not a tax-deductible expense, as are the interest payments to a conventional bank. This causes a major disadvantage to the clients of Islamic banks.
9. **Global auditing standards.** These standards are developed for the conventional banking system, and do not always fit in with or serve the Islamic banking industry. The Islamic auditing and standard setting bodies are still very new and do not yet have the total confidence of the global industry.

ISLAMIC FINANCE AND THE FINANCIAL CRISIS

The last major global financial crisis of 2007–2008 has changed fundamentally some of the thoughts related to the world of finance and the principles that guide it. The crisis started from a housing crisis in the USA and the resultant impact was worse than the Great Depression of the 1930s. Most countries around the world were affected to some extent by this crisis. A major source of the crisis was the interest-based financial securities linked to home mortgages. According to J. M. Keynes in the *General Theory of Employment, Interest and Money*, the schedule of profit rates is rarely in sync with the schedule of interest rates; and when profit rates are much higher than interest rates this can lead to inflation, while when they are much lower they cause deflation and unemployment. This boom and depression can affect the stability of the economy (Hasan, 2014). This shifts significantly in favour of profit and loss-based Islamic banking over interest-based conventional banking. In conventional finance, owned and borrowed funds are treated differently. On the governmental policy level, owned funds receive variable income, which is profit, while borrowed funds receive fixed interest. Further, interest, the cost of borrowed funds, is considered a tax-deductible cost while dividends, the cost of owned funds, are not tax deductible.

Islamic banking has held up well during the global financial crisis. Some of the reasons linked to this are that Islamic banking is more conservative than conventional banking; all Islamic financial transactions require to be linked to real assets, thus there is less uncertainty with them; furthermore, Islamic banking does not permit many of the instruments that were to some extent considered as causes for the crisis, like short selling and mortgage-based securities.

INTERNATIONAL ISLAMIC REGULATORY AND STANDARD SETTING BODIES

The Islamic finance and banking industry consists of the Islamic banks, the Islamic insurance or Takaful companies, the Islamic capital markets and the Islamic non-bank financial institutions. The Islamic non-bank financial institutions provide supportive functions for Islamic economic activities, like liquidity needs, and include Islamic finance companies, housing cooperatives, private equity and venture capital firms, microfinance institutions, charitable endowment or Waqf management institutions and Hajj and Zakat management bodies. Moreover, these IFIs operate in purely Shariah-based jurisdictions, in dual-banking jurisdictions and in non-Muslim jurisdictions without formal recognition of the Shariah rulings. The global standards of accounting reporting under the guidelines of the IFRS and the banking supervisions under the Basel rules were designed for conventional financial activities and are not always applicable to the participants of the Islamic finance and banking industry. Owing to the Shariah restrictions in their operations, IFIs often require special treatment which cannot be accommodated by either the IFRS or the Basel regulations. To overcome these problems, the Islamic finance and banking industry globally took the initiative to set up regulatory and standard setting bodies especially for its participatory institutions to self-regulate and develop appropriate standards. Efforts were also made to cooperate and coordinate with the global regulatory bodies in the formation of these international Islamic regulatory and standard setting institutions, to enhance acceptability and trust amongst the conventional and Islamic sectors. The role of the international Islamic regulatory and standard settings institutions is to safeguard the deposits and partnerships of the financial institutions and ensure efficient profit and loss sharing amongst the institutions, their depositors and shareholders. The two main bodies are the AAOIFI and the IFSB, with several other supportive institutions. These are elaborated below.

Accounting and Auditing Organization for Islamic Financial Institutions (AAOIFI)

The AAOIFI was set up in 1991 in Bahrain. It is one of the leading standard setting bodies in the global Islamic finance and banking industry and is an autonomous, non-profit institution. These standards are developed to bring harmony to the principles and practices of the global Islamic finance and banking industry and ensure uniformity and transparency in their financial reporting. AAOIFI is the Islamic counterpart of the IASB and its standards derive significantly from the IFRS. AAOIFI members originate from 45 countries and include banks, central banks, other regulatory authorities, non-banking financial institutions, accounting and auditing and legal firms. AAOIFI standards are not mandatory on countries or institutions, though increasingly more are opting to self-regulate themselves based on the AAOIFI issued standards.

Main Functions of AAOIFI

1. Develop standards related to accounting, auditing, governance, ethics and Shariah compliance.
2. Through the above standardizations increase confidence of ultimate users of financial statements of the IFIs.
3. Design rulings that clearly identify the IFIs' assets, liabilities, cash inflows and outflows and any related risk.
4. The rulings also search and separate out any prohibited income or expenditure.
5. Ensure the distribution of reasonable returns to the investors.
6. Report on the global IFIs' achievements related to social responsibilities and Zakat obligations.
7. Research and develop new ideas related to banking as well as accounting and auditing.
8. Review and adjust existing standards in the conventional sector to make them appropriate to IFIs.
9. Reduce inconsistency amongst the Shariah rulings passed by various SSBs and achieve conformity to standards.
10. Provide regulatory guidelines to central banks of Muslim countries and encourage them to accept standardization.
11. Encourage ethical practices by providing a standard code of ethics for IFIs.
12. Disseminate the regulatory and standard setting information and ideas via training of relevant professionals and organize seminars, conferences and publications.

Islamic Financial Services Board (IFSB)

The IFSB was established in 2002 and is based in Kuala Lumpur, Malaysia. For the global Islamic finance and banking industry it is one of the main standard setting bodies that stabilizes the industry by developing prudent and transparent standards and

Shariah governance. Its role is like that of the BIS. IFSB members consist of the Islamic Development Bank and the central banks or main regulatory authorities of Muslim countries, especially those where Islamic banking has a significant presence. According to the IFSB website as of April 2017, the IFSB has 183 members, including 70 central banks and regulatory authorities, 7 inter-governmental organizations, 106 financial institutions, professional firms, stock exchanges and industry associations.

Main Functions of IFSB

1. Develop new or adapt existing Shariah standards to build a prudent and transparent Islamic finance and banking industry.
2. Guide IFIs to develop in-house risk-management facilities, identify and report risk exposures from all Islamic financial instruments used and try to reduce these risks.
3. Set up standards to supervise, control and regulate all Islamic banking practices in coordination with the Basel requirements.
4. Dictate an acceptable capital adequacy ratio for Islamic banks.
5. Encourage cooperation amongst the member countries and build a global database of IFIs and Islamic finance experts.
6. Liaise and coordinate with the global conventional finance standard setting institutions.
7. Conduct relevant research and publications.

Liquidity Management Centre (LMC) and International Islamic Liquidity Management (IILM)

The LMC was established in 2002 in Bahrain and its main shareholders are the Bahrain Islamic Bank, Dubai Islamic Bank, Islamic Development Bank and Kuwait Finance House. The IILM is based in Kuala Lumpur and its current shareholders are the central banks and monetary authorities of Malaysia, Indonesia, Kuwait, Luxembourg, Mauritius, Nigeria, Qatar, Turkey and the UAE. The key purpose of both organizations is to create an interbank money market and issue short-term Shariah-compliant instruments to invest short-term liquidity surpluses of IFIs and facilitate liquidity management of the IFIs.

International Islamic Financial Market (IIFM)

The IIFM was set up in Bahrain in 2002 through the joint efforts of the central banks of Bahrain, Brunei, Indonesia, Malaysia, Sudan and the Islamic Development Bank. The key purpose of the IIFM is to set standards applicable to the Islamic capital markets. It focuses on the standardization of the Islamic capital market products, related documents and processes and is working towards the self-regulation and promotion of Islamic capital and money markets. The IIFM aims to develop both national and international trading infrastructures with transparent and standardized regulations and knowledge sharing amongst the various participants.

International Islamic Rating Agency (IIRA)

The IIRA was established in 2005 in Bahrain. It is the only rating agency whose sole purpose is to provide rating services for Islamic banking and for Islamic capital and money markets. The IIRA also aims to make its ratings acceptable by regulators in different jurisdictions. Its key functions are to set up benchmarks for issue and issuer ratings, ratings of timely repayments of debt obligations of sovereigns, corporates and banks, and assessment of the level of Shariah compliance and corporate governance. The IIRA also aims to publish reliable data about research, analysis and evaluation of sectors, industries and individual enterprises.

General Council for Islamic Banks and Financial Institutions (CIBAFI)

The CIBAFI was established in 2001 and is based in Bahrain. It acts like a bankers' association. It has nearly 120 members spread over 30 jurisdictions and includes IFIs, international inter-governmental organizations, professional firms and industry associations. The council was set up to represent and promote the Islamic financial services industry globally and enhance cooperation amongst its members. It advocates regulatory, financial and economic policies that would benefit its members. The CIBAFI distributes appropriate and accurate data amongst all stakeholders of the Islamic finance industry and promotes sound industry practices.

International Islamic Centre for Reconciliation and Commercial Arbitration for Islamic Finance Industry (IICRCA)

The IICRCA was established in 2003 and is based in Dubai. Its key function is to mediate in case of financial and commercial disputes amongst IFIs and commercial institutions.

Islamic Development Bank (IDB)

The IDB is part of the pioneering stage of the global Islamic finance and banking industry. It was set up in 1975 in Jeddah, KSA as a multilateral development bank. Currently the IDB's members are 57 countries, a requirement for membership is that the country needs to also be a member of the OIC. Within the IDB it has established the Islamic Research and Training Institute (IRTI), which aims to promote Islamic economics and finance via various academic endeavours like research, training, publications, seminars and conferences.

Main Functions of IDB

1. To foster economic development and social progress in member countries and in Muslim communities.
2. To participate in equity capital and to grant loans for productive purposes in member countries.
3. To provide financial assistance to governments of member countries.
4. To establish and operate special funds for specific purposes, like the assistance of Muslim communities in non-member countries.
5. To accept deposits and to mobilize financial resources through Shariah-compatible modes.
6. To promote foreign trade, especially in capital goods, among member countries.
7. To provide training services to assist with Shariah compliance in member Muslim countries.

International Islamic Fiqh Academy

The Fiqh Academy was created by the decision of the OIC in 1974 and was inaugurated in Jeddah, KSA in 1988. It is an institute of advanced learning on Islamic studies and Shariah law.

Regulatory Issues for IFIs in Non-Muslim Jurisdictions – A UK Example   The following discussion is based on material covered in Kettel (2010).

The UK's regulatory body, the FSA, authorizes all financial institutions operating in the UK irrespective of their country of origin, the sector they operate in or their religious principles. The FSA's approach towards Islamic banking is neither to create any obstacles nor to provide any special favours. Islamic banks appear to face three types of difficulties in the UK, or for that matter in most Western jurisdictions.

1. **Regulatory definition of products.** The economic impact of Islamic banking products is like that of conventional banking ones, but they are structured in a significantly different manner. As such, Islamic banks need to take extra care to ensure that their product structure is acceptable within the regulatory framework of the country.
2. **Role of Shariah scholars.** The FSA has issues with the role of the Shariah scholars of an Islamic bank, whether it is purely advisory or if they play some executive role also. The SSB often plays a hands-on role in product development, to ensure that products are structured in a Shariah-compliant manner and will not be rejected by the SSB on Shariah grounds later. Such executive responsibility of the SSB may cause conflict with the management or BOD. On the other hand, these Shariah scholars would be discouraged from being involved in the SSB of more than one institution to avoid conflicts of interest, and this would create a problem due to the shortage of scholars.
3. **Financial promotions.** Islamic banking products need to include the risks as well as the benefits in their promotion material, as many investors or clients are inexperienced in Islamic banking and the product structure is quite different from that in conventional banking counterparts.

The UK's FSA identified five different issues related to Islamic banking. First, Shariah compliance introduces some risks for Islamic banks but these are not too high and as such the FSA agrees to authorize Islamic banks. Second, the FSA defines Islamic demand deposits as simple non-interest-bearing accounts where the bank promises capital repayment and investment accounts as profit and loss-based Mudaraba accounts where the account holder accepts the risk of losing their original capital. Third, related to Shariah compliance and the role of the SSB, since the FSA is a financial regulator not a religious body, it prefers the appointment of internal auditors with Shariah knowledge to monitor Shariah compliance. Fourth, the FSA regulates Islamic banking instruments but not the Islamic products traded in the capital markets, like Sukuks. Fifth, the corporate governance issue which arises from the need of Islamic banks to create reserve funds to smooth the income to investment account holders; since the reserves lead to conflicts of interest between the investment account holders over shareholders or between the present investment account holders over future investment account holders, which can only be controlled through strict unambiguous rules to be followed.

KEY TERMS AND CONCEPTS

Adverse selection risk

Application of funds

Arbun

Bank–client relationship

Central bank

Cheque clearing services

Current accounts

Financial intermediation

Hawala

Hiba

Investment accounts

Kafala

Lender of last resort

Moral hazard risk

Muawadat

Musawama

Profit and loss
  sharing

Qard Hasan

Rahn

Sarf

Savings accounts

Shariah compliance
  risk

Shirkah

Sources of funds

Two-tier Mudaraba

Two-windows model

Wad

Wadia

Wakala

Waqf

Wassiyyat

CHAPTER SUMMARY

Islamic banking is an alternative to conventional banking, based on Shariah law, prohibiting interest and designed on the profit and loss basis. Both Islamic and conventional banks need to be licensed by the central bank, offer products for various customers and manage their liquidity via the interbank market. Some of the differences between the two types of banks are related to interest versus profit and loss, guarantee to depositors, bank–client relationship and default payments, etc.

The relationship of both conventional and Islamic banks to the central bank is more similar than different. In both cases the central bank acts as the supervisor, lender of last resort, provides cheque clearing services and dictates the statutory cash reserve and other controls. The differences come only from the Shariah compliance and different product structure of the Islamic banks. Both types of banks face liquidity, excess liquidity, credit, settlement, market, currency and operational risks. Only conventional banks have interest rate risk, while Islamic banks have adverse selection, moral hazard, equity investment, default penalty, higher cost, Shariah compliance and rate of return risk.

Financial intermediation is the core business of banking and is the matching of fund savers with borrowers or entrepreneurs. Conventional banks do this using interest, while Islamic banks use the profit and loss mechanism and the models used can be two-tier Mudaraba, two-window Mudaraba or the Wakala model. Today, conventional banks are also participating in Islamic finance and banking via a separate window, branch or subsidiary. The differences in the financial intermediation of conventional and Islamic banks are in the areas of religious, social, ethical, environmental and fiduciary requirements; in the manner of project selection and monitoring; in the terms of financing and related to leverage versus risk sharing.

The sources of funds of an Islamic bank include current, savings and investment accounts, while the application of funds involves a variety of products including Murabaha, Mudaraba, Musharaka, Ijara, Salam and Istisna. Shariah compliance of all financial contracts requires two or more parties, mentally sound; the subject matter should be Shariah compliant, devoid of Riba, Gharar and Maysir, linked to real assets and for sales contracts the asset should exist, be owned and be physically or constructively possessed by the seller. Unilateral contracts include Wad, Hiba, Qard Hasan, Wassiyyat and Waqf and bilateral contracts include Muawadat, Shirkah, Dhamanah, Wakala, Wadia, etc. Islamic banks serve individuals, corporates and governments.

Globally standardized financial accounting and reporting does not always fit Islamic banking operations, requiring the development of Islamic financial accounting which is tailored to Shariah-based operations and products of the industry. Besides the auditory standards and regulatory issues, other challenges faced by the Islamic finance and banking industry include applying the profit and loss system, default penalty, partnership ventures, tax treatment and the lack of qualified employees as well as Shariah scholars. On the upside though, Islamic banking held up well during the last financial crisis. To be more acceptable in the global finance industry, various international Islamic regulatory and standard setting bodies are being established, bringing more acceptability and reliability to this niche segment. These bodies include the AAOIFI, IFSB, LMC, IILM, IIFM, IIRA, CIBAFI, IICRCA, IDB and the International Islamic Fiqh Academy.

END OF CHAPTER QUESTIONS AND ACTIVITIES

Discussion Questions

1. Define Islamic banking.
2. What are the core objectives of an Islamic bank?
3. Discuss the similarities and differences between a conventional and an Islamic bank.
4. Describe the relationship of banks with the central bank.
5. What are the generic risks faced by all banks? Briefly explain each.
6. Discuss the risks specific to Islamic banks.
7. Compare 'risk sharing' in Islamic banking versus conventional banking.
8. Define financial intermediation in modern banking and why it is important.
9. What is financial intermediation in conventional banks?
10. Explain financial intermediation in Islamic banks.
11. What financial intermediation models can an Islamic bank use?
12. How do Islamic banks smooth out the profits given to depositors? Why is this important?
13. Conventional banks are also participating in Islamic finance and banking. What are the different distribution options used by them?
14. Contrast conventional financial intermediation with Islamic financial intermediation.
15. Discuss the main sources of funds for Islamic banks.
16. What are the common applications of funds of an Islamic bank? Which products are deferred exchange contracts, and which are equity-based products?
17. What are the requirements of a valid Shariah-compliant contract?
18. Briefly discuss a few unilateral contracts used in Shariah-compliant commerce.
19. Describe examples of bilateral Shariah-compliant contracts.
20. Discuss the common exchange contracts used in Islamic finance and banking.

21. What is the Shariah position on buying and selling of foreign exchange, especially forward transactions?
22. Discuss common retail and corporate products and services offered by an Islamic bank.
23. Why is it important to develop Islamic financial accounting procedures?
24. What are the objectives of Islamic financial accounting?
25. Describe the features of Islamic financial accounting.
26. Standardization in Islamic banking is required to reduce confusion. Briefly discuss any one confusion.
27. Discuss the challenges faced by Islamic banks today.
28. How did Islamic banking fare during the financial crisis of 2007–2008?
29. List the most important international Islamic regulatory and standard setting bodies.
30. Discuss the AAOIFI and its main functions.
31. Discuss the IFSB and its main functions.
32. Briefly describe the LMC, IILM, IIFM and IIRA.
33. What roles do CIBAFI and IICRCA play in Islamic finance and banking?
34. Discuss the IDB and its main functions.
35. What is the International Islamic Fiqh Academy?
36. How does the FSA in the UK deal with Islamic banks?

Multiple Choice Questions

Circle the letter next to the most accurate answer.
1. Which of the following principles applies to Islamic banking and finance?
   a. Prohibition of speculative behaviour
   b. Only Sharia-approved activities are permissible
   c. All profit-making is impermissible
   d. a and b
2. Islamic banks:
   a. Pay interest to their depositors
   b. Charge interest to their lenders
   c. Do not provide financing without collateral
   d. Base their investing criteria on the investment potential of the project and not just on collateral
3. Which of the following is a characteristic that differentiates Islamic banks from conventional banks?
   a. The absence of interest in all financial dealings
   b. Making profit from trade
   c. Allocation of funds to areas that increase economic activity and benefit society
   d. Provide home financing via mortgages
4. Islamic banks:
   a. Base their investment decisions entirely on the collateral submitted by the client
   b. Base their investment decisions on the investment potential of the project and not just on collateral
   c. May accept interest on their liabilities but donate it to charity
   d. Both a and c

5. Applying Islamic finance principles means:
   a. Islamic banks cannot provide lines of credit that bear interest
   b. Islamic banks can make money out of money
   c. No restriction on speculative behaviour
   d. Avoiding all kinds of risks by the Islamic bank

6. The main objective of Islamic banks is to:
   a. Provide funds for Muslims
   b. Make maximum profits for shareholders
   c. Finance building of Masjids and other Muslim religious institutions
   d. Provide an alternative to interest-based banking

7. The main objective of Islamic banks is to:
   a. Ensure Halal activities are not financed
   b. Finance the building of Islamic schools and colleges
   c. Provide Riba-free banking products and services
   d. Develop the retail and consumer banking in Muslim countries

8. Which statement below does not apply to an Islamic bank:
   a. Does not charge interest on funds given as loans
   b. Does not pay interest to its depositors
   c. Provides collateral-free loans to Muslims only
   d. Ensures no Haram business activity is financed

9. Which of the following is a Shariah rule applied to Islamic banking?
   a. Selling money for money is permitted
   b. Any profits made are not permitted
   c. A deferred sale at a price higher than the cost is not permitted
   d. A deferred sale at a price higher than the cost is permitted

10. The main Islamic banking products are:
    a. Musharaka, Mudaraba and Murabaha
    b. Ijara and Istisna
    c. Salam
    d. All of the above

11. An Islamic bank is a business, and so must make profit. Which of the statements below best explains the mechanism by which the Islamic bank earns profit?
    a. The Islamic bank charges a low interest on loans, and thus remains profitable without overcharging its clients
    b. The Islamic bank charges a competitive fee on loans and most of its profit comes from the fees
    c. The Islamic bank finances various needs of customers, linked to assets, on the basis of sale, leasing or partnership and earns a share of the profit from the transaction
    d. The Islamic bank does not lend money but instead acts as an agent between seller and buyer and receives a fee for its services

12. Sharia-compliant sales contracts have three requirements. Which of the following is not one of them?
    a. Assets need to be in existence
    b. Sales profit should be reasonable
    c. Owner should own the asset
    d. Asset should be in physical or constructive possession of owner

13. Abdulla agrees to sell his house to Ahmed at the market price. Is the sale valid under Islamic finance?
    a. Yes, the sale is valid because it is not fair that Abdulla loses money should the market price go up. At the same time, it is not fair that Ahmed pays too much for the house should the market price go down
    b. No, the sale is not valid because Abdulla and Ahmed did not sign a written bilateral contract agreement specifying this condition
    c. Yes, the sale is valid because both Abdulla and Ahmed agree to this condition and therefore they enter into a bilateral contract agreement
    d. No, the sale is not valid because the specific price has to be stated under the Islamic finance contract requirements
14. Rafe took a loan of £10,000 from Helen for a small business. The business incurred a loss and the capital reduced to £5,000. Can Rafe ask Helen to share in the loss? Which statement below is the best answer?
    a. Yes, because Rafe took the loan for the growth of his small business. Rafe does not have to pay the full amount back to Helen
    b. Yes, because in Islamic finance two parties always share the profit and loss because it is just and fair. Rafe does not have to pay the full amount to Helen
    c. No, because the transaction between the two of them is that of a loan and not any form of partnership. Rafe is liable to pay £10,000 to Helen
    d. No, because the transaction between the two of them was not recorded by the Shariah Supervisory Board. Rafe is liable to pay £10,000 to Helen
15. In Badr's grocery store there is surplus flour currently. He decides not to sell it now and to do so in the future, when there is a deficit of flour, so he can make a higher profit. Is this transaction acceptable under the principles of Islamic economics? Why?
    a. Yes, because taking advantage of a deficit of goods will result in higher profits for Badr
    b. Yes, because Badr speculates for changes in commodity supply, which is a proper business risk he is taking
    c. No, because Badr is hoarding food, and hoarding food and other necessities is unlawful under Islamic economics
    d. No, Badr is making the decision based on the issues of supply and demand of flour, which is unacceptable in Islamic economics
16. Noor purchased 1,000 bags of sugar from Islamic Bank on credit. While transporting the bags to her factory, the sugar was destroyed by heavy rains. Choose the statement that correctly explains who bears the loss.
    a. Noor bears the loss because she is the owner of the goods
    b. Noor bears the loss because she was transporting the goods at the time of the rain
    c. Islamic Bank bears the loss because it is the owner of the goods sold to Noor on credit
    d. Islamic Bank bears the loss because the heavy rains were an act of God and nature, and there was no insurance in place to cover the loss of the goods
17. As per the OIC Central Bank Governors declaration of 1982, which one below is not an aspect of the relationship between central banks and Islamic banks?
    a. Lender of last resort
    b. Supervisor regarding monetary policy
    c. Shariah supervisory
    d. Clearing house

18. Which international IFI is based in Dubai?
    a. LMC
    b. IFSB
    c. IICRCA
    d. GCIBFI
19. The key function of the IIFM is to:
    a. Create an interbank money market
    b. Set up accounting standards
    c. Mediate in IFI disputes
    d. Develop, regulate and promote Islamic capital and money markets

True/False Questions

Write T for true and F for false next to the statement.
1. The creditor–debtor relationship does not apply to Islamic banking.
2. Islamic banks use a high level of expertise and technical know-how to evaluate and monitor financing projects to ensure profitable use of funds.
3. Islamic banking transactions have to be based on tangible assets and not on intangible assets.
4. Conventional banks and Islamic banks cooperate on various issues.
5. Compared with conventional banks, Islamic banks take more risk.
6. Under central bank supervision in Muslim-majority countries an Islamic bank can operate without a Sharia Supervisory Board.

CHAPTER 4

Murabaha

Learning outcomes

Upon completion of this chapter, you should be able to:
  1. Define Murabaha, the types of Murabaha, including Tawarruq or reverse Murabaha, and key conditions of the Murabaha contract.
  2. Describe the Murabaha process for a standard contract and the Murabaha process commonly used by Islamic banks.
  3. Discuss the practical applications of Murabaha and the challenges and problems faced by the product.
  4. Compare the Murabaha contract with conventional loans.

INTRODUCTION TO MURABAHA

Conventional banking treats money and commodities and their trading as the same. As discussed in earlier chapters, Islam views money differently from commodities. Money is only a medium of exchange with no intrinsic value, and on its own it does not satisfy any need. Meanwhile commodities have intrinsic value and satisfy some need. Commodities have differing qualities and can be identified by specifications when they are traded. A new or a used car of the same model are not the same, or of the same value, but a new or an old bank note are the same. As such, money cannot be treated as a commodity. Hence, pure lending of money and earning a fixed return on it, which is interest, is prohibited. Islamic finance requires each financial transaction to be linked to a real asset. When commodities are traded for credit, an excess can be charged according to the majority of Muslim scholars. The seller can charge a different price for a cash sale or a credit sale, where the credit sale price would be higher.

According to Shariah rule, a sales contract can be executed only when the item already exists, is owned by the seller at the time of sale and is in the physical or constructive possession of the seller. Two exceptions to this rule are the contracts of Salam and Istisna, to be covered in Chapters 8 and 9, respectively.

In Islamic commerce, sales can be classified according to delivery and payment as:

1. Immediate delivery with spot payment.
2. Immediate delivery with deferred payment.
3. Immediate payment with deferred delivery.

Sales can also be classified based on disclosure of cost to the customer as:

1. **Musawama or bargain sale.** In this sale, the seller and buyer agree upon a price without any reference to the cost, because a seller is not obliged to reveal it. When we buy something from a shop we are aware of the price but do not know the cost. We either decide to buy at the given price or try to bargain on the price.
2. **Murabaha or trust sale.** Murabaha is the simplest Islamic banking instrument and is a widely used product. Islam prohibits charging fixed interest on money, but permits charging fixed profit on sale of goods. Islamic banks therefore use a sale-based transaction – Murabaha – instead of a term loan for financing. Murabaha is a sales contract where profit is made by selling at a cost-plus basis. It is an agreement where the bank purchases a specified item at the request of the customer, adds a pre-agreed profit to it and sells it to them at the marked-up price.

Murabaha is also called trust sales, since the distinguishing feature of Murabaha from regular sales is that the seller discloses the cost to the buyer and a known profit is added; the buyer puts their trust in the seller to buy the required item and to disclose to the client the quality or specification of the item and the actual cost as well as the markup added. If there is any storage, transportation or other cost incurred by the seller in delivering the item to the buyer, that will be added to the cost. The markup can either be a lump sum or a percentage of the price of the goods. The delivery of the goods is immediate. The client can pay on spot or pay deferred. Sales mostly is on deferred payment, so credit is extended, and this is used as a method of finance when the customer requires funds to buy goods. Deferred payment also has the option of the full amount at a deferred period or in instalments, the latter being more common. Thus, Murabaha provides the customer with the advantage of acquiring and using the asset, earning profit from it and using this profit to repay in deferred instalments. Murabaha is a Shariah-compliant instrument since the bank first acquires the asset for resale at profit along with the risk associated with purchase and resale, so an asset is sold for money and the transaction is not an exchange of money for money. There are two types of Murabaha.

- **Ordinary Murabaha.** The client asks the bank to acquire an asset that they would like to purchase without making any promise to buy it.
- **Murabaha sale with a promise (also called Murabaha to the purchase order).** The client makes a promise to buy the item once the bank acquires it. This type is more common as Islamic banks want to guarantee that the client will buy what they asked the bank to acquire for them.

In Murabaha with a promise the client has the risk of the goods not being delivered as per specification and at contracted time, while in the case of ordinary Murabaha the entire non-delivery risk is with the bank.

So, Murabaha is a sale and purchase agreement between the bank and its client. The bank sometimes may not prefer to buy the item itself due to legal restrictions, or because it does not have sufficient knowledge, and appoints the client as an agent to make the purchase. In such a situation, the client may take delivery of the item but the ownership will go to the bank. The bank may take security as a mortgage, guarantee, charge or lien to protect itself against default of the deferred payments. In case of default the bank may sell the security and recover its dues, but will make no profit and any excess remaining from the sale of the security will be returned to the client. Under Shariah rulings Islamic banks cannot charge a late payment fee, or if they do charge the bank cannot benefit from it and it is given away to charity. On the other hand, Islamic banks can charge for any costs they incur to recover the payments from the client.

Figure 4.1 is an overview of a Murabaha contract.

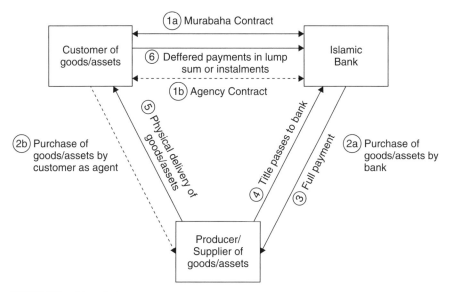

FIGURE 4.1   Murabaha contract

CONDITIONS RELATED TO MURABAHA

Murabaha contracts executed between an Islamic bank and a client are characterized by various conditions.

1. **Conditions of sale contract.** Murabaha from an Islamic bank is not a loan in exchange for interest payment as in a conventional bank, but the sale of a good or service. As such, Murabaha needs to fulfil the Shariah requirements of a valid sale – that is, the item of sale must exist at the time of the sale and be owned by and in the physical or constructive possession of the seller at the time of the sale.
2. **Goods subject to Murabaha contract.** These items need to be legal and Halal, having real commercial value. The items can be tangibles like vehicles, machinery, equipment and intangibles like brand name, trademark, copyright, patent, royalties, etc. Currencies and other mediums of exchange, like gold or silver, cannot be traded by Murabaha as they cannot be exchanged on a deferred basis.

3. **Costs related to the Murabaha item.** All direct and indirect costs, including the original cost of the item plus all other costs (e.g. packaging, transportation, delivery, installation and any agency costs), need to be identified and both the buyer and the seller should be aware of them and mutually agree to them.

4. **Markup or profit.** This can be a fixed amount or a percentage of the cost of the Murabaha item. This amount will constitute the Islamic bank's profit and for the Murabaha client or buyer it is the extra cost incurred for the advantage of deferred payment. The markup or profit will be clearly stated and mutually agreed by the bank and the client and cannot be changed later.

5. **Third-party seller.** The seller of the good or service in a Murabaha needs to be a third party, besides the client and the Islamic bank.

6. **Client's promise.** To reduce its risk, the bank may require the client to sign a unilateral promise to buy the goods once they have been acquired by the bank and in Western jurisdictions like the UK or the USA, this promise is binding. This is called Murabaha with a promise.

7. **Binding promise.** In Murabaha, when the two parties contract it is morally binding on both. However, if the bank – while relying on the promise – takes the necessary steps to acquire the property then the promise becomes legally binding.

8. **Defects in the item.** If there are any defects in the Murabaha item, the seller needs to inform the buyer or else it would be a betrayal and the buyer can demand compensation or the sale can be cancelled. Moreover, any risk of loss of the asset before delivery, or risk related to any concealed defects in the asset, are borne by the bank.

9. **Ownership of the item.** Murabaha is Shariah compliant because the bank needs to acquire the ownership and physical or constructive possession of the asset, thus assuming that all risks associated with it before reselling to the client; in contrast, the conventional bank simply lends the money to the client to acquire the asset without taking any risk related to the asset.

10. **Advance payment or deposit.** The client may be required, or want, to make an advance payment or a deposit, which is part of the price and is adjusted from the price during repayment. This is allowed by Shariah.

11. **Delivery of the item.** This is immediate, and after delivery the client bears the risk of the item as the sale has concluded.

12. **Repayment.** This can be spot or deferred, made in a lump sum or in instalments. The payment schedule and sequence of transactions should be mutually agreed upon before Murabaha is concluded.

13. **Security.** The Islamic bank may ask the client to provide some security or guarantee, or sign a promissory note to fall back on in case of non-repayment. The asset purchased via the Murabaha transaction can serve as the collateral.

14. **Delayed repayment.** If repayments are delayed, then conventional banks charge interest on interest but Islamic banks cannot increase the price or the markup. This may sometimes motivate customers to delay payments. To discourage this, Shariah scholars allow the Islamic bank to charge a penalty for delayed payment, but they cannot benefit from this money and it is donated to charity.

15. **Failure to repay.** According to Shariah rulings, if a solvent debtor deliberately delays or fails to repay, then legal action can be taken; if the debtor is insolvent, leniency in repayment is recommended.

CALCULATION OF MURABAHA PROFIT

The Arabic root word Ribh means gain or profit and is the foundation for the term Murabaha. Murabaha is an Islamic banking contract of sale, where the bank purchases an item at the request of the client and resells it to the client at a mutually agreed profit or markup. Outwardly the critics of Islamic banking find Murabaha markup to seem the same as interest, especially since the markup amount is fixed. The markup amount can be calculated in two ways. It is either a lump sum amount or it can be a percentage of the cost of the item of sale. For example, a client may purchase a car worth £100,000 and the markup may be decided as a lump sum amount of £8,000 or it could be decided as 8% of the original cost of the item, making the final sale price £108,000. In both cases the client and the bank are both aware and mutually agree to the original cost and the markup method and amount. A Murabaha contract and the markup added to the cost of the item of sale are both Shariah compliant because the Islamic bank is required to buy, own and bear all ownership risk of the item before selling it to the client. To compare: in the case of a conventional bank it sells the funds to the client at the price of interest, which is the time value of money; in the case of an Islamic bank it sells the asset to the client at a marked-up price and hence is Shariah compliant as this is not the same as selling the money. The deferred instalments of repayment of Murabaha usually include in proportion both the cost and the markup of the item of sale. The margin of profit, or net margin, is a ratio calculated by dividing net profits by sales and in case of the Murabaha it is calculated by dividing the markup amount by the sales price and it shows the degree of profit made in the contract.

In case of deliberate delay or failure to repay the due instalments by the Murabaha clients, as per Shariah rulings a penalty can be charged, to discourage clients from delaying, but the penalty cannot benefit the Islamic bank and is required to be distributed to charity. Moreover, legal proceedings and court action can also be taken against the client. In the case of insolvency of the client, the Islamic bank does not have the authority to charge the client with a penalty.

THE MURABAHA PROCESS

The steps involved in an **ordinary Murabaha** contract are as below:

1. A prospective client or buyer requests the Islamic bank to buy a specific item or asset, promising to buy it from the bank for a profit. According to Shariah scholars this is an invitation by the client to the bank to enter a contract, but not a commitment yet.
2. If the bank accepts this invitation they are required to source the item or asset as per client specifications, pay for the item and buy and own it with all ownership-related risks.
3. The bank then makes the formal offer to the prospective buyer.
4. The prospective buyers have the option to accept the offer and buy the item or asset or go back on their word. If they accept the offer a Murabaha contract is executed.

This leaves the bank with a major risk of being left with items or assets that were purchased for prospective clients who finally did not buy them. Since the bank is not a retailer of commodities, this can cause major problems. To avoid this, Shariah scholars have allowed banks to accept requests from clients tied up with a promise to buy. In contemporary Islamic banking, most Murabaha contracts are executed on this basis and the steps to be followed for a **Murabaha with a promise** contract are as below.

1. The client approaches the bank with a request to purchase a specific item or asset.
2. The Islamic bank sources the appropriate vendor for the item and identifies the total relevant cost.
3. The bank then negotiates with the client on the item, its costs and the applicable markup.
4. If the client agrees to the above conditions, it makes a request with a promise to buy.
5. The bank and the client sign a joint agreement, by which the bank agrees to buy the specified item and sell it to the client at the cost plus an agreed markup and the client promises to buy the item once the bank has acquired it. Alternately, the bank may assign the client as the agent to buy the asset on behalf of the bank, especially if the client has some experience, skill or other advantages with the vendor or in purchase of the asset. In this case, a separate agency or Wakala contract would be drawn up between the bank and the client.
6. Whether the bank buys directly from the vendor or buys via the agent, the client, a sales contract is executed between the bank and the vendor.
7. The bank or its agent, the client, then purchases the asset from the vendor, pays the original price and all other relevant costs.
8. A Murabaha contract is drawn up between the bank and the client for purchase of the asset at the original price, plus all other relevant costs, and a markup. The contract also clearly details the repayment schedule.
9. The bank delivers the asset to the client, or the client takes delivery directly from the vendor and is in physical possession of the asset, but the ownership title passes to the bank.
10. The client next accepts the Murabaha contract and the sale is executed between the bank and the client and ownership of the asset is transferred to the client.
11. The client pays the bank over the contract period either as a lump sum in the future or in instalments over the deferred period.

Three parties are involved in completing the Murabaha contract involving the purchase and sale – the bank, the vendor and the client. The Murabaha contract may include an advance deposit called the Arbun. This is an amount of money that the client pays to the bank in advance when signing the agreement but before the bank purchases the asset. Arbun is paid on request by the bank and it ensures the client's commitment and seriousness in acquiring the asset. If the client completes the Murabaha contract, the Arbun will be considered as part payment against the agreed price of the asset. If the client does not fulfil the Murabaha contract, the Arbun would be treated differently, depending on the type of Murabaha contract. If the contract was binding as in the Murabaha with a promise, and the client later refuses to purchase the asset, the bank can use the Arbun amount to cover any loss it incurred in purchasing the asset and not being able to sell it. If the Arbun is not sufficient to cover the bank's loss, it can demand the balance from the client. On the other hand, if the Murabaha contract is not binding (it is an ordinary Murabaha), the Arbun needs to be returned to the client.

PRACTICAL APPLICATIONS OF MURABAHA

Being a simple cost-plus sale with deferred repayment, Murabaha is widely used by Islamic banks. Some common uses of the Murabaha are as follows.

1. **Retail finance.** Includes home financing, vehicle financing, other personal durables financing for households, to finance their medium and long-term needs for assets like cars, homes, household furniture, equipment, etc.
2. **Working capital financing.** Businesses purchase raw materials and meet other working capital and short-term needs with Murabaha.
3. **Business medium and long-term financing.** Businesses use Murabaha to purchase land, buildings, equipment, machinery and vehicles with medium and long-term repayment schedules.
4. **Syndicated loans.** When the financing needs of the business are large, or the project is too risky for one Islamic bank, two or more Islamic banks come together for a joint Murabaha financing, called a syndicate. One of these banks, called the lead bank, is appointed to manage the Murabaha contract and liaise with the client.
5. **Trade finance.** This includes imports, exports, bills of exchange and letters of credit. The process of letter of credit (L/C) financing using the Murabaha contract involves:
   a. The importer or customer asks the Islamic bank to open a L/C to import goods and provides all necessary information.
   b. The bank checks the application and documents, secures the necessary guarantees and then opens the L/C in favour of the customer.
   c. Copies of the L/C are sent to the correspondent bank and the exporter.
   d. A Murabaha with a promise contract is signed between the Islamic bank and the importer, where both parties mutually agree on the costs of the goods and all other delivery costs and conditions.
   e. The exporter ships the goods and hands over the shipping documents to the correspondent bank.
   f. The correspondent bank sends the shipping documents to the Islamic bank.
   g. The Islamic bank's ownership of the goods is confirmed once it accepts the documents.
   h. The Islamic bank finally sells the goods to the importer on a cost plus markup basis.
   i. The importer pays the bank on a deferred basis – lump sum or instalments as per the mutually agreed schedule.

TAWARRUQ, REVERSE MURABAHA OR COMMODITY MURABAHA

Tawarruq or reverse Murabaha is a financial instrument where the client purchases a commodity from a seller, via an Islamic bank, on a deferred payment basis and then the client appoints the Islamic bank to sell the commodity to a third party on a spot payment basis. In a practical sense, the client raises immediate cash and will repay it in the future in instalments. Tawarruq is used by retail customers to raise personal finance and for businesses to raise short-term liquidity as well as working capital. Islamic banks themselves use Tawarruq to manage their short-term cash shortage or surplus. This provides an alternative to the conventional interbank liquidity market.

As in any Murabaha contract it involves a sale with deferred payment in instalments. Usually, to provide this short-term financing, a base metal is used as the underlying asset, and as such this product is also called commodity Murabaha. The price of the commodity, the markup amount or percentage, the purchase date and the repayment schedule are all mutually decided between the two parties. Once purchased via Murabaha on deferred payment, the Islamic bank sells the commodity on spot in the market and thus raises short-term funds for its own liquidity management or as an agent for its client. The commodities suitable for Tawarruq are those that are widely available, unique and not perishable. As per Shariah restrictions, commodities previously used as money (gold, silver, barley, wheat, etc.) cannot be used for Tawarruq. A disadvantage of Tawarruq is that some cost is involved for both the buy and sell part of the transaction.

From the Shariah-compliance perspective Tawarruq is a controversial product, since the client does not purchase the commodity for their use and the transaction is not linked to any real economic activity, so some scholars believe it is just raising cash and thus creates Riba. Other scholars permit it since it involves two Shariah-compliant contracts, the first being a Murabaha and the second being pure sales, and provided that clear ownership transfer of commodity happens and purchase and sales transactions are independent of each other. The AAOIFI has also permitted Tawarruq and developed a set of standards for Tawarruq. This product is used more in South-East Asian countries, rather than in GCC countries.

Tawarruq is allowed if built as a hybrid sale, where the customer buys the item (usually a commodity) from the bank on deferred instalment payments, then sells the commodity to a third party for immediate cash. Controversy exists about Tawarruq since on the surface it appears that money is currently being exchanged for money that will be paid later. Some Islamic scholars consider Tawarruq acceptable if the client requires the money for themselves and not to lend it to someone else, have no other cash financing option available, the sale has no link to Riba and the client takes possession of the item, physically or constructively, before selling it again.

CHALLENGES AND PROBLEMS ASSOCIATED WITH MURABAHA

Even though Murabaha is the simplest of the Islamic banking products being used today, and is widely used, it is not without criticism or issues. Some of the frequently discussed challenges and problems faced by Murabaha are listed below.

1. **Murabaha assets.** A Murabaha contract can only be executed for a permissible Halal asset.
2. **Appears like interest.** Outwardly, to someone not very familiar with the construction of Islamic banking products, the fixed repayment instalments may appear like interest, which can cause doubts amongst Muslim customers or be the reason for criticism from those who do not agree that Islamic banking is any different from conventional banking. In reality, the markup is determined as a lump sum amount or as a percentage of the cost of the item and added to the cost to derive the Murabaha price that is repaid, deferred in fixed instalments. Both parties are aware of and mutually agree to the cost as well as the markup.

3. **Interest-based benchmark.** One of the challenges for Islamic banks related to Murabaha is to decide the markup. Whether to use a lump sum amount or a percentage of the cost of the item. In case of a percentage, what percentage should be used? Due to the absence of an internationally accepted Islamic profit benchmark, and to stay competitive with conventional banks, most Islamic banks use the LIBOR as a benchmark to decide the markup. For example, the markup could be LIBOR +3%. This practice is not against the Shariah according to scholars, since interest is not being used, it only serves as a guideline for choosing a markup that will be competitive with the conventional banks, while all other Murabaha conditions are followed. The use of an interest-based benchmark to identify market acceptability of the Islamic banking profit does not make the Murabaha contract invalid.

4. **Uncertainty or Gharar.** LIBOR is a variable interest rate and using it to decide the Murabaha markup can introduce uncertainty or Gharar, which is prohibited in the contract according to some critics. Meanwhile other scholars opine that both parties agree on the LIBOR benchmark in advance, thus there is no uncertainty. To remove this doubt further, Islamic banks sometimes use the LIBOR to identify the markup at the onset of the contract only, add it to the cost and calculate fixed repayments over the deferred period. There is then no uncertainty, as the variability of LIBOR over the period of the Murabaha does not affect it.

5. **Risk of ordinary non-binding Murabaha.** In case of an ordinary Murabaha, once the bank acquires the asset, the client may refuse to buy it from them. The bank would then be left with an asset for which it may not be able to find another buyer soon, thus incurring other costs for holding the asset. To avoid this risk, Islamic banks mostly execute the Murabaha with a promise which is binding on the client once the asset has been acquired.

6. **Legal implications of the Murabaha with a promise.** The Islamic Fiqh Academy's opinion is that any commercial promise is binding on the promisor when the promise is one-sided as it is in Murabaha. When, due to this promise, the second party buys something and if the promisor goes back on their word, then the second party is liable to loss. In this case the Shariah courts can enforce the purchase of the asset or require the promisor to compensate the second party.

7. **Ownership risk.** When the bank acquires the Murabaha asset, any risk related to ownership is the bank's risk till the sales contract is completed and the asset is delivered to the client. The asset may have defects, or the quantity may be less, and these are all the bank's risks. The bank needs to provide acceptable quality and required quantity of the asset to the client as per the specifications in the Murabaha contract.

8. **Rescheduling of payments or rollover.** Conventional banks usually have no issues with rescheduling or rolling over loans, since they charge interest as the time value of money and with the expansion of the repayment period they earn more interest, and may even apply a new interest rate for the new period. Islamic banks cannot rollover Murabaha since it is a sale and not a loan, and the ownership has already passed to the client. If, considering the client's inability to repay on time, they allow rollover, they cannot increase the markup amount as this will be tantamount to the time value of money and prohibited in Shariah.

9. **Deliberate delay in payments.** Murabaha is a sales transaction with deferred payments, and as such Islamic banks cannot increase the sales price or markup amount

in case of delayed payments, unlike conventional banks that charge additional interest. Dishonest clients sometimes take advantage of this. To reduce or avoid this tendency, Shariah scholars allow charging of a penalty for delayed payment or default to discourage unnecessary delay in payments. As per Shariah requirements though, Islamic banks cannot benefit from this penalty and are required to give it away to charity.

10. **Collateral or guarantee.** Contemporary Shariah scholars have allowed Islamic banks to ask the client to provide some sort of security, for example a mortgage on the asset purchased by the Murabaha or any other kind of lien, to provide some protection to the bank against default or deferred payments. Security can be taken from the customer only after the sales transaction has happened in Murabaha and the client has a liability to repay, but the details of the security can be provided earlier. Moreover, third-party guarantees are also allowed in case of Murabaha under certain specific conditions, where the guarantor is required to make the deferred payments if the client fails to do so.

11. **Early payment discount.** This is allowed in conventional banking, but in case of Islamic banking a compulsory discount, if the client pays before the scheduled date, is not permissible and as such cannot be part of the Murabaha contract. The bank may voluntarily pay the client some discount for early payment.

12. **Buy-back arrangement.** These are prohibited in Shariah as such Murabaha contracts cannot be implemented for assets already owned by the client, where the client first sells to the bank and then buys back.

13. **Tax implications and ownership issues in non-Muslim jurisdictions.** The two levels of sales transactions – between vendor and bank and then between bank and client – involve two tax events, thus causing double taxation, which makes Murabaha transactions more expensive than conventional loans in Western jurisdictions. Moreover, the markup may also be viewed as a capital gain, leading to capital gains tax in non-Muslim jurisdictions that do not formally recognize Islamic banking. Another challenge in these jurisdictions is that Western banks are not allowed to act as principles in taking title to properties and this can cause major problems in Murabaha where the Shariah requires the bank to take title to the asset and then sell it to the client.

14. **Securitization of Murabaha.** Murabaha cannot be securitized as a negotiable instrument like Sukuk and traded in the secondary market, the reason being that once the Murabaha sale has been implemented the client owns the asset and also has a liability for deferred payments to the bank. This constitutes a certain amount of money, which cannot be traded as this amount is fixed and cannot be traded at a higher or lower price.

COMPARISON OF MURABAHA WITH CONVENTIONAL LOANS

A Murabaha contract is most commonly compared with regular loans from conventional banks. Table 4.1 highlights the most common differences between these.

TABLE 4.1 Differences between Murabaha and conventional loans

Factors	Murabaha	Conventional loan
Type of contract	Sales contract.	Loan contract.
Product description	The client requests the bank to acquire and sell an asset to it. The bank buys and resells the asset to the client at the cost and markup price, where both the original cost and markup are known to both parties and mutually agreed.	The client asks the bank for a loan and the bank lends the agreed amount of money, charging interest at a fixed or variable rate on the principal amount.
Repayment	Repayment is specified in a schedule and is most often deferred, either as a lump sum or as instalments.	Repayment is specified in a schedule. If interest is fixed, the schedule will be unchanged over the period. If interest is variable, the schedule will also be variable.
Relationship of the bank with the asset	A major requirement of Murabaha is for the bank to own the asset, physically or constructively, and then resell to the client. In summary, the bank sells the asset.	Conventional banks only lend the funds and have no relationship to the asset. In summary, the bank sells money.
Profit margin for the bank	The bank has a fixed margin since the cost plus the markup is decided at the onset of the contract.	The bank usually has a variable margin, since most often the interest rate is variable. Even if the rate is fixed, it is usually fixed for a limited period and then becomes variable.
Risk related to the asset for the bank	If the asset delivered by the vendor has any defect or deficiency, the bank bears the risk and cost as owner.	The bank only provides the funds; the client is the owner of the asset and bears all risk or cost of defect or deficiency in the asset delivered by the vendor.
Extension of repayment	The bank may extend the repayment dates but no additional markup or penalty can be charged.	Repayment date extension is technically an extension of the loan and will lead to an increase in interest.
Early payment discount	An early payment discount cannot be built into the Murabaha contract as per Shariah rulings and cannot be mandatory. The bank may provide some discount voluntarily.	In most loan contracts, an early payment discount is built in and early payment also leads to less interest expense.
In case of default	The bank can sue the client and demand payment.	The bank can sue and demand payment as well as additional charges.

KEY TERMS AND CONCEPTS

Binding promise

Markup or profit

Murabaha or trust sale

Murabaha process

Murabaha sale
  with a promise

Ordinary
  Murabaha

CHAPTER SUMMARY

Murabaha is one of the simplest and most widely used Islamic banking products. It is an alternative to conventional loans. In the Murabaha contract the bank purchases the asset required by its customer and then resells at a marked-up price. Important conditions related to the Murabaha contract are that it needs to meet the Shariah requirements of a valid sale, be only for Halal items and all direct and indirect costs related to the item and the lump sum or percentage of markup should be known to both parties. Other conditions are that the original seller of the item needs to be a third party, the bank may demand a promise to buy from the client, all risk of the item prior to sale to the client is the bank's, the bank may ask for an advance deposit or collateral from the client, delivery is immediate while repayment is spot or deferred, as a lump sum or in instalments.

The ordinary Murabaha process involves a client requesting the bank to acquire and resell to it any specific asset without a concrete promise to buy, leading to significant risk for the bank. In contrast, the more commonly used Murabaha sale with a promise includes a binding promise by the client to buy the asset once the bank has acquired it, thus significantly reducing bank risk. Murabaha is widely used for both retail and corporate customers as well as in trade finance and syndicated financing. Controversially, reverse Murabaha is used as personal finance or short-term financing for corporates or as a liquidity management instrument for the banks themselves.

Despite its simplicity, Murabaha faces challenges related to being applicable for Halal assets only, the markup appearing like interest, LIBOR being used as a benchmark, variability of LIBOR causing Gharar or uncertainty, ownership risk of the bank for defects in the item, delay or default in repayment and, unlike conventional finance, that Murabaha does not allow a compulsory early payment discount, buy-back arrangement, rescheduling of repayments, etc. Murabaha also faces tax issues in non-Muslim jurisdictions, since the markup is not treated with tax exemption as is interest for conventional loans.

Murabaha and conventional loans though are used as alternatives in the industry; they differ from each other in relation to the type of contract created, the relationship and risks of the bank related to the asset, early repayment, delayed payment or default and, of course, the contrast of interest versus markup.

END OF CHAPTER QUESTIONS AND ACTIVITIES

Discussion Questions

1. What are the three requirements of a Shariah-compliant sales contract?
2. Define Musawama.
3. What does a Murabaha contract mean?
4. What are the types of Murabaha contract? Describe them all.
5. Which kind of Murabaha contract is more commonly used by the banks? Why?
6. Write down any 10 conditions related to a valid Murabaha.
7. How is the Murabaha profit calculated?
8. Describe the process for ordinary Murabaha.
9. Describe the process for a Murabaha sale with promise.
10. Discuss some practical applications of the Murabaha contract in modern Islamic banking.
11. What is Tawarruq? Discuss the controversy related to this product.
12. Discuss the challenges and problems related to the Murabaha contract in modern Islamic banking.
13. Compare the Murabaha contract with a conventional bank loan.
14. Suppose that bank A buys a car for client B, and resells the car to the client. The bank and the client are both aware of the sales price to the client and mutually agree, but the cost of the car to the client is not disclosed to the client and is known only to the bank and the car dealer. Does this transaction meet the requirements of a valid Murabaha contract? Explain your answer.

Multiple Choice Questions

Circle the letter next to the most accurate answer.
1. Which one below is not a Shariah requirement for Murabaha?
   a. Existence of the asset
   b. Existence of a sales contract
   c. Sales price to be specified later
   d. Sales is on deferred payment
2. Murabaha is executed when:
   a. Money is sold for money
   b. A good or service is sold for money
   c. A commodity is sold for a commodity
   d. A commodity is sold for a service
3. Which restriction below is not applicable for Murabaha:
   a. No rollover is allowed
   b. No late penalty can be paid to the bank for its income
   c. No price renegotiation is allowed
   d. No profit can be charged on the asset sold by the bank

4. Tangible and non-tangible goods subject to Murabaha must be:
   a. Halal
   b. Real
   c. Have commercial value
   d. All of the above
5. Which statement below is most applicable for a Murabaha?
   a. Murabaha is a sale of items at a price including cost of purchase minus profit margin, mutually agreed by buyer and seller
   b. Murabaha is a sale of items at a price including cost of purchase plus profit margin, mutually agreed by buyer and seller
   c. Murabaha is rent of an asset
   d. Murabaha is a loan of funds
6. A Murabaha transaction is considered as Shariah compliant if:
   a. It deals with either tangible or intangible goods
   b. The buyer is aware of the original cost of the goods and any additional costs incurred in the process of procuring the goods
   c. The margin of profit on the goods is mutually agreed between the buyer and seller at the beginning of the contract
   d. All of the above
7. If the buyer defaults:
   a. The bank can renegotiate the price
   b. The bank can charge late payment fees
   c. The buyer pays a penalty that is donated to charity
   d. The bank can do nothing
8. Eman wants to purchase a car, priced at (Qatari rial) QAR100,000 with a Murabaha contract from Q Bank. The bank's required markup is 5%. How much will Eman pay each month if the total repayment period is 5 years?
   a. QAR2,500
   b. QAR1,750
   c. QAR1,500
   d. QAR1,250
9. A customer needs financing to purchase a machine for their factory and plans to use a Murabaha. Which structure below appears most accurate?
   a. A Murabaha is structured between the Islamic bank, the manufacturer of the machine and the customer and the manufacturer sells the machine directly to the customer while the bank pays the manufacturer directly
   b. A Murabaha is structured between the Islamic bank, the manufacturer of the machine and the customer, creating two sales contracts: one where the manufacturer sells to the bank and the second where the bank sells to the customer
   c. A Murabaha is structured between the Islamic bank, the manufacturer of the machine and the customer such that the bank lends money to the manufacturer to build the machine and then the bank sells it to the customer
   d. A Murabaha is structured between the Islamic bank, the manufacturer of the machine and the customer such that the bank lends money to the manufacturer to build the machine and then rents the machine to the customer

10. A corporation contracted with an Islamic bank using the Murabaha contract to purchase a fleet of trucks from a manufacturer. Is it allowed for the corporation to take delivery of the trucks directly from the manufacturer?
    a. Allowed, if legal title to the trucks passes to the bank prior to delivery to the corporation
    b. Allowed, if legal title to the trucks passes to the bank after delivery to the corporation
    c. Not allowed, because the bank must take both legal title and physical possession of the trucks before delivering them to the corporation
    d. Not allowed, because the bank must take physical possession of the trucks before delivering them to the corporation, while legal title can pass directly to the corporation

True/False Questions

Write T for true and F for false next to the statement.
1. Musawama and Ijara are two types of Murabaha.
2. Murabaha is usually a deferred credit sale.
3. Murabaha profit is mutually agreed between bank and client.
4. The bank acts as a middleman in Murabaha.
5. In Murabaha, the client is informed of the cost of the asset, the markup is not required to be disclosed.
6. In Murabaha, the price of goods is decided later.

Calculation Problems

1. Bintang has arranged to purchase a house costing (Indonesian rupiaya) IDR2 million on a Murabaha basis from Indonesia Islamic Bank. All other indirect costs of acquiring the property are IDR50,000. The bank agreed on a reasonable profit rate of 8%. The repayment will be made monthly over 20 years. How much will the price of the house be to Bintang? How much will Bintang have to pay each month?
2. Shamma wants to purchase a Nissan Patrol SUV, priced at (Pakistani rupee) PKR360,000 at Pak Automobiles. She wants to finance the car on a Murabaha basis from Pak Islamic Bank. The bank's required profit markup for the car finance is 3.5% per annum for a repayment period of 5 years. Compute the total cost of the car with the markup. How much will the monthly payment on this Murabaha auto-financing be?
3. Adam approaches the Islamic Bank of Arlington in the USA to finance the purchase of an industrial washer-dryer for his laundry business at USD10,000. The bank agrees to purchase the machine from the manufacturer and then sell it to Adam for USD12,000, which is to be paid by Adam in equal instalments over the next 3 years. What type of Islamic financing is being offered by the bank to Adam and how much is the monthly instalment?

CHAPTER 5

Mudaraba

Learning outcomes

Upon completion of this chapter, you should be able to:
1. Define Mudaraba and elaborate its role in the financial intermediation of Islamic banking.
2. Describe the different Mudaraba contracts available in modern Islamic finance and banking.
3. Explain the Shariah compliance and other regulatory conditions that develop the Mudaraba contract.
4. Discuss the challenges faced by Mudaraba, its practical applications today and its differences from conventional banking.

INTRODUCTION TO MUDARABA

Mudaraba is the first of the two equity-based contracts that are popular in modern Islamic finance and involve some sort of partnership. Mudaraba is a form of trust financing, while Musharaka is a joint-venture partnership (dealt with in Chapter 6). Islamic banks have successfully transformed these partnership contracts into financial instruments. In Mudaraba, one party provides the entire capital while the other provides time and effort in the business venture. The capital provider is called the Rab al Maal while the entrepreneur who manages and runs the business using their time, expertise, management and entrepreneurship skills is called the Mudarib. The Rab al Maal does not interfere in the day-to-day running of the business, but may specify some conditions related to management of the business. Rab al Maal trust their capital with the Mudarib, hence the name of 'trust financing'. Mudaraba can also be called a passive partnership, since one party is involved actively while the other is not. Rab al Maal is not involved in the actual management of the business activity and as such is called the sleeping partner, while the Mudarib is the managing partner.

The capital injected into the venture by the Rab al Maal is called Ras al Maal. Rab al Maal has the right to information and to monitor activities. They are like the limited partner in a limited liability company or an investor in a mutual fund company. The two parties mutually agree to a profit-sharing ratio at the onset of the contract which is based on the actual profit made by the business excluding the original capital invested. The monetary loss though is borne entirely by the financier, the Rab al Maal; the Mudarib would lose their time and effort in managing the business and would not be earning any profit, unless the losses were due to misconduct, negligence or violation of conditions by the Mudarib. In Mudaraba, the Rab al Maal's liability is limited to their capital contribution only. The Mudaraba contract can be terminated by either party unilaterally, after providing a reasonable period of notice, or it can be mutually terminated at any time.

USE OF MUDARABA FOR FINANCIAL INTERMEDIATION OF ISLAMIC BANKS

The major application of Mudaraba as an instrument is in the way Islamic banks perform their financial intermediation role, as discussed in Chapter 3. Mudaraba is used on both the asset and the liability side of an Islamic bank. Islamic banks, the same as conventional banks, are set up as corporations with initial capital sourced from shareholders. Financial intermediation, that is the matching of surplus units with deficit units, is the core business of banking. Islamic banks source funds from depositors on a Mudaraba basis and then supply the funds to borrowers or entrepreneurs using the Mudaraba instrument again. This system of Mudaraba is called two-tier Mudaraba, and Islamic banks use two-tier Mudaraba to replace conventional interest-based financial intermediation with the profit and loss-sharing mechanism of financial intermediation. Two-tier Mudaraba includes three parties: the depositors or investors, the borrowers or entrepreneurs and the Islamic bank which serves as the intermediary between the other two parties.

On the liability or deposit side of the Islamic bank's balance sheet, which constitutes tier one of the Mudaraba, the bank receives funds from the depositors into current, savings and investment accounts. The depositors are the Rab al Maal, the capital provider or financier and the bank is the Mudarib, the capital user. Current and savings accounts are demand deposits and can be withdrawn anytime. Current accounts are placed with the bank for safekeeping and do not earn any profit. Savings accounts are placed for safekeeping as well as a small profit. Meanwhile clients place their funds in investment accounts expecting a return. Investment accounts are based on the Mudaraba contract and can be either of restricted type (specific investment accounts) or unrestricted type (general investment accounts). The restrictions are related to how the Islamic bank can use the funds in these accounts. More details of these restrictions will be covered in the types of Mudaraba later in this chapter.

On the asset or financing side of the Islamic bank's balance sheet, which is tier two of the Mudaraba, the bank's role is reversed. The bank now acts as the Rab al Maal and provides capital to borrowers or business ventures, who are the capital users. Islamic banks have funds available from their own share capital, as well as funds in the current, savings and investment accounts to use as the funds for financing. According to central bank regulations, only a prescribed portion of the funds in current accounts can be used by the banks for financing and that too at the bank's own risk, since these funds can be withdrawn on demand and are placed with the bank based on safekeeping only. In case of restricted investment accounts, as per the client preference they mutually agree with the bank to apply the funds in these accounts only to certain types of businesses, during certain periods and at certain locations. For savings accounts and unrestricted investment accounts depositors place no such restrictions and their funds can be co-mingled with the bank's own funds, its share capital and can be applied to any venture that is Halal, Shariah compliant and deemed appropriate by the bank. Islamic banks also provide financing to certain entrepreneurs according to the restricted Mudaraba, limiting the choice to specific activities, duration and location and retaining the right to monitor the activities of the project. These restrictions though do not interfere in the operations and day-to-day management of the project, which is the responsibility of the entrepreneur.

In conventional banking all deposits, current, savings and term accounts are capital guaranteed but this is not allowed by Shariah in Islamic banking. Only current accounts held as Amanah or safekeeping are without risk for the depositors. To compensate for the lack of absolute capital guarantee, Islamic banks take other measures to reduce depositors' risk and ensure a competitive profit. Shariah scholars recommend that Islamic banks mix their own capital with depositors' funds to improve the efficiency in project selection. On the asset side of the bank's business, the Islamic bank itself is the Rab al Maal and is exposed to the loss of its entire capital when it finances borrowers or entrepreneurs. The measures taken by Islamic banks to protect their capital outlay, as well as indirectly to protect depositors' funds and ensure a reasonable profit for themselves and their depositors, include maintaining adequate capital, investing in a diversified portfolio of projects, selecting each project with a thorough study of its feasibility and profitability, asking for collateral or third-party guarantees, as and when possible within Shariah boundaries. In Mudaraba, Rab al Maal cannot demand a guarantee from the Mudarib for the repayment of the capital or for a fixed profit. The entrepreneur's liability is limited to their time and effort only, unless the loss has been caused by negligence or mismanagement of the entrepreneur, which will require the entrepreneur to compensate the financier. On the other hand, if the entrepreneur deliberately fails to make repayments to the bank, the bank can initiate legal proceedings and recover its dues from the collateral or guarantees, but it cannot ask the Mudarib to guarantee against business risk. The Rab al Maal's liability towards the project is limited just to the funds invested by them.

PROFIT CALCULATION IN MUDARABA

In contemporary Islamic banking, the bank's gross profit comes from its sales, investing and financing transactions related to the common Islamic banking products, acting as seller, lessor, partner, etc. All fee-based income is added to the profit, and all expenses – including overheads and Zakat (Islamic tax) – are deducted to arrive at the gross operating profit or loss of the bank. The Islamic banks share their gross operating profit with the savings and restricted and unrestricted investment account holders as per the pre-agreed profit-sharing ratio of each category of product and the deposit holders' proportional contribution of deposits. The bank receives the residue of the profit and distributes dividends to their shareholders or retains the profit in the business.

On the deposit side, the Islamic bank as Mudarib receives the funds from depositors against an anticipatory return, which is not guaranteed. The bank can aggregate the funds of various depositors to apply them to various financing and investment projects from which the bank earns a profit, which can also be aggregated together. In case of loss in any financing project of the bank it bears the loss as Rab al Maal, and if this leads to total loss for the bank, the depositors will also lose a proportional part of their deposits or the entire amount as they also are the Rab al Maal to the bank on the liability side of the balance sheet of the Islamic bank. The Mudarib, which is the bank on the liability side, and the entrepreneur or borrower on the asset side only lose their time and effort. The only exception to this is when the Mudarib is charged with misconduct, negligence or violation of conditions agreed in the Mudaraba contract. To be Shariah compliant, shared profit cannot be a fixed amount or a fixed percentage of the capital contribution, but needs to be a percentage of the profit earned.

PROVISIONS AND RESERVES RELATED TO MUDARABA

Since Islamic banks operate on profit and loss sharing, unlike interest-bearing conventional banks, the return to account holders is not fixed. As such, Islamic bank account holders bear higher risk. To reduce this risk and provide more stability to the return of the account holders, most modern Islamic banks include certain provisions and reserves within their operations. The international Islamic finance regulators AAOIFI and IFSB have both allowed such reserves and provisions. Moreover, in most countries the central bank or other regulatory body usually encourages the reserve fund as a mechanism that allows Islamic banks to stabilize their profit and loss and better compete in the global finance industry.

Common provisions set aside by Islamic banks are for doubtful accounts, a permanent decline in the value of investments like real estate, long-term investment, etc. and any contingent liabilities. The provisions are not fixed, but based on best judgment and management's decision on how conservative the provisions should be. The provisions need to be disclosed to all stakeholders including the auditor, the shareholders, the regulators and the investors.

Islamic banks allocate a percentage of their profit to a reserve fund before sharing it with depositors and distributing to shareholders. The purpose of this fund is aimed at smoothing the profit distributed to account holders between high-profit and low or no-profit years. Strict accounting rules need to be followed in allocating profit to the reserve funds, as this affects both the bank, its account holders and finally the shareholders. The approval of the account holders, mainly the investment account holders, who are the Rab al Maal, is required for the reserve allocation. Islamic banks and other Islamic financial institutions usually maintain two kinds of reserves.

- **Profit equalization reserve.** The allocation for this reserve from the Mudaraba profit is made before allocating any amount to the Mudarib. This reserve aims to maintain the level of return for investment account holders.
- **Investment risk reserve.** The allocation for this reserve from the Mudaraba profit is done after the share of the Mudarib has been allocated and it aims to protect investment account holders from future losses.

MUDARABA AS A LIMITED RECOURSE DEBT FINANCE

According to Kettel (2011), the Rab al Maal of the Mudaraba contract provides the entire capital and as such the Mudarib is indebted to the Rab al Maal who has first claim to the cashflows of the business till their original capital is recovered. After this the profit-sharing mechanism takes place. This debt is limited recourse, since it applies only to the cashflows of the project and not to other assets of the entrepreneur in case the cashflows are insufficient. On the downside, the claim is like a debt investment and the investor has priority till its investment is paid off. Rab al Maal has a claim to the profit of the project only, but not to the Mudarib's personal assets to recover their investment. Once this breakeven point is reached, on the upside, the investor no longer has any priority and it becomes like an equity investment rather than a limited recourse debt; the profits of the business are shared with the entrepreneur in the pre-agreed ratio. Usually the calculation and distribution of Mudaraba profit is done at regular periods. If both Rab al Maal and Mudarib agree to it, then part of the profit from the venture is used to repay the initial capital of the Rab al Maal and the remainder of the profit is shared between the two parties in the pre-agreed ratio.

TYPES OF MUDARABA

The most important classification of the Mudaraba is based on the mandate of limitations provided by the Rab al Maal to the Mudarib. According to this classification, there are two types of Mudaraba.

- **Mudaraba al Muqayyadah.** This is also called the restricted Mudaraba. In this case the capital provider, the Rab al Maal, provides certain parameters or restrictions within which they would prefer the Mudarib to invest their funds. These restrictions are usually about the type of investment, the place or location of the investment, and the time of the business venture. Besides these restrictions provided at the beginning of the contract, the Rab al Maal does not interfere in the everyday operations of the business, which is completely the responsibility of the Mudarib. In case of an Islamic bank, the restricted Mudaraba is applied for restricted or specific investment accounts where the depositors specify the projects in which they prefer their funds to be invested.
- **Mudaraba al Mutlaqah.** This is also called the unrestricted Mudaraba, where there are no restrictions imposed on the Mudarib. The Mudarib has complete authority and freedom to choose any type of project, provided it is Halal, Shariah compliant and legal. The location and time of the venture are also up to the Mudarib to choose. The unrestricted Mudaraba is applied to unrestricted or general investment accounts, where the bank co-mingles the funds of many depositors and invests according to the bank's own judgement and criteria.

Besides these main two classes of Mudaraba, from the operational viewpoint the following types of Mudaraba transactions are being used in modern Islamic banks:

- **Bilateral or simple Mudaraba.** In this case there are only two parties, one is the capital provider or Rab al Maal while the other is the entrepreneur or Mudarib.

- **Multilateral Mudaraba.** In this case there are several capital providers, whose funds are collectively provided to one Mudarib or entrepreneur.
- **Two-tier Mudaraba or re-Mudaraba.** In this case there are three parties involved in two Mudaraba contracts, as discussed in the 'financial intermediation' section above. There is Rab al Mal and Mudarib in the first Mudaraba. The Mudarib of the first contract becomes the Rab al Maal in the second Mudaraba and provides capital to a second Mudarib.

SHARIAH CONDITIONS RELATED TO MUDARABA

Mudaraba is one of the earliest and purest Islamic finance instruments that provides an alternative to interest-based finance. The Prophet served as a Mudarib, with his wife Khadija as Rab al Maal, when he conducted trading on her behalf. Some of the Shariah rules identified by the scholar Muhammad Taqi Usmani in 1999 and discussed in Kettel (2011) are given below.

- **Capital.** The total amount of capital must be known to both parties and needs to be returned to the Rab al Maal on settlement of the Mudaraba. Capital is calculated in the normal currency of the land. Capital could include tangible or intangible assets, but their value in the normal currency of the land must be calculated and stipulated in the contract. Rab al Maal gives the capital to the Mudarib on trust as investment, not as debt.
- **Profit sharing.** Shariah treats the shared profit as protection of the capital and this allows the investor to recover capital first from the profit and only then is the profit shared with the Mudarib. An exception to this is only allowed if the Rab al Maal permits it. Profit sharing is based on a pre-agreed ratio or percentage, but is never a lump sum. If the Mudaraba contract includes more than one Rab al Maal, then profits are distributed amongst them in the proportion of their capital investment, after deducting the Mudarib's portion.
- **Financial loss.** The capital provider is completely responsible for any financial loss, the capital user or entrepreneur does not own any capital and so loses none. The entrepreneur is liable to lose their time and effort and would not be getting any profit in case of loss.
- **Restrictions.** The Rab al Maal can invest their funds in a restrictive manner that can limit the Mudarib to use the funds in specific types of projects, in specific locations and within specific time periods to ensure efficient use of their funds. These restrictions should not prevent the Mudarib from executing their business activities and earning a profit. The Rab al Maal, which can either be the depositors or the Islamic bank, does not get involved or interfere in the management of the business invested in. The Mudarib is not permitted to lend or donate the Mudaraba capital or to enter into partnership with other Rab al Maal without the permission of the original Rab al Maal.
- **Security or guarantee.** The Rab al Maal cannot ask for any security or guarantee from the Mudarib against repayment of capital or for a fixed profit amount. However, a security or guarantee can be taken by the Rab al Maal from the Mudarib against losses that may occur due to negligence or mismanagement of the Mudarib.

- **Termination.** A Mudaraba contract can be terminated anytime by mutual consent or the contractual relationship can be cancelled by any one party by giving a reasonable notice period to the other party. At termination, the non-cash assets are liquidated, though most Islamic scholars recommend the method of calculating the worth by the net asset value method and agree that the Mudarib can buy the Mudaraba units from the Rab al Maal instead of liquidating the project if they prefer.

Additional Conditions Related to Mudaraba

In addition to the Shariah conditions listed above, some other conditions are imposed on Mudaraba contracts in most Islamic banks.

1. **Liability of the Rab al Maal.** This is limited to the capital invested by them only. The capital provided by the Rab al Maal can be cash or tangible or intangible assets and can be disbursed as a lump sum or in instalments.
2. **Liability of the Mudarib.** This is only limited to the labour, time and skills they applied to the Mudaraba venture.
3. **Responsibility.** The Mudarib cannot pass on their responsibility to another Mudarib without the permission of the Rab al Maal.
4. **Mixing of funds.** The Mudarib cannot mix the investment funds in a specific Mudaraba contract with their own funds or with the investment funds of one or more additional Rab al Maal without the consent of the original Rab al Maal. The only exception to this rule are the Islamic banks, who can pool the funds of several depositors who are the Rab al Maal and provide the funds to one entrepreneur or Mudarib.
5. **Pooling of profits.** Islamic banks also pool together the profit earned from various Mudaraba investments they finance as Rab al Maal and, after deducting all operational costs, they share this profit in a pre-agreed ratio with the depositors.
6. **Reserve funds.** Shariah boards and the AAOIFI allow Islamic banks to build reserve funds during years of high profit to compensate for low or no profits in some years. This income smoothing process gives more confidence to the depositors with more consistency to their profits and allows the Islamic banks to compete better with their conventional counterparts.
7. **Loss of the depositors and of the Islamic bank.** If the Islamic bank suffers a loss, then depositors will lose in proportion to the amount they deposited. The bank will lose their time and effort and will also make no profit. The exception to this is the case in which the Mudarib is found guilty of negligence or mismanagement that caused the financial loss. In this situation the Mudarib, that is the Islamic bank, is liable to compensate the depositors or Rab al Maal pro-rata to their deposits.
8. **Ordinary and capital losses.** The loss suffered by the Mudaraba venture can be either ordinary loss or capital loss. Ordinary loss is that which arises in the process of the business activity and can be offset against prior-period undistributed profits, carried forward to the next year or recovered from the previously distributed profits. Capital loss is the partial loss of the Mudaraba funds before the business venture started and requires the Rab al Maal and Mudarib to renegotiate their financing position and the profit-sharing ratio.

CHALLENGES AND PROBLEMS RELATED TO MUDARABA

Mudaraba is one of the purest forms of profit and loss-sharing Islamic finance products. In today's modern financial sector it is a high-risk method of financing. The Rab al Maal needs to put complete trust in the honesty, ability and performance of the Mudarib with their investment and in earning a reasonable profit from the venture. Islamic banks use the Mudaraba contract on both sides of their balance sheet in the two-tier Mudaraba. On the liability or supply side they collect funds from the depositors via the Mudaraba contract acting as the Mudarib and on the demand or asset side they provide funding to entrepreneurs or users of funds as the Rab al Maal. Islamic banks find the Mudaraba contract quite difficult to apply and unpopular on the demand side, since in current socio-cultural and business environments the fund provider is required to place absolute trust in the fund user, and this is often not realistic. Sufficient legal protection is also often not available for the Rab al Maal. Due to its profit and loss-sharing characteristics on both the demand and the supply side of the Islamic bank, Mudaraba finance is neither pure debt nor pure equity. Entrepreneurs or borrowers prefer to consider it as equity, while the banks prefer to consider it as debt. Mudaraba can still be used by taking measures to reduce the risk as far as possible. These measures involve financing only those borrowers who are highly reliable (like governments or corporations with transparency of financial information), by closely monitoring the business activities of the borrower and by taking collateral and guarantees against any negligence or mismanagement of the borrower.

PRACTICAL APPLICATIONS OF MUDARABA

The most common application of the Mudaraba contract is in the financial intermediation process of Islamic banks, mainly in their relationship with the investment account holders, for both general and specific investment accounts. The Mudaraba structure also works well in the financing of venture capital, project financing, formation of unit trusts as well as real estate investment trusts.

COMPARISON OF MUDARABA WITH INTEREST-BASED CONVENTIONAL BANKING

As can be seen from Figure 5.1, in the case of interest-based conventional banking depositors place their funds with the conventional banks on the basis of fixed or market-based variable interest rates for both savings accounts and term deposits, while current accounts are deposits without any interest payments. The bank then lends the funds, or the part of it allowed by regulations, to borrowers again at fixed or market-based interest rates. This interest rate paid by the borrower to the bank is not in any way linked to the profit earned by the borrower's business venture. Similarly, the interest paid by the bank to the depositors is not related to the bank's profit. Let us assume that the average interest paid by the bank to the depositors is 2%, and that

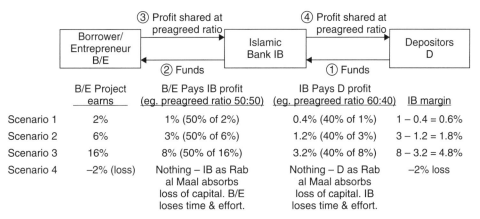

Interest-Based Financial Intermediation

	B/E Project earns	B/E Pays CB (eg. 6% fixed)	Profit/loss of BE	CB Pays D (eg. 2% fixed)	CB margin
Scenario 1	2%	6%	2 – 6 = –4%	2%	6 – 2% = 4%
Scenario 2	6%	6%	6 – 6 = 0%	2%	6 – 2% = 4%
Scenario 3	16%	6%	16 – 6 = 10%	2%	6 – 2% = 4%
Scenario 4	–2% (loss)	6%	–2 – 6 = –8%	2%	6 – 2% = 4%

Note: No link between B/E project income (Real economy) and conventional bank and depositors income.

Mudaraba-Based Financial Intermediation

	B/E Project earns	B/E Pays IB profit (eg. preagreed ratio 50:50)	IB Pays D profit (eg. preagreed ratio 60:40)	IB margin
Scenario 1	2%	1% (50% of 2%)	0.4% (40% of 1%)	1 – 0.4 = 0.6%
Scenario 2	6%	3% (50% of 6%)	1.2% (40% of 3%)	3 – 1.2 = 1.8%
Scenario 3	16%	8% (50% of 16%)	3.2% (40% of 8%)	8 – 3.2 = 4.8%
Scenario 4	–2% (loss)	Nothing – IB as Rab al Maal absorbs loss of capital. B/E loses time & effort.	Nothing – D as Rab al Maal absorbs loss of capital. IB loses time & effort.	–2% loss

Note: Clear link between B/E project income (Real economy) and Islamic bank and depositors income.

FIGURE 5.1 Comparison of Mudaraba-based financial intermediation with interest-based financial intermediation

the average interest received by the bank from the borrowers is 6%. The interest margin earned by the bank is 4% (6%–2%). The business venture may earn a profit of, for example, 2% or 6% or 16%, or may even have a loss. Irrespective of the borrower's business profit, they are required to pay the bank the fixed 6% interest. As such the loan has no connection to the real venture in which the funds were applied. The bank earns its due even when the profit of the borrower is less or none. But it does not earn more than the prescribed interest when the venture earns much more, as in the case of 16% profit.

In contrast, in the case of the Islamic bank, the depositors place their funds with the bank based on a pre-agreed profit-sharing ratio and they also share in the risk in case the bank loses money, where the depositors are the Rab al Maal and the bank is the Mudarib. Islamic banks then use the funds to finance entrepreneurs or borrowers, and this time the bank is the Rab al Maal and the entrepreneur is the Mudarib and there is a pre-agreed profit-sharing ratio as part of the contract. Let us assume this ratio is 50:50. If this business venture now earns a profit of, for example, 2% or 6% or 16%, or even has a loss, what will the entrepreneur have to pay the bank? No matter what amount of profit the business earns, it shares 50% with the bank so the bank will be paid 1% or 3% or 8%, respectively and in the situation where the business makes a loss the bank will not earn anything. So, we can see that what the bank earns is directly linked to the real economic activity and results of the business. The bank may earn less or nothing in some scenarios compared with a conventional bank, but it also has the opportunity to earn much more when the business venture is very successful. On the other hand, the bank shares its profit – after deducting all operational expenses – with the depositors as per the pre-agreed profit-sharing ratios. These ratios can be different for different types of depositors. The depositors' income varies with the variation in the bank's actual profit and is indirectly linked to the real economy too.

ACCOUNTING ISSUES RELATED TO MUDARABA

Accounting standards set by the Islamic regulatory bodies require the banks to recognize the assets and liabilities of the bank, value the assets, clearly identify income and expense, as well as profit or loss, and provide standard disclosure to the relevant stakeholders. At the end of each financial year the Islamic banks take account of the below:

1. The initial book value of capital is calculated.
2. Repayment of capital deducted from the Mudaraba financing is made.
3. Any loss of capital, happening before the Mudarib starts work and not attributed to mismanagement or negligence of the Mudarib, is deducted.
4. The Mudaraba capital may be cash or in kind, either tangible or intangible assets, is valued at fair market price and any difference with the book value is recognized as a profit or loss for the bank.
5. The loss of Mudaraba capital is borne by the Rab al Maal and may lead to the contract being terminated.
6. At liquidation or termination of the Mudaraba contract, accounts are fully settled between the Rab al Maal and the Mudarib.

KEY TERMS AND CONCEPTS

Bilateral Mudaraba	Mudaraba al Muqayyadah	Profit equalization reserve
Investment risk reserve	Mudaraba al Mutlaqah	Two-tier Mudaraba
Mudaraba	Multilateral Mudaraba	

CHAPTER SUMMARY

Mudaraba is one of the two main equity-based Islamic banking products. It is also called trust financing since one party, the Rab al Maal, pays the entire capital and trusts the other party, the Mudarib, to use the funds to generate profit. The two parties share the profit according to a pre-agreed ratio. While any financial loss is borne by the Rab al Maal, the Mudarib loses their time and effort and gets no profit. Mudaraba is the main instrument used to design Islamic financial intermediation. Depositors as Rab al Maal provide funds to the bank, as Mudarib, on the liability side. Meanwhile the bank, as Rab al Maal, provides the collected funds to borrowers or investors, as Mudarib, on the asset side. This is called the two-tier Mudaraba, where the bank as intermediary connects the surplus units with the deficit units. To compete with the conventional banks' guaranteed interest payments, Islamic banks build reserve funds to stabilize profit payments between high and low years.

When the Rab al Maal provides funds with restrictions related to type, place and time of investment it is called Mudaraba al Muqayyadah and without such restrictions it is called Mudaraba al Mutlaqah. Based on the operations, Mudaraba are also classified as bilateral, multilateral or two-tier. Specific Shariah conditions related to Mudaraba require both parties to be aware of the capital amount, which can be cash or tangible or intangible assets, but valued in local currency; profits from the Mudaraba project would first pay the Rab al Maal's capital and then be shared between the two parties as agreed, with loss according to each party's contribution of capital or effort. Shariah also allows the Rab al Maal to provide funds with general restrictions, but not interfere in the day-to-day management or require security. Termination can be mutually agreed at any time or if a unilaterally decided reasonable notice period has to be given.

Mudaraba is a pure form of Islamic finance. Islamic banks mainly use it for the liability side of their balance sheet but due to its risky nature, especially for the Rab al Maal, on the asset side it is less frequently used. In modern Islamic banking, a Mudaraba contract is applied in investment accounts, venture capital and project financing, as well as in real estate investment trusts.

END OF CHAPTER QUESTIONS AND ACTIVITIES

Discussion Questions

1. Define a Mudaraba contract.
2. How is Mudaraba used in Islamic financial intermediation?
3. Describe the characteristics of a Mudaraba agreement. Why is it called a silent partnership?
4. What are the liabilities of the Rab Al Maal and the Mudarib in case of loss? Are there any exceptions?
5. Discuss the process of profit calculation in case of a Mudaraba contract.
6. What provisions and reserve funds are related to the Mudaraba contract used by the Islamic banks? What are their importance?
7. Why is Mudaraba called a limited recourse debt finance?

8. Describe in detail a two-tier Mudaraba structure.
9. Describe the restricted Mudaraba. What is the Arabic name for it?
10. Describe the unrestricted Mudaraba? What is the Arabic name for it?
11. What is the difference between restricted and unrestricted Mudaraba?
12. What are the types of Mudaraba when classified based on the operational perspective?
13. Discuss the main Shariah conditions related to Mudaraba identified by the Shariah scholar Muhammad Taqi Usmani.
14. Discuss all the conditions related to the Mudaraba contract.
15. What challenges and problems does the Mudaraba contract face in Islamic banking?
16. What are the key applications of the Mudaraba contract in current Islamic banking?
17. Compare the Mudaraba contract with interest-based conventional banking.

Multiple Choice Questions

Circle the letter next to the most accurate answer.

1. Loss of capital prior to commencement of the Mudaraba venture is called:
   a. Operating loss
   b. Capital loss
   c. Business loss
   d. Non-operating loss
2. Mudaraba profit is arrived at after:
   a. All costs are deducted
   b. Direct costs are deducted
   c. All capital is recovered
   d. All of the above
3. Which relationship does not fit with a Mudaraba?
   a. Between investment account holders as Mudarib and the bank as Rab al Maal
   b. Between the bank as Rab al Maal and the parties to whom finance is provided
   c. Between the bank depositors as Rab al Maal and the Islamic bank as Mudarib
   d. Between credit card customers of the bank as Rab al Maal and the bank as Mudarib
4. Rab al Maal in a Mudaraba contract is the:
   a. Working partner
   b. Sleeping partner
   c. Sharia scholar
   d. Seller of assets
5. Mudarib in a Mudaraba contract is the:
   a. Sleeping partner
   b. Working partner
   c. Sharia scholar
   d. Buyer of assets
6. A Mudaraba contract is also called a:
   a. Full partnership
   b. Silent partnership
   c. Corporation
   d. Sole proprietorship

7. In Mudaraba the Rab al Maal provides:
   a. The entire capital for the project
   b. Part of the capital for the project
   c. Only time and effort for the project
   d. No capital for the project

8. In Mudaraba the Mudarib provides:
   a. Total time and effort for the project
   b. Part of the time and effort for the project
   c. Part of the capital for the project
   d. The entire capital for the project

9. Profits in the Mudaraba contract are shared:
   a. In a ratio of 50:50
   b. In a pre-agreed ratio
   c. In a ratio varying from year to year depending on the profits
   d. All profits to the capital provider

10. Financial losses in the Mudaraba contract are always:
    a. Shared in a ratio of 50:50
    b. Shared in a pre-agreed ratio
    c. Borne entirely by the Rab al Maal
    d. Borne entirely by the Mudarib

11. The liability of the Mudarib is limited to:
    a. All financial losses
    b. All time and effort contributed
    c. Part of the time and effort contributed
    d. No liability

12. In tier one of the Mudaraba for Islamic banking:
    a. The depositor is the Rab al Maal
    b. The Islamic bank is the Mudarib
    c. The Mudarib contributes expertise but no capital
    d. All of the above

13. In tier two of the Mudaraba for Islamic banking:
    a. The depositor is the Mudarib
    b. The Islamic bank is the Mudarib
    c. The borrower or investor is the Mudarib
    d. The contract has no Mudarib

14. In restricted two-tier Mudaraba:
    a. Investments can be made in areas dictated by the Islamic bank only
    b. Only Halal business can be invested in
    c. The entrepreneur or Mudarib has the right to manage the investment
    d. All of the above

15. In a Mudaraba, the Rab al Maal's risk of financial loss is for:
    a. The entire period of the contract
    b. A short period at the beginning of the contract
    c. A short period at the end of the contract
    d. A short period in the middle of the contract

True/False Questions

Write T for true and F for false next to the statement.

1. Mudaraba is a sales contract at the price of cost plus a markup.
2. Mudaraba is a partnership contract with both partners contributing capital.
3. Mudaraba is a partnership contract with one partner contributing the entire capital.
4. In restricted Mudaraba the Rab al Maal chooses the type of business to invest in.
5. In unrestricted Mudaraba the Mudarib is not allowed to choose the type of business to invest in.
6. Mudarib cannot mix their own funds with those of the Rab al Maal.
7. The Mudarib needs to guarantee the capital contributed by the Rab al Maal.
8. The Mudarib needs to guarantee a minimum profit for the Rab al Maal.
9. The Mudarib needs to compensate the Rab al Maal for any loss caused by their negligence or dishonesty.
10. In Mudaraba profit and loss is shared by the two parties in a pre-agreed ratio.

Calculation Problems

1. Kariem is the Rab Al Maal and Roaa is the Mudarib for a college snack shop in Khartoum. The table below shows various investment splits between the Rab al Maal and the Mudarib, as well as the possible Shariah-compliant profit and loss sharing. Identify the correct one. Briefly explain your answer.

	Investment contribution (Rab al Maal/Mudarib)	Profit sharing agreed (Rab al Maal/Mudarib)	Capital loss sharing agreed (Rab al Maal/Mudarib)
a.	70/30	60/40	70/30
b.	60/40	70/30	70/30
c.	100/0	60/40	100/0
d.	100/0	30/70	70/30

2. Nahla is the Rab Al Maal and Essa is the Mudarib for an office supplies shop in Kuwait City. The table below shows various investment splits between the Rab al Maal and the Mudarib, as well as the possible Shariah-compliant profit and loss sharing. Identify the correct one. Briefly explain your answer.

	Investment contribution (Rab al Maal/Mudarib)	Profit sharing agreed (Rab al Maal/Mudarib)	Capital loss sharing agreed (Rab al Maal/Mudarib)
a.	80/20	60/40	80/20
b.	60/40	70/30	70/30
c.	100/0	60/40	40/60
d.	100/0	30/70	100/0

3. Mahira is the Rab Al Maal and Anfal is the Mudarib for an accounting consultancy firm in Karachi. The table below shows various investment splits between the Rab al Maal and the Mudarib, as well as the possible Shariah-compliant profit and loss sharing. Identify the correct one. Briefly explain your answer.

	Investment contribution (Rab al Maal/Mudarib)	Profit sharing agreed (Rab al Maal/Mudarib)	Capital loss sharing agreed (Rab al Maal/Mudarib)
a.	100/0	50/50	100/0
b.	70/30	60/40	70/30
c.	60/40	70/30	70/30
d.	100/0	30/70	70/30

4. Fatma wants to start a daycare business and she has decided to get Mudaraba financing of (Omani rial) OMR500,000 from Oman Islamic Bank. The annual sales revenue expected from the business is OMR120,000 and the expected operational expenses are OMR50,000. Fatma's salary of OMR18,000 per annum is also deducted to arrive at the net profit. Each year half of the net profit is used to repay the capital of the bank. The remaining half is distributed as per the pre-agreed percentage of profit sharing between the bank and Fatma, that is 70:30. Calculate how much the bank will be paid as capital repayment and as a profit percentage and how much Fatma will get from the business as salary and profit.

5. KL Bank finances a business venture company with (Malaysian ringgit) MYR500,000 under a Mudaraba contract. The bank is the Rab al Maal and the company is the Mudarib. The total sales revenue of the company is MYR300,000 per annum. The cost of goods sold and other general expenses are MYR140,000 per annum. Capital repayment to the bank is a quarter of the profit generated. The balance of the profit is shared between the bank and the company in a ratio of 2:1. Assuming sales revenue and all costs to remain constant, how long will it take to repay the original capital to the bank? Calculate the profit amounts the bank and the company receive each year minus the capital repayment.

6. Dhaka Bank showed the following financial data at the end of the year (in Bangladeshi taka, BDT).

Dhaka Bank balances:

Current account	15,000,000
Unrestricted investment accounts	60,000,000
Dhaka Bank equity	40,000,000
Equity already invested in various fixed assets:	30,000,000
Annual profit (revenue minus expenses) from investment of the above amounts:	8,600,000

Bank policy regarding percentage of funds to be invested:

Current accounts (at bank's own risk)	40%
Unrestricted investment accounts	90%
Equity available for investments	100%

Dhaka Bank deducts 5% of the Mudaraba net revenue as profit equalization reserve and 5% of the investors' share of profit as investment risk reserve. The profit sharing as per the Mudaraba contract is 75% for investors, 25% for the bank.

Calculate the Mudaraba annual profit distributed between the investment account holders and the equity holders. Also, calculate the profit equalization reserve and the investment risk reserve allocations.

CHAPTER 6

Musharaka

Learning outcomes

Upon completion of this chapter, you should be able to:
   1. Define the Musharaka contract and describe the types of Musharaka in modern Islamic finance and banking.
   2. Explain Shariah compliance and other principles guiding Musharaka contracts.
   3. Discuss the problems related to the use of Musharaka contracts in Islamic banking.
   4. Describe the practical uses of Musharaka contracts and their differences from conventional banking and the Mudaraba contract.

INTRODUCTION TO MUSHARAKA

The term Musharaka is derived from the Arabic word Shirkah, and means partnership. Musharaka is a partnership of two or more, who put together their capital and labour based on mutual trust, share in the profit and loss of the joint venture and have similar rights and liabilities. It is the purest form of Islamic finance instrument. In Musharaka the risks and profit or loss are distributed more equitably between the investors, determined by the proportion of the investment of each partner, rather than in a conventional interest-based loan where interest is calculated based on the principal amount, the interest rate applied and the period of the loan, without any link to the risk or profit–loss scenario of the venture.

From the Shariah perspective, Musharaka is a simple partnership. But designing a banking product from it is not easy. Banks prefer to enter into a partnership for a limited period only. Yet Musharaka is considered the most viable Islamic banking product, with future growth potential. Islamic banks enter into a Musharaka contract with their clients, each contributing capital, in equal or varying quantities, and contributing their skills and expertise, also in varying quantities, to start a new joint venture or be part of an existing one. A partner may decide not to be involved in the day-to-day operations or management, thus becoming a silent partner. The profits of the venture do not have to be shared pro-rata to the capital contribution, but are shared according to a pre-agreed ratio which is decided at the initiation of the contract. Financial losses, though, are borne in proportion to the capital contribution of each partner. The return of the Musharaka venture cannot be guaranteed, like an interest-based loan, and may even lead to loss of the contributor's capital. As such, the product involves risk and since banks want to be involved for a limited period only, the product can be quite complex.

TYPES OF MUSHARAKA

Musharaka can be classified into diverse types. Based on the liability of the partners, it can be unlimited or limited. Based on the permanency of the Musharaka, it can be permanent or constant, temporary or diminishing. A special kind of Musharaka is Wujuh. As the industry is researching the potential of Musharaka as the purest form of Islamic finance, innovation continues and more varieties are expected in the future. The types currently in existence are discussed below, though all are not of equal popularity or use in the Islamic banking industry. Equity-based products like Mudaraba and Musharaka are challenging for Islamic banks to implement due to the problems of asymmetric information, where the fund user or customer has much more information about the operations and risks of the business venture than the Islamic bank and may decide not to disclose these to the provider of funds or the bank.

Mufawada or unlimited Musharaka. In this kind of Musharaka all the partners or participants rank equally in every respect – in their initial contributions of capital, in their privileges, in their rights and liabilities. The partners have equal roles in management, and equal rights in the profits and disposition of the assets of the venture. The liabilities of all the partners are unlimited, unrestricted and equal. They are all the agent and guarantor for each other. The Mufawada form of Musharaka is not very common or popular in the Islamic banking industry.

Inan or limited Musharaka. In this kind of Musharaka two or more partners contribute capital in varying amounts, which can be cash or kind, and may or may not contribute their labour, effort, skills and enterprise. Each partner is only the agent for all the others but is not a guarantor. The rights of the participants are different. In Inan Musharaka profit is shared according to a pre-agreed ratio, and the partners are at liberty to decide this ratio as they prefer; it may be different from the ratio of capital contributions. Any partner who is not involved in the management of the Musharaka business venture is not allowed a profit share that is more than their capital contribution. Inan or limited Musharaka is commonly used in the Islamic banking industry.

Constant or permanent Musharaka. In this kind of Musharaka the partners' shares in the capital remain constant or permanent throughout the contract period. The partners can sell their shares in the Musharaka capital to a third party. As in all Musharaka products, profit sharing is at a pre-agreed ratio and losses are borne in proportion to the capital contribution. Application of constant or permanent Musharaka amongst business partners is feasible and can be applied to other forms of partnership, like a law firm or a doctors' clinic, etc. Since Islamic banks want to finance projects for a limited period only, a constant form of Musharaka is not often applied.

Temporary Musharaka. This kind of Musharaka involves a single transaction or short-term financing, which concludes within one year. The Musharaka could be renewed each year if required. Common uses of temporary Musharaka are as working capital financing.

Wujuh Musharaka or partnership of goodwill. In this type of Musharaka one or more of the partners do not contribute financially but they contribute their goodwill, brand name or track record. Wujuh Musharaka is very suitable for financing franchising projects.

Musharaka Al Milk. This is a Musharaka partnership which involves ownership of common property that the partners may have acquired through a specific contract or via inheritance.

Musharaka Mutanaqisa, Musharaka Muntahiya Bittamleek or diminishing Musharaka. Diminishing Musharaka has widespread application in various financing contracts and its popularity is continuing to increase. This type of Musharaka is a joint-ownership contract at the very onset of which it is agreed that one party has the right to purchase the shares of the other partners over a prescribed contract period at a pre-agreed price. The repurchase can be at regular intervals or could be according to the financial convenience of the purchasing partner. Commonly, in Islamic banking, the borrower or entrepreneur is the party that gradually purchases the units in the Musharaka venture owned by the Islamic bank as partner. The result is that the Islamic bank's share in the Musharaka declines, finally becoming zero, while the other partner's share increases, reaching 100%, resulting in the latter owning all units of the venture and becoming the sole proprietor.

Musharaka Mutanaqisa is widely used by Islamic banks to provide long-term finance to retail customers for fixed assets like real estate, vehicles, etc. It is also used in corporate banking in the areas of project finance, trade finance and working capital finance. Profit is shared in a pre-agreed ratio and revised after each purchase instalment of the client that changes the ownership percentages. The liabilities and loss potential also change with the changes in ownership.

Diminishing Musharaka involves the parties entering into three contracts. The first contract is one of joint ownership between the client and the Islamic bank. The second contract is a lease contract between the bank and the client, where the bank agrees to lease its portion of the asset to the client. The third contract is a sales contract, which stipulates that the client would purchase the bank's share in the venture gradually and at pre-agreed intervals and price.

Figure 6.1 is an overview of a Musharaka Mutanaqisa.

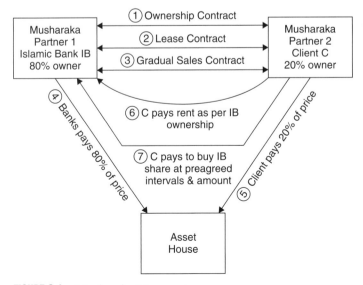

FIGURE 6.1 Musharaka Mutanaqisa

SHARIAH RULES AND GENERAL PRINCIPLES GUIDING MUSHARAKA CONTRACTS

Important principles and Shariah rulings that define the Musharaka contracts are discussed below, a large part of which has been derived from the work of Sheikh Muhammad Taqi Usmani (Usmani, 1999) and discussed in Kettel (2011):

1. **Musharaka venture and partners.** As in the case of all Islamic finance contracts, partners in Musharaka ventures are required to be competent to enter a contract. Moreover, the project or business to be financed by Musharaka should be Halal and Shariah compliant.

2. **Capital.** The capital of the Musharaka venture needs to be specifically defined, should be in existence and immediately available. The partners may or may not contribute capital in equal proportions. Capital can be in the form of money and/or tangible assets like goods, machinery or real estate. Some scholars allow intangible assets like brand name, patents, etc. to be considered as capital. The value of any such tangible or intangible asset needs to be clearly defined and agreed upon.

3. **Management and labour.** All partners can work in the Musharaka venture and it is not permissible to forbid any partner from being involved in the management or operations of the business. On the other hand, if all partners agree then any one partner may manage the business alone.

4. **Guarantee.** Each partner serves as a trustee of the funds of all other partners but provides a guarantee for the funds only against negligence or mismanagement. The Musharaka venture may take a security or mortgage or guarantee against negligence and mismanagement, but Shariah does not allow a security to be taken to guarantee the capital or a certain amount of profit.

5. **Profit and loss.** At the onset of the Musharaka contract the profit-sharing ratio is agreed upon. Usually it is in proportion to the capital contribution, but according to some scholars it may be different from the capital contribution if all partners agree. Any one partner may singly manage the business, or may be more involved in the operations and management of the venture or may have greater relevant expertise for the business, thus justifying earning a ratio of profit greater than their capital contribution. On the other hand, a partner who does not participate in management cannot demand a profit ratio higher than their capital contribution. The return of the Musharaka partners is based on the actual profit earned by the Musharaka joint venture and Shariah insists that it is a ratio or percentage of the actual profit earned and not a lump sum. In the case of loss in the Musharaka venture, each partner bears losses proportional to their capital contribution in the joint venture.

6. **Changes in partnership.** Generally, partnership is a permissible and non-binding contract. As such, any partner may decide to leave the partnership if they so wish, but this needs to happen with the knowledge of the other partner or partners so that the partnership and the interest of the other partners is not harmed. Some scholars' opinion is that the Musharaka joint-venture contract is binding till the project agreed upon at the start of the contract is completed or if the venture is liquidated with the agreement of all partners. If any partner wishes to exchange or sell their share in the partnership to a partner within the Musharaka or to a new partner, the

value of the share should not be based on the original capital contribution but be based on the fair value of the share at the time of sale. Moreover, any new partner can be introduced with the agreement of all other partners.

7. **Termination.** The Musharaka contract comes to an end either after completion of the prescribed project or if liquidation is executed, and this happens either if the project is declared bankrupt or if all partners wish to end the venture. At the termination of the Musharaka venture, a final profit and loss account is prepared and any amount held in the special reserve account is added to it. After paying off all creditors, the remaining balance is distributed amongst the partners pro-rata to their original capital contribution.

PROBLEMS RELATED TO MUSHARAKA

As discussed earlier, Musharaka is one of the purest forms of Islamic finance products but not easy to implement in Islamic banks. As such, in the initial years of Islamic banking Musharaka was rarely used by the banks. Though Musharaka is a simple partnership, with two or more parties contributing capital to a joint venture, developing it into a banking product is not easy since banks prefer to be involved in any kind of ownership, as in the case of a Musharaka, for only a temporary period. Moreover, the client partner has more information on the business than the bank, leading to asymmetric information and high moral hazard. Finally, the ownership role of the bank leads to the risk of bearing losses.

Other specific problems related to the product as discussed in Kettel (2011) are as follows.

Confidence of depositors. There is a risk that the managing partner in the Musharaka venture, in the event of loss of the venture, would pass the loss to the financing bank which usually has contributed the largest share of the capital. Any loss suffered by the Islamic bank would then pass on to its depositors. As such, depositors would be apprehensive about placing their funds with a bank that is involved in equity participation in products like Musharaka.

To avoid or reduce this problem, Islamic banks apply stringent due diligence by evaluating the business feasibility as well as the skills and character of the client in all Musharaka ventures they finance. Moreover, the Islamic banks do not finance just the one Musharaka but participate in a diversified portfolio of them, and it is unlikely that all or most of them will suffer a loss. Much more likely is that only a few of the Musharaka projects will suffer a loss. On the other hand, if the successful ventures make high profits as equity participants then the Islamic banks can benefit from this, unlike a conventional bank that only earns fixed interest no matter how much profit is made by the project it financed. As such, a well-chosen Musharaka project portfolio could yield higher returns than fixed interest.

Dishonesty of client. Another risk to the Islamic bank is that the managing partner of the Musharaka venture may not be honest in sharing business information and may 'cook the books' and falsely claim that the business has suffered a loss to deprive the Islamic bank of its profit, or may even claim such high losses that the original capital of the bank could be at risk.

To avoid or reduce this risk, Islamic banks need to efficiently monitor and audit all Musharaka ventures they contribute capital to, to prevent any misinformation or hiding of relevant information by clients. Moreover, the original Musharaka contracts should have measures built in that provide clear penalties and guarantees or security against any losses arising from negligence, misconduct or dishonesty of the client. Another protective measure Islamic banks can take is to provide Musharaka financing only to selective clients, especially those with whom the bank has a long-term relationship and whose integrity is beyond doubt. Finally, the Islamic bank may participate in Musharaka ventures in specific sectors only, which are easier to monitor and audit and which provide the client with less room for dishonesty. Export financing can be one such sector; since the exporter gets a specific order from abroad, specifying the final prices, costs are easy to determine, payments are secured by a letter of credit and made through the involved bank itself.

Secrecy of the business. Another risk related to Musharaka is from the perspective of the client. When the Islamic bank becomes a partner with the client in a joint venture, some business secrets of the client may have to be disclosed to the bank and sometimes from the bank to the investors whose funds the bank is applying. Such confidential business information may then reach the competitors and adversely affect the joint venture. To avoid this the client may introduce conditions to provide only necessary business secrets to the bank. Such information should be dealt with in the utmost confidence and not shared unnecessarily with investors or anyone else without the client's permission. Moreover, the bank should not interfere in the management of the venture and only a limited number of bank staff would be involved with the project, signing a confidentiality clause.

PRACTICAL USES OF MUSHARAKA

Despite the challenges and risks involved for an Islamic bank when it participates in the equity of its clients' ventures in Musharaka financing, this product is true to the principles of Islamic finance. In the early years of the development of modern Islamic banking very few Islamic banks applied Musharaka financing in their activities. In recent years, the Islamic banks globally are innovating in the area of Musharaka financing and using the product for various retail and business financing needs. Some of the common uses of Musharaka financing today are discussed below.

Working capital finance. The process of providing working capital finance by Islamic banks to their business customers using the Musharaka contract is similar to the working capital financing of conventional banks. Both types of bank deposit the agreed working capital funds into the client's account with the bank. The client uses the funds as and when needed. Conventional banks charge the amount with a predetermined interest rate, while Islamic banks charge the amount with a predetermined profit rate, based on the profit the client is expected to make and the pre-agreed profit ratio for the Musharaka financing, and this profit rate is subject to change (usually quarterly).

At the completion of the financial year, the actual profits earned by the client are calculated and the bank's share as per the pre-agreed ratio is calculated. If the amount already collected by the Islamic bank is less than the amount due to it, the client pays the difference into a special reserve account of the bank. On the other hand, if the amount taken by the Islamic bank is more, then the bank refunds the requisite amount into the client's account. If the client's business incurs a loss, the special reserve account is reduced by the amount of the loss. In case the reserve account amount is not sufficient to compensate for the loss, the bank would return part or all of the profit it had already collected during the year.

Domestic trade. Islamic banks finance domestic trade activities using the Musharaka contract. The bank enters into the Musharaka partnership agreement with the client for the purchase and sale of local goods whose specifications are provided by the client. The total cost of the goods purchased for domestic trade is divided between the client and the bank to contribute as capital. A special Musharaka account is opened at the bank into which the funds are deposited. After the goods are sold, each party receives their share of the profit as per a pre-agreed ratio; and if there is any loss, each partner bears the loss in proportion to their capital contribution.

Import finance. Islamic banks also finance imports using the Musharaka contract. Once the total cost of an import agreement is calculated, the bank provides part of the capital required to finance the import agreement. The cost of the import transaction is designated in the appropriate foreign currency.

The bank also opens a special Musharaka account and opens a letter of credit in favour of the importer or client. It is the responsibility of the Islamic bank to pay the exporter in full after receiving the shipment documents. The client or importer is responsible for arranging the import and the clearance and sale of goods. Once all operational costs (including shipment, insurance, etc.) are deducted from the sales revenue, the remaining profit is shared between the importer and the Islamic bank in the pre-agreed proportion. If any loss was incurred in the import contract, the loss would be shared between the importer and the bank according to the capital contributed by them.

Letters of credit. Musharaka is also used by Islamic banks to provide letter of credit facilities for trade finance. The process involves the customer informing the bank of their need for an L/C. Next, the terms of the Musharaka are negotiated. The customer's share of the capital contribution (which is part of the cost of goods to be imported) is deposited with the bank, based on the Wadia principle – that is, as keeper and trustee of the funds. The Islamic bank adds its own contribution of capital to the funds, issues the L/C and pays the proceeds to the negotiating bank and then provides the customer with the relevant documents. The customer uses the documents to release the goods and sells or disposes of them according to the Musharaka agreement. The profit earned from the transaction is divided between the bank and the customer as per a pre-agreed ratio. If any loss is incurred it would be borne by the partners pro-rata to their capital contribution.

Credit facilities. Islamic banks provide contingency financing for corporate customers as well as small and medium enterprises, for a variety of purposes and for different maturities using the Musharaka joint-venture contract. The client can use the Musharaka credit facility for working capital, or to purchase goods or equipment or other fixed assets. Each customer is assigned a certain credit line as a single or multiple Musharaka contract for various purposes and to be used once. Musharaka can also be designed as revolving credit, where it is used more than once during the period of the facility and could be renewed in the future.

Agriculture finance. Musharaka financing is progressively being used in agriculture financing around the world by Islamic banks. Under this scheme, the bank and the farmer become partners in a Musharaka joint venture. The bank contributes agricultural fixed assets to the venture (such as sprayers, ploughs, tractors, irrigation pumps, etc.) and may also contribute working capital in the form of seeds, pesticides, fertilizers, fuel, etc. The farmer's contribution to the venture would usually be land, actual labour, skills and management. The profits of the agricultural project are shared between the farmer and the bank according to the ratio agreed between them at the onset of the contract, while any loss would be shared proportional to the value of the capital contributed.

Diminishing Musharaka. Diminishing Musharaka is a special application of the Musharaka contract. In this type of Musharaka the bank or financier and the client contribute capital for the joint ownership of a property, which could be retail or commercial real estate, or could be equipment or a commercial enterprise. At the beginning of the contract the contribution of the bank is divided into equal units, and it is agreed that the client would purchase the units of the bank periodically. The number of units to be purchased at each period and the interval between any two periods are commonly the same, but the client and the bank could negotiate for intervals as well as units purchased to vary to match the ability and convenience of the client. Resultant to this process, at each interval the percentage ownership of the bank will decrease and that of the client will increase until finally the client purchases all units owned by the bank and becomes the sole owner of the property, equipment or enterprise. Diminishing Musharaka and its application to various financial needs of both retail and business clients of the bank is growing significantly.

Examples of the Use of Diminishing Musharaka

Purchase of a House Let us assume that a customer of the Islamic bank is interested in purchasing a house, but does not have adequate funds and needs bank financing. The bank and the customer mutually decide to apply a diminishing Musharaka contract. In this case the bank will participate with the customer in purchasing the chosen house. Let us further assume that the client contributes 20% and the bank puts in 80% of the price of the house; this leads to the client owning 20% and the bank owning 80% of the house. The property is jointly owned but the client intends to live in the house. In this case the client is required to pay rent to the bank commensurate to the bank's share in the ownership. The next step for both parties would be to determine the fair rental value for the property. One way to determine the rental value is for both the client and the bank to survey the market to obtain estimates for comparable properties in the same neighbourhood and negotiate an agreement. For this example, and for simplicity, we assume that the fair rental value will remain constant over the life of the contract. In the real world, the rental may be adjusted periodically.

The bank and the client also decided at the onset of the diminishing Musharaka that the share of the bank would be divided into eight equal units of 10% ownership of the house. The agreement is that the client would purchase one unit annually, and

TABLE 6.1 Payment schedule for the house purchase example

Year	Rent payment to bank by client (£)	Client pays 10% purchase price of the house to bank (£)	Total payment to bank (£)	Ownership of bank	Ownership of client
Start of contract	none	none	none	80%	20%
End of year 1	80,000	100,000	180,000	70%	30%
End of year 2	70,000	100,000	170,000	60%	40%
End of year 3	60,000	100,000	160,000	50%	50%
End of year 4	50,000	100,000	150,000	40%	60%
End of year 5	40,000	100,000	140,000	30%	70%
End of year 6	30,000	100,000	130,000	20%	80%
End of year 7	20,000	100,000	120,000	10%	90%
End of year 8	10,000	100,000	110,000	0%	100%

each year the ownership of the bank would reduce by 10% while that of the client would increase by 10%. The rent payable to the bank would also be reduced in accordance with the reduction in ownership. This process continues for eight years, by which time the client has purchased the 80% ownership share of the bank and becomes the sole owner of the house, while the bank's ownership reduces to zero. This method allows the client to receive financing for the property purchase, and use it as their residence, while paying rent to the bank as per the bank's share in the property and, over a period of eight years, repay the financing by purchasing the bank's share in annual instalments. The table above shows the calculations and changes in the ownership and payments from the onset to the conclusion of the diminishing Musharaka for the house purchase, when it is assumed that the purchase price of the house was £1 million and the annual rent for the property is £100,000. So, the bank pays £800,000 and client pays £200,000 to purchase the property. Each year the client pays £100,000 to the bank to purchase a further 10% of the property. The client also pays the bank rent for the bank's share in the property.

Table 6.1 shows the payment schedule for this example.

Service Sector Example   Let us discuss a service sector example to further elaborate the use of diminishing Musharaka. Let us assume Adam wants to purchase a taxi to provide transport services and to earn an income from the fares. The cost of the taxi is £200,000. Adam does not have sufficient funds to buy the taxi by himself. His savings are only £100,000. He needs financing from a partner or a bank for the balance of £100,000. Adam approaches his friend Baseer to be his partner. Baseer agrees to provide 50% value of the taxi (£100,000) for a period of 5 years. During this period Adam will share the profit of the taxi, according to Baseer's ownership percentage in the taxi. Moreover, every 6 months Adam will pay for 5% of the ownership share of Baseer, thus purchasing the entire 50% over a period of 5 years. The taxi profit due to Baseer during this period will be as per his ownership percentage. The approximate monthly profit made by the taxi is expected to be £2,000. The table below shows the calculations and changes in the ownership and payments from the onset to the conclusion of the diminishing Musharaka for the taxi purchase. The purchase price of the taxi was £200,000, of which Adam and Baseer contributed £100,000 each. The taxi makes £2,000 profit per month and £12,000 in 6 months. Part of this profit Adam will pay to Baseer every 6 months, commensurate to his ownership percentage. Adam has agreed to purchase 5% value of the taxi from Baseer every 6 months, and will make payment of £10,000 towards that (£200,000 × 5%).

Table 6.2 shows the payment schedule for this example.

The above simplified examples do not consider the fees and payments charged by the Islamic banks, such as insurance, project evaluation and monitoring fees.

The examples also show repayments annually or biannually to keep the tables manageable, while most repayments would be monthly and would have a longer duration.

In case of non-payment of rent by the client, the bank would assess the reason for the non-payment and, if it was valid, some leniency would be shown to ensure the client is not overburdened and may be given extra time to make the payment. If there was no genuine reason for the delayed payment, the Islamic bank may demand a penalty that will be donated to charity.

Similarly, diminishing Musharaka can be applied for various retail and business financing needs, like in small or medium business set-ups or for operational expenses, for agriculture, for domestic or international trade, or for retail purchase of fixed assets, etc.

TABLE 6.2 Payment schedule for the service sector example

Year/month	Taxi profit payment to Baseer by Adam (£)	Adam pays 5% purchase price of taxi to Baseer (£)	Total payment to Baseer (£)	Ownership of Baseer	Ownership of Adam
Start of contract	none	none	none	50%	50%
Year 1, month 6	6,000	10,000	16,000	45%	55%
Year 1, month 12	5,400	10,000	15,400	40%	60%
Year 2, month 6	4,800	10,000	14,800	35%	65%
Year 2, month 12	4,200	10,000	14,200	30%	70%
Year 3, month 6	3,600	10,000	13,600	25%	75%
Year 3, month 12	3,000	10,000	13,000	20%	80%
Year 4, month 6	2,400	10,000	12,400	15%	85%
Year 4, month 12	1,800	10,000	11,800	10%	90%
Year 5, month 6	1,200	10,000	11,200	5%	95%
Year 5, month 12	600	10,000	10,600	0%	100%

Securitization of Musharaka

Musharaka can easily be securitized into Sukuk certificates that are sold in the primary Sukuk market, especially when the project size is large and the amounts involved are huge. Musharaka Sukuks are a useful way of raising funds from the public in small amounts. Each subscriber to the Musharaka is given a Sukuk certificate that represents their proportional investment and ownership in the Musharaka assets. Once the Musharaka project has been initiated, the certificates represent ownership of real assets and are treated as negotiable instruments which can be bought and sold in the secondary market. Trading of the Sukuk certificates is not allowed while the Musharaka assets are still in liquid form, like cash or receivables or advances due from others. Contrary to a bond, which is a debt from the bondholder to the bond issuer, a Musharaka certificate or Sukuk gives the holder proportional ownership in the project's assets. Moreover, the issued bond certificate and its holder have no link to the actual business undertaken with the borrowed money. The bond interest and its principal repayment are liabilities for the issuer irrespective of the profit and loss scenario of the venture, while the Sukuk income is directly related to the profit and loss of the venture. Sukuks will be discussed in more detail in Chapter 11.

COMPARISON OF MUSHARAKA WITH INTEREST-BASED FINANCING

The difference between Musharaka and an interest-based loan lies, to a significant extent, in the manner in which the two products are designed and operated and the products' relationship with the depositors and borrowers. The differences between the two instruments are highlighted in Table 6.3.

TABLE 6.3 Comparison of Musharaka financing with interest-based financing

Features	Musharaka	Interest-based financing
Type of contract	Equity participation contract.	Debt financing contract.
Profit sharing/fixed interest payment	The profit of the venture is shared at a pre-agreed ratio between the borrower and the bank. The borrower pays no fixed interest.	No sharing of profit with the bank. The borrower pays fixed interest irrespective of the profit or loss of the venture.
Loss of the venture	Any loss in the Musharaka venture is borne by both the bank and the client borrower in proportion to their respective capital contribution, unless the loss is due to negligence or mismanagement by the client. In that case, the client is liable to compensate the bank.	The bank provides the loan on fixed interest and has no link to any loss incurred by the venture, which is still liable to pay the interest and principle of the loan.

(Continued)

TABLE 6.3 *(Continued)*

Features	Musharaka	Interest-based financing
Yield of the venture	Cannot be guaranteed, depends on the profit and loss situation of the venture.	Is guaranteed as it is fixed interest and will be collected irrespective of the profit and loss situation, unless the venture goes bankrupt.
Security and guarantee	The profit amount or return of the capital contribution cannot be secured by collateral or guarantee. The only purpose of any collateral or guarantee, if taken, is to compensate the bank in case of any negligence or mismanagement by the client leading to lack of profit or actual loss or inability to return the bank's original capital.	The loan principle and its interest are not contingent on the profit or loss of the venture but most commonly secured by collateral or guarantee. Thus, the final negative impact of any loss falls on the borrower only.

COMPARISON OF MUSHARAKA WITH MUDARABA FINANCING

Table 6.4 highlights the differences between Musharaka and Mudaraba financing.

TABLE 6.4 Comparison of Musharaka and Mudaraba financing

Features	Musharaka	Mudaraba
Source of financing	All partners contribute capital to the venture as its source of financing.	Financing is provided solely by the Rab al Maal.
Partners' right to participate in the management of the business	All partners have the right to participate in the management of the venture, though they may choose not to, or all partners together may assign the management to a single partner.	The Rab al Maal has no right to be involved in the management, which is the responsibility of the Mudarib only. The Rab al Maal has the right to apply conditions on the Mudaraba venture and demand information to safeguard their investment.
Period of the venture	As an equity participation product, it is more suitable for ongoing businesses and for the long term.	Since the entire funding comes from Rab al Maal without any management role, it is more suitable for short-term and/or projects with a specific purpose (like constructing a building or manufacturing a machine).

TABLE 6.4 (*Continued*)

Features	Musharaka	Mudaraba
Sharing profits and losses	All partners earn profit in ratios agreed at the onset of the contract and this may not be exactly as the ratio of capital contribution, while losses are shared in accordance with the capital contribution.	Profits are shared as per a pre agreed ratio, while monetary loss is borne only by the Rab al-Maal; the Mudarib loses time and effort and cannot claim any profit.
Liability of the partners	Usually unlimited, borne by all partners pro-rata.	The Rab al-Maal's liability is limited to their investment amount only.
Capital/ownership of assets	All assets of the venture are jointly owned by all partners. In case of disposition of the assets, any increase in value is jointly shared by them pro-rata to their original capital contribution.	All assets are owned only by the Rab al-Maal, who contributed capital solely. In case of sale of the assets with profit, the Mudarib can share in the profit in the pre-agreed ratio but cannot claim the assets.

KEY TERMS AND CONCEPTS

Constant or permanent Musharaka	Musharaka Al Milk	Temporary Musharaka
Inan	Musharaka Mutanaqisa, Musharaka Muntahiya Bittamleek or diminishing Musharaka	Wujuh
Mufawada		
Musharaka		

CHAPTER SUMMARY

Musharaka is a partnership of two or more parties based on mutual trust and is one of the equity-based products in Islamic finance. From the Shariah perspective it is one of the purest Islamic finance products. In modern Islamic banking various Musharaka contracts – Mufawada, Inan, constant and temporary – are used. Wujuh, Musharaka al Milk and diminishing Musharaka are other special types of Musharaka contracts.

Special Shariah compliance and general rules related to Musharaka involve the types of ventures and partners permissible, the contribution of capital and management of labour, the sharing of profit and loss, the guarantees of the partners, changes in the partnership and termination of the contract. Musharaka contracts are highly recommended by the Shariah but suffer from asymmetric information and moral hazard, as well as issues of depositor confidence due to risks, dishonesty of the client and lack of control over business secrets.

The major uses of Musharaka contracts by Islamic banks are in the areas of working capital, domestic trade, import finance, credit facilities for small and medium enterprises, agricultural finance and other financing of assets for both retail and corporate customers, especially using diminishing Musharaka. Musharaka contracts can raise finance through the mechanism of securitization.

Musharaka contracts differ from interest-based financing in the areas of profit versus interest payments, loss sharing, yield of the venture and the roles of security and guarantee. Mudaraba and Musharaka contracts differ in the sources of financing, partners' role in management, the preferred period of the venture, sharing of profit and loss, liabilities and ownership of assets by the partners.

END OF CHAPTER QUESTIONS AND ACTIVITIES

Discussion Questions

1. What is a Musharaka? Why is it called a full partnership?
2. What are the types of Musharaka available with the Islamic banks in these times?
3. Describe the Mufawada and the Inan form of Musharaka.
4. Explain the constant and temporary forms of Musharaka.
5. What are the uses of the Wujuh and the Musharaka Al Milk?
6. Explain what you understand by the diminishing Musharaka. What are the other terms that describe this product?
7. Discuss the important Shariah and general principles that guide the Musharaka contract.
8. What are the problems faced by the Islamic banks and/or their clients in using Musharaka contracts?
9. Briefly discuss any one problem related to the Musharaka contract and how it can be minimized.
10. Discuss the practical uses of Musharaka in modern Islamic banks.
11. Compare Musharaka with interest-based financing.
12. Compare the Musharaka contract with the Mudaraba contract.

Multiple Choice Questions

Circle the letter next to the most accurate answer.
1. Musharaka is also called:
    a. Silent partnership
    b. Full partnership
    c. Sole proprietorship
    d. Guarantee
2. Profits in a Musharaka are shared:
    a. Always in proportion to the capital contribution
    b. In a pre-agreed ratio
    c. In a 50:50 ratio
    d. Decided annually

3. In a Musharaka, the Islamic bank has a:
   a. Certain rate of return throughout the entire period
   b. Uncertain rate of return throughout the entire period
   c. Certain rate of return for a limited period
   d. Uncertain rate of return for a limited period
4. In a Musharaka, investors' capital is:
   a. Exposed to total loss
   b. Exposed to partial loss
   c. Exposed to no loss
   d. Exposed to loss at the beginning only
5. Which of the following is the most appropriate definition of Musharaka?
   a. Musharaka is a deferred payment sales contract of an item
   b. Musharaka is an advance payment sales contract of an item
   c. Musharaka is a partnership between two or more parties, all contribute capital but only one party can manage the venture
   d. Musharaka is a partnership between two or more parties, all contribute capital and can manage the venture
6. Inan Musharaka is a partnership with:
   a. One partner providing the entire capital
   b. Unlimited liability
   c. Limited liability
   d. Equal capital contribution
7. The Musharaka capital contribution determines:
   a. Profit-sharing ratio based on agreement
   b. Loss-sharing ratio based on outstanding capital
   c. Profit and loss-sharing ratio based on agreement
   d. None of the above
8. Diminishing Musharaka reduces:
   a. Capital loss exposure of entrepreneur
   b. Capital loss exposure of financier
   c. Profit rate of entrepreneur
   d. Profit rate of financier
9. Which of the following is a difference between Musharaka and Mudaraba?
   a. Profit-sharing ratio only
   b. Management role of entrepreneur
   c. Management role of capital provider
   d. Loss-sharing ratio only

True/False Questions

Write T for true and F for false next to the statement.
1. Musharaka is Sharia compliant because the bank and its customer both bear losses in proportion to their contribution to the capital.
2. Risks and losses in Musharaka are always shared in proportion to capital invested.
3. In diminishing Musharaka the share of one partner reduces periodically as repayments are made by the other partner.

4. In diminishing Musharaka the bank's share usually increases after each repayment is made.
5. Rab al Maal only bears the loss of capital in Mudaraba, while all capital providers bear the loss in proportion to their investment in Musharaka.
6. Profit is shared according to a pre-agreed ratio in Mudaraba, while in Musharaka it is in proportion to the capital invested.

Calculation Problems

1. Given the investment ratio of two partners in a Musharaka, identify the correct profit and loss sharing. Briefly explain your answer.

	Investment contribution	Profit sharing agreed	Loss sharing agreed
a.	40/60	50/50	50/50
b.	60/40	70/30	75/25
c.	75/25	50/50	75/25
d.	100/0	60/40	100/0

2. Given the investment ratio of two partners in a Musharaka, identify the correct profit and loss sharing. Briefly explain your answer.

	Investment contribution	Profit sharing agreed	Loss sharing agreed
a.	40/60	50/50	50/50
b.	60/40	70/30	60/40
c.	75/25	50/50	25/75
d.	100/0	60/40	100/0

3. Latifa purchased an apartment using the diminishing Musharaka method of financing from Egypt Islamic Bank. The value of the apartment is (Egyptian pound) EGP500,000. Egypt Islamic Bank requires 20% deposit. The repayment period is 10 years. The market rental value for the apartment is estimated at EGP30,000 per year. Repayment is annual.
   ▪ How much will Latifa have to deposit for the purchase of the apartment?
   ▪ How much will Egypt Islamic Bank finance?
   ▪ Complete the table below for the diminishing Musharaka. Year 1 is completed.

Year	Rent payment to bank	Annual repayment of purchase price to bank	Total payment to bank	Bank ownership (%)	Latifa ownership (%)
Start of contract	none	none	none	80	20
1	24000	40000	64000	72	28
2					
3					
4					
5					
6					

Year	Rent payment to bank	Annual repayment of purchase price to bank	Total payment to bank	Bank ownership (%)	Latifa ownership (%)
7					
8					
9					
10					

4. Ramizah purchased a pizza shop using diminishing Musharaka financing from Brunei Islamic Bank. The shop cost (Brunei dollar) BND400,000. The bank paid BND300,000 and Ramizah used BND100,000 of her own money. The shop is expected to earn BND2,000 each month. Ramizah will buy the bank's share by paying annually over a period of 6 years. Calculate and build a table as in the diminishing Musharaka examples (Tables 6.1 and 6.2).

5. Hayat purchased a vegetable farm with diminishing Musharaka financing from Jeddah Bank. The farm cost (Saudi rial) SAR500,000. The bank paid SAR400,000 and Hayat used SAR100,000 of her own savings. The farm will earn SAR1,000 each month. Hayat will buy the bank's share by paying annually over a period of 4 years. Calculate and build a table as in the diminishing Musharaka examples (Tables 6.1 and 6.2).

6. Adilah wishes to start a ready-made garments business but lacks the required funds. Bariah agrees to participate with her for a specified period of 4 years. Adilah contributes 40% of the investment and Bariah contributes 60%. Both start the business based on diminishing Musharaka. The proportion of the profit allocated for each of them is expressly agreed upon and is 50% each till the end of the Musharaka period of 4 years, since Adilah will also manage the business. Bariah's share in the business is divided into 8 equal units and Adilah purchases these units every 6 months from Bariah till all units are owned by Adilah. So, each 6 months Bariah earns part of the profits and the purchase price of 1 unit of ownership. (Moroccan dollar) MAD1 million was invested in the garments business. The business earns MAD10,000 each month. Prepare the payment schedule of the diminishing Musharaka.

7. Assume that a potential buyer is interested in purchasing a home worth (US dollars) USD150,000. The buyer approaches an Islamic financial institution for the purchase of the property and puts down 20% of the price (USD30,000). The financial institution provides the other 80% of the price (USD120,000). This agreement results in 20% of the home belonging to the client and the remaining 80% to the financial institution. The next step is to determine the fair rental value for the property based on the estimates of other properties in the same neighbourhood. A fair rental value of USD1,000 per month is determined. As such, the client pays USD800 as rent for the 80% share of the financial institution at the start of the contract. The two parties then agree on a period of financing of 15 years, that is 180 months (12 × 15 = 180). Based on the rental value and the financing period, the financial institution then determines the fixed monthly payments the client would have to make to own the house by paying the required rental amount each month and an equal monthly amount to repurchase the bank's share. Prepare an excel spreadsheet of the monthly payments as in Tables 6.1 and 6.2.

CHAPTER 7

Ijara

Learning outcomes

Upon completion of this chapter, you should be able to:
1. Define Ijara in comparison with a conventional lease.
2. Describe the types of Ijara offered by modern Islamic banks.
3. Explain the Shariah rules and general principles that guide Ijara contracts and the documents related to Ijara.
4. Discuss the differences of Ijara from a conventional lease, a loan and diminishing Musharaka.

INTRODUCTION TO IJARA

The term Ijara is derived from the root word 'ajr', which means reward or wages for work done or services rendered. In the financial world, Ijara is a bilateral contract involving transfer of the use of an asset for an agreed period for a consideration. It involves two parties: the lessor or Muajir, who is the owner of the asset and the lessee or Mustajir, who uses the asset. The owner of the object temporarily transfers its usufruct to the lessee for the agreed period and the lessee should be able to derive benefit from it without consuming it. The ownership of the leased asset remains with the lessor, along with all risks pertaining to ownership. The physical possession of the asset is held on trust by the lessee, who is not liable for any loss, destruction or reduction in value of the asset, unless caused by misuse or intentional negligence by the lessee.

In Islamic jurisprudence, the term Ijara is used for two different situations. One, as in the case of a conventional lease, is the transfer of the usage of an asset, while the other is where a person is employed for some service in exchange for wages, like teachers, lawyers, and doctors. According to Islamic scholars, the Ijara contract consists of three main elements. Like all contracts Ijara also involves offer and acceptance – Ijab and Qabul. There are the contracting parties, the lessor and lessee; the subject matter of the contract, including the consideration or rent (called Ujrah) that the lessee pays for the right to use and derive benefit from an object owned by the lessor. The asset is called the Majur and the benefit derived from the asset is called Al Manfaah. It is important to note that the benefit from use of the asset is the subject matter of the contract, not the asset itself, and this benefit is guaranteed by the contract.

Ijara is very similar to a conventional lease. The majority of Islamic scholars consider Ijara as a Shariah-compliant financial instrument if the object in consideration has beneficial use and is Halal. Not every object or asset is suitable for Ijara or leasing. It needs to be tangible, non-perishable, valuable, identifiable and quantifiable. For example, perishable items like food, fuel, etc. cannot be leased, neither can money be leased.

IJARA IN ISLAMIC BANKS

Ijara is a service-based contract, used significantly to meet short and medium-term financing needs, involving either rent or hire purchase of an asset based on an agreed rental fee and period. Islamic banks offer this product to retail and business customers and some common applications involve rental of fixed assets, rental of a package of services, property financing, vehicle financing, project financing and personal financing.

To offer the Ijara mode of financing, the Islamic bank buys the object of the Ijara and leases it to its client, who may only rent the item for the concerned period or may decide to buy the item eventually. In the former case, the monthly lease payments (Ujrah) would be the rent for use of the item only; in the latter case, the monthly payments will consist of two components, the rent as in the former situation plus instalments towards the purchase of the item. After the lease period expires, the asset either reverts to the lessor, the lease is renewed or the ownership is transferred to the lessee if so agreed.

TYPES OF IJARA

Islamic banks currently offer two main types of Ijara. These are called Ijara and Ijara wa Iqtina, and most Islamic scholars unanimously consider both forms of Ijara as Shariah compliant. Like Murabaha, Ijara was not considered originally as a mode of financing, rather it was a business transaction between two parties to transfer the usufruct of an asset from one person to another for an agreed period against an agreed consideration. In conventional finance, this is the operating lease. Now, many Islamic financial institutions have adopted Ijara or leasing as a mode of financing, as an alternative to interest-based loans, and this is called a financial lease. The types of Ijara are discussed in detail below.

IJARA, REGULAR IJARA OR OPERATING LEASE

Ijara or regular Ijara are like a conventional operating lease and can also be called a true lease. These are contracts of rent only, and do not end in the transfer of ownership of the leased asset from the lessor to the lessee. Rather, the asset is returned to the lessor at the end of the Ijara period. In this kind of Ijara, the Ujrah or rentals that are charged over the Ijara period are not sufficient to recover the full value of the asset. The owner or lessor can recover the remaining value of the asset by re-leasing the asset or selling it.

Both the lessee and the lessor may cancel the contract, but with due notice to the other party. Ijara can be used for renting an apartment to a tenant by a landlord or by car rental companies to rent out vehicles. The rental can be fixed for the entire lease period or may be adjusted periodically as agreed between the parties at the onset.

Banks often use a conventional index like LIBOR to determine a competitive profit rate in arriving at the Ujrah, and LIBOR may also be used to adjust the Ujrah at agreed intervals. At the end of the lease period the lessee can either return the asset or ask for an extension of the lease. An Ijara or operating lease is suitable for expensive assets such as ships, aircraft, large-scale machinery and equipment. The bank's advantage is that it retains ownership during the lease period and yet earns a good return, while the lessee is saved from an expensive purchase. The risks and responsibilities of ownership are placed on the lessor, while the lessee is liable to use and take care of the asset in a proper manner. The lessee will have to compensate the lessor for any damage caused by misuse or negligence, and not because of regular wear and tear. Depreciation and any impairment loss in the value of the asset is borne by the lessor. Any additional cost incurred directly for the processing of the Ijara will be amortized into the rental payments. Any repairs that are required during the lease period, and which are undertaken with the lessor's consent, would be the responsibility of the lessor.

IJARA WA IQTINA, IJARA MUNTAHIA BITTAMLEEK OR FINANCIAL LEASE

When the ownership of the leased asset passes to the lessee at the end of the lease period it is called Ijara wa Iqtina or Ijara Muntahia Bittamleek. This kind of Ijara is comparable with a conventional financial lease or hire purchase. The Arabic word Tamleek means ownership. This transfer of ownership may be with or without additional payment at the end of the lease period. In a financial lease, the lessor amortizes the asset over the term of the lease and at the end of the period the asset will be sold to the lessee. The lessee provides a unilateral purchase undertaking to the lessor with the purchase price specified.

There are several types of Ijara Muntahia Bittamleek, which are characterized based on the method by which the ownership is transferred between lessor and lessee. Under the rulings of the Islamic standards setting body, the AAOIFI, the transfer of ownership in case of Ijara wa Iqtina, Ijara Muntahia Bittamleek or financial lease can be done in a variety of ways. Firstly, the lessor completely amortizes the value of the asset during the lease period in the regular rental payments and no additional payment is required at the end of the lease period, allowing the lessor to gift the item to the lessee. Secondly, a fixed amount, decided at the beginning of the contract, is paid by the lessee at the end of the contract through a legal sale to become the owner of the asset. Thirdly, through a legal sale before the end of the period of the lease at a price equivalent to the remaining Ijara instalments. Fourthly, an amount decided by the market value of the asset at the end of the lease period is paid by the lessee for the ownership transfer. Fifthly, gradual transfer of the ownership of the asset is made to the lessee as the rental payments include payments towards the price of the asset. In the Islamic banking industry, the first and second options are more common.

In this kind of Ijara or financial lease the bank buys the asset based on the purchase promise included in the lease agreement with the customer. In such an Ijara, once the asset is provided to the customer for lease it is not returned to the bank at the end of the lease period, as is commonly the case in an operational lease. As such it is more convenient for banks to apply, since they are not in the business of owning assets or managing them. The Ijara Wa Iqtina, Ijara Muntahia Bittamleek or financial lease is completed when the ownership of the asset is transferred to the lessee along with all the risks and rewards incident to ownership. The lease payments are calculated considering the purchase price of the asset which is financed, the rental value of the asset and the lease period. The lease rentals can be fixed or floating. As in the case of an operating lease, LIBOR could serve as a benchmark. The Ujrah or rentals collected recover the usage rent and the purchase price of the asset in diverse ways.

1. The periodic payments made by the lessee during the lease period could include both the rent element for the use of the asset and part of the purchase price of the asset; at the end of the lease period ownership of the asset passes to the lessee.
2. On the other hand, the periodic payments made by the lessee during the lease period may consist of the rental element for the use of the asset only and the purchase price of the asset or its residual value is paid by the lessee at the end of the lease period, leading to transfer of ownership of the asset from the lessor to the lessee.
3. The Ijara contract may be renewed at the end of the lease period with new rental negotiated and the transfer of ownership may be agreed to be at the end of this lease period with rentals including portions of the purchase price of the asset, or this amount may be paid at the end of the lease period.

IJARA THUMMA AL BAY

A third name for the Islamic financial lease, or more specifically the Islamic hire purchase, being offered by the industry is Ijara Thumma al Bay. This is more commonly offered in Malaysia. Ijara Thumma al Bay consists of two totally separate contracts. The first one is an operating lease contract while the second one is a sale contract, with an agreed price to be executed at the end of the lease period.

Figure 7.1 is an overview of the Ijara contracts.

SHARIAH RULES AND GENERAL PRINCIPLES GUIDING IJARA CONTRACTS AND THEIR CHARACTERISTICS

The Shariah rulings related to Ijara contracts as identified by Sheikh Muhammad Taqi Usmani (Usmani, 1999) and other principles developing the characteristics of the Ijara contracts being offered by the Islamic banking industry are discussed below.

1. **Majur or Ijara asset.** Ijara can only be done for assets which have beneficial value and are Halal. Items having no usufruct at all cannot be leased. The Ijara contract must clearly stipulate that the leased asset remains under the ownership of the lessor, and only the usufruct of the asset is transferred to the lessee. As such, anything which cannot be used without consuming it is not suitable for leasing. Consumables like food or fuel cannot be leased. Similarly, money cannot be leased.

Regular Ijara or operating lease – No transfer of ownership

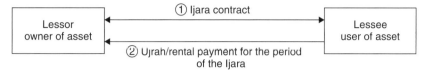

Ijara wa Iqtina or Financial lease – Transfer of ownership

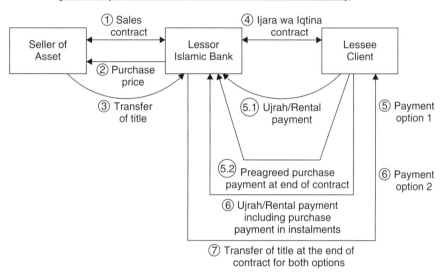

FIGURE 7.1 The Ijara contracts

2. Moreover, the Ijara asset needs to be known to both the lessor and the lessee. The asset returned at the end of the lease should be the same one that was originally leased. The lessee may lend the leased object to a third party, but cannot rent it out or give it as a pledge or security. Any asset jointly owned by more than one person can also be leased, with the Ujrah or lease rentals being distributed to the owners in proportion to their ownership share.

3. **Tangible versus financial asset.** Shariah allows tangible assets to be leased but not financial assets and encourages financial capital to be converted to tangible assets, with the financier assuming the risks of ownership and then earning from them via the Ijara contract.

4. **Usufruct and purpose of the Ijara asset.** Al Manfaah, or the benefit derived from the Ijara asset or its usufruct, should be clearly defined to avoid any uncertainty. The Ijara asset can be used only for the purpose specified in the Ijara contract and none other. Usage of the asset should be Shariah compliant and not Haram, for example a machine cannot be leased for a pork processing factory. If no such purpose is specified in the contract, the lessee can use the asset for any purpose in the normal course of the business. However, if the lessee wishes to use it for a purpose that may be categorized as abnormal, clear permission of the lessor is required. The usufruct should be attainable from the asset; as such, perishable items or faulty

items cannot be Ijara assets. Usufruct can be used by more than one lessee, but the purpose for which the asset has been leased should stay the same.

5. **Ownership versus usufruct.** During the lease period, ownership of the asset would be with the lessor while only the usufruct is transferred to the lessee; as such, consumables like food, money, fuel, etc. are not suitable Ijara objects.

6. **Acquisition of the asset.** To be Shariah compliant an Ijara contract concerning a specific asset should happen only after the asset has been acquired or is already in the ownership of the lessor, which could be the bank.

7. **Ujrah or lease rentals.** The lease rental needs to be calculated and decided at the time of the contract and should be known to both the lessee and the lessor in an unambiguous manner, either for the full term of the lease or for a specific period in absolute terms. The AAOIFI has allowed LIBOR as a benchmark to determine the percentage of profit the bank may ask for in calculating the lease rentals. The two main reasons to allow this are the absence of any internationally accepted Islamic profit benchmark and so that Islamic banks can compete in the lease or Ijara business with conventional banks. When rentals are flexible, they are adjusted periodically with the movement of LIBOR. This raises the question of Gharar or uncertainty. The argument is that since both parties agreed on LIBOR which is known to them, this does not amount to Gharar.

8. Shariah requires the lessee to know the price of the asset, the bank's profit margin included in the price and the amount of rent the lessee would pay. Normally, lease rentals do not become due and payable until the lease asset is delivered to the lessee. If the rent or any part of the purchase price is paid in advance before delivery of the asset to the lessee, the amount is held with the lessor 'on account' and adjusted against the rental payments after it becomes due. The lessor is not allowed to increase the lease rental unilaterally.

9. **Period of lease.** The period of the lease must be determined in clear terms. The lease period commences from the date on which the leased asset has been delivered to the lessee, irrespective of whether the lessee has started using it or not. The Ijara period is usually of short or medium term, but can also be long term if the banks are comfortable with such a contract.

10. **Maintenance.** The major maintenance and insurance of the leased asset is the responsibility of the lessor as owner, which could be the bank. The lessor may delegate to the lessee the task of carrying out such maintenance at the lessor's cost. Meanwhile the lessee is responsible for day-to-day operating or periodical maintenance, and keeping the asset in good condition for continued usage. The lessor is responsible for any loss, unintentional destruction or damage, depreciation of the asset, payment of taxes, etc., while the lessee is liable for any damage caused by negligence or misuse and would need to compensate the lessor.

11. **Risks and liabilities related to the Ijara object.** All risks and liabilities related to ownership are the lessor's, while those related to physical possession and usage of the asset are the lessee's. The lessee will compensate the lessor for any damage to the asset due to misuse or negligence, but not for the regular wear and tear related to usage. Meanwhile any damage beyond the control of the lessee will be borne by the lessor. The risk of obsolescence is also there. The leased asset shall remain at the risk of the lessor throughout the lease period in the sense that any harm or loss, caused by factors beyond the control of the lessee, shall be borne by the lessor.

12. **Lessor's obligations.** The lessor is required to make the leased asset available for the lessee. The lessor also needs to guarantee the asset against any defects, and is also obliged to pay for all major maintenance expenses and for the insurance of the leased asset.

13. **Lessee's obligations.** The lessee's obligations include using the leased asset according to the contractual conditions and safeguarding the asset. They are also required to make the lease rentals on time and are responsible for operational expenses related to the asset. The lessee is also responsible for all risks and consequences related to third-party liability, arising from or incidental to the use of the leased assets. Moreover, all obligations arising from the lessee using the asset for non-customary use, and for use not stipulated in the Ijara contract without mutual consent, will be borne by the lessee.

14. **Sub-lease.** The lessee is permitted, only with the consent of the lessor, to sub-lease the asset to a third party. If the asset is jointly owned, then the consent of all lessors is required.

15. **Default.** If the lessee defaults, then the lessor has the right to repossess. All expenses related to repossession are the responsibility of the lessee. Default by the lessee can happen if they fail to make the regular lease payments, or do not maintain the asset in the condition agreed in the contract, or fail to observe or perform any of the provisions of the lease, or if the lessee is going through a winding-up process, etc. The lease agreement could include in advance a penalty for delay in lease payment. In case of Ijara, the bank can enforce the lessee to pay this penalty for a delay in making the lease payments calculated at the agreed rate (%) per day/annum, but the bank or lessor cannot benefit from it and needs to give it to charity to meet with Shariah requirements. If required, the lessor or bank can take the issue to the relevant courts for award of damages from the lessee, decided at the discretion of the courts, and based on the direct and indirect costs incurred due to the default.

16. **Guarantee or security.** When funds are supplied by financiers like banks or are invested in assets that are leased, these funds are owned by depositors, and therefore the bank has a prime responsibility to protect its interests and those of its depositors, by securing its investments and reducing the credit risks. In Islam, the concepts of guarantee or Kafalah and security or Al-Rahn are allowed under certain conditions to provide safety to the financier's investments. In case of the Ijara contract, the lessor can ask for either a personal or corporate guarantee from the lessee or ask for some form of security to secure the rental payments, or as security against misuse or negligence and subsequent damage of the asset. A physical asset can be taken as security or mortgage, like land, buildings, machines, etc. Lien or charges can be taken as security also. A guarantee can be taken by the lessor in the form of a sum of money from the lessee that would be held against any damages to the leased asset, with no amount deducted from this sum except for any actual damages suffered by the asset. A penalty can also be charged for delayed payment of rentals, though this needs to be given to charity. Security or collateral can also be sold by the lessor or bank without the intervention of the court to recover unpaid rentals or damages to the asset.

17. **Sale of leased asset.** The lessor has the right to sell the leased asset but needs to inform the buyer of the lease agreement and ensure the lease continues as binding and irrevocable. All terms and conditions, rights and liabilities agreed upon in the

lease contract are transferred to the new owner. In case the original lessor or the new owner would like to cancel the lease agreement, due notice as stipulated in the Ijara contract must be given.

18. **Termination.** The Ijara contract terminates naturally once the lease period is over. It can also be terminated for various other reasons. The Ijara contract terminates if the asset is destroyed without the fault of either the lessor or the lessee. The lease contract automatically terminates, and the lessee does not need to pay any further rentals if the leased asset loses its functionality and cannot be repaired, due to no fault of the lessee. In case the loss of functionality is due to misuse or negligence of the lessee, compensation needs to be made to the lessor for the loss of the value of the asset and its rentals. However, if the leased asset is damaged but can be repaired, the Ijara contract will remain valid. The Ijara contract can also be terminated before the end of the term of the lease with the mutual consent of both parties. The two parties may mutually agree to terminate the Ijara contract before it begins to operate.

DOCUMENTATION RELATED TO THE IJARA CONTRACT

Ijara agreement. The main document to be created for the Ijara contract would be the Ijara agreement, including all terms and conditions of the Ijara. This agreement is signed by the two parties only after the lessor is in possession of the lease asset and not before. Documents to be added to the Ijara agreement would be as follows.

1. **Description of the Ijara asset.** Providing complete specifications of the asset.
2. **Schedule of Ijara rentals.** Providing the exact dates of the start and end of the Ijara contract as well as the specific dates of the lease rentals and amounts.
3. **Receipt of asset.** Confirms that the lessor has acquired and delivered the asset to the lessee and is an acknowledgement of receipt by the lessee.
4. **Demand promissory note.** Once the asset is accepted by the lessee the rental payments are due and this is an acknowledgement of this and a promise to pay on time.

Undertaking to purchase leased asset. This document is an undertaking from the lessee to purchase the leased asset on an agreed purchase date and at an agreed purchase price. The document would also include a schedule of the various dates at which instalment payments build up to the purchase price, or the lump sum paid in one go.

Other documents. Besides the two documents mentioned above, an Ijara contract may also require the lessee to sign an undertaking to use the Ijara for personal purposes if they are a retail client. The lessor would provide an authorization to the lessee to take possession of the asset and both parties would sign a sales deed when the Ijara concludes in transfer of ownership, as is most common when the lessor is a bank.

MAIN DIFFERENCES BETWEEN IJARA AND A CONVENTIONAL LEASE

Although Ijara has many similarities with leasing in conventional banking there are some differences also, and these are highlighted in Table 7.1.

TABLE 7.1　Differences between Ijara and a conventional lease

Factor	Conventional lease	Ijara
Religious requirements	Does not follow any religious rulings. Based on the finance and banking laws of the country.	As all Islamic finance products, based on the rulings of Shariah law.
Signing of lease contract	Lease agreement can be signed by the lessee and lessor even before the asset has been acquired by the lessor.	Lease agreement can only be signed by the two parties after the Ijara asset has come into existence, is owned by the lessor and is in physical or constructive possession of the lessor.
Types	There are two types of contracts – financial lease and operational lease. Both contain conditions that contravene Islamic Shariah law, especially interest.	The Ijara can also be of two main types – regular Ijara and Ijara wa Iqtina – and both are designed to ensure they do not contain any condition that is against Shariah law.
Purchase of the lease asset	The leased asset for a financial lease is automatically transferred to the ownership of the customer upon completion of the lease period.	No such automatic transfer of ownership. A separate sale agreement needs to be executed between the lessor and the lessee to finalize the purchase of the asset by the lessee.
Registration charges	Any registration required, like the registration of a leased vehicle, is the responsibility of the lessee.	The leased asset, like a vehicle, is registered in the name of the financier who is responsible for any charges. Registration expenses are considered when lease rentals are calculated.
Rights and liabilities of lessor and lessee	The client is responsible for all kinds of loss or damage to the leased asset, irrespective of the circumstances. In case compensation is not provided by the insurance company, the client is liable to the full amount or to pay the balance after insurance compensation.	The lessor bears all risks related to the ownership of the asset and as such bears all loss or damage beyond what is compensated by the insurance company. The lessee only bears usage-related risks and any dues for negligence or mismanagement.
Rental payments	Based on applicable interest rate and principle amount invested in the asset and the lease period.	Agreed rental payment as in the contract, based on the amount invested in the asset, the rental value of the asset and the profit margin of the bank.

(Continued)

TABLE 7.1 (*Continued*)

Factor	Conventional lease	Ijara
Commencement of rentals	Usually starts after the lessor has acquired the asset by paying the manufacturer or dealer.	Usually starts after the asset is delivered to the lessee.
Rental recovery in case of theft and loss	If the leased asset is stolen or destroyed, the financier continues to charge lease rental till the settlement of the insurance claim.	In Shariah rulings, the lease rental is directly related to the usage of the asset and if the asset is stolen or destroyed, or temporarily out of order, rental cannot be charged.
Insurance premium	The insurance expense is independent of the lease contract and is borne directly by the lessee or added to the rentals paid by the lessee.	Shariah rulings require the lessor of the Ijara contract to be responsible for the insurance premium as the owner. The insurance expense can be considered as part of the cost of acquiring the asset for Ijara and included in the rental payment calculation though.
Rescheduling of the rentals	Allowed with additional interest charged commensurate to the increase in the period.	Not allowed, as charging extra for extension of the period would be tantamount to interest.
Late payment penalty	Penalty interest charged by calculating original payment and the default interest on the due amount and an additional penalty could be applied.	Fixed amount could be charged as penalty, but bank cannot benefit and it is given to a charitable fund, often managed by the bank.
Transfer of ownership	Happens automatically in financial lease.	Separate sales contract needs to be concluded.

DIFFERENCES BETWEEN IJARA AND A CONVENTIONAL LOAN CONTRACT

In Ijara the ownership of the borrowed item is not transferred to the borrower, who needs to return the same item at a stipulated time. Meanwhile, in a loan, ownership of the borrowed money is transferred to the borrower, which does not have to be returned as the same notes of money. As in borrowing of consumables like food items, once they are consumed the same items are not returned. In the case of physical property like a vehicle in Ijara, the same property is returned.

DIFFERENCES AND SIMILARITIES BETWEEN IJARA WA IQTINA AND DIMINISHING MUSHARAKA

In Ijara Wa Iqtina, ownership of the asset remains with the lessor during the entire lease period. In contrast, in diminishing Musharaka, the ownership percentages are clearly defined and at each payment schedule the financier's percentage reduces and the client's percentage increases. The similarity between the two products is that in each payment made by the client there are two parts, one part is a rental payment for the part of the property owned by the Islamic bank and the second part is an instalment towards purchasing the asset or part of it owned by the bank.

PRACTICAL APPLICATIONS OF THE IJARA CONTRACT

Ijara contracts are used by banks to finance, most commonly, the short and medium-term financing needs of retail and business customers. Common lease assets are consumer durables like TVs, fridges, vehicles, computers, equipment, machinery, etc.

The Ijara or operating lease is usually executed to rent out property, by 'rent-a-car' companies, for agricultural equipment and major assets like aircraft. A financial lease, Ijara wa Iqtina or Ijara Muntahia Bittamleek can serve as an alternative measure of financing retail or business needs.

Calculation of Lease Rentals

A specific formula is used to calculate the lease rentals, called the Ijara formula:

$$TLR = CF + (CF * i * n)$$

where:

TLR = total lease rentals (total amount of rentals paid over the entire lease period)
CF = cost of finance or cost of acquiring the lease asset (total cost of asset in Ijara wa Iqtina, or part of the cost in operating Ijara)
i = rate of return per annum (flat per annum profit rate the bank intends to make)
n = period of financing in years (the total lease period in years)
Monthly lease rentals = TLR/n × 12

Practice Calculations

1. Arbaz Bank provides leasing facilities to both its retail and business customers. A bank client applies for Ijara wa Iqtina to acquire specialized equipment for its food processing business. Let us assume that the total cost to the bank to purchase, deliver and set up the equipment at the client's premises is €50,000. The total lease period

agreed is 5 years and the agreed profit rate for the facility is 6% per annum. Calculate the total lease rentals and monthly lease payment the client is required to make.

TLR = CF + (CF*i*n)

TLR – 50,000 + (50,000*6%*5) = €65,000

Monthly lease payment = 65,000/(5 × 12) = 65,000/60 = €1,083

Total profit earned by bank = 65,000 – 50,000 = €15,000

2. Jacob enters an operating or regular Ijara contract with Independent Islamic Bank to rent a machine for his car repair business. The cost of the machine is USD250,000. The rate of profit is 8%. The lease period is 5 years. The total useful life of the machine is 20 years. Calculate the monthly lease payment for Jacob.

TLR = CF + (CF*i*n)

TLR = 250,000 × 25% + (250,000*8%*5) = 62,500 + 100,000 = $162,500

Monthly lease payment = 162,500/(5 × 12) = 65,000/60 = $2,708.33

KEY TERMS AND CONCEPTS

Ajr	Ijara Muntahia Bittamleek or Ijara wa Iqtina	Operating lease or regular Ijara
Al Manfaah		
Conventional lease	Lessee or Mustajir	Ujrah
	Lessor or Muajir	Usufruct
Ijara	Majur	

CHAPTER SUMMARY

Ijara is a financial contract where the owner of an asset, the lessor, allows the lessee to use the asset in return for a consideration for a specific period. Ijara is a service-based contract used by Islamic banks to meet the short and medium-term needs of retail and corporate customers. Islamic banks offer regular Ijara, which is like an operating lease, involving renting only and Ijara wa Iqtina or Ijara Muntahia Bittamleek, which is like a financial lease, where ownership of the asset is transferred along with renting.

The Shariah rules and general principles that guide the Ijara contract include the Ijara asset, which should be beneficial and Halal and a tangible rather than a financial asset. The lessor owns the asset while the lessee has the usufruct of the asset in exchange for a lease consideration for a lease period. The ownership-related risks and liabilities, as well as insurance expenses, are the responsibility of the lessor, while those related to the usage of the asset are the responsibility of the lessee. The lessee may sub-lease with the consent of the lessor, and the lessor may demand a security or guarantee from the lessee and charge a penalty for default, but this needs to be given away to charity. An Ijara contract may terminate before the end of the contract term if both parties agree mutually, or if terminated unilaterally reasonable notice must be given.

An Ijara contract involves an Ijara agreement, description of the asset, rental payment schedule, receipt of the asset and a promissory note from the lessee to pay the rentals, as well as an undertaking to purchase the asset in case of Ijara wa Iqtina.

The main differences between Ijara and a conventional lease involves the link to religion, signing of a contract after acquiring and registering the asset, differences in the rights and liabilities of the lessor and lessee, start of the rental payments, rescheduling of the rentals, penalty in case of default in payment and rentals in case of theft or loss of the asset. The differences also involve insurance and maintenance responsibilities, and the manner in which the ownership of the asset is transferred.

END OF CHAPTER QUESTIONS AND ACTIVITIES

Discussion Questions

1. Define the Ijara contract.
2. Ijara is an alternative to which conventional finance product? Justify.
3. What are the parties in an Ijara contract?
4. What is the main difference between an operating lease and a financial lease? Is regular Ijara an operating or a financial lease?
5. Why is Ijara permitted in Shariah?
6. What are the types of Ijara contract? Discuss each type.
7. Describe the process through which ownership can be transferred to the lessee in Ijara wa Iqtina.
8. Discuss the key Shariah rules and general principles guiding the characteristics of the Ijara contract.
9. What documents are required for an Ijara contract?
10. Discuss the main differences between a conventional lease and Ijara.
11. Distinguish between Ijara and a conventional loan.
12. What are the similarities and differences between Ijara wa Iqtina and diminishing Musharaka?
13. How is Ijara Wa Iqtina different from Murabaha?
14. What are the common uses of an Ijara contract in modern times?
15. Explain the Ijara formula.
16. A small start-up construction company has won the bid to build a school playground. The company needs one excavator to dig the ground at the start of the construction project. The company does not have the finances to buy the excavator. Suggest two possible products from Islamic finance to the company. Of the two solutions, which is better and why?

Multiple Choice Questions

Circle the letter next to the most accurate answer.
1. The lessor is:
   a. Owner of the asset
   b. User of the asset
   c. The agent to buy an asset
   d. Value of the asset

2. The lessee is:
   a. Owner of the asset
   b. User of the asset
   c. The agent to buy an asset
   d. Value of the asset
3. Which one below is not a rule of Ijara?
   a. Owner of the asset sells the asset along with all liabilities
   b. Owner of the asset transfers the use of the asset for an agreed period at an agreed rent
   c. Owner of the asset transfers the liability related to the use of the asset for an agreed period at an agreed rent
   d. Owner of the asset retains the ownership of the asset and liabilities related to ownership
4. Ijara is Shariah compliant because:
   a. It is interest free
   b. The rent is charged for the use of a tangible asset not for lending money
   c. The rent will be charged after the asset has been delivered to the lessee
   d. All of the above
5. Which characteristic below is not a Shariah-compliance requirement for an Ijara contract?
   a. The product must be a tangible asset
   b. The usage of the leased asset should not be in a forbidden way
   c. A personal or corporate guarantee cannot be provided to the lessor
   d. The lessor can lease the asset only after acquiring it
6. Capital loss in Ijara is a risk borne by the:
   a. Lessee during the lease period
   b. Lessee for the full lease period
   c. Lessor for part of the lease period
   d. Lessor for the full lease period
7. At the end of the regular Ijara period:
   a. The lessee is always given the option to purchase the asset at a pre-agreed price
   b. The lessee is never given the option to purchase the asset at a pre-agreed price
   c. The lessee is sometimes given the option to purchase the asset at a pre-agreed price
   d. The lessee is sometimes given the option to purchase the asset at a nego-tiated price
8. At the end of the Ijara wa Iqtina period, what does not happen?
   a. The ownership of the asset passes to the lessee
   b. The lessee is never given the option to buy the leased asset
   c. The lessee is offered to buy the asset at a pre-agreed price
   d. The lessee is offered to buy the asset at the market value of the asset
9. Zuthimalin plans to lease a car from Algerian Islamic Bank using the Ijara wa Iqtina contract. The price of the car is (Algerian dinar) DZD20,000. The lease period is 5 years, during which 50% of the value of the asset will be used up. The bank wants a profit rate of 6% in the lease contract. What is the TLR?
   a. DZD6,000
   b. DZD20,000
   c. DZD26,000
   d. DZD16,000

10. Amna plans to lease a car from Gulf Bank using an operating Ijara contract. The price of the car is (UAE dirham) AED100,000. The lease period is 5 years, during which 50% of the value of the asset will be used up. The bank wants a profit rate of 6% in the lease contract. What is the TLR?
    a. AED100,000
    b. AED130,000
    c. AED 80,000
    d. AED120,000
11. The term usufruct is used in which Islamic finance contract, meaning right to use an asset owned by someone else?
    a. Salam
    b. Wakala
    c. Ijara
    d. Istisna
12. The lessee is offered the option of buying the leased asset at a pre-agreed price at the end of the lease period in:
    a. Ijara wa Iqtina
    b. Operational or regular Ijara
    c. Musharaka
    d. Murabaha
13. Ijara is a:
    a. Lease contract in which the owner of the asset rents it to the lessee for a specified period and at a specified rent, without transferring the ownership
    b. Sale contract in which the seller sells the asset to the buyer, and transfers ownership immediately, while the buyer pays in deferred instalments
    c. Lease contract in which the owner of the asset rents it to the lessee for a specified period, but the rent is variable, without transferring ownership
    d. Borrowing contract in which the owner of the asset lends the asset to the other party, without any consideration
14. A mine operating company approaches an Islamic bank for lease financing of large, expensive and specialized equipment. The bank is worried it will not be able to sell or re-lease the equipment once this lease is completed. What should it do?
    a. The bank should provide no lease finance to avoid the risk
    b. The bank should offer an operating Ijara lease for the specified period and commit the mining company to purchase the equipment at the end of the lease
    c. The bank should offer the mining company an Ijara wa Iqtina lease for the specified period and commit the mining company to purchase the equipment at the end of the lease
    d. The bank should offer to sell the equipment with a Murabaha contract

True/False Questions

Write T for true and F for false next to the statement.
1. In case of Ijara, if the lessee does not pay on time, no penalty can be charged.
2. In case of Ijara, if the asset is damaged during the lease period, due to negligence or misuse by the lessee, the lessee is liable.
3. A guarantee cannot be demanded by the lessor.
4. Ijara wa Iqtina does not involve transfer of ownership at the end of the lease period.
5. Operating Ijara does not involve transfer of ownership.

Calculation Problems

1. Shamma approaches Al-Meezan Islamic Bank to lease a car using an Ijara wa Iqtina contract ending in the ownership transferring to Shamma. The price of the car is AED100,000. The lease period is 4 years, during which 40% of the value of the asset will be used up. The bank wants a profit rate of 7% in the lease contract. Calculate the monthly lease payment for the customer.
2. A customer approaches an Islamic bank to lease a car using regular Ijara. The price of the car is £100,000. The lease period is 2 years, during which 10% of the value of the asset will be used up. The bank wants a profit rate of 6% in the lease contract. Calculate the monthly payment for the customer.
3. A customer approaches an Islamic leasing company to lease a van for her garments factory, using operating Ijara. The price of the van is (Malaysian ringgit) MYR200,000. The lease period is 3 years, during which 30% of the value of the asset will be used up. The bank wants a profit rate of 8% in the lease contract. Calculate the monthly payment for the customer.

CHAPTER 8

Salam

Learning outcomes

Upon completion of this chapter, you should be able to:
1. Define the Salam contract and explain its important characteristics.
2. Discuss the history, Shariah acceptability and benefits of the Salam contract.
3. Describe the role of Islamic banks in the process of Salam and parallel Salam and their practical applications.
4. Elaborate the problems faced in Salam contracts and contrast them with conventional banking.

INTRODUCTION TO SALAM

Under Islamic Shariah law, to be valid, all sales contracts need to meet certain conditions. These are that the asset, which is the subject of the contract, needs to exist at the time of the contract. Moreover, the asset should be owned by the seller and be in physical or constructive possession of the seller. Islam allows practical flexibility in its rules, as needed by the community to perform various business transactions legally and conveniently. Salam and Istisna are the two Islamic finance products that do not follow these Shariah regulations, and they are the permitted exceptions.

In the case of a Salam contract, the payment is made fully in advance at the time of the contract and the delivery of the asset is deferred to a specific time in the future. A Salam contract is like a forward sale contract in conventional finance, with advance payment and deferred delivery. The buyer of the asset is called the Muslam, the seller is the Muslam Ileihi, the payment for the asset is called the Ras al Maal and the purchased asset or commodity is the Muslam Fihi.

Most Salam contracts are short term, though they can be for the medium or long term, and are used for production finance. As such, Salam is more of a trade contract and not a loan. Salam contracts are most suitable for homogenous goods, which have commodity-like characteristics and are freely available in the market, like sugar, coffee, oil, cotton, etc. Any assets that have unique characteristics (farm animals, precious stones, etc.) are not suitable for Salam contracts. Though the asset or commodity does not exist at the time of the contract, a detailed description, quality and quantity needs to be specified in the contract. Salam contracts are suitable and commonly used to finance transactions in agriculture, trade, construction, manufacturing, project finance and working capital.

In the Murabaha contract as elaborated in Chapter 4, the asset is delivered in spot while the payment is a deferred lump sum or instalments and the price includes a markup, and thus is higher than the spot price. A Salam contract is the opposite of Murabaha, where the payment is made in spot in advance and delivery is in the future. The price paid with Salam is often a discounted price, which is less than the price if delivery is made in spot.

IMPORTANT CHARACTERISTICS OF THE SALAM CONTRACT

Goods suitable for Salam. Not every asset or good is suitable for Salam. Goods that are homogenous in character and which are traded by counting, measuring or weighing according to usage and the customs of trade are more suitable for Salam. These goods should normally be expected to be available at the time of delivery. Commodities like oil, wheat, sugar, etc. can be transacted easily using Salam, and as such it is commonly used for agriculture and trade financing. Goods whose quality or quantity cannot be determined by exact specifications cannot be sold through the contract of Salam. Also, goods that are not the same cannot be sold using Salam. For example, farm animals which are each different, precious stones which are each of distinct size, shape, clarity, etc.

Clear specifications of the goods, including description, quantity and quality, should be provided to avoid any uncertainty or Gharar. When goods are sold by Salam, it is essential to clearly specify the attributes of the contracted goods, but none of these goods can be directly tied up to any specific source of supply, like a specific farm for an animal, a specific tree for fruit or a particular oil field for oil. Any source should be acceptable if the goods meet the required specifications. Salam cannot be used for items that are termed Ribawi items (money-like items), which can be exchanged only at spot – for example gold and silver.

Price of the Salam contract. The buyer pays the price fully in advance at the time of the contract. If the full amount is not paid in advance, then the debt of future payment is exchanged for the debt of supply of goods in the future, and this is tantamount to a sale of debt against debt and thus is prohibited. The price in Salam is most often set at a level lower than the price of the same commodities delivered at spot; the difference between the two prices is the benefit for the buyer.

Delivery date and place. The exact date and place of the delivery needs to be mutually agreed between the seller and the buyer, and should be clearly specified in the contract. On that date in the future and at the designated place, the seller commits to supply a specific quantity and quality of certain goods to the buyer, who has already paid the price in full in advance at the time the sales contract was made. The date and place of delivery can only be changed by mutual consent of the two parties. For the contract to be completed, there should be actual delivery of the goods. A Salam contract cannot be executed for items which must be delivered on spot and not in the future.

Moreover, the goods should be such that they are readily available on the date of delivery.

Buy-back condition. In a Salam contract, the buyer cannot demand a buy-back condition from the seller, which would require the seller to buy back the goods delivered. Shariah ruling does not allow the buyer to sell back the commodity to the original seller. However, some scholars opine that once the buyer has taken delivery of the items, with physical or constructive possession, the buyer can enter into a separate sales contract with the original seller which is completely independent of the original Salam contract.

Security and guarantee. It is permitted in a Salam contract for the buyer to ask the seller to provide security to ensure timely delivery of the commodity. Acceptable securities could be a guarantee, a mortgage, a hypothecation or a performance bond. A Salam contract is not a liability of money but is a debt obligation of the contracted goods. If the seller fails to deliver the commodity as per specifications on the assigned delivery date, and at the assigned delivery place, the buyer may reject the contract and execute the performance bond, or may sell a mortgaged asset or the hypothecated items to recover their original price and any other incidental loss, or may require the guarantor to pay the requisite amount. Since a Salam contract is a debt obligation of goods not money, it is permissible to take a guarantee or security up to the value of the goods. Guarantees, security or performance bonds can be taken to ensure delivery on the due date, failure of which can lead to cancellation of the contract and exercise of the security.

Penalty. A penalty can be agreed upon in the Salam contract at the onset which is liable on the seller if there is any delay in delivery of the contracted commodity to the buyer. The seller may also be liable to pay a penalty for delayed delivery, calculated as a percentage per day of delay, but this penalty needs to be donated to charity. The buyer can also approach the relevant courts for an award of damages, at the discretion of the courts and determined based on all direct and indirect costs incurred, but excluding any time value of money. The courts may also provide permission to sell the security provided by the seller to recover the losses of the buyer.

Termination. Once the Salam contract has been signed, none of the parties can revoke it unilaterally. Termination can only be executed with mutual consent of both parties.

HISTORY OF THE SALAM CONTRACT AND ITS SHARIAH ACCEPTABILITY

During the time of the Prophet, Salam contracts were used in agriculture. When the Prophet migrated to Medina, it was common for people there to pay in advance the price of fruits to be delivered later. The Prophet specifically said that whoever pays in advance for dates, to be delivered later, should have a contract that clearly specifies the weight and measure of the dates.

A Salam contract was allowed by the Prophet subject to certain conditions. The main utility of the Salam contract was to meet the needs of small farmers who needed money to pay for the expenses of growing their crops, especially dates, and to provide for their families till the harvest period. With the advent of Islam, when Riba or interest was declared prohibited, these farmers could not accept any interest-based loans. As such, they were permitted to sell their agricultural produce before they harvested it. During the same time, Arabian traders were involved in exports of certain commodities from their home country to other places and imports of other goods from those places to their own country. These traders were also in need of funds to conduct their export and import business and were not able to approach the interest-based money lenders. Salam financing was applicable for the traders also. Salam is a kind of debt, since the seller is liable to provide for the contracted goods, at the specific date. To remove all uncertainty, the Prophet said that all who sell based on Salam must sell a specific volume and a specific weight, on a specific due date.

The delivery date is very important in the Salam contract, since the asset needs to be delivered to the buyer on that date, and if the seller has not been able to acquire or produce by the contracted date, they may have to purchase it from the open market and deliver on the due date. Both the buyer and the seller are aware of the price and the date of delivery of the contract. Moreover, the seller is taking the risk of not delivering on the due date and being required to pay a higher price in the open market, while the buyer takes the risk of the asset being cheaper in the spot market on the contracted future delivery date. Since both parties assume risk and are aware of all details, the Salam contract is free of Gharar and Maisir.

BENEFITS OF THE SALAM CONTRACT

The Salam contract along with Istisna, to be introduced in Chapter 9, are the two exceptions to the Shariah conditions of a valid sales contract of the asset being in existence, owned and in physical or constructive possession of the seller at the time of the contract. This flexibility in the Shariah rules is beneficial when executing various business transactions where the seller requires advance payment to produce or acquire the asset to sell. A Salam contract is beneficial to the sellers because they receive the price for the commodity in advance and can utilize it as a Shariah-compliant financing alternative, and are able to avoid any involvement with interest-based financing.

A Salam contract also benefits the purchasers by providing assets or goods at a discounted price, since the advance price is lower than the spot price. This is possible since the purchaser is willing to pay in advance and thus is providing financing for the business venture producing or acquiring the asset or commodity, which encourages the seller to offer a price discount. Usually, the Salam buyer expects the price to increase in the future.

ROLE OF ISLAMIC BANKS IN SALAM AND THE PARALLEL SALAM CONTRACT

Salam contracts are gaining in popularity amongst the modern Islamic banks operating around the world. Islamic banks can provide Salam financing by entering into two separate Salam contracts: the first is called a Salam contract and the second is called a parallel Salam contract. A second way for Islamic banks is to participate in one Salam contract and then in an instalment sales contract, like Murabaha.

The Islamic bank acts as the buyer of the asset or commodity in the first Salam contract and then enters into the second Salam contract, the parallel Salam, as a seller of the acquired asset or commodity from the first Salam contract that it will now sell and deliver to the buyer in the parallel Salam. Shariah rules require these two Salam contracts to be completely independent of each other. There must be two different and independent contracts, they cannot be tied up and the performance of one should not be contingent on the other. Parallel Salam is allowed with a third party only. Any liability arising from either contract would not affect the other contract.

The Salam and parallel Salam contracts together would involve three parties, the bank being the common party in both contracts. In the Salam contract the bank would commit to buy a certain quantity and quality of the asset or commodity from the supplier or manufacturer that will be delivered in the future at a specific date and place, and pay the full contracted price in advance upfront. This price is usually less than the spot price at the time of the contract. The bank then enters the parallel Salam contract as a seller of the exact same quantity and quality of the asset or commodity it purchased earlier in the Salam contract; the other party in this contract is the client, the buyer, who pays the full price in advance to the bank for delivery at a date and place which is the same as in the Salam contract.

The actual sequence of events is that the client first approaches the bank to buy the asset using Salam financing and, based on this application, the bank then contracts with the supplier or manufacturer on one side in the Salam contract and with the client on the other side in the parallel Salam contract. The specifications of the asset or commodity, the delivery date and place of both contracts, are identical. The objective of the bank in entering the Salam contract is to be able to fulfil the parallel Salam contract only. The period of the parallel Salam contract is much shorter and usually the price would be higher, compared with the original Salam contract with a longer period and lower price. The bank pays the supplier a lower advance price but pays it much earlier in time compared with when the client pays the bank the full price in advance, which is slightly higher. The difference between the two prices constitutes the profit earned by the bank. When an Islamic bank gets involved in a Salam contract it is basically providing purchase finance or forward finance to the client.

Islamic banks have the choice of also purchasing the commodity with a Salam contract executed with the supplier/manufacturer. Then, instead of entering a parallel Salam contract with the client, it may decide to use a Murabaha contract, resell the commodity with a markup and provide the client with the opportunity to pay in deferred instalments, thus technically providing purchase finance.

SALAM AND PARALLEL SALAM DIAGRAM AND PROCESS

A diagram of the Salam process is shown in Figure 8.1.

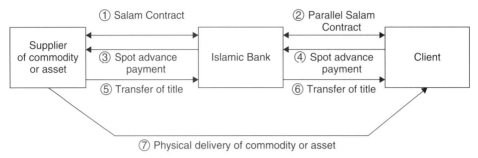

FIGURE 8.1 Salam and parallel Salam contracts

1. The client approaches the bank for financing the purchase of a specific quantity and quality of a commodity or asset.
2. The bank agrees and the client completes the application.
3. The bank signs a Salam contract with the relevant supplier or manufacturer for the commodity or asset for a specific date and place, where the bank is the buyer, the supplier is the seller, based on the client's application.
4. In the parallel Salam contract signed with the client as buyer and the bank as seller, the quantity, quality and specifications are exactly the same as in the Salam contract.
5. The duration of the Salam contract is much longer than the parallel Salam contract.
6. The bank orders the supplier and pays in advance, on behalf of the client, the required asset or commodity.
7. The client makes the advance payment for the parallel Salam much later while the delivery date and place are the same, thus technically the client is receiving purchase finance from the bank.
8. Often the bank only receives the ownership title and then passes it on to the client, while the physical delivery of the asset is made directly to the client.

PRACTICAL APPLICATION OF SALAM

Salam is used where the asset is not ready, and payment can be made in advance. Salam contracts are most commonly used for financing agriculture, natural resources and international trade, providing advance funds to farmers, miners and exporters to finance their activities. It can also be used as working capital finance for businesses.

A Practical Example

Alpha Superstore (A) approaches Big Bank (B) on 1 September to purchase 10,000 boxes of candy using the parallel Salam to be delivered on 31 December of this year, while the payment of USD50,000 will be made on 1 November as the contract is signed. B enters into the Salam contract for the exact same 10,000 boxes of candy with manufacturer Candy Maker (C) on 2 September, paying on spot USD45,000 in advance with delivery to be on 31 December. On the delivery date, physical delivery is directly from C to A, though actually legally two sales contracts were implemented from C to B and then from B to A. B makes the payment earlier and at a lesser amount. The price difference is the bank's profit. The customer needs to pay later and thus gets purchase funding indirectly.

The parallel Salam delivery to A from B is not conditional on C delivering to B. If C does not deliver in time or of the required quality, quantity or specification, B needs to buy from the market and deliver to A and thus bears the risk of making a loss. A, B and C need to be three independent parties.

PROBLEMS RELATED TO SALAM CONTRACTS

Credit risk – seller's default. The supplier manufacturer in the Salam contract may not deliver on the specified date and at the specified place, and this could force the bank to purchase from the market to deliver to its client in the parallel Salam contract.

Market risk. The price of the commodity may change in the market and the bank can lose, either if it is forced to buy at a higher price from the market or if the price goes below the price at which the bank buys from the manufacturer in the Salam contract.

Mismatch of quality and quantity. If the commodities specified in the Salam and parallel Salam contracts do not match completely, or the delivered goods do not match with the specifications, the supplier or manufacturer would be in default with the bank, but the bank still has to supply to the client by purchasing from the open market.

COMPARISON OF SALAM CONTRACT WITH CONVENTIONAL BANKING

As discussed in Chapter 3, the main difference between Islamic banking and conventional banking comes from the differences in financial intermediation applied in the two systems, and this is carried into the application of various Islamic banking products vis à vis conventional bank loans. As explained earlier in Chapter 3, conventional bank depositors provide their funds to the bank against a fixed interest rate. The conventional bank applies these funds to finance various loans on fixed interest again. The borrower may earn less or more but will pay the fixed amount to the bank, which in turn pays a fixed amount to the depositors. The bank shares no risk with the borrower and similarly the depositors share no risk with the bank. In contrast, in the Islamic bank, the depositors share the profit and loss earned by the bank, while in case of the Salam contract the bank buys the good by paying in advance and resells it to the client at a higher price and thus earns a profit which it shares pro-rata with its depositors.

KEY TERMS AND CONCEPTS

Buy-back condition	Muslam Fihi	Ribawi
Mismatch of quality and quantity	Muslam Ileihi	Salam
	Parallel Salam	Seller's default
Muslam	Ras al Maal	

CHAPTER SUMMARY

Salam is one of the two Islamic finance products that are the exception to the Shariah requirement of a valid sales contract – that the asset should exist, be owned by and be in the physical or constructive possession of the seller. In Salam, the buyer makes the full payment in advance to the seller for a specific amount of good, to be delivered at a specific future date.

Goods with homogenous characteristics, that can be counted, measured or weighed, rather than those with unique characteristics, are suitable for Salam. The price, delivery date and place need to be clearly stipulated. No buy-back condition is allowed, though security or guarantee is permitted, and a penalty can be charged for delay of delivery but needs to be donated to charity. Termination of the contract is only allowed with mutual consent.

The Salam contract was used during the time of the Prophet, especially in agriculture and trade. It benefits the seller in the form of advance funding to produce, while the buyer benefits from a discounted price. In modern Islamic banking the banks play middlemen by contracting with the original manufacturer in the Salam contract and with the original buyer in the parallel Salam contract.

Some problems related to Salam contracts are the credit risk or seller's default, market risk and mismatch of quality and quantity. Salam differs from conventional banking financial intermediation, where the bank receives deposits and gives loans on fixed interest and earns from the margin of the two interest rates. In Salam the bank as buyer pays in advance to the manufacturer, and in parallel Salam the bank as seller receives advance payment from the client buyer. Usually the Salam contract has longer duration and less advance price compared with parallel Salam, thus the bank provides purchase finance and earns profit from the difference in price.

END OF CHAPTER QUESTIONS AND ACTIVITIES

Discussion Questions

1. Define the Islamic banking instrument of Salam.
2. What are the various parties in a Salam contract?
3. Discuss the characteristics of a Salam contract.
4. How was Salam used during the time of the Prophet?
5. What benefits do the buyers and sellers in Salam derive?
6. Discuss the role of Islamic banks in Salam.
7. Explain how an Islamic bank gets involved in a Salam and a parallel Salam contract, discuss the parties and the differences of these two contracts.
8. Explain and draw the process of Salam and parallel Salam.
9. What problems do Salam contracts face?
10. Compare Salam with conventional banking.

Multiple Choice Questions

Circle the letter next to the most accurate answer.

1. Which of the following is a characteristic of the Salam contract?
   a. The buyer pays the seller part of the price of the asset in advance
   b. The buyer pays the seller the full price of the asset in advance
   c. The asset is delivered at the time the contract is signed
   d. The goods must exist at the time of signing the contract

2. Which of the following is not a characteristic of the Salam contract?
   a. The goods must be homogenous or identical
   b. Quality and quantity must be determined at the time of contract signing
   c. Salam cannot be tied to the produce from a specific farm, field or tree
   d. Date and place of delivery is determined later, not at the time of the contract signing

3. Which statement below is true about the Salam contract?
   a. The seller will provide a specific commodity to the buyer, with delivery and payment both in the future
   b. The seller will provide a specific commodity to the buyer, with delivery in the future and payment in advance today
   c. The seller will provide a specific commodity to the buyer, with delivery now and payment in the future
   d. The seller will provide a specific commodity to the buyer, with delivery and payment both today

4. The Salam contract resembles which conventional finance product?
   a. Loan contract
   b. Forward contract
   c. Options contract
   d. Swap contract

5. Under the Salam contract the seller is at risk:
   a. For the entire period of the contract
   b. For a very short period at the beginning of the contract
   c. For a very short period towards the end of the contract
   d. At no point during the contract

6. The two Islamic banking products that are exceptions to the Shariah rules of goods being in existence and possession of the seller are:
   a. Salam and Murabaha
   b. Mudaraba and Musharaka
   c. Ijara and Murabaha
   d. Salam and Istisna

7. In a Salam contract the Muslam is:
   a. The buyer
   b. The seller
   c. The goods under contract
   d. The payments made during the contract

8. In a Salam contract the Muslam Ileihi is:
   a. The buyer
   b. The seller
   c. The goods under contract
   d. The payments made during the contract

9. In a Salam contract the Ras al Maal is:
   a. The buyer
   b. The seller
   c. The goods under contract
   d. The payments made during the contract
10. In a Salam contract the Muslam Fihi is:
    a. The buyer
    b. The seller
    c. The goods under contract
    d. The payments made during the contract
11. In which Islamic banking contract is the purchase and sale of a commodity done for deferred delivery in exchange for immediate payment?
    a. Istisna
    b. Salam
    c. Ijara
    d. Musawama

True/False Questions

Write T for true and F for false next to the statement.
1. Salam is a sales contract where the seller supplies specific goods to the buyer in the future against full advance payment on spot.
2. The deferred delivery for immediate payment in Salam is an exception allowed by Shariah.
3. In Salam the seller is exposed to a total loss of capital.
4. In a Salam contract delivery of the goods on the due date is a must.
5. Using a Salam contract, an exporter can be paid in advance and can use these funds to buy the raw material to manufacture the items of the export contract.
6. In a Salam contract, the seller can decide to sell their goods to a different buyer if the sales price increases in the future.
7. A Salam contract can be cancelled unilaterally with due notice.
8. The buyer of a Salam contract pays, on spot, the full price in advance for future delivery of the goods, expecting the price to be less in the future.
9. Salam can only be used for goods that are very standardized.

CHAPTER 9

Istisna

Learning outcomes

Upon completion of this chapter, you should be able to:
1. Define Istisna and describe the Shariah rules and general principles guiding its characteristics.
2. Discuss the role of Islamic banks in Istisna and parallel Istisna and the problems related to these contracts.
3. Elaborate the Istisna financing process and compare it with a conventional loan.
4. Compare Istisna with Salam and Ijara and describe the practical applications of Istisna.

INTRODUCTION TO ISTISNA

Istisna is the second sales contract, in addition to Salam, that is an exception to the Shariah requirements for a valid sales contract. These Shariah requirements are that the asset being sold must exist at the time of the contract, the seller should be the owner of that asset and the asset should be in the possession or control of the seller, either physically or constructively. The word Istisna is derived from the Arabic word Sina'a, which means to manufacture a specific commodity. Shariah scholars allow the Istisna contract as an exception to a valid sales contract since it helps meet the needs and requirements of individuals and organizations which cannot be financed through standard sales contracts.

Istisna is a sales contract in which the buyer contracts with the seller to manufacture, produce, construct, fabricate, assemble or process any asset in accordance with given specifications, descriptions, quality and quantity identified, and within a specified period and at an agreed price. The asset is produced using the seller's raw materials and/or effort, labour. All these conditions and details are discussed and agreed in advance, with the mutual consent of both parties. Wherever possible, a sample or model needs to be provided to reduce ambiguity.

The parties in the Istisna contract are the buyer (al Mustasni) and the seller (al Musania), and the specific asset to be manufactured is the al Masnu. Istisna is the sale of an asset which does not exist yet, similar to a Salam contract. The main difference is that, in case of a Salam contract, the price is paid in advance at the time of the contract while delivery is made in the future, while in case of an Istisna contract the order is provided for a specific manufacture, with delivery in the future and the payment being at spot or deferred in the future.

Istisna is one of the most flexible Islamic finance contracts with regard to payment and delivery. The buyer has various options to pay in a lump sum or instalments during construction, at delivery, or deferred in the future, according to a pre-specified payment schedule or in payments linked to progress in the construction or manufacture of the asset. The contract cannot be cancelled unilaterally by either party once work on the asset has started. The flexible payment options make Istisna a suitable form of contract for construction and project financing, and it is applied to long-term projects involving building or manufacturing a capital item.

If the buyer does not specify it as a condition in the contract that the seller is required to manufacture the item itself, the seller has the right to contract with a third party to manufacture, produce, construct, fabricate, assemble or process the asset. In this case the seller enters into a second Istisna contract, as a buyer this time, and the manufacturer of the asset is the seller in this second Istisna, which is called the parallel Istisna. Usually, when an Islamic bank is involved as the seller in the Istisna contract, it enters the parallel Istisna as the buyer while the manufacturer is the seller.

SHARIAH RULES AND GENERAL PRINCIPLES GUIDING ISTISNA CONTRACTS AND THEIR CHARACTERISTICS

The Shariah rulings related to the Istisna contracts as identified by Sheikh Muhammad Taqi Usmani (Usmani, 1999) and other principles developing the characteristics of Istisna contracts being offered by the Islamic banking industry are discussed below.

1. **Exception to valid sales contract.** Istisna is an exception to the rules under Shariah that need to be met for a sales contract to be valid. These rules are that the asset involved in the sales should exist at the time of the contract, should be owned by the seller and should be in physical or constructive possession of the seller.
2. **Specifications of the asset to be provided.** To reduce or remove all ambiguities related to a yet-to-be-manufactured asset, significant specifications related to the asset's description, quality and quantity need to be included in the contract and be mutually agreed between the parties. This also serves the purpose of removing any uncertainty or Gharar in the contract.
3. **Material sourcing.** This is the responsibility of the manufacturer and should match the asset specifications as agreed.
4. **Price.** This is decided mutually between the two parties and included in the contract. Any change required later can only be made with mutual consent.
5. **Delivery.** A specific date of delivery is agreed in the contract and the seller is obliged to meet this delivery date. The buyer, on the other hand, is obliged to take delivery of the asset at the prescribed date, provided the asset matches the specifications in

the contract. The buyer cannot refuse to accept the asset once it has been manufactured, unless it has an obvious defect.

6. **Payment options.** An Istisna contract can be designed with a variety of payment options. The buyer has the option to pay in full at the time of the contract, in instalments during the construction period, in full at the time of delivery, or deferred in the future either in a lump sum at a specific date in the future or in instalments over a defined period after delivery. The payments can also be made progressively in accordance with the progress in construction or manufacture of the asset.

7. **Cancellation or termination of contract.** The parties can cancel the contract unilaterally only prior to the start of work on the manufacture. Once work starts, no unilateral cancellation is allowed. The parties can mutually agree to cancel.

8. **Default.** Default can occur in four ways in the case of Istisna. It can happen before delivery or after delivery, by the buyer and by the seller.

   a. **Default before delivery by seller.** If the before-delivery default is caused by the seller, by not delivering on the due date or the delivered asset not matching the specification or being damaged, the buyer can terminate the contract and demand return of any payments already made, and even damages if due to the default the buyer would lose.

   b. **Default before delivery by buyer.** If the before-delivery default is caused by the buyer, for instance failing to or refusing to take delivery of the asset when the specifications are met by the seller, the seller can claim damages from the buyer. In case the buyer has already partially paid, and the value of the instalments paid by the buyer is greater than the damages, the seller will deduct its damages and return the excess to the buyer, but if the value is less than the damages, the buyer needs to pay the additional amount.

   c. **Default after delivery by seller.** If the after-delivery default is due to the seller, for example when the seller fails to meet commitments relating to post-construction or after-sales service, in such a manner that the asset cannot be used by the buyer as was intended, the buyer can terminate the Istisna and claim return of the purchase price from the seller as well as damages for any loss incurred.

   d. **Default after delivery by buyer.** On the other hand, if the default happens because the buyer fails to make repayments as they fall due, the seller cannot take the asset back since title has already passed to the buyer, but they can claim damages and recover their dues from the collateral or security or through a court procedure.

9. **Penalty.** If the seller fails to deliver the asset on the agreed delivery date, then the price of the item can be reduced by a specific amount each day. This is not the time value of money, but compensation to the buyer for loss of the benefit or value that the buyer could have derived from the asset if it was delivered on the due date. On the flip side, a penalty can also be applied to the buyer for delayed repayment. This penalty could be applied as per the contract specifications, as a percentage per day for delayed repayment or a fixed amount, but the seller cannot benefit from this penalty and it needs to be donated to charity.

10. **Security or collateral.** As seller, the bank often takes security or collateral from the buyer. In case of delayed payment or non-repayment, the asset provided as security or collateral can be sold to recover the payments and this can be done without the intervention of the courts.

11. **Insurance of the Istisna asset.** During the manufacture or construction of the asset the manufacturer, the seller of the parallel Istisna contract, is responsible for the insurance. After the delivery of the asset the customer, the buyer of the first Istisna contract, is responsible for insuring the asset.
12. **Independence of Istisna and parallel Istisna contracts.** The two Istisna contracts need to be completely independent of each other and the rights and obligations derived from each contract are in no way dependent on each other.

ROLE OF ISLAMIC BANKS IN ISTISNA AND PARALLEL ISTISNA

Theoretically, Istisna is a contract between a buyer and a seller, where the buyer requires the seller to construct, fabricate, assemble, produce or manufacture an item, equipment, building, etc. In modern Islamic banking, Istisna has three parties, consisting of two Istisna agreements. The buyer, being the customer, approaches the Islamic bank which acts as an intermediary. Banks are not in the business of manufacturing any item, but rather in the business of financing such a manufacture. The bank agrees to deliver the required asset as per the detailed specifications provided by the customer by entering into an Istisna contract with the customer playing the role of a seller but entering into a second back-to-back Istisna contract called the parallel Istisna. The bank acts as the buyer in the parallel Istisna and contracts with the manufacturer, producer, assembler, fabricator or constructor for the exact same item as required by its customer, providing the exact same specifications. The bank adds its profit margin to the price at which it contracts the manufacturer and sells the item to the customer at this higher price. The price difference between the two Istisna contracts is the spread or margin earned by the bank. The delivery date on both Istisna contracts is often the same. The physical delivery of the item is made directly to the customer, while ownership of the asset passes from the manufacturer to the bank. On the parallel Istisna contract, the bank pays the cash in advance at the time of entering the contract or in instalments during the manufacturing process. On the Istisna contract, the bank offers the customer a variety of payment options including spot or deferred, lump sum and instalments. Thus, the main role of the Islamic bank is to provide financing for the manufacture of the asset required by the customer.

The first Istisna contract is drawn up between bank and customer; the bank is the seller and the customer the buyer. The customer provides full specifications, description, quality and quantity of the item, including design details, material to be used, also maybe the raw material supplier and manufacturer to be assigned, the performance standards to be met, completion time and appropriate costing. The repayment period for this contract will usually be long term with a variety of options available to the customer to pay a lump sum on spot at delivery, or deferred to the future as a lump sum at an assigned period, or in regular instalments over an agreed repayment schedule.

The second Istisna contract is drawn up between the bank and the assigned manufacturer; the bank is the buyer and the manufacturer is the seller. The bank approaches the manufacturer with the exact same order and specifications that the customer has provided to the bank in the first Istisna. When the bank receives the quote from the manufacturer, it adds its own profit and quotes to the customer for the first Istisna.

If the customer agrees, then the first Istisna is contracted. The bank then goes back to the manufacturer and enters the contract of the second Istisna agreement, the parallel Istisna. The bank makes the payment to the manufacturer either in full when signing the contract or in instalments during the manufacture, or sometimes in full at delivery. The parallel Istisna can be called a sub-contract, but to be Shariah complaint the two Istisna contracts must be completely independent of each other with respect to rights and obligations.

The term period of the parallel Istisna is much shorter than the first Istisna, since the manufacturer wants to be paid in advance, or during construction, or at delivery or soon after. On the contrary, the customer usually requires a longer period to make the payment and this is the main reason for having to approach the bank, to receive financing for purchase of the asset. Hence, the bank allows the customer a much longer payback period and various repayment options, including lump sum payment on spot at delivery, deferred lump sum or instalments. The price difference between the two Istisna contracts is the margin or profit made by the bank, basically by paying for the asset and providing the customer with the opportunity for delayed payment, thus in practice providing the financing for the asset.

Description of the Process

Figure 9.1 shows a diagram of the Istisna and parallel Istisna processes.

1. The Istisna process usually starts when the customer approaches the bank to finance any asset to be produced, manufactured, constructed, fabricated or assembled. For example, a new building. A conventional bank at this stage would offer a loan, while an Islamic bank could suggest an interest-free Shariah-compliant Istisna contract.
2. The customer would then provide the bank with a detailed description, specifications, quality, quantity, time to develop and expected cost estimate. In the case of the building example, the customer would provide other documents like the plan, layout and blueprints, as well as government permits. The customer may also identify the preferred construction contractor and preferred suppliers of materials.
3. The Islamic bank would then approach the manufacturer, builder or producer with the above specifications provided by the customer for a quote.

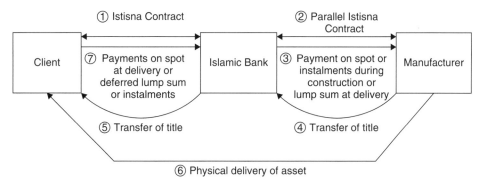

FIGURE 9.1   Istisna and parallel Istisna contracts

4. When the bank receives the quote for the development of the prescribed asset from the manufacturer, which is usually valid for a few months, the bank adds its own profit or margin to the price quoted and takes it to the customer.
5. If the quoted price and the delivery time are acceptable to the customer, then the bank and the customer would enter into the Istisna contract, the customer being the buyer and the bank being the seller.
6. Once the Istisna contract is completed, the bank goes back to the manufacturer, accepts its quote and enters the parallel Istisna, the bank being the buyer and the manufacturer being the seller.
7. The delivery time for both contracts is usually the same; the bank takes over the title from the manufacturer and the delivery is made directly to the customer.
8. Istisna allows a variety of payment options. In the parallel Istisna contract the bank may pay the manufacturer the full price at the time of the contract, or pay in instalments during the period of production (these payments could be tied up with progressive completion of the production), or pay in full on delivery, or pay deferred in full or in instalments after delivery. Usually in this contract the deferred payment is less common, and even if it is deferred the repayment period would be short. On the contrary, in the Istisna contract the buyer has the option to pay in full at delivery, or pay deferred in full or in instalments. Usually the deferred payments are more common in this contract, and the repayment period is much longer than in the first Istisna contract.
9. As such, it is evident that through the mechanism of Istisna and parallel Istisna contracts for the exact same asset and the same delivery period, the customer acquires the asset without having to pay for it immediately. In this case the customer is being financed by the Islamic bank, which pays the manufacturer upfront or within a shorter period and delivers the asset to the customer, allowing the customer a much longer deferred period to make payments.

PROBLEMS RELATED TO ISTISNA AND PARALLEL ISTISNA

Default risk of banks. Banks serve as an intermediary between the Istisna and the parallel Istisna contracts and they carry default risk from the counterparty on both contracts.

Credit risk of banks. In the Istisna contract the bank has the risk of non-payment by its customer, called credit risk. To deal with this, banks can ask for security or collateral from their customers, which can be used to recover any amounts that are not paid by the customer.

Performance risk. In the parallel Istisna contract the bank is exposed to the risk of the manufacturer not delivering the asset in the required specification, quality and quantity and at the designated time and price, called performance risk. To manage the manufacturer's performance risk, banks may demand performance bonds and warranties after delivery. Any delay due to negligence of the manufacturer allows the buyer, the bank, to claim compensation. The bank may reject the asset if it does not meet the Istisna specifications as detailed in the contract, and may also demand compensation from the performance bond. Any failure to provide after-delivery services can be compensated by the warranties. Shariah compliance requires the two Istisna contracts to always remain separate, however, and the liability of one cannot be related to the liability of the other.

COMPARISON OF ISTISNA WITH INTEREST-BASED FINANCE, SALAM AND IJARA

Istisna is one of the Shariah-compliant deferred sales contracts and can be compared with the standard interest-based financing provided by a conventional bank. The two forms of financing are compared in Table 9.1.

TABLE 9.1 Differences between Istisna and conventional interest-based loans

Features	Conventional interest-based loan	Istisna
Type of contract	Contract of loan.	Sales contract.
Number of contracts and parties	One contract only. Two parties, lender and borrower.	Two contracts – first Istisna and then parallel Istisna. Three parties in the two contracts – customer, bank, manufacturer.
Bank–customer relationship	Lender–borrower.	Seller–buyer.
Bank relationship with asset	None other than as collateral, when asset purchased with borrowed funds is taken as security.	Bank is responsible to contract manufacturer for the purchase of the asset and then sells the asset to the customer.
Bank risk	Conventional banks face credit risk from the borrower. The borrower may fail to repay. In the absence of any security, the bank may lose its money.	Islamic banks face credit risk from the customer's failure to repay on the Istisna contract. They also face performance risk from the manufacturer in the parallel Istisna contract from any shortfalls with respect to delivery time, or meeting specifications of the asset. The defaults faced on the two Istisna contracts are completely independent of each other, as per Shariah rulings. As such, banks cannot pass on the loss in one contract to the other contract and may lose their money on both contracts, unless they take security or collateral from the customer and a performance bond or warranty from the manufacturer.
Penalty	The bank can charge interest on interest, as well as an additional penalty from the borrower in case of delayed payment.	The Islamic bank can also charge a penalty from the customer for delayed payment but cannot benefit from this and needs to give it to charity.

DIFFERENCE BETWEEN SALAM AND ISTISNA

Salam and Istisna are both Shariah-compliant deferred sales contracts. Both are exceptions to Shariah rulings for valid sales. That is, in both cases the asset does not exist at the time of the contract, and as such it is neither owned nor physically or constructively in the possession of the seller. In both Salam and Istisna, the possibility of Gharar is avoided by providing detailed specifications of the asset. Beyond these similarities Salam and Istisna contracts have the differences listed in Table 9.2.

TABLE 9.2 Differences between Istisna and Salam contracts

Features	Salam contract	Istisna contract
Type of asset	Salam can be for any item that needs to be manufactured or not. More often Salam contracts are conducted for homogenous commodities.	An Istisna contract is only for items that have to be manufactured as per specific quality, quantity and specifications.
Specific manufacturer	The item of the Salam contract can be sourced from any supplier, since they are homogenous in nature. The buyer cannot dictate a specific manufacturer.	In case of an Istisna contract, the buyer can recommend a specific manufacturer and specific suppliers of raw materials.
Payment method	The price of the asset in the Salam contract is paid in full in advance.	The price of the asset does not have to be paid in advance. Various payment options are available. In the parallel Istisna contract, the bank or buyer can pay the manufacturer in advance at the time of the contract, in instalments during construction, in spot at the time of delivery or in instalments after delivery. The buyer or customer in the Istisna contract can pay spot at delivery, a deferred lump sum or in instalments.
Subject matter of contract	Called Muslam Fihi.	Called Al Masnu.
Time of delivery	This is an essential feature for the Salam contract and is very crucial in Salam.	The time of delivery has more flexibility in the case of Istisna.
Cancellation	A Salam contract, once made, cannot be cancelled unilaterally.	An Istisna contract can be cancelled unilaterally till the manufacturer starts work on the assigned asset.

TABLE 9.2 (*Continued*)

Features	Salam contract	Istisna contract
Bank's involvement	The bank acts as an intermediary by contracting with both the buyer and the seller through the Salam and parallel Salam contracts.	The bank acts as an intermediary by contracting with both the buyer and the seller through the Istisna and parallel Istisna contracts.

COMPARISON OF ISTISNA WITH IJARA

In case of the Istisna contract, the manufacturer uses their own materials to produce, manufacture, construct, fabricate or assemble the asset. If the raw material is not already in the possession of the manufacturer, they are required to obtain it as per the specifications provided by the bank or buyer and develop the asset in accordance with the Istisna contract. If the raw material required for production is provided by the buyer and the manufacturer only applies their labour and/or skill, the transaction can no longer be termed Istisna but rather becomes Ijara, where the services of the manufacturer to produce the asset have been hired through the payment of a specific fee.

PRACTICAL APPLICATION OF ISTISNA

Istisna is a financing method offered by Islamic banks that is specifically designed to offer clients funding for assets that are yet to be constructed, manufactured, produced, fabricated or assembled. Unlike Murabaha, which is the purchase of an existing asset or Ijara, which is the renting of an existing asset, Istisna is the purchase of an asset that is yet to be developed. Thus, it allows the client to acquire an asset that has been tailor made to their requirements and built to detailed specifications. Istisna contracts are usually for the longer term and are for assets of significant value. Most commonly, Istisna financing is used for construction finance, project finance, trade finance, machinery for specific purposes and capital equipment such as aircraft, ships, oil rigs, etc. Due to its longer term, and since the asset will be built and delivered in the future, significant risk is involved in Istisna financing. Islamic banks have innovated various measures to minimize these risks. Two measures gaining a lot of popularity are described below, as detailed in Kettel (2011).

Parallel phased Istisna (PPI). This technique was first introduced by the ABC International Bank, based in the UK and a subsidiary of the Arab Banking Corporation of Bahrain. Construction projects with Istisna can be risky and expensive, as they are often drawn out over an extended period and subject to various kinds of delay. To reduce this risk ABC broke the construction period into multiple Istisna contracts, each linked to staggered financing, conditional on the completion of the previous phase.

Buy, operate, transfer (BOT). Istisna can also be used for projects in BOT mode. For example, a government may contract a manufacturer to build a bridge. Once the bridge is completed, the builder operates it, collecting toll, which in turn pays off the builder. Once the toll money repays the builder completely, it hands over the bridge and its operations to the government. In this way the asset pays for itself, moreover it is operated by the manufacturer during the early part of its lifetime to assist with any trouble-shooting required.

KEY TERMS AND CONCEPTS

Al Masnu	Default after delivery	Performance risk
Al Musania	Default before delivery	Parallel Istisna
Al Mustasni	Default risk	
Credit risk	Istisna	

CHAPTER SUMMARY

Istisna is the second exception to the Shariah-compliant sales contract, where the buyer contracts the seller to manufacture, produce, fabricate, assemble or process a specific item with descriptions, quality and quantity identified. A specific delivery period and price are also mutually decided. Istisna is the most flexible Islamic finance product with respect to repayment options.

The Shariah rules and general principles guiding the characteristics of the Istisna contract include the exception from the valid Shariah sales of the asset being in existence, owned and in possession of the seller, providing detailed specifications to avoid any Gharar, also rules related to material sourcing, price, delivery and payment options, cancellation and termination of contract, default and penalty, security, insurance and the independence of the Istisna and parallel Istisna contracts from each other.

The Islamic bank serves as an intermediary between the buyer and the seller by entering into the Istisna contract as seller with the client and into the parallel Istisna contract with the manufacturer as buyer for the same items, with the same delivery period. The price and payment options would differ in the two contracts, and the price difference is the profit made by the bank for providing the financing. Islamic banks face credit risk in the Istisna contract and performance risk in the parallel Istisna contract, and default risks in both contracts.

Istisna differs from conventional loans with respect to the type and number of contracts, the parties, the bank's relationship to the customer, the asset and the risks and penalty. The differences of Istisna from Salam, the other exception to the Shariah sales contract rulings, include the suitable type of subject matter, manufacturer, payment method, delivery, cancellation and bank involvement.

Istisna contracts usually involve larger funding and longer term. To minimize the risk, modern Islamic banks break the contract into phased smaller contracts with staggered financing conditional on completion of the previous phase; they also use the BOT mechanism of financing with Istisna contracts.

END OF CHAPTER QUESTIONS AND ACTIVITIES

Discussion Questions

1. Define the Istisna contract.
2. Discuss the major Shariah rules and general principles guiding the Istisna characteristics.
3. Why is Istisna considered as a manufacturing contract?
4. Discuss the role of Islamic banks in Istisna and parallel Istisna contracts.
5. What are the challenges faced by an Islamic bank in playing the role of an intermediary in Istisna contracts?
6. Draw a flowchart for a suitable Istisna financing contract.
7. Describe the steps in the Istisna and the parallel Istisna process.
8. Describe the back-to-back or parallel Istisna contract in the financing of the construction of a house for a client.
9. What are the differences of Istisna in comparison with a conventional loan?
10. Contrast the differences between Salam and Istisna contracts.
11. Differentiate between direct sale and parallel Istisna sale.
12. Differentiate Istisna with an Ijara contract.
13. Istisna is a long-term contract for major assets. What are the challenges related to this?
14. Explain the parallel phased Istisna.
15. Discuss buy, operate, transfer as a mode of Istisna.
16. Alpha Company would like to purchase a shopping mall using Istisna financing. The total project will cost around €25 million. Draw a flowchart showing the parties involved in the contract and the steps of Istisna and parallel Istisna financing.
17. Beta Car Leasing Company owns land on which it plans to build its office and garage. The company approaches its bank, Delta Islamic, for financing. The bank agrees to carry out the project, and they mutually agree on the price, date of delivery and the parties involved. Beta has requested from the bank the option of instalment payment after delivery in the future, instead of full payment of the price. The bank has agreed.
    a. What is the Islamic product appropriate for financing this project?
    b. Who will own the office and garage at the end of the project?
    c. Describe the parties involved and the respective contracts necessary to complete the project.
    d. What can the bank demand to protect itself from the possible risks in this project?
18. Abdulla wants to manufacture specialized coffee machines for his Coffees of the World shop in Abu Dhabi. He contacted the Shariah Bank and requested the bank to finance his acquisition of these customized machines. Abdulla provided the bank with the specifications, quantity and other details of the machines to be manufactured. The bank contracted the Middle East Machine Suppliers to manufacture the machines with the exact details as provided by Abdulla. The bank signed the purchase agreement with Middle East Machine for payment during manufacture in instalments and the bank also signed the sales agreement with Abdulla for instalment payments after delivery.
    a. What type of Islamic banking contract is this?
    b. Explain if this is an asset-based or equity-based Islamic banking contract.

Multiple Choice Questions

Circle the letter next to the most accurate answer.

1. In an Istisna contract the Mustasni is:
   a. The asset
   b. The buyer
   c. The manufacturer
   d. The seller

2. In an Istisna contract the Musania is:
   a. The asset
   b. The buyer
   c. The manufacturer
   d. The seller

3. In case of Istisna the Masnu is the:
   a. Buyer
   b. Manufacturer
   c. Asset
   d. Payments

4. In the Islamic finance contract of Istisna, _____ is a buyer and _____ is a manufacturer.
   a. Mustasni, Musania
   b. Musania, Mustasni
   c. Bank, client
   d. Masnu, client

5. Which is the most appropriate definition of Istisna?
   a. Istisna is a contract for producing or constructing goods, for future delivery; payment can be during construction or deferred to the future
   b. Istisna is a contract for producing or constructing goods, allowing cash payment in advance with future delivery, but does not allow future payment with future delivery
   c. Istisna is an interest-free loan made for charitable purposes
   d. Istisna is a contract where Islamic banks provide advice to customers

6. Istisna is most suited for the following activities except:
   a. Project finance
   b. Construction
   c. Providing financial consultancy
   d. The buy, operate, transfer mode of financing

7. Istisna is a product where:
   a. The payment is made now, and the product delivered in the future
   b. The product is manufactured and delivered in the future and payments are deferred
   c. The product exists now and is sold on a cost-plus basis
   d. The product is rented to the customer

8. Istisna is an exception to the Shariah rulings related to sales contracts. Which statement below is related to these exceptions?
   a. The subject matter of the contract is not in existence at the time of the contract
   b. The subject matter is in existence at the time of the contract
   c. The seller sells from their ready stock of the subject matter
   d. None of the above

9. Which of the following statement(s) is/are correct?
   a. Istisna is most suitable for manufacturing projects
   b. In Istisna the buyer buys the goods after they are constructed
   c. Istisna is a contract for producing or constructing goods, for future delivery; payment can be during construction or deferred to the future
   d. All of the above

True/False Questions

Write T for true and F for false next to the statement.
1. In Istisna the buyer buys the goods after they are constructed.
2. Normally, Shariah does not allow selling goods that are not in existence.
3. Normally, Shariah allows selling goods that are still not in the possession of the seller.
4. In parallel Istisna, if the manufacturer delivers faulty goods or does not deliver them on time, the client who is the buyer in the Istisna contract can hold the bank liable.
5. A major difference between Murabaha and Istisna is that in Istisna goods can be purchased only after they have been manufactured.
6. In Istisna the item needs future manufacturing while in Salam it does not.
7. In a Salam contract the price is paid on delivery or in deferred instalments like Istisna.
8. Istisna allows both deferred lump sum payment in full and deferred payment in instalments.

Calculation Problems

1. Arif owns land in Delhi, India and approaches an Islamic housing cooperative (IHC) for financing the construction of his house by Reliable Builders (RB). Arif and the IHC sign an Istisna contract and then the IHC signs a parallel Istisna with RB.

   The details included in the Istisna and parallel Istisna contracts are:
   - Construction cost at actuals of the house (Indian rupee) INR2,500,000
   - Financing period 10 years
   - Repayment quarterly instalments
   - Detailed specifications of the asset – house
   - IHC profit margin 5% of construction cost
   - RB will take 8 months to build the house
   - RB profit margin also 5% of construction cost
   - RB requires downpayment of 20% of construction cost at contract
   - Balance 80% payment to RB in eight equal instalments over the 8 months of construction
   a. What is the price at which the IHC will buy the house from RB?
   b. What is the price at which the IHC will sell the house to Arif?
   c. How much downpayment will the IHC pay to RB?
   d. How much will be each instalment paid during construction to RB?
   e. What will be the instalment amount that Arif will pay each quarter to the IHC over the 10 years?

2. Fatima owns land and plans to build a small factory to produce imitation jewellery. She needs financing for the construction of this factory and has signed an Istisna contract with Turki Islamic Bank (TIB). The bank has contracted Turkish Construction (TC) for the job.

The details included in the Istisna and parallel Istisna contract are:
- Construction cost at actuals of the factory (Turkish lira) TRL1,000,000
- Financing period 10 years
- Repayment quarterly instalments
- Detailed specifications of the asset – jewellery factory
- TIB profit margin 8% of construction cost
- TC will take 6 months to build the factory
- TC profit margin also 6% of construction cost
- TC requires downpayment of 10% of construction cost at contract
- Balance 60% payment to TC in six equal instalments over the 6 months of construction. Final 30% at delivery

a. What is the price at which the TIB will buy the factory from TC?
b. What is the price at which the TIB will sell the factory to Fatima?
c. How much downpayment will the TIB pay to TC?
d. How much will be each instalment paid during construction to TC?
e. How much will the TIB pay TC at delivery?
f. What will be the instalment amount that Fatima will pay each quarter to the TIB over the 10 years?

CHAPTER 10

Takaful

Learning outcomes

Upon completion of this chapter, you should be able to:

1. Introduce the historical background of Takaful, the modern Takaful industry and parties in the Takaful contract.
2. Explain the Shariah rules and general principles guiding Takaful contracts and characteristics.
3. Discuss the development of Takaful over the centuries.
4. Describe the types of Takaful, the operational structures, the Takaful models and the underwriting surplus and deficit.
5. Compare Takaful with conventional mutual insurance as well as with commercial conventional insurance.
6. Compare Retakaful with reinsurance.

BACKGROUND OF TAKAFUL

Takaful is the Islamic alternative to conventional insurance and is a major part of the current Islamic finance industry. The word Takaful is derived from the Arabic word 'Kafalah', which means joint guarantee or guaranteeing each other. The earliest origin of insurance in Islam can be seen in the practice of Aquila, by Muslims in Makkah and Medina, and was approved by the Prophet. In this system, if anyone was killed by someone from another tribe, blood money was paid to the victim's family by the killer's tribe, who pooled together the required amount. Blood money is the compensation paid to the family of anyone killed, and is the responsibility of the killer or their family or tribe. The original objective of Aquila was to ensure that the victim's family did not suffer loss of income from the death of the earner. Some Arab Muslim countries still use the blood money system. A more sophisticated insurance scheme was used by Muslim traders, mostly travelling to Asia. These traders contributed to a common fund that was used to compensate anyone in their group who suffered a loss from robbery or any other disaster in the process of exporting or importing goods.

Is risk protection acceptable in Islam? Muslims believe that all that happens in this world, whether good or bad, is by Allah's will. So, is it permissible to try to protect against something going wrong? The answer is that Islam teaches its followers to make all efforts to avoid or reduce the possibility of risk. The Hadith related to the camel and Bedouin is major evidence to support this (Hassan, Kayed & Oseni, 2013). This Hadith states that when the Prophet Muhammad (PBUH) saw a Bedouin leaving his camel in the desert without tying it up, he asked him why he was not tying the camel. The Bedouin replied that he had his trust in Allah. The Prophet advised him to tie his camel first and then put his trust in Allah. This suggests that Muslims are encouraged to make all efforts to avoid or reduce risks. Since risk brings unwanted or negative consequences, Muslims are permitted to reduce or remove the risks by managing them; and conventional insurance or Takaful are measures to manage risk.

MODERN TAKAFUL INDUSTRY AS AN ALTERNATIVE TO CONVENTIONAL INSURANCE

In today's world, insurance is a major mechanism via which risk protection is accomplished. Conventional insurance contains elements of Riba, Gharar and Maysir, which are all prohibited by Shariah law. Islamic scholars state that Maysir and Gharar are interrelated, and if elements of one exists, the other is usually present too. Gharar is uncertainty or doubt in terms of the transaction, and exists in conventional insurance since the premium paid is for an uncertain benefit which may or may not happen, and the insured loses the premium if it does not happen.

Maysir is all about gambling or games of chance. Maysir means that when one party gains, the other party loses. In case of conventional insurance, the insurance company collects premiums with the expectation that the claims made over the period will be far less than the premiums collected, providing them with a profit. Viewed from the perspective of the insured, they pay a small amount of premium with the expectation that they may be compensated for their loss when the unexpected loss happens in a much larger amount, or they may end up losing their premium. This is like Maysir, and is most evident in life insurance. Conventional insurance companies also usually apply their funds to interest-based products, thus involving Riba in their income.

As with conventional insurance, the objective of Takaful is also to provide reasonable financial protection against unpredicted risks or disasters faced by people in their lives, or with their property or faced by businesses. Unlike conventional insurance though, which is purely based on profit maximization objectives, rather than the well-being of the insured, Takaful is a form of mutual help – as the word Takaful implies. The insured jointly guarantee each other. Takaful is based on the principles of Taawun, which is mutual cooperation and Tabarru, which means a donation, gift or contribution. In Takaful each participant contributes their premium into a fund in the form of a donation, and the Takaful fund supports or compensates any participant who faces an uncertain risky event. The participants of the Takaful fund donate their premiums into the fund to protect themselves from any kind of uncertainty and to protect anyone else, who is also part of the fund and has donated their premiums. The participants in the fund, therefore, are jointly guaranteeing each other and sharing the risk of potential loss of anyone in the group by contributing enough premiums to cover the expected claims of all. Conventional insurance also originated as mutual insurance, which involved the pooling of funds of policyholders for the risk protection of all.

The main reason that Takaful is free from Gharar and Maysir, uncertainty and gambling, is because of the use of the Tabarru or donation mechanism. All the participants of the Takaful fund seeking protection against the prescribed risk for themselves are also sincerely motivated to donate their premiums towards compensating other participants facing difficulties, thus achieving cooperation and unity amongst the Takaful fund participants. The Tabarru mechanism removes Gharar and Maysir from the transactions, since there is no uncertainty about the donated premium – it will benefit one or the other participant. Any surplus remaining in the fund after meeting the needs of all eligible participants is shared between the participants and the Takaful company. More details of this process will be discussed later in this chapter. Meanwhile in conventional insurance, once the insured purchases the insurance and pays the premium, the risk is transferred from the policyholder to the insurance company and whether the policyholder will finally benefit from the premium or lose it depends on future uncertain risky events, thus containing Gharar and Maysir. Takaful or Islamic insurance is acceptable in Islam when it is based on mutual cooperation, and the common welfare and good of society, which has similarities with the mutual form of conventional insurance but is significantly different from the commercial form of insurance more evident in the world today.

Even though Takaful is based on cooperative risk sharing and not profit maximization, to participate and compete in the global platform some amount of commercialization is acceptable, to allow Takaful operators to earn a reasonable profit from their underwriting activities. The Takaful industry has not grown at the same speed as the Islamic banking and Sukuk markets, but significant potential exists, especially since it is quite similar to the ethically popular mutual insurance concept of the conventional market. Most major Islamic banks also offer Takaful products or are aligned with a Takaful operator. The Sudanese Islamic Insurance Company, set up by the Faisal Islamic Bank of Sudan in 1979, was the first Takaful company. In the same year, the Dubai Islamic Bank established the Arab Islamic Insurance Company and the Saudi Arabian government founded, under 100% ownership, the National Company for Cooperative Insurance. In 1992 the Bahrain Islamic Bank established the International Islamic Insurance Company and the Jordan Islamic Bank set up the Islamic Insurance Company.

PARTIES IN TAKAFUL

Takaful consists of four parties.

- **Participants.** Those individuals who contribute to the Takaful fund, as a gift or donation under the Tabarru mechanism.
- **Insured.** The participants who face the risky event and who would be compensated or helped in case they suffer from any loss from the Takaful fund into which they have also contributed.
- **Beneficiaries.** Those participants who are going to benefit from the Takaful fund or else those people or institutions which have been identified or nominated by the insured to benefit from the Takaful fund in case the risky event happens.
- **Takaful operator (TO).** A registered and licensed body or corporation responsible for managing the operations of the Takaful fund on behalf of the participants.

SHARIAH RULES AND GENERAL PRINCIPLES GUIDING TAKAFUL CONTRACTS AND THEIR CHARACTERISTICS

1. **Taawun – mutual assistance, responsibility and protection.** Takaful participants agree to mutually guarantee each other against risks from uncertain events. This is similar to conventional cooperative or mutual insurance, where participants pool their funds together to indemnify each other and share each other's risks. Policyholders or participants mutually guarantee each other, and as a result each one of them is both the insured (protected against unforeseen losses) and also the insurer (providing protection to others participating in the fund). Takaful operations earn a profit but that is not their prime objective, their main purpose is to mutually help and protect each other and be responsible for defined losses that anyone in the group may face.

2. **Tabarru – donation.** In Takaful the participants do not just pay a premium to purchase risk protection against any uncertain risk, rather they contribute their premium as a donation or gift into the Takaful fund. Such donation of the premium is aimed not only at providing loss protection for the participant but for others too in the group, thus including cooperative risk protection, social responsibility and caring for others in the process. Moreover, the donation of premiums provides the certainty that the premiums would benefit someone – the total collection of premiums either meets the loss claims currently or any excess premium remains in the fund to benefit someone in the future. Through this mechanism, both Gharar and Maysir are eliminated from Takaful.

3. **Compliance with Shariah law.** To be Shariah compliant, Takaful operations need to ensure that they are devoid of the Gharar, Maysir and Riba that exist in conventional insurance. Riba, Gharar and Maysir are major prohibitions in all Islamic finance transactions. To ensure proper Shariah compliance, Takaful operators need to put in place a standard Shariah governance system and an SSB has to be set up which would oversee all operations and transactions of the Takaful operator to ascertain that Shariah rules are followed. Gharar or uncertainty is removed from Takaful since the premiums are voluntary donations or Tabarru, which certainly benefit someone, and there is a clear definition of the types of loss that the protection is for. As such, the Takaful operations leave no uncertainty related to premiums and compensation.

   Maysir or excessive risk taking is also removed from the Takaful contracts, since the premiums are paid by policyholders for the mutual benefit of the participants of the Takaful fund and not for any speculative profit making by the insurance companies. Any losses incurred are divided amongst all participants and any liability of the Takaful fund is spread amongst them as per the community pooling system, ensuring that no one gains an advantage at the cost of someone else.

   Additionally, measures should be taken to ensure that the underwriting policies, investment strategies and all products and processes are Shariah compliant. Conventional insurance companies, including mutual companies, invest their liquid funds in interest-bearing products to earn income and increase the funds available to meet claims. These companies also borrow funds, if required, on an interest basis. On the contrary, Takaful funds avoid Riba in both their investments and borrowing. All investments made by the Takaful operator should be free of Riba and in an ethical business that does not harm people or the environment.

4. **Clear financial segregation.** Conventional insurance companies are the insurer and profit-making entities that bear the financial losses arising from policyholders' claims. The shareholders own these insurance companies and any profit or loss made by the companies at the end of the year, after meeting claims and all other expenses, belong to them.

In contrast, Takaful companies are not the insurer, the participants themselves insure each other and the Takaful companies are operators of the Takaful fund on behalf of the participants. As such, it is imperative to manage clear financial segregation of the Takaful fund owned by the participant and the operational funds that belong to the Takaful operator on behalf of the shareholders, and as such also called the shareholder fund. In Takaful, the contributions made by the participants are normally put into two funds, the underwriting fund and the investment fund. The underwriting fund is the one in which the participant's contribution is made as a Tabarru or donation, and this is used for the mutual assistance of the claims arising from losses of the participants in the fund. The investment fund is used for savings and investment purposes on behalf of the participants who share in its profit and loss. This division of responsibilities and segregation of funds is the reason for which a Takaful company is usually called a Takaful operator rather than an insurance company.

5. **Four key conditions of Takaful.** Takaful companies also operate under four special conditions, which stand them apart from conventional insurance companies.

   a. **The specialty condition** – the joint guarantee and common risk taking of the participants of the Takaful fund towards each other.

   b. **The partnership condition** – the Takaful operator and all the participants in the fund are partners and share in any profit or loss made by the fund, and since the excess premium (if any) remains in the fund for future claims, the fund is self-sustaining also.

   c. **The investment condition** – to be Shariah compliant all investment activities of the Takaful company should be in Halal products and with Halal procedures.

   d. **The management condition** – allows the participants, who are both the insured and the insurer, to participate in management and review the operations and accounts of the Takaful operator if they so wish.

6. **Significant insurable interest.** Takaful contracts, as in the case of conventional insurance, are only taken out when the event for which the Takaful is executed has significant insurable risk. Insurable risk means the possibility of causing loss to the insured who is being protected by the contract arising from an uncertain future event, and the insured can be financially compensated by the Takaful fund.

7. **Indemnity.** This means that the insurance or Takaful contract will compensate the insured for the actual loss that has happened. In case of conventional life insurance, the contract can be for any amount and anyone can be assigned as beneficiary, even if they have no insurable interest in the person whose life has been insured. In contrast, in case of family Takaful, which is an alternative to conventional life insurance, only those who have a close family relationship to the insured can be assigned as beneficiary and the insurable amount is based on the income loss from the death of the person insured.

8. **Utmost good faith.** In case of all forms of insurance, all relevant information related to the uncertain risky event and its relationship to the insured is best known to the insured rather than the Takaful operator, and due to this imbalance in available information the parties need to have trust in each other. By law the Takaful operator accepts the information from the insured in good faith and it is the responsibility of the insured to be truthful; if they are not, all liability arising from the risky event would be theirs.

9. **Insurance premium and claim.** The premium is the consideration paid by the insured to the insurer, which in case of conventional insurance is paid by the policyholder to the insurance company and in case of Takaful is paid into the Takaful fund as a donation. Upon the occurrence of the risky event covered under the Takaful policy, the insured or participant claims the amount of compensation from the Takaful fund.

THE DEVELOPMENT OF TAKAFUL

During the Time of the Prophet

The earliest evidence of insurance in Islam was seen amongst the Muslims in Makkah and Medina during the Prophet's time in the practice of Aquila. According to Aquila, if someone was killed then the accused's family or tribe were required to pool together the required blood money as compensation to ensure that the victim's family did not suffer from loss of income. Besides this the Prophet also employed two other mechanisms to deal with distressful situations that are cooperative risk sharing – Fidya, a ransom paid to free prisoners of war and a cooperative scheme to provide help to the poor, needy and ill people of the community by contributions from the community members. Muslim traders also contributed to a common fund, used to compensate anyone in their group who suffered a loss from robbery or any other disaster, appearing very similar to the concept of Takaful.

The 18th and 19th Centuries

A Hanafi lawyer, Ibn Abidin (1784–1836) was the first person to discuss the legal basis for insurance rather than just depending on the customs prevailing (Klingmuller, 1969). Early development of insurance was seen in Malaysia during the colonial era of the 18th and 19th centuries.

20th Century

Islamic scholars began to issue Fatwas that conventional insurance as a commercial exchange contract for risk mitigation was not acceptable by Shariah law, and discussed Takaful as an alternative based on a contract of donation. Some of the major events at which these issues were discussed, and the Fatwas issued in chronological order, are listed below.

1926	Supreme Court of Egypt
1965	Muslim League Conference in Cairo
1972	National Religious Council of Malaysia; Muslim scholars at a seminar in Morocco
1976	Higher Council of Saudi Arabia
1977	Judicial Conference in Makkah; Fiqh Council of the Muslim World League
1984	Takaful Act by the government of Malaysia; Fiqh Council of the Organization of the Islamic Conference
1985	Grand Counsel of Islamic Scholars, Makkah

Most major Islamic banks also offer Takaful products or are aligned with a Takaful operator. Institutional development in the Takaful industry globally achieved some of the following milestones.

1979	The first Takaful company was set up in Sudan by the Faisal Islamic Bank and was called the Islamic Insurance Company; followed by the establishment of the Islamic Arab Insurance Company in Saudi Arabi
1980	Islamic Arab Insurance Company later established in the UAE
1981	Dar Al Mal Al Islami, Switzerland
1983	Bahrain Islamic Insurance Company; Islamic Takaful Company, Luxembourg; Saudi Islamic Takaful and Retakaful Company, Bahamas

The Takaful operations in Malaysia grew during the 1980s to satisfy the Muslim population, and this complemented the actions of Bank Islam Malaysia Berhad (BIMB) in 1983.

1984	Al Barakah Insurance Company, Sudan; Syarikat Takaful, Malaysia
1985	Islamic Insurance and Reinsurance Company, Bahrain
1986	National Company for Cooperative Insurance, Saudi Arabia
1992	International Islamic Insurance Company set up by Bahrain Islamic Bank, Bahrain; Islamic Insurance Company, established by Jordan Islamic Bank; Al Rajhi Islamic Company for Cooperative Insurance, Saudi Arabia
1993	Takaful IBB Berhad and Takaful TAIB Berhad, Brunei; National Insurance Takaful Company, Malaysia; Alborz Insurance Company, Iran
1994	PT Syarikat Takaful and Asuransi Takaful, Indonesia
1995	Syarikat Takaful, Singapore; Islamic Insurance Company, Qatar
1997	Dubai Takaful Insurance Company, Dubai; First Takaful, USA

The 21st Century and Moving Forward

In 2002 Lebanon, a major player in the Middle East and North Africa MENA region, as well as the Levant region, entered the Takaful industry by setting up Al Aman Takaful, while Pakistan established Pak Kuwait Takaful Limited, which is considered the first Takaful company.

Europe also entered the Takaful industry around this time and major developments were witnessed, especially in the Retakaful areas in 2006 when Germany's Hanover Re and Switzerland's Swiss Re entered the Retakaful business. Germany's Munich Re followed in 2007 and Britain joined in by establishing the Salaam Insurance Company in 2008. European insurance companies today play a major role in Retakaful business.

The IFSB and AAOIFI represent the main global standard setting bodies for the Islamic finance industry and have played major roles in regularizing the Takaful industry via the IFSB's *Guiding Principles on Governance for Takaful* in 2006 and the AAOIFI's *Islamic Insurance Standard no. 26* in 2010. Malaysia plays a key role globally in the development of the Takaful industry, and the new Malaysian IFSA (Islamic Financial Services Act) 2013 came into force on 30th June 2013. Its main objectives are to promote financial stability and compliance with Shariah, thus strengthening consumer protection and further increasing the confidence of the public in Takaful.

The Takaful industry still targets mainly the global Muslim population. As a proponent of an ethical form of mutual insurance, it may target people from all faiths for Takaful products in the future as the industry develops and innovates. The world Muslim population at end 2016 is estimated to be about 2.14 billion, more than a quarter of the global population estimated at 7.5 billion. According to the Pew Research Center (2011), the Muslim population is expected to increase at 35%, twice the rate at which the non-Muslim population is growing, reaching 2.2 billion by 2030 (Shamma & Maher, 2012). They constitute the majority in more than 50 countries (Damirchi & Shafai, 2011) and a significant minority in another 15 countries (Fisher & Taylor, 2000). The *World Takaful Report 2016* (Finance Forward, 2016) estimated global Takaful assets at around USD33 billion by the end of 2014. Global Takaful revenues were estimated to be USD14.9 billion in 2015, showing a double-digit 14% growth in 2015 (Global Takaful Report, 2017).

The main concentration of the Takaful market is in the GCC and South-East Asia. Saudi Arabia, Malaysia and the UAE are in the forefront. Takaful comprises about 1% of the global insurance industry, while the population of Muslims is currently more than a quarter of the world population. The Takaful industry has not grown at the same speed as the Islamic banking and Sukuk markets, but significant potential exists, especially since it reflects the characteristics of the ethically popular mutual insurance concept of the conventional insurance market. Its popularity may thus extend beyond the Muslim world. The *World Takaful Report 2016* identifies a total of 174 Takaful operators participating in the market, of which 34 are in Saudi Arabia, 43 in the rest of the GCC countries, 11 in Malaysia, 29 in other ASEAN countries excluding Malaysia, 12 in South Asia, 36 in Africa and 9 in the Levant area. The growth in the Takaful industry is estimated at 10–20% per year.

CHALLENGES FACED BY THE MODERN TAKAFUL INDUSTRY

Irrespective of the Takaful industry's significant growth, it needs to overcome several challenges to maintain its acceptance and position in the global insurance industry. Some of these challenges and their solutions are listed below.

1. **Lack of awareness.** Enhance awareness of the Takaful industry and its products amongst Muslims as well as potential non-Muslim customers.
2. **Lack of interest amongst Muslims.** Promote the benefits of Takaful and risk protection amongst the Muslim population, the main target group, who have a significantly lower affinity towards risk protection.
3. **Shariah scholar lack of consensus.** Build harmony amongst the various schools of thought of Shariah scholars and the resultant differing accounting practices.
4. **Shariah scholars lack of Takaful knowledge.** Provide training related to general insurance and Takaful principles to the Shariah scholars on the boards who often lack this, resulting in lack of innovation in product development.
5. **Copying of conventional insurance.** Encourage product innovation rather than imitation of conventional insurance products.
6. **Size problems.** Attract greater capital to the industry to overcome the size weakness compared with conventional counterparts.
7. **Regulatory challenges.** Mostly, in non-Muslim countries, regulatory challenges are faced and should be dealt with by dialogue between the regulatory authority of the land and the international Islamic regulatory and standard setting bodies, like the IFSB and the AAOIFI.
8. **Weak Retakaful industry.** Significant efforts should be exerted to increase the underwriting capacities of the Retakaful industry.

TYPES OF TAKAFUL

Takaful operators offer Islamic alternatives for most types of insurance offered by the conventional insurance companies. The Islamic banks have played a significant role in developing the Takaful business globally. As with conventional insurance, Takaful products are divided into two groups – non-life or general Takaful products and life or family Takaful.

General Takaful

General Takaful products are offered both to individuals and to commercial entities. Most common general Takaful insurance products are car or motor, home and content, health, fire, burglary, marine, education, machinery breakdown, worker compensation, employers' liability, etc. Some important characteristics of the general Takaful products are listed below.

1. **Short term.** Most general Takaful policies are short term and are renewed periodically, mostly annually.
2. **Compensation for material loss.** General Takaful policies provide cover for any material loss or damage to the assets and other belongings of the participants.
3. **Takaful fund.** A general Takaful fund is established from the participants' contributions, as a gift or donation.
4. **Shariah compliance.** The Takaful fund is invested in a Shariah-compliant manner and provides for any claims from the participants.
5. **Excess in Takaful fund.** Any excess in the Takaful fund after meeting the claims within the prescribed period either remains in the fund or is distributed to the participants annually.

Family Takaful

Family Takaful is a substitute for conventional life insurance. Life insurance is not accepted in Islam. We need to understand the life insurance product to understand on what grounds it is not acceptable under Islamic Shariah law. A typical life insurance is a long-term policy, maybe 20, 30 or more years, the insured paying regular premiums. Sometimes it is also used as a savings plan. Its main cover is the risk of premature death. If the insured dies before the maturity period, the beneficiary gets the full value of the policy. If premature death does not happen, then at the end of the maturity period the insured receives the full value of the policy.

Life insurance is different from all other types of insurance. The indemnity and insurable interest features are dealt with differently in case of life. The insured is not compensated for the loss, determined at the time of an uncertain risky event. Rather, the payment amount is decided at the time of the contract. The reasoning behind this is that loss of life cannot be measured and compensated accordingly, so the amount is chosen in advance by the insured and a commensurate size of premium decided. The amount of life insurance can be unlimited, unlike in case of say home insurance, where the maximum amount cannot exceed the value of the property. Additionally, the insured can choose anyone to be beneficiary and this has no link to the person having an insurable interest or being liable to any loss from the risky event. These are the reasons for which Islam does not accept life insurance. Moreover, death is a certain event, and insurance is supposed to be for uncertain events. This further makes life insurance, in its traditional form, Shariah non-compliant. Life insurance can also be purchased for someone else. Though not for just anyone; the law allows this only for some relations – husbands and wives, parents and children, corporations and their executives, debtors and creditors.

Family Takaful needs to be structured carefully to be Shariah compliant. Shariah allows savings plan-type policies which have a maturity date with specified benefits and may also be designed to help the insured's family in case of the death of the insured before the maturity period by compensating financially for the loss of income. Family Takaful includes two parts. The first part is the savings part, where the insured regularly saves a certain amount which accumulates over time and grows with Shariah-compliant investments; the second part is the risk-sharing part, where all Takaful participants donate their premium to a common pool which provides collective financial protection for the insured in case of disability or compensates the family of the insured for income loss in case of death prior to the maturity of the policy. There are limitations on the amount of the policy and the beneficiary choice. In life insurance the amount can be unlimited but in family Takaful it is limited to the maximum income loss that may happen in case of death of the insured. Additionally, in life insurance anyone can be the beneficiary but Shariah rules dictate that the beneficiaries of the family Takaful can only be immediate family members like parents, siblings, spouse, children, cousins, etc.

Family Takaful is not yet well known amongst the Muslim population, who often do not participate in life insurance due to religious restrictions. Amongst those who are aware of the existence of family Takaful, an alternative to life insurance, many affluent Muslims do not feel it is necessary to participate in family Takaful or think that the risks it covers are not so likely. Awareness-building drives and greater emphasis on its benefits, both as a long-term savings product and as family protection against financial risk, can increase the usage of family Takaful amongst people from all walks of life. Reasons for using family Takaful are savings for the future, health care, disability plans, children's education, property purchase, performance of hajj, retirement income, leaving an inheritance for heirs, providing for Waqf charity, etc.

When participants of family Takaful contribute their regular instalments, the fund is divided and credited into two separate accounts. The first account is called the participants' account and a substantial proportion of the instalments is credited into this account for savings and investment; at maturity of the family Takaful the accumulated balance of the account is delivered to the insured or to the assigned beneficiary of the insured. The second account is called the participants' special account. The smaller balance portion of the regular instalment is credited into this account based on the Tabarru or donation mechanism, and the fund created from all participants' special accounts is used by the Takaful operator to pay the Takaful benefits to the heirs of any participant who may die before the maturity of their contract.

Family Takaful can be of three types.

1. **Ordinary collaboration.** In this kind of family Takaful the participants usually contribute to a common pool of funds as a donation or Tabarru. The contributions do not have a savings element, rather the contributed premiums are used to provide mutual protection via an underwriting fund to compensate the members of the fund if any unforeseen loss or disaster affects them; the compensation is paid to the participants or, in case of death, to their assigned beneficiary.

2. **Collaboration with savings.** In this kind of family Takaful the participants usually contribute a premium that has two parts. One part is contributed as a donation to a common pool of funds used for underwriting purposes to compensate any member of the fund or their beneficiary in case of unforeseen loss or disaster. The second part of the premium is used to build up a savings or investment fund for each participant, accumulated over the life of the policy; the final balance is handed over to the participant at maturity or, in case of premature death, the accumulated amount is handed over to the assigned beneficiary. The underwriting fund and the savings/investment fund are kept separate. The participants of this type of family Takaful gain benefits individually from the savings fund and collectively from the underwriting fund.

3. **Collaboration based on specific groups.** In this kind of family Takaful the participants belong to a common group which could be built based on community, ethnicity or even employment in the same organization. This is the closest Islamic alternative to group life insurance. Membership of this kind of collaboration is limited to those who come from the same group. The premium contributions to the underwriting fund may be made by the participants individually or jointly by the organization on behalf of the participants, or can be a combination of both (like the individual contribution and the organizational contribution to group life insurance). The fund is used solely to provide benefits to any participant or their assigned beneficiary in case of any risky uncertain event, disability or death, as covered by the Takaful contract.

OPERATIONAL STRUCTURE OF TAKAFUL

Takaful operations are like those of mutual insurance but involve a two-tier structure. The Takaful operator is a licensed body or a limited liability company, thus either acting as an agent or as a company with share capital. The main purpose of the Takaful operator is to manage the Takaful activities. The Takaful operator is responsible for two separate funds – the underwriting fund and the investment fund, both owned by the participants or policy-holders of the Takaful operations. The first tier involves these two funds, while the second tier in case of a limited liability Takaful company is the shareholders fund.

The underwriting fund is responsible for meeting claims arising from the participants. If the claims arising in a specific period are higher than the premiums collected, basically being greater than the underwriting fund, then a deficit condition is created. If any reserves built into the underwriting fund are also not sufficient, then the shareholders' capital can be utilized. Other sources of additional funds to meet the deficit of the underwriting fund are interest-free Shariah-compliant financing arrangements with any financial institution, interest-free loans from the Takaful operator as Qard Hasan or even additional contributions required from the participants. As such, a major economic reason to have the two-tier structure is that the share capital of the Takaful operator can be a final source to make up the deficit of the underwriting fund and thus prevent the fund from being declared insolvent. The Qard Hasan from the Takaful operator is repaid from subsequent surpluses in the underwriting fund. The Takaful operator does not bear the risk of the underwriting fund, since the temporary support provided is only in the form of a Shariah-compliant loan and is repaid from the underwriting fund. But this role of the shareholders fund is a major reason for Takaful regulators requiring the Takaful operator to have adequate capital.

The legal framework of the country in which the Takaful operation is being executed may dictate the acceptable structure of the Takaful operator. In countries where cooperative or mutual forms of company are legally accepted, the underwriting fund formed from the participants' contributions is included in the Takaful company, though this fund is kept separate from the shareholders fund. On the other hand, in countries where companies can only be formed with shareholders' capital, the underwriting fund cannot be included in the company itself, but is maintained separately and only managed by the Takaful operator. The Takaful operator's functions can be divided into two categories. Firstly, managing the underwriting services, which includes preparing insurance policies, collecting premiums as donation, assessing the claims and distributing the compensations. Secondly, the Takaful operator also manages the investment fund, by investing the money in the fund in various Shariah-compliant products and monitoring the investments. The Takaful operators can be set up as cooperatives or mutual companies operating as licensed bodies; they can also be independent profit-oriented companies or can be just a Takaful window within a conventional insurance company.

Takaful participants contribute to the Takaful fund and their contributions or premiums are calculated based on the type of risk they are protecting themselves from and the probability of that risky event happening to the participant during the period covered. A common pool of underwriting fund is created from the contributions, and the fund is invested in a Shariah-compliant manner. All claims arising from the group covered are paid from this fund. Any surplus in the fund at the end of the financial year, after meeting all claims and expenses, can either be kept in reserve for future need or distributed to the participants as a regular discount or no claim discount. The Takaful industry uses the below formula to calculate the underwriting ratio:

$$\text{Underwriting ratio} = \text{Underwriting profit or loss}/\text{Premium}$$

An insurance company's main source of income is from the underwriting surplus, but it can still make a profit after a negative underwriting ratio by making up from its investment income. The underwriting ratio and net income from investment together determine whether the company will make a profit or a loss. In case of a Takaful operator, its income and its profit or loss scenario can be different depending on its operational structure, which is called the Takaful model. The main models and their resultant income are given below, while more details about the models are discussed in the next section.

- **The Mudaraba Model:** It is based on the Mudaraba concept. The participants are the Rab al Maal, who provide the capital and the Takaful Operator is the Mudarib, who provides the effort and skill, and they share the profit at a pre-agreed ratio. In case of a loss, the participants lose their capital and the Takaful Operator is not compensated for their work.
- **The Wakala model.** Based on the Wakala or agency concept. The participants are the principal and the Takaful operator acts as agent or Wakeel. The Takaful operator earns an agency fee for their services and may also earn an incentive in the form of a performance fee.
- **The hybrid model.** Based on a combination of Mudaraba and Wakala. Usually the underwriting services of the Takaful operator are compensated by a Wakala fee, while for its management of the investment services the Takaful operator shares the profit or loss with the participants on a Mudaraba basis.
- **The Waqf model.** A special Takaful model developed for non-profit Takaful activities for government or other non-profit organizations. The Takaful fund's surplus is neither distributed to the participants nor taken by the Takaful operator, instead it is held in the fund for social welfare activities benefiting the community.

TAKAFUL MODELS

Pure Wakala Model

Wakala is the Arabic for agency. Wakala or agency is a contract where the first party, the principal, delegates their business to the second party, the agent or Wakeel, to provide their effort and skill towards achieving the assigned responsibility. The Wakala contract bounds both the principal and the agent equally to the contract.

The Wakala model of Takaful is also based on the principal–agent relationship, where the policyholders or participants are the principal, the real owners, providing the funds through their contributions which constitute the underwriting and investment funds. The participants jointly own the underwriting fund and its sole purpose is to mutually indemnify the participants; the investment fund is individually owned by the participants for their own benefit. The Takaful operator acts as the agent who manages both funds on behalf of the policyholders. The principal–agent relationship strictly built into and enforced in the contract of the Wakala Takaful model clearly outlines the rights and duties of both the principal and the agent. The policyholders bear all risks related to the funds and any profit or loss generated by the investment fund or any surplus or deficit in the underwriting fund at the end of the specific period are their responsibility. As compensation for its work, the Takaful operator is paid the Wakala or agency fee. The agency fee must be clearly specified in the Takaful contract and can be a fixed amount, a percentage of the contributions made by the policyholders or an agreed ratio of the profit made by the investment fund. This fee may be charged as income upfront or after the contract is completed. An additional performance fee may also be given to the Takaful operator as an incentive for above-average and efficient management. The IFSB recommends that the agency fee should be sufficient to cover all expenses of the Takaful operator, like management expenses, distribution costs, any payments to intermediaries, and should include a margin of operational profit for the Takaful operator. The Wakala contract may also be designed in such a manner that all operational expenses are paid by the principle at actuals, while the

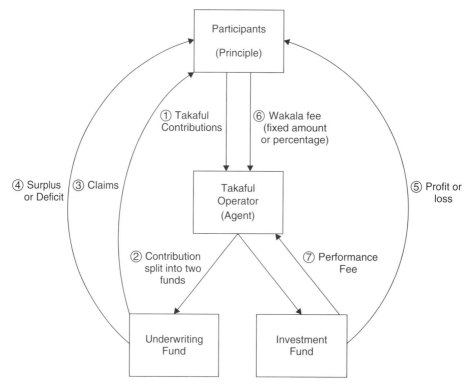

FIGURE 10.1   Pure Wakala model

Wakala fee constitutes the income of the Takaful operator only. To generate profit from its efforts, the Takaful operator must manage all operational expenses like salaries, overheads, sales commissions and marketing expenses within the disclosed amounts. The Wakala model is a transparent model since the Wakala fees and all operational costs are specified and related to each other. This model is moderately popular in the global Takaful industry.

Some of the reservations of Shariah scholars related to the Wakala model are about the distribution of the underwriting surplus to the participants in proportion to their contributions, like a conditional gift, which is not allowed. Moreover, the provision of Qard Hasan from the shareholders of the Takaful operator to make up the deficit in the underwriting fund is not correct when the operator is only an agent or Wakeel.

Figure 10.1 illustrates the pure Wakala model.

Pure Mudaraba Model

The Mudaraba contract in Islamic finance is based on trust financing. The capital or funding is provided entirely by the Rab al Maal, while the Mudarib provides their effort and skill for the enterprise. The profit is shared between the Rab al Maal and the Mudarib according to a pre-agreed ratio, while any financial loss is entirely the capital provider's. The Mudarib loses their time or effort only unless there is negligence or misconduct. In case of the Mudaraba model of Takaful, the participants or policyholders are the Rab al Maal or the capital providers and the owners of the Takaful undertaking. The Takaful operator is the Mudarib, considered as the business partner of the participants in the investor–entrepreneur relationship under the Mudaraba contract. As the entrepreneur, the Takaful operator would accept the contributions made by the participants, called the Ras al Maal or Takaful premium, which forms the underwriting fund according to the Tabarru or donation concept and may also include a portion that would form the investment fund.

The contract specifies how the surplus from the underwriting fund, after the Takaful claims and other expenses are met, would be shared between the Takaful operator and the participants, and the pre-agreed ratio at which the profit of the investment fund would be shared. All financial losses in both the underwriting and investment funds are borne completely by the policyholders. The Takaful operator would only lose their time and effort, and not be compensated for their efforts. If the Takaful operator is responsible for negligence or misconduct, they will have to compensate the policyholders. To protect the interests of the participants, the Takaful operator is required to observe certain prudential rules of operations. Additionally, in case of a deficit in the underwriting fund there is the provision of Qard Hasan or a no-cost loan from the Takaful operator to meet the claims. Usually the income to the Takaful operator or Mudarib is calculated at the end of the Takaful contract. Supporters of the Mudaraba model claim that since the Takaful operator shares in the profit or surplus of the underwriting fund it is an incentive for efficient management of the fund and judicious distribution of claims as well as careful expenditures.

Shariah scholars, though, have many reservations about the pure Mudaraba model of Takaful and because of these the method is not very popular in the market. It was first used in Malaysia and some Takaful operators in Brunei also follow this

Malaysian model. According to some scholars, the contributions given as donations by the participants cannot become the capital of a commercial enterprise like the Mudaraba. The profit of a Mudaraba enterprise is considered as the income earned after recovery of the initial capital. In insurance or Takaful for the underwriting fund, no profit is really earned; rather it is a surplus left from the original capital that was not fully exhausted after paying off claims. Another criticism is that in Mudaraba the Rab al Maal is liable for all losses up to their share capital contribution and not beyond, whereas in the case of Takaful the participants are liable for unlimited losses and may be obliged to provide additional contributions to make up the losses. Another reservation, as discussed earlier in the pure Wakala model – the distribution of surpluses from the underwriting fund to the participants as a conditional gift – applies in the Mudaraba model too. Also, some scholars opine that the risk of the Takaful operator is quite high since it shares in the profits of both the underwriting and the investment fund. Provision of Qard Hasan from the shareholders fund in case of a deficit in the underwriting fund is also not a suitable expectation from the Mudarib, whose role is not that of a guarantor.

Figure 10.2 illustrates the pure Mudaraba model.

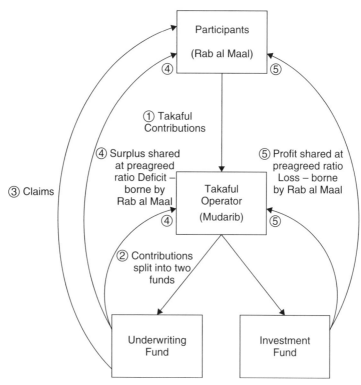

FIGURE 10.2 Pure Mudaraba model

Wakala and Mudaraba Combined or Hybrid Model

This Takaful model utilizes both the Wakala and Mudaraba concepts and this twin role makes the model unique. The Wakala model is used for the underwriting fund and the Mudaraba model is used for the investment fund. As the agent or Wakeel for the underwriting activities, the Takaful operator receives an agency fee mutually agreed between the participants and the Takaful operator; as the Mudarib of the investment activities, it shares in the profits with the capital providers, the participants, at a pre-agreed ratio. The Takaful operator may also get the performance fee for above-average results. In case of a deficit in the underwriting fund or a loss in the investment fund, the financial loss is that of the policyholder and not that of the Takaful operator, unless the deficit or loss was caused by the negligence or misconduct of the Takaful operator. Normally, the Takaful operator is liable to lose its time and effort in case of the Mudaraba-based investment activities; in case of the Wakala-based underwriting activities, if there is a deficit the agent will not receive its fee or may be required to provide an interest-free loan called Qard Hasan. The Wakala–Mudaraba hybrid model is preferred by some financial regulators. International Islamic finance organizations like the AAOIFI also recommend this model and it is becoming the most popular method, used by most Takaful operators in the Middle East. Bahrain Central Bank only allows this model.

The Takaful operator plays a twin role in this hybrid structure, making it quite unique. It is entitled to the mutually decided agency fee or commission as the agent for the underwriting activities and is entitled to a predetermined ratio of any profits realized by its management of the investment activities. Therefore, the sources of income of the Takaful operator in the combined Wakala–Mudaraba model include the agency fee, the incentive or performance fee and the share in the profit of the investment fund. A major advantage of the hybrid model is that it achieves clear segregation between the shareholders fund and the participants' funds.

This model resolves the criticism of the Mudaraba model related to the excessive risk of the Takaful operator participating in the profit and surplus of the investment and underwriting operations. According to these scholars, the underwriting surplus is not the same as profit and should belong to the policyholders only. Surpluses should be utilized to build up reserves that would cover the deficits in later years.

Figure 10.3 illustrates the combined Wakala–Mudaraba model.

Waqf–Wakala–Mudaraba Model

Waqf is a charitable endowment under Islamic law, which involves donating any asset (land, a building or an amount of money) for charitable, social or religious purposes. The individual or organization making the donation has no intention and cannot reclaim the asset back.

The Waqf–Wakala–Mudaraba model of Takaful is a recent form of Takaful operation and was established for the social welfare objectives of governments, charitable institutions and social enterprises. It is initiated when a company is formed by its

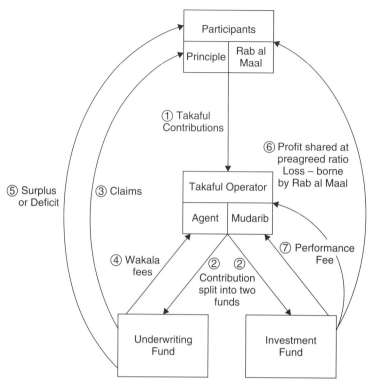

FIGURE 10.3 Wakala and Mudaraba combined model

shareholders donating contributions to establish a common pool designated as the Waqf fund. The donations can be of any reasonable amount or may be specified by the SSB. The Waqf fund's objective is to meet the claims of participants, especially needy participants who may not have been able to make their own contributions, against defined losses. The Waqf-based underwriting fund may also enrol participants who contribute premiums as well as those who are not financially capable to contribute. Both the shareholders and the participants lose the ownership rights to their contribution once it becomes part of the Waqf fund. The capital in the Waqf fund is invested and the claims are only met from the income earned by the fund, while the original capital remains in the fund for reinvestment and for the continuity of the Waqf fund. The company serves as the agent of the shareholders and manages the Waqf fund. The company earns a mutually agreed and specified agency or Wakala fee for acting on behalf of the shareholders. Besides managing the Waqf fund and meeting the claims of enrolled participants, the company is also responsible for managing the investment activities of the Waqf fund in a Shariah-compliant manner. The investment function is carried out as a Mudaraba and the company, as Mudarib, shares in the profit from the investments at a pre-agreed ratio. An additional performance fee may also be paid as an incentive for excellent performance. The remainder of the investment profit goes back to the Waqf fund to top up the initial Tabarru or

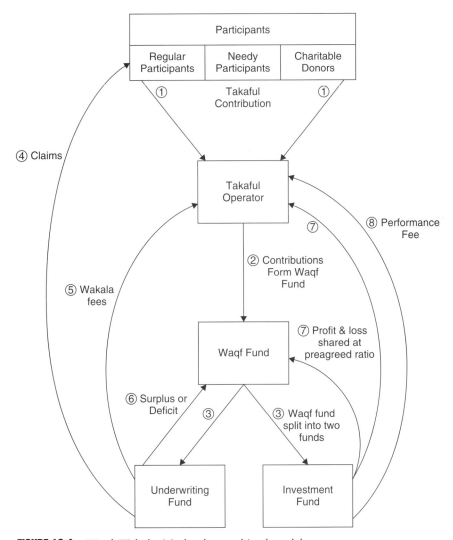

FIGURE 10.4　Waqf–Wakala–Mudaraba combined model

donation made by the shareholders for the benefit of the participants, and to ensure the continuity of the Waqf fund. The Waqf fund is set up as a separate legal entity formed by the initial donation of the shareholders. This model is often used by social and governmental institutions to provide Takaful protection for those who otherwise may not be able to access it.

Figure 10.4 illustrates the combined Waqf–Wakala–Mudaraba model.

Comparison of the Different Takaful Models

Table 10.1 gives an overview of the differences between the Takaful models discussed.

TABLE 10.1 Comparison of the Wakala, Mudaraba, Wakala–Mudaraba hybrid and Waqf–Wakala–Mudaraba models (Hassan, Kayed & Oseni, 2013)

Feature	Wakala model	Mudaraba model	Wakala–Mudaraba hybrid model	Waqf–Wakala–Mudaraba model
Contracts used	Wakala only.	Mudaraba only.	Wakala and Mudaraba.	Wakala, Mudaraba and Waqf.
Investment strategy	Shariah-compliant assets.	Shariah-compliant assets.	Shariah-compliant assets.	Shariah-compliant assets.
Takaful operator's responsibility	Manages the underwriting and the investment fund.	Manages the underwriting and the investment fund.	Manages the underwriting and the investment fund.	Manages the underwriting, the investment and the Waqf fund.
Initial capital	Participants' premium.	Participants' premium.	Participants' premium.	Participants' premium and charitable donations.
Benefits	Mutual guarantee against any risk for participants and end of year surplus. Takaful operator gets agency fee.	Mutual guarantee against any risk for participants and end of year surplus. Profits to be shared between participants and Takaful operator.	Mutual guarantee against any risk for participants and end of year surplus. Profit to be shared between Takaful operator and participants. Takaful operator also gets the agency fee.	Mutual guarantee against any risk for participants. The Takaful operator gets the agency fee for managing the underwriting activities. The profit from investment of the Waqf fund is shared with the Takaful operator at a pre-agreed ratio and remainder added to the fund. The surplus in the underwriting fund is added back to the fund.

UNDERWRITING SURPLUS OR DEFICIT AND TECHNICAL PROVISIONS

The Takaful operations are executed with the use of the underwriting fund, formed by the Tabarru contributions of the participants. The claims made to this fund over a specific period are uncertain, depending on the risky events affecting the enrolled participants in the Takaful. As such, the fund may either have a surplus or a deficit at the end of the period and managing both is a major part of the Takaful operations. The AAOIFI has issued Standard 13, which comprises regulations related to the determination and disclosure of both the surplus and deficit in the underwriting fund of the Takaful companies. In a simplistic manner, the underwriting surplus is the excess that remains from the contributions made by the participants after the deductions of all claims, expenses and management fees for the Takaful operator. As per regulations, the underwriting surplus or deficit is calculated for each financial year using the following technique:

Premium contributions received for the period

Plus income from investments made by the underwriting fund

Minus (all indemnities paid out for acceptable claims made during the period + any Retakaful expenses + underwriting expenses + underwriting fee paid to the Takaful operator)

Plus or minus changes in technical provisions (technical provisions include estimates of future claims related to events that have already happened. Any amount previously allocated but not as yet used up in claims is added back. This also requires adjustments for any unpaid claims and unearned premiums).

The result of the above calculations is a surplus when it is a positive amount and a deficit when it is a negative amount.

In Takaful operations there is a clear separation between the assets, liabilities and income from operations of the participants or policyholders and the shareholders. The shareholder is not entitled to any surplus in the underwriting fund; it belongs exclusively to the policyholders. This is a collective right of the participants originating from their respective contributions during the financial year. Shareholders earn from any Wakala or performance fees and share in the profit from the operations of the underwriting and/or investment fund as the Mudarib. In some special cases the SSB may allow the shareholders to share in the surplus of the underwriting fund with the policyholders at a pre-agreed ratio.

Allocation of Underwriting Surplus

Any surplus in the underwriting fund may be utilized to build the reserve fund to meet the underwriting needs during a deficit, or it may also be used to repay the Takaful operator for any previous interest-free loan or Qard Hasan. If the surplus is distributed amongst the policyholders, according to AAOIFI regulations the following methods are used for allocation.

1. Allocate surplus to policyholders in proportion to premium contributions irrespective of whether they have had any claims during the financial year or not.
2. Allocate surplus only to those policyholders who had no claims during the financial year in proportion to their premium contributions.

3. Allocate surplus to those policyholders who had no claims in proportion to premium contributions, as well as those who had claims and will receive the allocated distribution in proportion to premium contributions minus the amount they received as claim.
4. Allocate surplus between both policyholders and shareholders according to a preagreed ratio.

Management of Underwriting Deficit

If, instead of a surplus, the underwriting fund has a deficit at the end of the financial year, then the AAOIFI proposes the following methods for covering the deficit.

1. The deficit may be made up from the reserve fund created from the policyholders' contributions, if such a fund exists.
2. A loan is made from any external financial institution and this loan is required to be repaid from future surpluses.
3. The policyholders are asked to meet the deficit by providing additional contributions in proportion to their original contributions.
4. Increased future premium contributions of policyholders on a pro-rata basis.
5. Meet the deficit by taking a benevolent loan called Qard Hasan from the Takaful operator and/or from the shareholders fund, which would be repaid from future surpluses.
6. The Retakaful or reinsurance companies may also be required to cover up the deficit amount, dependent on the Retakaful or reinsurance policy in which the said Takaful operator is participating.

The deficit may happen either in the underwriting fund or in the investment fund. It is usually the responsibility of the Takaful operator to meet any deficiency or loss in the underwriting fund. If the claims are greater than the contributions, then the Takaful operator may provide Qard Hasan to be repaid from future surpluses. If the deficit is due to negligence, misconduct or mismanagement of the Takaful operator, then the deficit will be met from the shareholders fund. On the other hand, if the deficit arises from the investment fund it is absorbed by the participants who are the capital providers. The Takaful operator as the entrepreneur cannot fix the deficit through Qard Hasan. If the deficit was caused by negligence, misconduct or mismanagement of the Takaful operator, then it would be covered from the shareholders fund.

CONVENTIONAL MUTUAL INSURANCE AND TAKAFUL

Takaful is very similar to conventional mutual insurance. In both conventional mutual insurance and Takaful, the insured or policyholders create a pool of funds by contributing their premiums; this fund belongs to the policyholders, who mutually insure each other. The fund is used to indemnify those policyholders who suffer any loss from the risks against which they have been insured. As such, there is no buying or selling of indemnities, which is prohibited in Islam. Any surplus or deficit in the underwriting fund is not commercial profit or loss, but belongs to the policyholders only. In case of a deficit, the members of the mutual fund or the Takaful fund are collectively responsible for payments of claims and may have to make additional contributions. In case of Takaful, a benevolent loan from the Takaful operator may also meet the deficit.

Conventional mutual insurances are governed by the secular law of the land and use a bilateral insurance policy, while the Takaful industry is governed (in addition to the secular law of the land) by Shariah law. Takaful utilizes the Wakala and Mudaraba concepts and unilateral contracts based on Tabarru or donations. The mutual fund could be invested in any kinds of assets, while the Takaful fund is required to be invested only in Shariah-compliant assets.

The conventional insurance industry originally started as a mutual, where the capital is owned by the policyholders who are both the insured and the insurer. Many of the mutual insurance companies have been converting over the years to limited liability commercial insurance companies, issuing their shares to the public. Some of the reasons for this changeover are that these mutual insurance companies needed additional capital to support their expansion plans, to increase in size, since this is very important in the global insurance industry, and regulatory requirements related to capital adequacy and solvency also push the need for additional capital.

SIMILARITIES AND DIFFERENCE BETWEEN TAKAFUL AND CONVENTIONAL INSURANCE

Similarities

The objectives of both insurance and Takaful are the same, to provide protection for the policyholders or participants against any financial loss arising from risky unexpected events. The contributions in the form of premiums in the case of insurance and Tabarru donations in the case of Takaful are made at the onset of the contract and the resultant coverage. The insured or policyholder must have a legitimate insurable interest in the risk against which the cover is being provided; that is they must be liable to suffer financial loss when the insured event occurs.

Differences

Table 10.2 summarizes the differences between conventional insurance and Takaful.

TABLE 10.2   Differences between conventional insurance and Takaful

Feature	Conventional insurance	Takaful
Source of law and regulations	Sources of laws and regulations are man-made and set by State, called the law of the land. They are based on common law principles. No religious law has any influence.	Sources of law are based upon the Quran and Sunnah. The regulations are derived from the Islamic Shariah law and based on the principles of Islamic contracts. Additionally, the Takaful industry is also subject to the governing law of the land.

(Continued)

TABLE 10.2   (*Continued*)

Feature	Conventional insurance	Takaful
Shariah prohibitions	Shariah prohibitions have no influence.	Shariah prohibitions of Riba, Gharar and Maysir need to be strictly followed.
Overseeing body	A technical committee oversees the operations of the insurance company.	The SSB oversees Shariah compliance of the Takaful operator, a technical committee may be an additional overseeing body.
Type of contract	The insurance contract is a bilateral exchange contract of sale and purchase, where the insurer or insurance company sells the risk protection and the policyholder or insured buys it.	Takaful is a combination of several contracts. The participants contribute their premiums based on the Tabarru contract or donation. The relationship with the participants and the Takaful operator is based on the Wakala or agency contract and the Mudaraba contract, depending on the type of Takaful model being applied. Moreover, in case of governmental, social or charitable use of Takaful, the Waqf contract may also be used.
Parties to contract	There are two main parties in conventional insurance, the policyholder or insured and the insurance company or insurer. The policyholders play no role in guaranteeing anyone other than themselves when they pay the premium.	In Takaful there are many parties. The participants who mutually insure each other and as such are both the insured and the insurer, plus the Takaful operator who is not the insurer but is responsible for managing the Takaful funds and the underwriting operations.
Enforceability of the contract	The insurance contract is binding on the insurer only, who is obliged to meet the legal claim if made, and not on the insured. The policy is enforceable only after the first premium is paid.	The Takaful contract is binding on all parties as soon as the contract is accepted. The contract enforces the participants to mutually indemnify each other and the Takaful operator to manage the Takaful operations in the most effective and efficient manner.

TABLE 10.2 (*Continued*)

Feature	Conventional insurance	Takaful
Basis of establishment	The insurance company is established solely for commercial purposes. The company aims to achieve the highest possible profit, so profit maximization is its main goal.	The Takaful company is established mainly for mutual cooperation amongst its members. The aim of the Takaful operations is community wellbeing, provision of affordable risk protection amongst the participants, making them self-reliant and self-sustainable rather than making any profit.
Insured–insurer relationship	There is a clear insured–insurer relationship. The interests of the policyholders and the insurance company are separate and different. The policyholders want risk protection while the company is interested in earning a profit.	Takaful operations do not include the insured–insurer relationship. Participants act as both insured and insurer. The interests between policyholders and operator are appointed by participants and according to the model applied.
Initial capital	The initial capital of the insurance company is supplied by its owners, the shareholders.	The initial capital of the Takaful company is supplied by the participants as their premiums when it operates as a licensed body or if it operates as a company it could be supplied by its shareholders, but the underwriting fund still comes from the participants' contributions.
Responsibility for providing protection	Insurance companies provide protection to policyholders in return for a premium. The policyholders have no relationship amongst themselves.	Participants are responsible for protecting each other through the Tabarru or donation. The role of the Takaful operator is only to manage the Takaful operations on behalf of the participants.

TABLE 10.2   *(Continued)*

Feature	Conventional insurance	Takaful
Premium contribution	The policyholders pay the premium to the insurance company and once paid it is the insurance company's income and as such belongs to their shareholders. In return, the insurance company bears the risk of compensating policyholders if the uncertain event happens.	The policyholders or participants pay the premium as Tabarru or donation into the underwriting fund, which mutually indemnifies all participants against any potential risk. The underwriting fund belongs to the participants and not the Takaful company, and is maintained separate from the shareholders fund.
Payment procedure of the premium	The premium is calculated based on the probability of the risky event happening and the amount of compensation claimed.	In case of Takaful, though the premiums are paid as a donation into a common fund by which the participants indemnify each other, the amount of premium contribution depends on the probability of the risky event happening and the amount of compensation claimed.
Premium forfeiture	The premium may be forfeited if utmost good faith is breached. If the risky event for which the premium provided cover does not happen, it is not returned, and this may lead to Gharar and Maysir.	The premium cannot be forfeited in the Takaful operations, since it is the capital of the underwriting fund and was given as a donation. In case of surplus in the underwriting fund it may be returned to participants.
Liability of insurer/operator	The insurance company is liable to pay the legitimate claims of the insured from the insurance funds or from the shareholders fund even at a loss.	The Takaful operator is liable to efficiently manage the Takaful funds and pay the legitimate claims from the underwriting fund and, if necessary, provide Qard Hasan in case of a deficit. Payment of losses can also be met through mutual contribution of the participants.

TABLE 10.2 (*Continued*)

Feature	Conventional insurance	Takaful
Investment of the funds	Investment of the funds owned by the insurance company is its own decision, with no involvement of the policyholders and no restriction (moral, religious or otherwise) except for those imposed by the regulators for prudential reasons.	The Takaful operator is obliged to invest the underwriting and investment funds as per Shariah guidelines, ensuring the avoidance of Riba, Gharar and Maysir, along with the prudence required by the regulators.
Right to determine the beneficiary	In most insurance contracts the insured and the beneficiary are the same. Life insurance does require identification of a separate beneficiary, since it also covers premature death. The insured has the right to nominate anyone they prefer.	In most Takaful contracts the participants are also the beneficiaries. Though in case of family Takaful, the Islamic alternative to life insurance, they can only nominate close family members as beneficiary.
Right to surplus of the underwriting operations and its distribution	All surplus of the underwriting operations, which is the excess of premium remaining after meeting the claims, constitutes the profit of the insurance company. It stays with the insurance company and does not go back to the insured.	Any surplus in the underwriting fund belongs to the participants, though since it was given as a donation it may be retained in the fund for future use or be diverted to a reserve fund or may be returned to the participants pro-rata to their original contribution. The Takaful operator earns fees from this fund. Any profit in the investment fund would be shared with the shareholders if the Mudaraba principle was applied.
Deficit of the underwriting operations and the transfer of loss	The insurance company is completely responsible for making up any deficit in the underwriting funds and any loss is transferred to the shareholders.	The deficit can be met from funds saved in the reserve fund, or from a benevolent loan from the Takaful operator or additional contributions from the participants. Losses are the sole responsibility of the participants.

TABLE 10.2   (*Continued*)

Feature	Conventional insurance	Takaful
Reserve fund	The insurance company may maintain a reserve fund for its own operational efficiency. This would have no link to the policyholders.	In Takaful operations the participants may choose to build the reserve fund from the underwriting surplus over the years, and this would be utilized in case of a deficit rather than collecting additional premiums.
Taxes	Insurance companies are liable to pay local, State and federal taxes.	Takaful operations are liable to pay any applicable local, State and federal taxes and also obliged to pay annual Zakat. In Muslim countries, the Zakat could be considered as part of the taxes.
Termination of contract	A lapse in premium payment or any kind of breach of utmost good faith would result in the termination of the contract and make the policy invalid. All reserves and surpluses in the underwriting activities would belong to the shareholders.	A lapse of premium payment does not make the policy invalid. Reserves and surpluses of the underwriting activities need to be returned to participants if the Takaful operations are dissolved.

RETAKAFUL

Retakaful is the Islamic alternative to reinsurance. Reinsurance basically means insurance for insurance companies. Insurance companies deal with large portfolios of risk and to protect themselves they buy reinsurance from large insurance companies or companies specialized in providing reinsurance only. These companies are basically underwriting the risks of the smaller insurance companies.

In the case of Retakaful, the individual Takaful operators are the participants, who contribute their agreed premiums to a common pool of underwriting fund to mutually protect each other. The operator of this underwriting fund is the Retakaful company which insures all the risks of the Takaful operators. To be accepted by Islamic Shariah law, Retakaful contracts are also required to be Shariah compliant and devoid of Riba, Gharar and Maysir. Their operations are very similar to those of the Takaful operators.

The global Takaful industry is still in the development stage, and there are very few Retakaful operators. Those available are very small and hence not very reliable. The Retakaful companies play a very important role when, due to unforeseen events, many

Takaful operators are required to meet large numbers of claims from their participants and they themselves could suffer from deficits or losses, and may even be financially incapable of meeting the claims made on them. As mentioned earlier, since most of the current Retakaful companies are small, their capital is not sufficient to achieve an 'A' rating, which is essential for reinsurance purposes. Owing to this extreme shortage, Islamic scholars have allowed Takaful companies to reinsure themselves with conventional reinsurance companies in the absence of Retakaful companies, with certain precautionary measures taken to remove or reduce any non-Shariah-compliant funds or income from the process. This process though is not free from controversy, and some Shariah scholars do not agree with it.

Retakaful operations have both similarities and differences with reinsurance, as discussed in Kettel (2011) and listed below.

Similarities Between Retakaful and Reinsurance

1. The regular insurance or the regular Takaful companies are the policyholders of the Retakaful or reinsurance companies.
2. In both cases, the objective to participate in reinsurance or Retakaful is due to the excessive risk an insurance or Takaful company takes in its underwriting activities for the policyholders, and to ensure that they can meet the claims even in case of major disasters that lead to excessive losses of the policyholders.
3. Only the insurance company or the Takaful company has the right to claim compensation from the reinsurance or Retakaful company; the original policyholders of the insurance or Takaful company have no rights on the reinsurance company or Retakaful operator.
4. Both the reinsurance company and the Retakaful operator are obliged to meet the claims of the insurance company or the Takaful company as per the reinsurance or Retakaful contract.

Differences Between Retakaful and Reinsurance

Table 10.3 lists the differences between the Retakaful and reinsurance industries.

TABLE 10.3   Differences between reinsurance and Retakaful

Features	Reinsurance	Retakaful
Regulations	Operates under the insurance regulations of the land as well as other financial regulations, including any from the central bank as well as common law.	Operations need to comply not only with the insurance regulations and other financial requirements (including any from the central bank or the common law of the land), but also need to comply with Islamic Shariah law.

(Continued)

TABLE 10.3   (*Continued*)

Features	Reinsurance	Retakaful
Shariah Supervisory Board	Operates under the supervision of the regulatory bodies discussed above only.	In addition to the supervision of the regulatory bodies discussed above, it is also under the supervision of the SSB which is the final authority on the legitimacy of operations of the Retakaful operator.
Investment of the underwriting fund and the reserves	The amounts in the underwriting fund and in the reserve fund can be invested in any income-generating product with due diligence.	The amounts in the underwriting fund and in the reserve fund can be invested only in Shariah-compliant products which need to be free of Riba in addition to basic due diligence.
Premiums	The premiums paid by the insurance companies are the price paid to purchase reinsurance protection and any amounts left over after paying claims belongs to the reinsurance company.	The premiums paid by the Takaful operators are in the form of Tabarru or donations to mutually indemnify each other; the Retakaful operator is only the manager of this fund. Any amounts left over after paying claims belong to the participating Takaful operators and are either retained in the reserves or distributed to the participating Takaful operators after paying the Retakaful operator its share of the profit or its agency fee, depending on the insurance model applied in the relationship.

KEY TERMS AND CONCEPTS

Aquila	Conventional insurance	Hybrid model
Bedouin	Family Takaful	Indemnity
Beneficiary	Fidya	Insurable interest
Clear financial segregation	General Takaful	Insurance claim

Insurance premium	Reinsurance	Underwriting deficit
Insured	Retakaful	Underwriting surplus
Insurer	Taawun	Utmost good faith
Kafalah	Tabarru	Wakala model
Mudaraba model	Takaful	Waqf model
Mutual insurance	Takaful model	
Participants	Takaful operator	

CHAPTER SUMMARY

Takaful is the Shariah-compliant alternative to conventional insurance. Though Muslims believe all that happens is the will of Allah, they are encouraged to avoid unnecessary risk and to do all to reduce or remove risk. Conventional insurance contains Riba, Gharar and Maysir, and Takaful contracts are designed to be free of them. Takaful is based on cooperative risk sharing, where the participants guarantee each other. Meanwhile the Takaful operator is responsible for managing the Takaful operations.

The Shariah rules and general principles guiding Takaful contracts and characteristics include mutual assistance, premiums as donation, compliance with Shariah law, clear financial segregation between the Takaful fund and the shareholders fund, operations of Takaful under the special conditions of specialty, partnership, investment and management, the Takaful contract having significant insurable interest, indemnity and involving premiums and claims.

Evidence of Takaful was there during the time of the Prophet in practices of Aquila and Fidya, as well as in trade and social welfare. During the 18th and 19th centuries the legal basis and early forms of Takaful were developed. During the 20th century various meetings and conferences of Shariah scholars and industry professionals took Takaful further, and the first Takaful company (Islamic Insurance Company) was set up in Sudan in 1979, followed by others set up in the Middle East, South-East Asia, Europe and the USA. In the 21st century the industry has moved further, with the emergence of Retakaful in major European reinsurance companies and regulation and standardization efforts made by the IFSB and AAOIFI. Major challenges faced by the Takaful industry today are the lack of interest and awareness amongst the Muslim community, lack of consensus and Takaful knowledge amongst the Shariah scholars, lack of product innovation, regulatory problems in non-Muslim countries and minimal Retakaful capacities.

Like conventional insurance, general and family Takaful are the main types of contract available. The Takaful structure resembles that of mutual insurance, with two tiers. The Takaful operator is a licensed body or limited liability company that manages the Takaful activities and the underwriting and investment funds, which are owned by the Takaful policyholders. Takaful operations are designed around four types of model: Wakala, Mudaraba, Wakala–Mudaraba hybrid and Waqf–Wakala–Mudaraba. The underwriting surplus or deficit and the technical provisions related to them are also an important part of the Takaful management, and specific regulations to deal with them have been provided by the AAOIFI.

Takaful is like conventional insurance with respect to risk protection objectives, premium contributions and specific coverage in case of financial loss. Takaful differs from conventional insurance in the areas of sources of law, prohibitions, overseeing body, contract type, parties and enforceability, the basis of the establishment of the organization, insured–insurer relationship, initial capital and responsibilities of risk protection, also with respect to premiums, liabilities, investments, choice of beneficiary, surplus and deficit handling, reserve fund, taxes and termination of contract.

Retakaful is the Islamic alternative to reinsurance, which is insurance for insurance companies. Minimal capacities exist for Retakaful, and major conventional reinsurance companies are serving the need. Owing to a shortage of Retakaful, this is allowed by many scholars.

END OF CHAPTER QUESTIONS AND ACTIVITIES

Discussion Questions

1. Define the concept of Takaful.
2. Muslims believe everything happens by Allah's will. Will they be interested in buying insurance or Takaful?
3. Why is conventional insurance not Shariah compliant?
4. Explain what Taawun and Tabarru are in the context of Takaful.
5. Discuss the parties in a Takaful contract.
6. Describe the important Shariah rules and the general principles that guide the Takaful contracts and their characteristics.
7. What does clear financial segregation of the Takaful fund and the shareholders fund mean?
8. Discuss the four key conditions of Takaful operations.
9. Discuss the chronology of development of Takaful from the time of the Prophet until current times.
10. What evidence of Takaful was seen in the Muslim world during the time of the Prophet in Arabia?
11. What are the main types of Takaful offered by the industry?
12. Describe the characteristics of general Takaful and the common risk coverage included under this.
13. What is family Takaful? Which conventional insurance product does it aim to substitute?
14. Explain the types of family Takaful the industry currently offers.
15. What are the differences between family Takaful and life insurance?
16. Discuss the operational structure of the Takaful contract.
17. What is the underwriting ratio?
18. What are the main Takaful models?
19. Discuss the Wakala model.
20. Discuss the Mudaraba model.
21. Discuss the Wakala–Mudaraba hybrid model.

22. Discuss the Waqf–Wakala–Mudaraba model.
23. Compare the various Takaful models.
24. What does the underwriting surplus or deficit mean?
25. How is the Takaful surplus or deficit calculated?
26. Discuss the AAOIFI recommended measures to deal with an underwriting surplus.
27. Discuss the AAOIFI recommended measures to deal with an underwriting deficit.
28. Compare Takaful with mutual insurance.
29. Compare Takaful with conventional insurance.
30. What is Retakaful?
31. What are the similarities between Retakaful and reinsurance?
32. What are the differences between Retakaful and reinsurance?
33. The Middle East Finance Group (MEFG) is planning to set up an insurance company. The BOD need to make the following decisions – provide answers to them as an Islamic finance expert.
    a. What are the Takaful models available to MEFG?
    b. Which model do you suggest for MEFG? Briefly explain the model.
    c. Which model is most popular in the Middle East?
34. Malaysia Islamic Insurance Company uses the Wakala model of Takaful. Draw the diagram of the model and label it clearly. In the Wakala contract of insurance, who is the principal and who is the agent? Briefly discuss any two operating features of the Takaful contract.
35. London Takaful Company uses the pure Mudaraba model of Takaful. Draw the diagram of the model and label it clearly. In the Mudaraba contract of insurance, who is the Rab al Maal and who is the Mudarib?

Multiple Choice Questions

Circle the letter next to the most accurate answer.
1. Takaful is the Shariah-compliant alternative to:
   a. Bonds
   b. Fixed deposit
   c. Insurance
   d. Mutual fund
2. Takaful involves:
   a. Mutual assistance
   b. Mutual responsibility
   c. Mutual protection
   d. All of the above
3. A conventional insurance company:
   a. Provides protection against specific risks to its policyholders
   b. Is owned by its shareholders who receive any underwriting surplus
   c. Can invest in interest-bearing products
   d. All of the above
4. Which one below is not a unique characteristic of Takaful?
   a. Cooperative risk sharing
   b. Profit and loss sharing with owners
   c. Clear financial segregation between policyholder and shareholder funds
   d. Shariah-compliant procedures

5. The premiums collected in Takaful are:
    a. Donations provided for mutual guarantee of all participants
    b. Paid for specific risk coverage of the specific policyholder
    c. Always belong to the participants and any surplus needs to be returned to them
    d. All of the above
6. Which of the below income of the Takaful operator will not be Shariah compliant?
    a. Wakala fee
    b. Profit share from the investment funds
    c. Fixed percentage return from the investment funds
    d. Incentive fee for good performance
7. Which Takaful model is called the hybrid model?
    a. The Wakala–Mudaraba model
    b. The Mudaraba–Musharaka model
    c. The Wakala model
    d. The Waqf–Wakala–Mudaraba model
8. The Wakala fee should cover which expenses of the Takaful operator as recommended by the IFSB?
    a. Management expenses
    b. Distribution costs, any payments to intermediaries
    c. Margin of operational profit for the Takaful operator
    d. All of the above
9. General Takaful covers all the below except:
    a. Education
    b. Fire
    c. Permanent disability
    d. Employers' liability
10. Health Takaful is an example of:
    a. Family Takaful
    b. General Takaful
    c. Social welfare Takaful
    d. Government Takaful
11. Family Takaful is of three types. Which of the following is not one of them?
    a. Ordinary collaboration
    b. Collaboration with savings
    c. Special collaboration
    d. Collaboration based on specific groups
12. Which type of family Takaful would be the best substitute for conventional group life insurance?
    a. Collaboration based on specific groups
    b. Ordinary collaboration
    c. Extraordinary collaboration
    d. Collaboration with savings

13. The AAOFI has determined the manner of distribution of Takaful surplus. Which of the following is not one of them?
    a. Allocation of surplus to all shareholders and policyholders in a pre-agreed ratio
    b. Allocation of surplus only among policyholders who have not made any claims during the financial period
    c. Allocation of surplus to all policyholders irrespective of whether they had any claim or not
    d. Allocation of surplus to all employees of the Takaful operator
14. The AAOIFI has determined the way to make up the Takaful deficit. Which of the following is not one of them?
    a. From the reserve fund created by policyholders
    b. By borrowing from the shareholders fund to be paid back from future surpluses
    c. By issuing new shares to raise funds
    d. By increasing future premium contributions of policyholders on a pro-rata basis
15. In current times, Shariah scholars:
    a. Allow Takaful operators to purchase policies with conventional reinsurance companies whenever needed
    b. Allow Takaful operators to purchase policies with conventional reinsurance companies under certain conditions only
    c. Do not allow Takaful operators to purchase policies with conventional reinsurance companies under any condition
    d. Allow Takaful operators to purchase policies with conventional reinsurance companies only once a year

True/False Questions

Write T for true and F for false next to the statement.
1. Takaful is the Islamic alternative to conventional insurance.
2. Takaful involves mutual assistance, mutual responsibility and mutual management of the finances.
3. Policyholders in Takaful are only the insured and not the insurer.
4. Takaful policyholders donate their contribution as premiums to a common pool for joint guaranteeing of all members of the pool.
5. Riba, Gharar and Maysir are not as strictly prohibited in Takaful as they are in Islamic banking.
6. The Takaful operator always shares in the surplus of the underwriting fund.
7. Shariah law does not allow the Takaful company to act only as an operator, managing the underwriting and investment funds on behalf of the participants.
8. Takaful companies operate to provide cooperative risk protection but are not concerned about profit-making at all.
9. A policyholder in conventional insurance pays a premium for risk coverage for themselves and has no concern about risk coverage of other policyholders.
10. Takaful operators and conventional insurance have no difference in the types of instruments they can choose for investment.
11. In Takaful the profit from the investment fund is shared between the Takaful operator and the participants based on a pre-agreed ratio.
12. The Mudaraba model of Takaful is the most popular in current times.

13. In the Wakala model, the Takaful operator only manages the underwriting and investment funds on behalf of the participants and bears no risk.
14. In the hybrid model, underwriting operations utilize the Wakala concept and investment operations use the Mudaraba concept.
15. The AAOIFI recommends the Wakala–Mudaraba model for Takaful companies.
16. Family Takaful of the ordinary collaboration type is where the policyholders pay premium donations to compensate any member, including themselves, in the event of any misfortune or disaster (or in case of death to pay the beneficiary).
17. Deficit occurs when the Takaful claims of the participants are less than the pool of funds for underwriting activities.
18. Both conventional insurance companies and Takaful operators minimize their risks from the underwriting operations by insuring themselves with a reinsurance or Retakaful company.
19. Shariah scholars absolutely prohibit Takaful operators from reinsuring with conventional reinsurance companies.
20. Most existing Retakaful operators are much smaller than most reinsurance companies.

CHAPTER 11

Islamic Investments and Sukuks

Learning outcomes

Upon completion of this chapter, you should be able to:

1. Discuss the conventional as well as the Islamic investment markets and products.
2. Describe Shariah-compliant stocks and the process of Shariah screening.
3. Explain Islamic asset management and the types of Islamic investment funds, including Islamic REITs.
4. Compare Islamic investments with their conventional counterparts and discuss the risks, challenges and Shariah governance and supervision related to Islamic investments.
5. Define Sukuks and their characteristics.
6. Describe Ijara, Istisna, Salam, Murabaha, Mudaraba and Musharaka Sukuks.
7. Discuss the controversies related to Sukuks, as well as their ratings, trading and comparison with conventional bonds.

INVESTMENT MARKETS AND PRODUCTS

The global financial system is a complex system of products, markets, institutions, transactions, legal systems, rules and regulations. A major anchor of the financial system is the financial intermediation by which money flows from those who have a surplus of it to those who have a shortage in an efficient manner and with benefits for both parties, as well as the intermediaries in the middle. The financial intermediaries include banks, as well as credit unions, insurance companies, investment companies, finance companies, brokers, stock exchanges, mutual funds, pension funds, etc. Other participants directly involved with the financial system are governments and their treasury, central banks and business corporations. The main markets involved in these movements of funds are the money market and the capital market. The key difference between these two markets is the period of the transaction. Money markets are for the short term – up to a year. Capital markets are for the longer term – more than a year. Parties with a fund shortage have two main options. Firstly, they can go directly to those with surplus funds and interested to invest these funds in the market, either the money market or the capital market. Secondly, they can borrow funds indirectly from financial intermediaries like banks.

The surplus fund owners in the conventional financial markets, therefore, have the option of investing mainly in the money and capital markets. Additionally, there are the commodity, foreign exchange and derivative markets. These markets all are further subdivided into the primary market where new securities are issued and the secondary market where the securities are traded after initial issue. Briefly, these markets can be described as follows.

- **Money market.** Investors and borrowers access the money market to invest or borrow for the short term. The period varies from overnight to a year. In most countries, primary and secondary money market transactions take place over-the-counter (OTC) using electronic measures, though some transactions happen at the stock exchanges. The conventional money market is an interest-based system used by financial institutions like banks to manage their asset and liability structure. Banks use the money market to manage their liquidity, adjusting the mismatch of assets and liabilities on their balance sheet by either investing their excess liquid funds in the money market for a short term or borrowing short term from the money market to manage a lack of liquidity. In addition to the banks, corporations and governments also utilize the money market for short-term investments and borrowing. Large corporations, with high credit rating, raise the required funds by issuing commercial paper, while governments issue bills. Investors can choose the money market instruments available to them as per the different risk levels, returns and maturity they prefer. The central banks also utilize the money market for their monetary policies and to stabilize the markets by influencing liquidity levels and short-term benchmark interest rates. They operate in the market by buying and selling relevant securities and funding banks to meet their short-term deficits.
- **Capital market.** Most instruments in this market have a maturity of more than a year. The transactions are both exchange traded and OTC. This market is further divided into the debt market (bonds), equity markets (shares) and markets for structured or hybrid products.
- **Commodity market.** This special market allows investors to trade in commodities, including precious metals. This market is utilized by traders and hedgers, and operates both via the exchanges and OTC.
- **Foreign exchange market.** Foreign currency transactions are conducted in this market, which are both spot and forward transactions. The foreign exchange transactions are only OTC, and executed in a variety of global currencies.
- **Derivative market.** This market involves special financial instruments whose values are derived from an underlying instrument that is traded in any of the other markets discussed above. The four main instruments traded in the derivative markets are forwards, futures, options and swaps, which deal with future delivery instead of spot delivery as done in the other markets above.

The financial markets serve a variety of functions for various players in the markets. Two main functions are providing savings and borrowing facilities for those with a surplus or deficit of funds. Another function is providing an efficient, effective, as well as trustworthy and fast payment mechanism for goods and services. The financial markets are a means for individuals and institutions to store wealth with the expectation of income and growth in value. Sometimes the savers or investors may own financial instruments but temporarily need ready cash to meet certain needs, and the financial markets can provide this liquidity also. The financial systems assist in risk reduction and protection for a variety of risks faced by individuals and institutions. Finally, governments use the financial markets to execute various policies to stabilize the economy and keep inflation under control.

ISLAMIC INVESTMENTS

The Islamic investment markets also consist of the money and capital markets, as well as the foreign exchange and commodities markets. The markets, intermediaries and functions of the Islamic investment markets are quite like those in the conventional case, although the instruments in these markets and the transactions taking place are required to meet Shariah compliance in addition to meeting the financial needs of various participants in the markets.

To be Shariah compliant the Islamic financial system and its products and procedures need to be designed to ensure they are devoid of Islamic prohibitions. Islam prohibits all forms of interest, whether simple or compound, fixed or floating, nominal or excessive; they are all Haram or prohibited and treated in the same manner under Shariah law. As such, all forms of investment under the Shariah compliance rule need to be free of interest or Riba, and these products should be able to make a profit or loss instead of the guaranteed interest income. All forms of speculation, including uncertainty or Gharar and gambling or Maysir, are also not allowed in Islam. Commonly used conventional investment products like bonds, bills, certificates of deposit, preferred stocks, warrants, derivatives, repos or buy-backs are not allowed in Islamic investment.

Islamic investments, therefore, are required to avoid excessive risk, uncertainty and speculation. As such, speculative conventional contracts like short selling and derivatives are prohibited. Short selling involves selling an instrument before it has been purchased, with the expectation that prices will go down. All investment contracts need to meet the Shariah requirements of a clear and unambiguous contract. Moreover, Shariah-compliant investments are also required to be socially responsible and ethical. Specifically, Shariah prohibits all forms of gambling, alcohol, pork, pornography and other unsocial or immoral activities, and encourages the fulfilment of various social responsibilities like Zakat, which is compulsory charity, Sadaqah, which is voluntary charity, Waqf or charitable endowment and Islamic cooperative insurance called Takaful.

Money Markets – Islamic Perspective

Money markets are extremely important, whether in the conventional or the Islamic financial system, for monetary stability and economic development. Central banks manage the liquidity issues of financial institutions like banks through reserves and short-term borrowing or investments in the money market. Islam prohibits the treatment of money as a commodity; it can only be considered as a medium of exchange. For banks to deal with their liquidity challenges, an efficient interbank market is required with very short maturities varying between overnight and a week. Developing a vibrant Shariah-compliant money market that enables market players to perform similar functions to those of conventional markets, without interest-based products or any form of Gharar or Maysir, is a major challenge of the modern Islamic finance industry. Islamic finance encourages developing financial instruments that are based on real assets such as certificates of Murabaha, Mudaraba and Wakala, as well as Ijara Sukuks. Islamic money markets extensively utilize the process of securitization of assets in a portfolio, and its risks and returns are assigned to the investors as owners of the securities, pro-rata to their ownership. These securities are traded both on exchanges and OTC. For the Islamic money market to be successful it needs the support of the government, the central bank and other regulatory bodies to ensure that it meets the needs of the participants and that the securities are Shariah compliant. An active money market indicates to the central banks the volume of open market operations that are required to ensure liquidity and monetary stability.

Thus, Islamic money market instruments are Shariah compliant, structured on assets, including both debt and equity, and require the approval of the financial regulators as well as of the SSB. On the other hand, conventional money market instruments are structured on debt only and require approval of the financial regulators only. Islamic treasury products are mostly in the form of deposit and investment instruments, and the instruments may have an underlying contract of Murabaha, Mudaraba or Wakala. Instruments currently used in the Islamic money market include Mudaraba-based accounts, negotiable Islamic debt certificates, Islamic treasury bills, Islamic accepted bills, commodity Murabaha, Islamic commercial paper, Salam and Ijara-based Sukuks.

Capital Markets – Islamic Perspective

Islamic capital markets include equity markets and asset-linked securities market, especially Sukuks. The Islamic capital market instruments are also required to be Shariah compliant and free of Riba, Gharar and Maysir. Major participants of this market are investment banks, brokers, fund managers and asset management institutions. The main international Islamic regulators involved in developing, regulating and promoting the Islamic capital markets are the IIFM, the IFSB and the AAOIFI.

Shariah-Compliant Stocks   A share is a unit of ownership that represents an equal proportion of a company's capital. It entitles the shareholders to an equal claim on the company's profit or growth, either through dividend or capital gains, as well as equal obligation in the case of losses. Two major types of shares are ordinary shares or common stock and preference shares. The main difference between the two types is with respect to the right to vote, which only ordinary shareholders have and the fixed dividend, which only preference shareholders have.

Equity or shares in a company is not debt and hence does not have the complication of Riba. Yet the shares of all companies are not acceptable as Shariah compliant. It is very difficult to find companies that are completely free from Shariah-non-compliant financial transactions. To deal with this significant investment challenge, the

Shariah scholars and the international Islamic regulatory and standard setting bodies have developed more flexible procedures to be able to identify some companies that can be considered within reasonable Shariah compliance. This process is called the **Shariah screening process for stock selection** and involves a set of guidelines that are provided to select such companies and identify Shariah-compliant stocks. The process has two stages.

Stage 1: Industry screening or business activity screening. This stage weeds out in general the companies that are in a Shariah-non-compliant industry or that are involved in activities that are against Shariah. The general guidelines for this screening are listed below.

1. Companies with mainly Halal business are separated from those that operate a non-Halal business like alcohol, pork, tobacco, gambling, prostitution, immoral media and entertainment, financial services based on Riba or interest, conventional insurance, stock broking or share trading in Shariah-non-compliant securities.
2. Select companies for investment that operate in local communities aimed to generate growth and prosperity.
3. Select companies for investment in socially and environmentally responsible companies.

Stage 2: Financial screening. This stage of the process evaluates the Shariah-non-compliant financial activities of the company. There are very few companies in the global markets that are fully Shariah compliant. The majority of Islamic scholars have identified a certain level of non-compliant financial activity as acceptable, provided the income earned from these companies is purified by donating the non-compliant proportion of income to charity. The guidelines for financial screening according to the AAOIFI standards are listed below.

1. The financial practice of the company, ideally, should be devoid of Riba, Gharar and Maysir, or any other prohibited commercial transactions. But in today's world conventional debt is so prevalent that Shariah scholars, after a lot of debate, have decided to allow some flexibility and declared acceptable debt ratios for selecting stocks for Islamic funds.
2. Conventional debt to total assets should be less than 30%.
3. Cash and interest-bearing deposits to total assets should also be less than 30%.
4. Accounts receivable to total assets should be less than 45%.
5. The total interest income and income from non-compliant activities should be less than 5% of total revenues.
6. Shariah-compliant investments should be in actual stock and not on a paper index.
7. Any dividend income earned by the company should go through the process of Shariah-compliant income purification.

Dealing with Non-compliant Stocks

With global markets changing and with mergers and acquisitions, Shariah-compliant stocks may become non-compliant, for example when a conglomerate with Shariah-compliant businesses acquires a subsidiary that deals with non-compliant business or which fails on the financial screening. Besides merger and acquisition, a company previously approved after industry and financial screening may change its area of business or its financial behaviour, making it unacceptable in the Shariah screening. In such cases, the following are recommended.

1. **Temporary non-compliance.** If the non-compliance appears to be unplanned and temporary, and the stock soon returns to compliance, the non-compliance is tolerated.
2. **Short-term non-compliance.** If the stock remains non-compliant for a brief period and then returns to compliance, the stock may be kept in the portfolio, but this non-compliance needs to be reported to the SSB and any income earned during the non-compliant period needs to be calculated and donated to charity to purify the income.
3. **Permanent non-compliance.** If it appears that the stock has become permanently non-compliant it needs to be sold off as unacceptable stock.

Purification of Income Distribution

Some scholars do not allow investment in stocks that involve any kind of conventional debt, while others allow such stocks with the condition that the income generated needs to be cleansed or purified in proportion to the Shariah-non-compliant activities. As such, any income that is interest or from any other non-compliant source is donated to charity. The view of Muslim jurists related to cleansing of capital gains is even more controversial. Some scholars feel that capital gains earning also needs to be purified by donating the proportion relevant to non-Shariah-compliant activities, while some scholars opine that no purification of capital gains is required since the company belongs to a Halal industry. Some scholars also allow the payment of Zakat as a measure of purifying the income.

Initially, Islamic equity funds were benchmarked against conventional indices like the Morgan Stanley Capital Index (MSCI). Over time, Islamic stock market indices were developed to provide benchmarks for Shariah-compliant investment in shares. Prominent Islamic indices include the Dow Jones Islamic Market Index, FTSC Global Islamic Index, S&P Global Investable Shariah Index, Kuala Lumpur Composite Index, Pakistan Meezan Islamic Fund, Global GCC Islamic Index, Jakarta Islamic Index, etc.

ISLAMIC ASSET AND FUND MANAGEMENT

An investment fund is a specialized firm into which many investors, individuals or corporations contribute a pool of funds to be managed professionally. The employees in the investment funds are professionals; they have a fiduciary responsibility towards the investors and their relationship is based on trust. An Islamic investment fund is a joint pool into which investors contribute their surplus money to be invested by professionals in accordance with Islamic Shariah guidance. The fund managers of an Islamic fund are responsible for ensuring Shariah compliance of the instruments and processes used to build and manage the fund, avoiding non-Halal industries like alcohol, pork, gambling, uncensored media and entertainment, pornography and other things Shariah clearly forbids.

According to the AAOIFI, 'Funds are investment vehicles, which are finally independent of the institutions that established them. Funds take the form of equal participating shares/units, which represent the shareholders/unitholders' share of the asset and entitlement to profit or losses. The Funds are managed based on either Mudaraba or agency contract'. The AAOIFI further elaborates that Shariah compliant Islamic investment funds are a form of collective investment, with the rights and duties of the participants clearly defined and restricted by the common interest of the participants, besides the Shariah objective.

Islamic investment funds started to appear from the late 1980s and the 1990s. Compared with the well-established investment funds in the conventional sector, these funds are still at a very early stage of development, and depend significantly on the experience and expertise of conventional fund managers. The development of the sector got a major boost after it received the ruling by the Islamic Fiqh Academy of the OIC providing standardization and guidance for the funds. As the Islamic investment sector is growing, demand for Shariah-compliant asset management and Islamic funds is also growing. According to Thomson Reuters (2017), assets invested in Islamic funds have reached USD60 billion and are forecast to reach at least USD77 billion by 2019, while the latent demand for Islamic funds is projected to grow to USD185 billion during the same period.

An investment portfolio is developed by investing in a variety of assets like shares, bonds, other securities, real estate, etc. as per the risk and return appetite of the participants of the fund. For the investment portfolio of an Islamic investment fund, the assets selected must be Shariah compliant, from Halal industries and need to be devoid of interest, and speculative activities involving Gharar or Maysir. The investments should not be unethical or unsocial. As such, an Islamic investment portfolio cannot use instruments like preferred stocks, warrants, treasury bonds and bills, certificates of deposit or derivatives. Additionally, an Islamic investment fund is not permitted to trade on margin or get involved in sale and repurchase agreements, that is repos and buy-backs. To avoid Gharar and Maysir, Islamic fund managers are not allowed to undertake excessive risks or speculations. The fund managers issue certificates of investment to investors, making them pro-rata owners of the fund, earning profit on a pro-rata basis.

Islamic Unit Trust or Mutual Fund

A unit trust or investment fund is a collective investment scheme in which many investors with similar financial goals, investment strategy and risk tolerance pool their surplus funds to invest in a large diversified portfolio of financial instruments, professionally managed on behalf of the investors. An Islamic unit trust is very similar, except that the portfolio would be built with Shariah-compliant instruments and the professional managers would be responsible for following Islamic guidelines in the procedures and management of the unit trust, in addition to following all due diligence for a regular unit trust. Unit trusts or investment funds can be open-ended or close-ended.

An open-ended unit trust is one with the authority to issue new units and redeem existing units at any time. The fund manager of such a unit trust publicly offers the units and any proceeds received are added to the collective fund. On the other hand, investors can purchase units in such unit trusts directly from the unit trust company or its authorized agent, and are able to sell back their units to the unit trust company at the existing market price, which fluctuates every day depending on the performance of the fund. A close-ended unit trust can issue a limited number of units only. Once the original investors have acquired these units, any subsequent buying and selling of units happens only on the secondary market – the stock exchange. An initial public offering (IPO) of a company's shares is a form of close-ended investment where the share purchaser provides their investments to the company for good and if at any point they want to sell their shares, they do not get their money back from the companies but rather go to the stock exchange and sell the shares at the current market price.

Investment funds are managed either actively or passively. In case of active management, the fund manager actively designs the portfolio and buys and sells actively to manage it. In case of passive management, the role of the fund manager is to design the fund as close to a chosen index as possible with the stocks included in the index; the fund's value then moves up or down with the index. The main benefit of investing in a mutual fund for investors is that they can diversify at relatively low cost with smaller investment amounts. Diverse types of mutual funds and Islamic mutual funds are available, as will be clear from the next segment of this chapter, developed to meet the different profiles of the investors, their risk and return appetite, time horizon, the amount available to invest and the liquidity they require. Other advantages include convenience of investment, professional management, transparent operations and supervision under governmental oversight. Disadvantages of investing in a mutual fund include the fees to be paid, sales charges (called load) that may be paid at the onset of the investment or when the investment is redeemed; some mutual funds may not require any load payment. Other disadvantages are that the investor may not be sure of how much income will be earned or will have far less say on the fund design and its updates.

A variation of the mutual fund is called the exchange traded fund (ETF). Mutual funds became very popular during the 1980s and 1990s and were priced based on the closing price of each day rather than priced during the day as trade moved. To deal with this limitation, ETF, which are also mutual funds, were created but were traded on the exchange like the shares of a company, with the price determined by market forces. ETFs have all the advantages of the mutual funds discussed above but additionally are highly tradable instruments. Shariah-compliant ETFs are called Islamic ETFs or I-ETFs. The first one listed was at the Istanbul Stock Exchange and was called the DJIM Turkey ETF.

Common Types of Islamic Investment Fund

Islamic investment funds can be divided into various types depending on the way they are structured.

- **Islamic debt fund.** Invested in fixed-income Islamic instruments like Murabaha, Ijara, Istisna or Salam, which are deferred payment sales contracts that yield a fixed income over a given period, thus providing stability to the income generated by the fund and shared by the investors in the fund after deducting all relevant expenses.
- **Islamic commodity fund.** In this case the fund manager uses the common pool of funds to purchase a variety of commodities that would be resold based on a deferred payment system and at a profit, which constitutes the main income of the fund and is distributed pro-rata amongst the investors after deducting all relevant expenses.

- **Ijara fund.** This fund is created by investing money in purchasing a pool of suitable physical assets that can then be leased out to a third party, who would be the ultimate user. The rentals earned from the lease or Ijara constitute the income of the fund, distributed amongst the investors of the fund after deducting all relevant expenses. This fund has slightly higher risk than the debt or fixed-income fund and higher returns are also expected.
- **Islamic equity fund.** The assets of the fund are invested mostly in shares, with a small amount possibly invested in cash and other fixed-income Islamic securities. The chosen shares would be Shariah screened, and this is the most common type of fund used by Islamic fund managers globally. The fund aims less for income from dividends and more for long-term growth and earnings through capital gains. An Islamic equity fund may be structured as a Mudaraba contract or a Musharaka contract. In the Mudaraba contract the investors of the fund are the Rab al Maal and the fund manager is the Mudarib, performing the managerial functions; in the Musharaka contract the fund investors and the fund manager are equity partners who own the assets of the fund to the extent of their financing ratio. Profit and losses are shared according to the proportion of capital invested in the fund, after deducting all relevant expenses.
- **Islamic balanced fund.** A mutual fund that invests its pool of money to purchase a combination of Shariah-screened shares, commodities and Islamic fixed-income instruments is called a Islamic balanced fund and provides investors in one common fund the goals of both short-term income and long-term growth and capital gains.
- **Islamic private equity.** Such a fund is created by investing in shares of private limited companies that are not traded on the stock exchange. The shares of such companies are usually owned by a few large individual or institutional investors. To belong to Islamic private equity these companies need to belong to the Halal industries and their operations need to be screened to be at the acceptable level of Shariah compliance.
- **Islamic venture capital.** Venture capital is financing provided to small, new and promising start-up businesses which have good entrepreneurial, managerial and technical skills, but lack financing. Investors may pool their money and structure a fund which invests in prospective ventures on a long-term basis but is not traded on exchanges. The ventures that receive funding and their operations have to be Shariah compliant.

Islamic Real Estate Investment Trusts

A real estate investment trust (REIT) is an investment vehicle which invests mostly in real estate. The regulatory requirement on the minimum percentage of assets in a REIT that should be real estate varies between jurisdictions. According to PriceWaterhouseCooper (2017), the minimum percentage of REIT income that should be generated from real estate, for example, is 75% in the UK and the USA while in Malaysia it is 50%, and the minimum distribution to investors in all three countries is 90%. The PWC REIT Report (2017) estimates the current market capitalization of REITs globally at USD1.7 trillion, up from USD734 billion in 2010, which is almost 230% growth.

Real estate investment could be through direct ownership of the real estate or through a single purpose company whose principal asset comprises real asset or items that relate to real estate, and whose main income is real estate rentals. Islamic REITs usually use Ijara contracts or Ijara–Istisna contracts. These are often designed as equity REITs, where investors may get proportional ownership of the underlying real estate and earn stable rent income. Islamic equity REITs are structured like an Ijara fund, the difference being that the Ijara fund has fixed maturity while that of the Islamic REIT (I-REIT) is long-term or ongoing. Like all other investment funds, the REITs and I-REITs are structured by individual investors placing their funds into a common pool, which is invested in a managed pool of real estate, generating income from renting, leasing and selling real estate. The income of the REIT or I-REIT net of all management expenses is distributed regularly amongst the investors pro-rata to their investment, including any capital gains generated by the fund.

Structured as limited companies, most REITs and I-REITs are listed on stock exchanges and those not listed are traded OTC as private REITs or I-REITs. According to their core function, REITs and I-REITs can be divided into (1) those that manage owned real estate, (2) those that provide financing for real estate owners or operators and (3) the hybrids that are involved in both types of function. The biggest advantage offered by REITs and I-REITs is the opportunity for investors to more effectively and efficiently diversify their real estate investment at a much lower amount compared with direct real estate investments, and to have a much higher liquidity since they are traded on the stock exchange and it is so much easier to sell the units of the REIT or I-REIT than to sell the actual property. Investors can also choose locations of REITS and I-REITs to achieve further diversification compared with their investments in other categories of instruments. REITs are usually treated differently for tax purposes and are exempt from corporate tax, provided 90% of the income is distributed to investors.

Similarities Between REITs and I-REITs

Table 11.1 lists the similarities between REITs and I-REITs.

TABLE 11.1   Similarities between REITs and I-REITs

Factors	Conventional REITs and I-REITs
Structure	REITs and I-REITs are both structured in the same manner, both invest mostly in real estate or real estate-linked assets and are required to have a trustee, a management company, property managers, valuations, etc. For REITs and I-REITs that are listed on the stock exchange, all their transactions need to follow relevant securities laws, guideline and rules. Meanwhile unlisted REITs and IREITs must ensure transactions are approved by the investors.
Size	Since investment is mostly in a portfolio of real estate, both need to have a significant size.
Tax treatment	Both types of REIT and I-REIT are treated similarly relating to corporate tax, stamp duty and capital gains tax.

TABLE 11.1 (*Continued*)

Factors	Conventional REITs and I-REITs
Distribution	A large part of the income realized from rental income, capital gains and other real estate-related income, often as high as 90%, is distributed amongst the investors pro-rata to their investment.
Investment in foreign real estate	This is allowed subject to strict regulations – considering the entry barriers, exit strategies, political, economic, operational, accounting and taxation issues, and other risk elements.

Differences Between REITs and I-REITs

Table 11.2 lists the differences between REITs and I-REITs.

TABLE 11.2 Differences between REITs and I-REITs

Factors	Conventional REITs	I-REITs
Regulatory framework	Involves the financial regulators for investment funds as well as the regulatory authorities related to real estate.	Involves the financial regulators for investment funds and real estate regulators, plus is regulated by Shariah law.
Shariah Supervisory Board	Not required.	Required.
Asset investment	No restrictions. Any real estate or real estate-linked asset can be invested in.	Any real estate or real estate-linked asset that is also Shariah compliant and used for Halal purposes can be invested in.
Rental restriction	No restriction on the tenant's nature of business as long as it is legal.	The tenant's business should be legal as well as Shariah compliant.
Financing instruments	Borrowing for assets of the fund is usually allowed up to a maximum percentage, usually around 50%. May vary in different jurisdictions, and all financing instruments are acceptable.	Borrowing for assets of the fund is usually allowed up to a maximum percentage, usually around 50%. May vary in different jurisdictions, and the financing instruments allowed must be Shariah compliant.
Insurance	All real estate included in the REIT must be protected with insurance, which can be Takaful or conventional insurance.	All real estate included in the I-REIT must be protected with insurance, which ideally should be Takaful. If Takaful is not available, conventional insurance may be used.

RISKS AND CHALLENGES INHERENT IN THE ISLAMIC CAPITAL MARKETS

Many risks faced by the Islamic capital markets are the same as in the conventional capital markets, although some may be different. Since interest or Riba is not allowed, Islamic capital markets do not face this major risk of the conventional markets. Some of the major risks facing the Islamic capital markets are as follows.

- **Market risk.** This risk is faced by the overall market, linked to any environmental factors like the economy, socio-political situation, etc.
- **Credit risk.** This risk is of a partner or customer failing to repay the due amount.
- **Foreign exchange risk.** This risk occurs when the relevant exchange rates have adverse effects on the capital market or the instrument under consideration.
- **Fiduciary risk.** This arises when the agent or Wakeel does not operate in the best interests of the principal.
- **Shariah non-compliance risk.** This risk is unique for the Islamic capital markets and does not exist in the conventional markets. Shariah non-compliance risk arises when financial instruments or procedures used in the capital markets have elements that go against Shariah rulings. This can happen for three common reasons: in the process of competing and copying conventional financial products or procedures; due to the influence of the conventional regulators or the court systems in non-Muslim or even Muslim countries sometimes; due to lack of Shariah scholars with significant knowledge and expertise in the areas of Islamic jurisprudence as well as in the disciplines of economics and finance.
- **Liquidity risk.** This is associated with temporary shortages of cash to meet short-term obligations and is a major issue for Islamic financial institutions due to the lack of Shariah-compliant short-term securities available in the market and the inability to utilize interest-based conventional products. Conventional investors use the overnight money market for very short-dated liquidity, yet there is no Shariah-compliant alternative for this.

The lack of Shariah-compliant instruments is a major challenge faced by fund managers in the Islamic capital markets and due to the inherent profit and loss-sharing mechanisms of Islamic financial instruments they may have greater risks compared with fixed-income instruments in the conventional markets. Conventional fund managers utilize derivatives like swaps, options, futures and forwards to minimize their risk exposure, which being Shariah non-compliant are not available to Islamic fund managers. Moreover, the secondary market for Islamic financial instruments is far less vibrant than the conventional markets, exposing Islamic fund managers to the risk of not being able to sell off instruments very quickly. Islamic fund managers are more prone to balance sheet mismatches since the Islamic money market is still in the developing stages and is not as active as the conventional money market. They may face higher cash outflows during downturns in the market when investors wish to liquidate their positions.

SHARIAH GOVERNANCE AND THE SHARIAH SUPERVISORY BOARD IN ISLAMIC INVESTMENT

One of the crucial reasons for investors to choose an Islamic fund is to be able to invest and earn in a manner acceptable to their religious beliefs and Shariah law, and as such investors need to be guaranteed about the Shariah compliance of the fund, its operations and income. It is highly recommended that the fund set up an SSB comprised of Shariah experts, or at least avail themselves of the services of a Shariah consulting firm to oversee the investment fund. The main job of the board is to set the compliance parameters before the fund builds up its portfolio. These parameters are clearly documented and shared with the fund's shareholders or investors. The legal responsibility for the fund's Shariah compliance rests with the BOD rather than with the SSB, since the latter is not involved in the day-to-day management and control of the fund. There is concern amongst international regulators about the conflict of interest between the fund manager and the SSB and to ensure proper adherence to both legal and Shariah regulations, the authority, roles and responsibilities of the SSB and of management need to be carefully outlined and segregated.

The Shariah experts' main functions are to ensure the fund's assets, operations and transactions are Shariah compliant, to monitor and oversee the purification of the portfolio from any Haram or non-permissible income or action, to prepare a Shariah compliance report, provide the necessary certificates and help the management of the fund understand and operate in a Shariah-compliant manner, by providing advice and training to staff and also advice on the Zakat and other social and charitable distributions. The BOD also helps identify appropriate charities to receive donations to purify non-compliant income and gains. The SSB or consultant should be able to operate independently of the management and without any kind of pressure.

Shariah supervision is an ongoing activity. The SSB, in consultation with the management, at regular intervals reviews the fund, its assets and transactions to ensure Shariah compliance is achieved and reports any breach of compliance and recommends solutions. The SSB also issues an annual Shariah audit of the financial statements.

COMPARISON OF ISLAMIC INVESTMENTS WITH CONVENTIONAL INVESTMENTS

Table 11.3 lists the differences between Islamic and conventional investments.

TABLE 11.3   Differences between Islamic and conventional investments

Features	Conventional investment	Islamic investment
Short-term interbank market	Mostly interest-based debt contracts are used.	Can only use Shariah-compliant contracts like Murabaha, Mudaraba and Wakala based on assets, equity and debt.
Risk allocation of the instruments	Risk transferred from seller to buyer.	Risk shared between the two parties.
Ownership of underlying assets	Instrument buyer does not have any ownership in the underlying assets.	Instrument buyer has ownership in the underlying assets.
Principal protection	Principal is usually protected irrespective of the value of the underlying assets.	Principal not protected but linked to the value of the underlying assets.
Price of the instrument	Based on expected yield, current interest rates and creditworthiness of the issuer.	Based on expected yield and market returns/market value of the underlying assets.

INTRODUCTION TO SUKUKS

A major product of the Islamic capital markets is the Sukuk, which can be described as an Islamic alternative to a conventional bond. The AAOIFI defines Sukuks as certificates of equal value representing undivided ownership shares in tangible assets, usufructs, services, specific projects or special investment activity (AAOIFI, 2008, p. 307). Meanwhile, according to the IFSB, another Islamic regulator, Sukuks are certificates representing proportional ownership in an undivided part of an underlying asset and the holder of the certificate has all the rights and obligations related to such asset (IFSB-2). The Islamic Fiqh Academy of the OIC declared the Sukuk to be a legitimate instrument.

In the 1st century, during the Umayyad Caliphate, there is evidence of Sukuk certificates being used as commodity coupons instead of cash payments to soldiers. During the mediaeval period they were used as the main instrument to transfer commercial payments between cities and reduce the use of cash, which was less safe. In current times, Sukuks are used in modern Islamic finance as an alternative funding source through asset securitization. To summarize, the Sukuk is a legal instrument, a financial certificate, which – unlike a conventional bond – needs an underlying asset in the form of ownership or lease agreement.

The Sukuk certificate provides ownership or beneficial interest in an asset or enterprise and is neither a share nor a bond but has characteristics of both. A bond is a contractual obligation of the issuer to pay bondholders a fixed interest, the coupon, on specified dates and the principle at maturity of the bond. As such, it is a debt instrument, the issuer being the borrower and the bondholder being the lender. In contrast, Sukuks are structured by setting up a special purpose vehicle (SPV) which acquires the underlying assets and issues financial claims in the form of tradable Shariah-compliant trust certificates to investors, providing them with undivided proportional ownership and the right to the Shariah-compliant income stream from the asset and any proceeds from the realization of the Sukuk assets. The Sukuk market grew phenomenally during the first decade of the 21st century. In 2011 a record-breaking USD84.4 billion Sukuks were issued globally, and Sukuks have become a popular investment vehicle in the GCC and South-East Asia (Hasan, 2014).

CHARACTERISTICS OF THE ISLAMIC INVESTMENT PRODUCT – SUKUK

1. **Investment process.** Each Sukuk holder mixes their funds with those of other investors to invest the common pool in an asset or enterprise to make profit. This process benefits small investors who can participate in such opportunities at small cost.
2. **Underlying asset.** The underlying asset could be a tangible asset, or the usufruct of an asset or services, or a specific project or special investment activity or an enterprise. When the Sukuk certificates are issued to investors, they represent equal and proportional ownership in the underlying asset.
3. **Ownership.** Sukuk certificates represent specific proportional ownership of the investors in the underlying asset and have the rights and obligations related to ownership.

4. **Shariah compliance.** The underlying asset and transaction on which the Sukuk is based are both acceptable in Islamic Shariah law. Income from Sukuk is Shariah compliant since the Sukuk holders are part owners of the underlying asset.

5. **Parties in Sukuk.** The parties in a Sukuk contract include the following.
   a. **Originator or obligor** – this would be the company or the government, in need of funds, that decides to issue a Sukuk.
   b. **Arranger or bank** – the originator approaches the bank to assist in the Sukuk issue and the bank creates the SPV, prepares the prospectus, underwrites and promotes the issue.
   c. **SPV or issuer** – the body that issues the Sukuk certificates to investors and collects funds from them.
   d. **Investors** – the buyers or holders of the Sukuk, who are providing the funds needed by the originator.
   e. **Manager of the SPV** – the Islamic bank can be assigned to this role and it serves as the representative of the Sukuk holders to ensure that the underlying asset and its utilization are as per the Sukuk contract.

6. **Profit and loss.** Usually, regular periodic income is generated from the Sukuk underlying asset and all returns and losses arising from the Sukuk assets are shared with the Sukuk certificate holders.

7. **Sukuk security.** The real underlying assets serve as security for the Sukuk holders and can be utilized to realize payments to the Sukuk holders.

8. **Trading.** Sukuks can be bought from the issuer at the primary market and bought or sold in the Shariah-compliant secondary capital market when an active secondary market exists.

9. **Sukuk rating.** The IIRA as well as the conventional rating agencies assess the Sukuks and rate them. Sukuk rating is more complex than conventional bond rating, since they are based on an underlying asset and can be modelled in a variety of ways.

10. **Sukuk payments.** Sukuk holders are paid an expected target return at regular intervals, which is not an interest obligation like the coupon. This payment is made after all expenses related to the management of the Sukuk are deducted. As owners of the underlying asset, the holders not only have the financial right to any return made on the asset but also bear the risk arising from their proportional ownership. The Sukuk holders' liability related to the underlying asset, though, is limited to the value of the Sukuk certificate owned by them. Moreover, any depreciation or appreciation in the value of the underlying asset also belongs to the Sukuk holder. While in conventional bonds the market value of the bond may change with respect to the difference between coupon rate and market interest rate, and this change belongs to the bondholder, any appreciation or depreciation of the assets of the issuer of the bond belong to the issuer only. Sukuks built on leased assets, or with partnerships in properties or projects, provide a stream of income to the Islamic investor as does the coupon of the bond, the difference being that this income is generated by the underlying asset or enterprise and may vary.

11. **Restrictions on Sukuks** (as listed in AAOIFI, 2008):

   a. **Purchase undertaking** – to be Shariah compliant, the Sukuk issuer cannot guarantee the Sukuk holders the return of their investment in the exact amount at the end of the Sukuk period, as in the case of bond principal payment at maturity. The only exception is Ijara Sukuk, which is based on a sale and lease-back transaction, with a pre-agreed purchase price. In case of all other types of Sukuk based on Mudaraba, Musharaka and Wakala, the issuer can provide a purchase undertaking but not at a pre-agreed price, rather the price is based on the market price of the asset at the time of maturity.
   b. **Sukuk manager guarantee** – the Sukuk manager cannot guarantee a fixed income to the Sukuk holders or make payment to compensate for any shortfall in their income. The Sukuk managers are allowed and encouraged to build up reserves from periods in which the underlying asset makes higher than expected profit, to top up the income of Sukuk holders in periods when the profits are less than expected. Reserve allocation needs to be done before the profits are distributed to the Sukuk holders.

TYPES OF SUKUKS

Sukuks are designed to provide an alternative to conventional bonds, ensuring that all Shariah-non-compliant features are excluded, including Riba and Gharar. A major advantage of most Islamic banking products is the ability of the bank to securitize the product and thus access a much larger source of funds from the public investors. To undertake securitization of any Islamic finance contract, a special entity is created – the SPV – which ceases to exist once the project is completed. The most common classification of Sukuks depends on the major Islamic finance product on which they are modelled using Islamic financial engineering. The various types of Sukuk under this classification are described below.

Ijara Sukuk

This is the most common form of Sukuk, based on the Ijara contract, and mostly used for leasing and project finance. In Ijara Sukuk, the issuer in need of financing first sells the asset to the investors, thus collecting the funds it needs. The issuer then leases the asset back from the investors based on the Ijara mode and issues the Ijara Sukuk certificates to the investors who are also the lessors now. The Sukuk certificates represent the undivided proportional ownership and right to lease in the leased asset of the investors/lessors. Ijara Sukuk are tradable on the secondary market, as they are backed by real tangible assets and are usually issued on stand-alone assets included in the balance sheet, like land, buildings, equipment, vehicles, etc. The lease payments can be variable based on the market rental rates and paid to the investors similar to coupons. Sometimes the Ijara Sukuk may include the right of the issuer to buy back the asset from investors at the end of the lease period, as in the case of an Ijara wa Iqtina contract. The purchase price either has to be pre-agreed or needs to be determined based on the market price. But this is a debatable feature amongst Shariah scholars, since it may represent a pure

buy-back clause that is not considered Shariah compliant and if included, all regulations to ensure Shariah acceptance need to be inserted. Some of the risks associated
with Ijara Sukuk are that the lessee defaults or is genuinely unable to pay rentals, the
lessee refuses to or is unable to buy back the asset at the end of the Ijara, or the asset
itself may be damaged through no fault of anyone or may become obsolete.

Ijara Sukuk is quite popular in mobilizing funds for long-term infrastructure projects and for subsequent trading in the secondary market. Some variations of the Ijara
Sukuk include the following.

1. **Sukuk of ownership in leased asset.** This Sukuk mainly aims to sell the asset with a
   title transfer to the Sukuk holders, who would then jointly own the asset through
   undivided proportional ownership and have the right to both any profit or loss
   arising from the asset. This type of Ijara Sukuk is used to purchase new assets.
2. **Sukuk of ownership of usufructs of assets.** This kind of Sukuk is issued to transfer the right of usufruct in an identified asset to the Sukuk holders, who become
   joint owners only to usufruct called Al Manfaah in Arabic, where the owners of
   the asset have only leased the usufruct to the Sukuk holders and not sold the asset
   to them. Sukuk holders may be allowed to sublease the usufruct of the asset to a
   third party.
3. **Sukuk of ownership of services.** This type of Ijara Sukuk gives the Sukuk holders the right to prescribed services and they may also sublease such services to a
   third party.

Figure 11.1 gives an overview of the Ijara Sukuk.

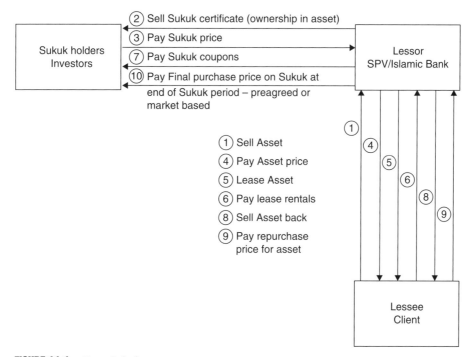

FIGURE 11.1   Ijara Sukuk

Istisna Sukuk

This form of Sukuk uses the Istisna mode of Islamic finance to fund manufacturing, real-estate development, large industrial projects, construction of major items like power plants, ships, aircraft, etc. To raise the requisite funds, the issuer or bank produces Sukuk certificates that provide the holders with proportional ownership in the asset to be manufactured or constructed. Once the asset is completed, its ownership may be passed on immediately to the ultimate client and the deferred payments made by the client are passed on to the Sukuk holders. Sometimes, instead of ownership transfer, the asset is leased to the client and the Istisna Sukuk converts into an Ijara Sukuk. The Istisna Sukuk is usually of long term. The detailed specifications and costs of the asset are mutually agreed between manufacturer and client. Once a Sukuk is raised, the full costs are provided to the SPV, who may pay the manufacturer in instalments in accordance with the production schedule. After production and delivery is completed, the buyer starts repaying the price in deferred instalments, which are passed on to the Sukuk holders as their payments. The risk involved could be a manufacturer failing to produce and deliver, the asset becoming damaged or obsolete, or the client defaulting on payments.

The steps of the Istisna Sukuk are given below.

1. The SPV raises funds by issuing Sukuk certificates to Sukuk holders.
2. These funds are used to finance the Istisna project by paying the constructor, manufacturer, producer, fabricator or assembler as per the parallel Istisna contract.
3. The contracted asset is then sold to the original bank customer as per the first Istisna contract.
4. The delivery of both Istisna and parallel Istisna contracts is usually at the same time. At delivery, the title to the asset is transferred to the SPV, while the asset is delivered to the original bank customer.
5. The customer makes payments through regular instalments.
6. The funds received from the payments are distributed to the Sukuk holders.

Figure 11.2 gives an overview of the Istisna Sukuk.

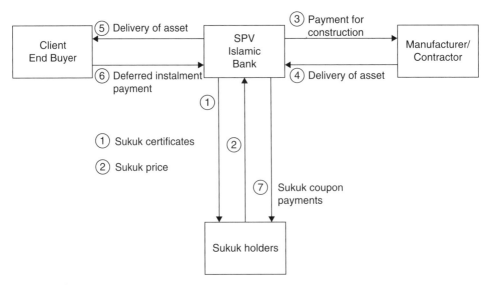

FIGURE 11.2 Istisna Sukuk

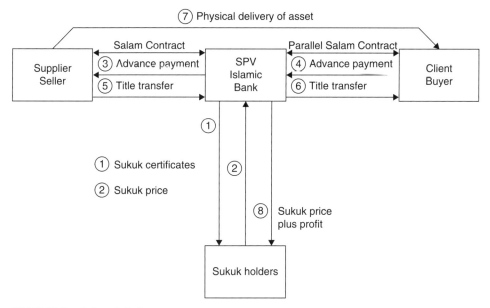

FIGURE 11.3   Salam Sukuk

Salam Sukuk

This is based on the Salam mode of financing, where the buyer pays the full price of the asset in advance on spot; usually the buyer gets a discount on the price for paying in advance. The seller would deliver at a mutually agreed future date. The contract is like a conventional forward contract. The majority of Salam Sukuks are short term. The SPV established for the Sukuk raises funds by selling the certificates to Sukuk holders and finances the seller on spot as advance payment to produce the asset under contract. Once production is completed, the seller sells the asset to the end buyer and pays the Sukuk holders the original finance amount plus a markup via the SPV. The asset in this case is not transferred to the Sukuk holder when the Sukuk is issued; as such, the Salam Sukuk cannot be traded and needs to be held till maturity. The Salam Sukuk has similarities to a conventional zero-coupon bond, where no payments are made during the life of the bond or Sukuk and a single payment is made at maturity. The risks that can occur are that the seller is not able to confirm a buyer for the asset or cannot deliver the asset on time, or is not able to sell it at a price to pay the Sukuk holders their original funds, the markup and make a profit itself.

   Figure 11.3 gives an overview of the Salam Sukuk.

Murabaha Sukuk

The Murabaha Sukuk is based on the Murabaha mode of financing, where a seller interested in acquiring assets to resell using the Murabaha mode may raise the cost to acquire the assets by issuing Sukuks. The Sukuk holders would own the assets till they are resold, and will be entitled to the marked-up sales price in proportion to the shares in the Sukuk issue.

   Figure 11.4 gives an overview of the Murabaha Sukuk.

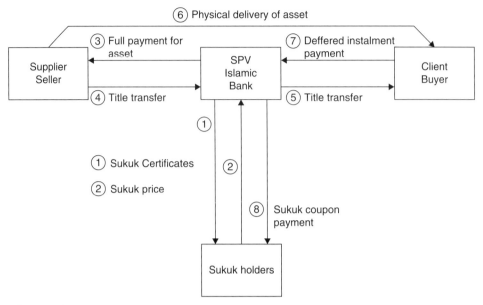

FIGURE 11.4   Murabaha Sukuk

Mudaraba Sukuk

Mudaraba Sukuks are equity-based, unlike the previous Sukuks discussed, which are a deferred payment debt like instruments or leasing. In Mudaraba one party, the Rab al Maal, pays the entire capital; the other party, the Mudarib, provides the effort and entrepreneurship. The two parties share the profit according to a pre-agreed ratio, but the entire financial loss is borne by the Rab al Maal and the Mudarib loses their effort. When the Sukuk is structured, it represents undivided ownership of units of equal value in the Mudaraba equity and these units are registered in the names of the Sukuk holders who contribute their capital into a specific project to be managed by the issuer or Mudarib. The Rab al Maal is the Sukuk holders, while the Mudarib could be the bank or SPV or an entrepreneur with a good business concept but in need of capital. Usually, the restricted Mudaraba concept is used, which provides clear guidelines on the type of business, the location of the business and the period during which the business will be conducted. The return on this partnership Sukuk is variable, and as such it is still not a very popular mode of constructing the Sukuk, since Sukuk holders prefer a regular stream of income.

The Islamic Fiqh Academy of the OIC, in its fourth session in 1988, stipulated the following resolutions related to the Mudaraba Sukuk.

1. The Mudaraba Sukuk represents common ownership of the Sukuk holders in the specific Mudaraba project.
2. The Sukuk prospectus should provide all details related to the Mudaraba project and its securitization.

3. The Mudaraba Sukuk is tradable and the holder has the right to transfer their ownership to anyone willing to buy in the secondary Sukuk market, provided the sale follows Shariah requirements. If the Mudaraba capital comprises money, then the exchange of money for money must be in accordance with the Shariah rules of Sarf; if the capital is in the form of debt, it must follow the principles of Islamic debt trading; if the capital is a combination of cash, receivables, tangible and intangible assets and benefits, the trade must be as per the market-based price reached through mutual consent.

4. The Sukuk manager or SPV who collects the contributions from the Sukuk holders may also invest their own funds in the Mudaraba project.

5. The issuer or Sukuk manager is not allowed to provide any guarantee, either for the capital of the Mudaraba project or for a fixed profit, lump sum or percentage. As such, the prospectus or Sukuk contract cannot stipulate any specific amount to be paid to the Mudaraba Sukuk holders, rather the profit is to be divided and distributed as per Shariah rules and the profit and loss-related information needs to be transparent, published and shared with the Sukuk holders.

6. Reserves can be created for the Sukuk, to deal with contingencies such as loss of capital or less than expected profits. The reserve is built by taking out a portion of the higher than expected profits in good years, but this process needs to be communicated to the Sukuk holders and have their consent.

Figure 11.5 gives an overview of the Mudaraba Sukuk.

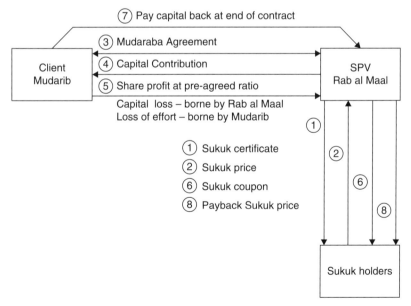

FIGURE 11.5 Mudaraba Sukuk

Process of Structuring the Mudaraba Sukuk

1. A company or business that requires funding approaches a bank to establish an SPV.
2. The SPV issues Sukuk certificates to investors raising funds, providing them with equal proportional ownership in the business.
3. Cash raised serves as capital in the Mudaraba contract between the SPV acting as agent for the Sukuk holders and the company acting as Mudarib to manage the business.
4. The profits earned are periodically distributed among the two major parties – the company and the SPV – as per the pre-agreed ratio.
5. The SPV then pays out the profit to the Sukuk holders according to the proportion of their individual shares in the invested capital.

Musharaka Sukuk

Musharaka is based on an equity partnership where all parties provide the capital and the profits are shared in a pre-agreed ratio, while the losses are borne according to the capital contribution. Musharaka Sukuks are structured to raise funds for new projects or to extend an existing project or for a huge business activity based on a joint venture. The Musharaka Sukuk certificate gives the Sukuk holders proportional ownership in the assets of the Musharaka equity partnership project, and these certificates are negotiable instruments which can be traded in the secondary capital market. Each shareholder of the Musharaka and the Sukuk holder in case of Musharaka securitization has the right to participate in the management of the enterprise or project if they so wish. The shareholders or Sukuk holders may also choose to appoint the issuer or SPV to act as their agent and manage the Musharaka venture. More often the company or business acts as the managing partner while the SPV, on behalf of the Sukuk holders, may act as the silent partner, not getting involved in the day-to-day business.

Figure 11.6 gives an overview of the Musharaka Sukuk.

Sukuks can also be classified or grouped as tradable, non-tradable, debt-based and equity-based. Tradable Sukuks are those that represent ownership in tangible assets or in an enterprise that can be bought or sold at the Islamic capital market – for example Ijara, Mudaraba and Musharaka Sukuks. Non-tradable Sukuks are those that represent receivables as cash or goods and hence not tradable – for example Murabaha and Salam Sukuks. Equity-based Sukuks are those that are modelled on partnership-based Islamic instruments, like Musharaka or Mudaraba. Debt-based Sukuks are based on receivables, like those arising from Murabaha or Salam.

Another classification divides Sukuks into three groups.

1. **Pure Ijara Sukuk.** These certificates are issued on underlying assets that are stand-alone on the balance sheet, like land or equipment, and the rental income can be fixed or floating and depends on existing market forces.
2. **Hybrid or pooled Sukuk.** These Sukuks are based on Istisna, Murabaha as well as Ijara contracts; the return on these Sukuk certificates is fixed and predetermined.
3. **Zero-coupon non-tradable Sukuk.** These Sukuk certificates are based on underlying assets that would be sold in the future (most probably assets being built under a Salam or Istisna contract) and therefore cannot be traded now.

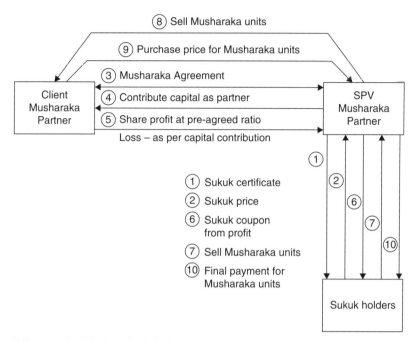

FIGURE 11.6   Musharaka Sukuk

Another manner of classifying Sukuks is related to what recourse is available to the Sukuk holders; Sukuks are grouped as asset backed and asset based. According to Dr Sayd Farook, Global Head, ICM, Thomson Reuters (Hassan, Kayed & Oseni, 2013), asset-backed Sukuk certificate holders rely on the underlying asset to generate yield and recover their investments. An example could be a building with rental income which provides the return to the investors but if the issuer fails to repay, the asset could be sold to return the investors' money. On the other hand, the asset-based Sukuk involves purchase and sale of the asset, as in Murabaha or Ijara contracts where the asset already exists, and the investors depend on this asset as the last resort to recover their investment. So, we can see that in case of the asset-backed Sukuk the asset is still in the ownership of the Sukuk holders and thus recourse to it is easier. On the other hand, in asset-based Sukuk the asset was purchased and sold, and its deferred payments make payments to the Sukuk holders so in case of non-payment, ownership of the asset is no longer with the Sukuk holders, thus the main recourse is the creditworthiness of the customer who purchased the asset.

CONTROVERSY RELATED TO SUKUKS

After their initial introduction into the Islamic financial markets, Sukuks earned tremendous popularity and many players entered the market. The regulatory environment was still not significantly developed, and doubts about the Shariah compliance of the Sukuk issues in the market began to circulate. Critics believed the Sukuks were sometimes being used unethically to take advantage of the demand for Shariah-compliant investment amongst Muslims in general and the affluent population in the oil-rich Muslim-majority countries of the Middle East specifically, and these hastily designed instruments were not fully following Shariah requirements.

In 2007, the Chairman of the AAOIFI, Sheikh Taqi Usmani, commented that 85% of all Sukuks in the market were not fully compliant with Shariah. This was a major set-back in the growth and acceptance of Sukuks. With nearly 200 members from 45 countries, the AAOIFI is the major international Islamic standard setting body and its regulations are mandatory in Bahrain, Dubai International Finance Centre, Jordan, Qatar, Sudan and Syria. Elsewhere the regulations are used as a guideline for the Islamic finance industry. As the Chairman of AAOIFI, Sheikh Usmani made the following comments related to Sukuks.

1. If Sukuks are issued on existing businesses then Sukuk holders must have complete ownership of real assets of the business whose profits will be the revenue of the Sukuk holders.
2. If any incentive is given to the Sukuk manager, it should be based on profit earned by the enterprise and not on any interest rate. Many Sukuks use LIBOR, which has no link with business efficiency, to stipulate their return, and this is not Shariah compliant. Rather, they should base incentives on the difference between expected and actual profits.
3. Sukuk managers cannot repurchase the Sukuk certificates at face value, rather the price should be decided based on the market value of the Sukuk certificates or the market value of the underlying assets at the time of repurchase. Then the principal payment is not irrespective of the performance of the asset, is not guaranteed or fixed, but is based on the profit and loss.

The AAOIFI declared five key Shariah implications for Sukuks.

1. All tradable Sukuks represent ownership of the Sukuk holders with rights and obligations in the physical assets, or in the usufruct or services, or the special investment activity or the specific project. This implies true sale of the asset to the SPV, and sovereign issuers may be reluctant to do that.
2. Tradable Sukuks should not represent any payables or revenues, and normally this would exclude Murabaha and Salam Sukuks, since these comprise fixed deferred payments. However, if these payments are based on the fixed pre-agreed revenue earned by the underlying asset, then it is acceptable in Shariah.
3. Sukuk managers cannot lend to Sukuk holders any amount to make up any deficit between expected and actual profits. This can be paid from a reserve fund only, which should be built from the contribution of the Sukuk holders and with their consent.
4. Sukuks should not be repurchased from the Sukuk holders at maturity at the face value, but the repurchase price should be based on the market value of the underlying assets at the time of maturity.
5. A properly established SSB with the requisite authority should review the Sukuk issue at all stages to ensure compliance with Shariah.

RATING OF SUKUKS

Bond rating is a very crucial factor in the issuance of bonds by governments or corporations, and for the investment by individuals and organizations into these bonds. The rating of a bond depends mainly on the creditworthiness of the issuing corporation or government, and varies from 'AAA', considered as the highest grade, to 'C', which is the lowest. Credit rating guides prospective investors to pick the bonds best meeting their risk–return appetite. Based on rating, bonds are mainly grouped into high-rated bonds called investment grade bonds and lower-rated or riskier bonds called junk bonds. Both in the conventional bond and the Islamic Sukuk market, the rating is closely linked to the price – a higher rating can demand a higher price for the bonds or Sukuk certificates.

Globally, more than 50 rating agencies operate, though the top three rating agencies are Moody's, Standard & Poor's and Fitch. In addition to rating conventional bonds, these three main rating agencies also rate Sukuks, which are the Islamic alternative to bonds. Additionally, some countries have their own localized rating agencies, as in Malaysia, India, Bangladesh and Sri Lanka. In 2005 the Islamic Development Bank established the International Islamic Rating Agency (IIRA), which has been striving to ensure greater reliability and quality in the Islamic finance industry. Bonds are very simple debt obligations and easy to evaluate and rate. In contrast, Sukuks are more complicated and can be constructed in a variety of different ways, and both the underlying asset of the Sukuk and the issuer needs to be rated.

Sukuk ratings are yet to earn the same reliability as bond ratings, due to a lack of efficient domestic specialized rating agencies and due to the inexperience of the international rating agencies in dealing with Sukuks. Over time, as the popularity of Sukuks increases, it is expected that the international agencies like Moody's, Standard & Poor's and Fitch will increase their involvement and expertise by setting up special departments dealing with Sukuks, and will also support the local rating agencies to improve, thus enhancing the transparency and safety in the Sukuk markets, benefiting the issuers, investors and regulators. Factors related to the issuer and the security that are considered in arriving at the ratings are the issuer's history in managing Sukuk issues, cash balances and reserves, amounts and consistency of cash flow, the issuer's business history, type of assets and repayment history, and the security provided by the underlying asset, project or enterprise involved in the Sukuk issue to repay the Sukuk holders.

TRADING OF SUKUKS ON THE SECONDARY MARKETS

The ability of Sukuk holders to trade their certificates on the secondary market has been a major issue to be dealt with for Shariah scholars. In general, Shariah does not permit the trading of debt. This can only be done under strict regulations outlined by the AAOIFI. These regulations are that the Sukuk holder own the Sukuk certificates with all ownership rights and obligations in the underlying assets, tangible or intangible, usufruct or services, but receivables or debts should be excluded from the assets. The Sukuk manager, as Mudarib or partner or agent, cannot add to the income of the Sukuk holders if the income is below expectations or they can repurchase the Sukuk from the Sukuk holder at the nominal value at maturity, but can repurchase at the current market value. In case of Ijara Sukuk though, the lessee can buy the underlying leased assets at their nominal value, provided that the lessee is not the Sukuk manager. Finally, a well-established SSB needs to be formed to ensure not only the structuring of the Sukuk, but also that all procedures related to its original sale, trading, accounting and auditing are Shariah compliant. Both the primary and secondary Sukuk markets are still small and underdeveloped. The cities of London, Luxembourg, Labuan in Malaysia, Dubai and Bahrain are developing as major global Sukuk centres, with regulations and tax issues being significantly supportive of the issue and trade of various types of Sukuks.

COMPARISON OF SUKUKS WITH CONVENTIONAL BONDS

Investors aim for safety of their capital, maximum return and want a balance between liquidity and profitability of their investment. Shariah-compliant investors prefer ethical and socially responsible investments that are devoid of all Shariah-prohibited items like Riba, Gharar, Maysir and restricted businesses like alcohol, pork, drugs, gambling, adult entertainment and pornography, etc.

Bonds are financial instruments issued by governments or corporations to raise funds, usually for the long term. Bondholders are creditors and paid interest by the issuers, which is called the coupon. The bonds are rated according to the credit rating of the issuer and they may also have collateral attached to them. Bonds are first issued and sold in the primary market and later traded in the secondary market. At the maturity date the principal amount is returned to the bondholder. The main Islamic prohibition in bonds is that they pay interest, and also they don't have any underlying asset. Sukuks, on the other hand, are based on an underlying asset and Sukuk holders own part of this asset and all risk and return related to the ownership.

Common Advantages of Both Conventional Bonds and Sukuks

Sukuks are called the Islamic alternatives to conventional bonds, and both products have similar advantages.

1. **Diversification of funding sources.** Bonds and Sukuks are both excellent techniques used by the issuer to raise large amounts of finance from the public instead of depending on a single financier, allowing governments and corporations to diversify their sources of funds.
2. **Traded in the secondary markets.** As we know, bonds are traded in the secondary markets and this adds to their attractiveness to investors. Similarly, most Sukuks are also traded in the secondary markets when they are monetized real assets, which are liquid in nature, and their ownership can easily be transferred to another.

3. **Liquidity management.** Banks and other financial institutions, as well as corporations, use bonds and Sukuks to manage their liquidity since both products are traded in the secondary market, so when they have excess cash they buy bonds or Sukuks and when they have a shortage of cash they sell them.
4. **Rated instruments.** Both bonds and Sukuks are evaluated and given a rating varying from 'AAA' to 'C', based on a range of factors that indicate reliability and risk–return expectations by various rating agencies, which can be global or local. A good rating increases the popularity of the bond or Sukuk.
5. **Various structures.** Both bonds and Sukuks can be structured in diverse ways to match the needs of the investor. Sukuks can be modelled on the various Islamic finance products and investors can choose from them, based on their legal and tax jurisdictions, and the requirement for variable or fixed income options. With conventional bonds we already know that they also come in fixed or variable rates, as zero coupon and with other options, designed to match the differing needs of investors.
6. **Attractive investment option.** Both bonds and Sukuks are ideal investment vehicles for investors who may participate with a small amount of funds, choose from a variety of structures available, having regular income and also easily divest themselves if needed by selling in the secondary market.
7. **Pricing benchmark.** Bonds provide a pricing benchmark for the conventional capital markets and with time, as the Sukuk market develops, they will also be a major benchmark for the Islamic capital markets.
8. **Recognition.** Since bonds and Sukuks are both sold in the exchanges and can be accessed by international investors, they enhance the global profile of the issuers.
9. **Government infrastructure funding.** Bonds help governments raise funds for infrastructure development and similarly Sukuks are being used by governments of Muslim countries to build up their infrastructure.

Additionally, Sukuks have another advantage and that is **equitable distribution.** Sukuks are an instrument which can be used for equitable distribution of wealth, since all investors benefit from the actual profit generated by the underlying assets.

Differences Between Conventional Bonds and Sukuks

Table 11.4 details the differences between conventional bonds and Sukuks.

TABLE 11.4 Differences between conventional bonds and Islamic Sukuks

Features	Conventional bonds	Islamic Sukuks
Definition of the instrument	Conventional bonds are pure debt of the issuer, with no ownership; representing a loan with periodic interest payable as well as the principal or face value payable at maturity.	Sukuks are an ownership stake in the underlying asset, its usufruct or services; representing undivided proportional ownership of the Sukuk holders.

(Continued)

TABLE 11.4   (*Continued*)

Features	Conventional bonds	Islamic Sukuks
Certificates issued	Conventional bonds represent a simple debt certificate.	Sukuks represent a trust certificate giving the Sukuk holders ownership rights to the underlying asset.
Type of contract	Bonds represent a loan contract creating indebtedness.	Sukuks rarely use a loan contract, since regular loans based on interest are Shariah prohibited. Rather, Sukuks utilize a variety of contracts creating financial obligations between issuer and investors, according to the Islamic financial instrument being used for securitization (Mudaraba, Ijara, Musharaka, etc.)
Asset linked to the instrument	Can be receivables or other financial assets.	Tangible or intangible asset, or its usufruct or services.
Return earned	Interest or coupon is the return earned by bondholders irrespective of the profit or loss made by the enterprise or project and the principal amount is also returned at maturity.	Sukuk holders or investors have the right to earn profit from the enterprise or project pro-rata to their ownership in the sale, lease or partnership contract, but are also liable to any losses incurred.
Asset-related expenses	Bondholders depend mainly on the creditworthiness of the issuer, not the asset-related expenses of the enterprise or project.	As owners of the assets, Sukuk holders are concerned about the asset-related expenses, their return being calculated only after the deduction of the relevant expenses.
Equitable distribution	Holders of bonds receive fixed interest only irrespective of the profit or loss made by the project or company, so neither gain nor lose from the company's or project's status since their rights are not linked to the assets of the company or project.	Sukuk holders participate in the ownership of the company or project that entitles them to any appreciation or depreciation of the underlying asset. This ensures more equitable distribution, where investors benefit from the actual profit and not a fixed interest rate, but bear any losses also.
Relationship	In case of conventional bonds, the contractual relationship between the issuer and the investor is that of debtor and creditor.	In case of Sukuks, the contractual relationship between the issuer and the investor varies with the Islamic finance instrument used to build the Sukuk and could be that of seller–buyer, lessor–lessee or partners.

TABLE 11.4   (*Continued*)

Features	Conventional bonds	Islamic Sukuks
Maturity	The term of the bond does not need to correspond to the term of the underlying project or enterprise.	The Sukuk maturity corresponds to that of the underlying project or activity.
Prospectus	The bond prospectus provides details of the issuer and the use of the funds raised by the bond, no Shariah constraints are relevant or mentioned.	The Sukuk prospectus provides details of the issuer, the underlying asset, usufruct or service as well as details of how Shariah compliance is achieved.
Ethics	Bond managers do not have to worry about the ethics of the project.	Sukuk managers need to ensure that the underlying asset, project or activity on which the Sukuk is based is ethical and not harmful to society or the environment, as Shariah requires.
Contractual obligation	The issuer of the bond has a contractual obligation to pay the bondholder the coupons on fixed dates and pay back the principal amount at maturity.	The issuer of Sukuk is contractually obliged to share the profit or loss of the underlying asset, project or activity with the Sukuk holder.
Say in the operations of the project or enterprise or asset	Bondholders, as creditors, do not have a say in how the bond proceeds from the bond issue are utilized or managed. The issuer has complete control on the operations and management, provided they pay the bondholders periodic coupon and the face value at maturity.	Sukuk managers serve as the representative of the Sukuk holders, responsible for ensuring their best interests are upheld in the operations and management of the underlying assets, project or activity. Sukuk managers may also be the issuer, and their right to retain this position depends on the Sukuk holders who have placed their trust in the manager as owners and not as creditors.
Recourse in case of default or loss	Conventional bonds may be backed by financial assets such as receivables, which cannot be used in Sukuks. If the issuer of the bond defaults, secured bondholders have recourse to the financial or physical asset provided as security, but unsecured bondholders are only part of the general creditors seeking the assets of the company after its bankruptcy.	Asset-backed Sukuk certificate holders have recourse to the underlying asset, which could be sold to recover their investments if the issuer fails to repay. For asset-based Sukuks, which involve purchase and sale of the asset, the underlying asset has already been sold so in case of non-payment, the asset cannot be sold and the only recourse left to the Sukuk holders is the creditworthiness of the issuer and the customer who purchased the asset.

TABLE 11.4　(*Continued*)

Features	Conventional bonds	Islamic Sukuks
Trading	Bonds are actively traded on the stock exchange and this amounts to trading of debts, normally with discounting.	Sukuks are not independent instruments but are based on an underlying Islamic finance instrument and, depending on which instrument they are linked to, some may be tradable or not. Tradability depends on the nature of the financial rights the Sukuk holders have on the underlying instrument. All Sukuks, except the Salam and Murabaha Sukuks, can be traded. In case of Salam and Murabaha Sukuks the ownership of the asset has already been transferred to the client, so they cannot be traded but need to be held till maturity.
Prices	Bond prices depend on the creditworthiness of the issuer.	Asset-backed Sukuk prices depend on the underlying assets, while asset-based Sukuk prices depend on the trustworthiness of the issuer.

When making investment decisions, Islamic investors also need to choose between the purchase of Sukuks or the purchase of Shariah-screened shares. Some differences between Sukuks and shares are listed in Table 11.5.

TABLE 11.5　Differences between Sukuks and Shariah-screened shares

Feature	Sukuk	Shares
Type	Sukuks are classified and regulated as debt instrument, though some types of Sukuks are built on equity-type financial instruments.	Shares are classified and regulated as equity instruments.
Risk	Considered as low-risk instruments with fixed or regular return, though some Sukuks have variable return.	Considered as high-risk instruments with variable return.
Maturity	All Sukuks have a limited maturity period.	Shares are an ongoing investment, having unlimited maturity period.
Security	Sukuks may be attached to some security or may be unsecured.	Shares are always unsecured.

KEY TERMS AND CONCEPTS

Al Manfaah

Asset-backed Sukuk

Asset-based Sukuk

Capital market

Close-ended fund

Commodity market

Debt-based Sukuk

Equity-based Sukuk

Financial screening

Foreign exchange market

Ijara fund

Ijara Sukuk

Industry screening

Islamic asset management

Islamic balanced fund

Islamic commodity fund

Islamic debt fund

Islamic equity fund

Islamic real estate
  investment trust

Istisna Sukuk

Money market

Murabaha Sukuk

Mudaraba Sukuk

Musharaka Sukuk

Non-compliant stocks

Non-tradable Sukuk

Open-ended fund

Purification of income
  distribution

Salam Sukuk

Shariah-compliant stocks

Shariah screening process

Special purpose vehicle

Sukuk

Tradable Sukuk

CHAPTER SUMMARY

The global investment industry is a complex system of products, markets, institutions, transactions and regulations, broken into the money, capital, commodity, foreign exchange and derivative markets. The Islamic investment industry has many similarities to its conventional counterpart, having the same markets but within Shariah restrictions.

All shares as equity are not acceptable Islamic investment tools but need to go through a Shariah screening process involving industry and financial screening. There are very few companies that are devoid of all Shariah prohibitions, and to manage this situation Shariah scholars and Islamic regulatory bodies have developed flexibilities within the screening process to allow those stocks that match Shariah compliance reasonably. As in the case of conventional asset management, Islamic asset and fund management involves investors pooling their funds which are professionally invested and managed by professionals, but with Shariah being a major objective. Common Islamic funds include debt, commodity, Ijara, equity, balanced, private equity, venture capital funds and REITs. As with all kinds of funds, I-REITs have similarities with as well as differences from conventional REITS.

Islamic capital markets face risks related to the market, credit, foreign exchange, fiduciary, Shariah non-compliance and liquidity. Investors who choose Islamic investment products or funds over conventional ones do so mainly for the religious requirements of Shariah compliance, and as such Shariah supervision of Islamic asset and fund management is very important. Islamic investments differ from conventional ones with respect to the interbank market, risk allocation, ownership of underlying assets, principal protection and price of the instrument.

Sukuks are the Islamic alternatives to conventional bonds. Important characteristics of the Sukuk include pooling of funds of multiple investors, ownership in the underlying asset, ensuring Shariah compliance, Sukuk parties of the originator, bank,

SPV, investors and SPV manager. Other characteristics are related to the sharing of profit and loss and Sukuk payments, securities offered, rating, trading and Sukuk restrictions. Sukuks are designed on a variety of Islamic financial products, including Ijara, Istisna, Salam, Murabaha, Mudaraba and Musharaka.

From the initiation of Sukuks in the markets during the 1980s and 1990s they became very popular, but in 2007 Sukuks faced major controversy when the Chairman of AAOIFI, Sheikh Usmani, commented that many of the Sukuks in the market were not totally Shariah compliant. The AAOIFI has since forwarded specific regulations to improve the Shariah compliance of Sukuk issues. Like bonds, Sukuks are also rated by major conventional rating agencies as well as the IIRA and localized Islamic rating agencies. Sukuks also trade in the secondary markets, as do bonds.

Sukuks share similarities to bonds with respect to providing a funding source, liquidity and trading in the secondary market, having various structures matching different investor profiles, being an attractive and rated investment instrument, providing a pricing benchmark and enhanced issuer profile. Sukuks differ from bonds with respect to the certificate and type of contract used, links to the underlying assets, return and expenses related to the assets, issuer–investor relationship and obligations, maturity of the instrument, ethics, recourse in case of default and pricing.

END OF CHAPTER QUESTIONS AND ACTIVITIES

Discussion Questions

1. Discuss the conventional investment markets.
2. Are the Islamic investment markets subdivided very differently or quite similarly as in the case of conventional investment markets? Discuss.
3. Are all stocks Shariah compliant for Islamic investments? Discuss.
4. Explain the Shariah screening process for stock selection.
5. Once screened as acceptable, do stocks need to be monitored for continuing Shariah compliance? Discuss.
6. How do fund managers deal with the non-compliance of stocks in their portfolios?
7. Explain the concept of purification of income distribution for Islamic funds.
8. Discuss Islamic asset and fund management.
9. What is the Islamic unit trust or mutual fund?
10. What are the types of Islamic funds? Describe each briefly.
11. What do you understand by the REIT?
12. What is an Islamic REIT or I-REIT?
13. Discuss the similarities and differences between REITs and I-REITS.
14. What are the challenges faced by Islamic investments and fund managers?
15. How important is the SSB for Islamic investment?
16. What are the differences of Islamic investments from conventional investments?
17. How did the AAOIFI define Sukuks?
18. Discuss the main characteristics of Sukuks.
19. What is an Ijara Sukuk? Describe.
20. What are the types of Ijara Sukuks?
21. Describe an Istisna Sukuk.
22. What is a Salam Sukuk? Explain.

23. What does a Murabaha Sukuk mean?
24. What is a Mudaraba Sukuk? What are the resolutions related to Mudaraba Sukuks put forward by the Islamic Fiqh Academy?
25. Describe the Musharaka Sukuk.
26. What does tradable, non-tradable, debt-based and equity-based Sukuk mean?
27. Explain pure Ijara, hybrid and zero-coupon Sukuks.
28. Define an asset-backed and an asset-based Sukuk.
29. Discuss the controversy faced by Sukuks during the early part of this century.
30. What are the Shariah implications put forward by the AAOIFI related to Sukuks?
31. How are Sukuks rated?
32. Can Sukuks be traded in the secondary markets like bonds?
33. What are the common advantages of both bonds and Sukuks as investment tools?
34. What are the differences between Sukuks and conventional bonds?
35. Compare Sukuks with Shariah-screened stocks.
36. Al Rashidiya Company produces furniture and is interested in purchasing a new plant that will automate the production process. The sophisticated plant is expensive, and they will need finance to purchase it. They are looking at Islamic finance and have chosen to finance the new plant by dividing the ownership of the machine into equal ownership parts as certificates and selling those parts to prospective investors. Answer the questions below related to this case.
    a. What Islamic financial instrument are they considering and what is the similar product under conventional finance?
    b. Discuss any two variations of this product that will be suitable for this financing.

Multiple Choice Questions

Circle the letter next to the most accurate answer.

1. Which one below is not a requirement of Shariah-compliant investment?
   a. Avoid all forms of Riba
   b. Avoid speculative investments
   c. Take no risk
   d. Be involved in socially responsible and ethical investing
2. Which one below is not a responsibility of the Islamic fund manager?
   a. Select investment instruments that are devoid of Riba, Gharar and Maysir
   b. Ensure the investment process does not involve any Shariah-prohibited elements
   c. Commit a reasonable return to their clients
   d. The contract signed with the client must follow Shariah guidelines
3. The most prominent Islamic indices are:
   a. Dow Jones Islamic Market Index
   b. FTSC Global Islamic Index
   c. S&P Global Investable Shariah Index
   d. All of the above
4. The Shariah screening process for stock selection involves:
   a. Industry screening
   b. Financial screening
   c. Income purification
   d. All of the above

5. Islamic investment funds can invest in the following instruments:
   a. Corporate bonds
   b. Treasury bills
   c. Certificates of deposit
   d. None of the above
6. Which one below cannot be an Islamic investment fund?
   a. Ijara fund
   b. Derivatives fund
   c. Venture capital fund
   d. I-REIT
7. Which fund below is formed with private limited companies with a few large individual or institutional investors?
   a. Islamic private equity fund
   b. Islamic venture capital fund
   c. Islamic debt fund
   d. Ijara fund
8. Which characteristic below is common to both a private equity fund and a venture capital fund?
   a. Not traded on exchanges
   b. Existing privately owned companies
   c. Provide funding to promising new and start-up businesses
   d. All of the above
9. Which Islamic product is a certificate of equal value representing undivided ownership shares in tangible assets, usufructs and services, specific projects or special investment activity?
   a. Ijara funds
   b. Sukuk
   c. Shariah-screened stocks
   d. Waqf funds
10. Common benefits shared by Sukuks and conventional bonds include:
    a. Liquidity management
    b. Issuer profile enhancement
    c. Diversification of funding source
    d. All of the above
11. Classifications of Sukuks include:
    a. Tradable and non-tradable
    b. Short term and long term
    c. Debt-based and equity-based
    d. a and c
12. Which one below is not a tradable Sukuk?
    a. Murabaha Sukuk
    b. Ijara Sukuk
    c. Mudaraba Sukuk
    d. Musharaka Sukuk

13. Which one below is not a type of Ijara Sukuk?
    a. Sukuk of ownership in leased assets
    b. Sukuk of ownership of usufructs of assets
    c. Sukuk of ownership of services
    d. Sukuk of ownership of bonds
14. The two most popular classifications of bonds and Sukuks related to investment quality are:
    a. Investment grade bonds and junk bonds
    b. Corporate bonds and government bonds
    c. Investment grade bonds and sovereign bonds
    d. None of the above

True/False Questions

Write T for true and F for false next to the statement.
1. Speculative investment activities may involve both uncertainty or Gharar and gambling or Maysir, and both are prohibited in Islam.
2. Islamic investing includes conventional insurance and derivatives.
3. Stocks in Halal industries, even if they are using conventional financial products, are allowed in Islamic investment funds.
4. A stock market index indicates the performance of stocks in a financial market.
5. Islamic fund managers are permitted to speculate but not to undertake any unnecessary risks.
6. Some scholars allow Zakat payment to be part of the purification process to remove Shariah-non-compliant income in Islamic investments.
7. Sukuks are negotiable instruments that cannot be traded in the secondary market.
8. A major issue Islamic fund managers face is related to liquidity when they want to sell their instruments quickly.
9. Sukuk holders do not need to have an ownership interest in the underlying asset.
10. Reserves cannot be created for Sukuk payments to even out the profit distribution.
11. The AAOIFI has developed standards and rulings related to various Sukuk issues and their trading in the secondary markets.
12. The rating agencies rate bonds as well as Sukuks in a range from 'AAA' which is the highest to 'C' which is the lowest.
13. Credit rating provides professional judgement to potential investors to make informed investment decisions.

Calculation Problems

1. Great Auto Repair (GAR) wants to expand its business significantly by adding an auto assembly plant at a cost of €100 million. The land for the plant, valued at €10 million, will be provided by GAR. When GAR approaches Islamic Bank (IB) for financing of the balance of €90 million the bank suggests a Musharaka Sukuk. The bank sets up the SPV which would raise the amount by issuing tradable Musharaka

Sukuks offering an expected 5% annual return. The SPV plans to set up a reserve fund from years of above expected return to compensate for years of below expected return. Profit and loss sharing will be as per capital contribution.

The GAR assembly plant makes a net profit after all expenses, including SPV management expenses, at the rate of 8%, 5% and 4% in the next 3 years. Calculate the below:

a. In each year how much return is earned in euros?
b. What amount is paid to GAR in each year?
c. What amount is paid to the Sukuk holders in each year?
d. What amounts are added into the reserve fund or allocated to Sukuk holders from the reserve fund?

2. The dividend received from a Shariah-screened stock is $10,000. The company belongs to a Halal industry but has some conventional financial transactions that contribute a 2% Shariah non-compliant portion to the net profit and hence the dividend. How much of the dividend (in dollars) has to be donated for income purification?

CHAPTER 12

Global Standing of Islamic Finance and Banking

Learning outcomes

Upon completion of this chapter, you should be able to:

1. Understand the background of Islamic finance and banking in comparison with its conventional counterpart.
2. Discuss the growth of Islamic finance and banking globally, and specifically amongst the Muslim community in the Middle East, South and South-East Asia.
3. Explain the achievements, opportunities and challenges of the global Islamic finance and banking industry.
4. Discuss the social responsibilities of Islamic finance and the key issues moving forward.

BACKGROUND OF MODERN ISLAMIC FINANCE AND BANKING

The idea of interest-free financing has existed since the birth of Islam, but its reintroduction into the world of finance is only a few decades old. The concept of modern Islamic finance emerged in the mid-20th century with Asian and Arab Muslim-majority countries gaining independence from Western colonial powers, searching for their own identity and inspired by Islamic economics distinct from both the Western capitalist and Eastern socialist models. Islamic economics, as a term, was first coined by Abul Ala Al Mawdudi, who sought to develop Islamic social science (Kuran, 2004). Islamic finance and banking evolved from the concepts of Islamic economics, based on the profit and loss system (which is considered more equitable and stable) and with the joint efforts of Islamic Shariah scholars and practicing professionals in the finance and banking industry.

The theory of Islamic banking forbids interest, and considers it neither necessary nor desirable for banking operations; instead, it recommends banks to use the PLS mechanism. The prohibition of interest is common to all three Abrahamic faiths – Judaism, Christianity and Islam (Ariss, 2010). According to the CIA World Factbook (2012), more than half of the world's population of 7 billion belongs to the Abrahamic faith, which prohibits interest, yet the international financial system has been operating mainly on interest for more than 200 years (Chapra, 2007). Aristotle condemned interest, which he said was the birth of money from money; Judaism forbade demanding any increase on the principal when lending among the Israelites, but allowed it in dealings between Israelites and gentiles. In Christianity, Christ said, 'lend freely, hoping nothing thereby' (Luke 6:35), while Islam strictly prohibited interest, in any form, small or substantial, fixed or variable. This clearly establishes that the prohibition of interest is not unique to Islam.

Criticism of interest and its detrimental effects exists in Western literature as well as in religious doctrines. According to Dar & Presley (1999), most Islamic finance researchers and writers often implicitly assumed that prohibition of interest was unique to Islam. As such, they failed to acknowledge Western literature, both religious and non-religious, which has been critical of interest for decades and failed to derive any advantage from such supportive Western published material towards its interest prohibition principle. Instead, most Islamic finance and banking scholars and researchers introduced it as a completely new system of finance, based on Shariah law.

CONVENTIONAL VERSUS ISLAMIC FINANCE

Islamic banking was introduced to the world only about five decades ago and the principles under which it operates are significantly different from those of conventional banking, which is a well-established and well-understood form of finance and banking globally. The guiding principle of Islamic finance and banking is the Islamic Shariah law, especially the portion of it that is applicable to commercial transactions. Shariah law prohibits the payment or receipt of interest or Riba in any form, and recommends sharing of risk and sharing of profit and loss between financial institutions like banks and their customers. Shariah law also prohibits transactions involving uncertainty where the features of the contract are not clear between the parties (Gharar) and unnecessary risk and speculation and activities like games of chance (Maysir). Shariah also prohibits industries involved with alcohol, pork, indecent media and entertainment, prostitution, etc. This is in stark contrast to the conventional finance and banking industry that primarily operates on interest and on the profit-maximization principle.

Before the revival of modern Islamic finance and banking, the prohibition of interest made banking activities difficult for the religiously oriented Muslims globally, and especially in the Gulf region. Often, these people either left their money in non-interest-bearing accounts in conventional banks or stayed outside the formal banking system altogether, which significantly hindered the free flow of capital between global financial markets and the GCC. The advent of affluence in the region, with the discovery of oil bringing in enormous amounts of petrodollars, magnified the problem further. Around this time the introduction of Islamic banking was viewed as a major solution, providing distinctive Shariah-compliant means of financial intermediation. Islamic banking was conceptualized through the efforts of Islamic political activists, Muslim legal scholars, economists and businessmen, applying Shariah law to the modern economy and innovatively structuring traditional Islamic financial instruments to provide customers with most of the services associated with conventional banks, within Shariah restrictions (Smith, 2006). Today, Islamic banking has established its place globally.

Islamic and conventional banks serve customers with the same banking needs. As such, Islamic banking often appears similar and at times identical to conventional banking, except that the contracts must comply with Islamic Shariah. Tahir & Umar (2008) identified some main differences between Islamic and conventional banks. Firstly, conventional banks finance customers by simply lending the money, where the bank is the creditor and the customer is the debtor, while Islamic banks finance customers on deferred sales contracts or on a partnership basis. The bank buys the goods or appoints the customer as agent to buy, and sells to customers at a markup, with repayment made in instalments over a specific future period, or provides the funds by partnering with the customer in the project. Secondly, Islamic banks share in the customer's activities, risks, profits and losses; conventional banks, on the other hand, earn fixed interest from customer loans. Thirdly, since Islamic banks are partners in customers' businesses, they need to understand the business well, while conventional banks only lend money and are concerned with getting the principal and interest back. Fourthly, Islamic banks cannot charge penalties from defaulters; profit, once agreed on, cannot be changed. If customers delay repayment and compensation is charged, such money is given to charity. Conventional banks can apply simple or variable interest rates and defaulters are penalized by compound interest. Fifthly, both Islamic and conventional banks face risks related to credit, capital adequacy, liability and asset matching, currency fluctuation and liquidity, although the risk for Islamic banks is higher because they are exposed to profit and loss in each customer deal. In the case of conventional banks, the risk of loss is completely the client's; on the other hand, interest rate risk is faced by conventional banks only while Islamic banks are free from it. Finally, Islamic banks cannot finance any activity which goes against Shariah law, while conventional banks have no such religious restrictions and may finance any profitable and legal activity.

GLOBAL GROWTH OF THE ISLAMIC FINANCE AND BANKING INDUSTRY

Islamic finance and banking is a new sector within the global finance and banking industry. The concept of Islamic banking emerged only in the mid-20th century, the first experimental Islamic bank was established in Egypt in 1963, and the first commercial Islamic bank was set up in Dubai in 1975. Being new and different from traditional conventional banking, there is a significant lack of awareness and knowledge of Islamic banking. According to Mishkin (2001), banking is an integral part of the service industry, its contribution increasing with time. Islamic banks perform operations very similar to those of conventional banks, except that their transactions need to be interest free and in accordance with Islamic Shariah law. Islamic banking has flourished globally over the past decades, becoming popular not only among Muslims, but non-Muslims as well (Rehman & Masood, 2012).

The global expansion of Islamic finance and banking over the decades after its re-emergence was majorly supported by the rise of the petroleum-based economies in the Middle East, mainly the GCC countries. Oil brought affluence to this region amongst the

Muslim-majority population, as well as budget surpluses for governments coming in from the export of oil and the rising oil price. The Muslim population of this region, coming out of colonial influence as well as acquiring wealth from the petrodollars, became more aware of the need for banking and preferred to bank according to Islamic beliefs. Initially, Islamic banking experiments were private initiatives of individuals, but later governments in some Muslim countries significantly encouraged their growth, by changing existing legislation to match the Shariah-compliant features of the Islamic banking operations, developing new legislation tailored to the Islamic banks and removing various handicaps in the predominantly interest-based environment (Ahmad, 1994). Islamic finance started as a niche market catering only to Muslims wanting to avoid interest-based banking. Today's modern Islamic finance, a blend of Islamic economics and modern financial principles, is able to serve both Muslims and non-Muslims, with wide product ranges. The Islamic finance and banking industry was able to face the global financial crises better than conventional banks, owing to stricter lending criteria and less risky alternatives, and offering ethical investments, thus aiming to rise above religious beliefs and gain greater market share (Abdullah, Sidek & Adnan, 2012). The current stage in Islamic banking development can be identified as global expansion and acceptance beyond that of the religiously motivated Muslims, as it gains customers amongst non-Muslims. This remarkable global growth of an industry only a few decades old indicates the tremendous opportunities existing in this niche business for the participating banks.

Almost non-existent five decades ago, the Islamic finance industry has emerged as one of the fastest-growing sectors of the global finance industry. Over the past five decades, it has been growing at about 15% per annum, reaching almost 500 institutions in 75 countries globally. The Shariah-compliant assets of the top 500 banks are expected to reach USD2.6 trillion by end 2017, with a further 191 conventional banks offering Islamic products, some on a limited scale via Islamic windows, or via subsidiaries or branches specifically established to offer Islamic banking products. Currently the Islamic finance and banking industry is spread over the Middle East, Asia, Africa, Europe and North America, the largest Islamic banks being located in the GCC countries (Abdullah, Sidek & Adnan, 2012; Duran & Garcia-Lopez, 2012; Hassan, Kayed & Oseni, 2013; O'Sullivan, 2009; Shamma & Maher, 2012; The Banker, 2010).

Modern Islamic banking was neither successful, fully understood nor appreciated from the inception of its introduction. Developments in the theory and practice of modern Islamic banking can be roughly divided into three periods. The first was a period of conceptualization (1950–1975), when Islamic scholars raised Muslim consciousness about prohibition of interest, mostly from the religious aspect; the second was a period of experimentation (1975–1990), profit and loss-sharing Islamic banks were set up, Islamic financial instruments and institutions were established, Western financial institutions entered the market and the sector was accepted as an interest-free alternative to conventional banking; the third period (1990–present) is about earning recognition, confidence and credibility in domestic and international markets, the innovation of products and the standardization of products and procedures (Iqbal & Mirakhor, 1999). The first Islamic banking experiment occurred in Mit Ghamr in Egypt in 1963 with the establishment of a cooperative savings bank, which could not, however, develop into a successful commercial bank. The world's first successful commercial Islamic bank was the Dubai Islamic Bank, which has grown with both governmental and public support since its inception in 1975.

Most Muslim countries apply Shariah law to some extent in their social framework. Its application to commercial activities like finance and banking varies between the Muslim-majority countries. Most countries operate on a purely interest-based banking system, some on a dual banking system, with both conventional and Islamic banking legislation, while only a handful, like Iran and Sudan, operate in an interest-free banking environment. During the 1980s there was movement to make Pakistan's banking sector fully Shariah compliant, but this initiative fell apart due to lack of significant practical steps and now Pakistan operates according to the dual banking mechanism (State Bank of Pakistan, 2008).

Although the global banking environment is predominantly interest-based, Islamic finance has proliferated in the Far East, the GCC, North Africa, the Indian sub-continent, as well as in the emerging CIS countries (Ariss, 2010). Many non-Muslim countries like the UK, the USA, Australia, Denmark, India, Liberia, Liechtenstein, Luxembourg, Philippines, South Africa, Thailand and Singapore have Islamic financial institutions (Ahmad, 1994). Major international banks like Citigroup, HSBC, Barclays, UBS, BNP Paribas and others are diverting some of their operations from conventional practices to set up Islamic windows or fully fledged Islamic subsidiaries (Ariss, 2010). Britain is aiming to convert London into a global Islamic finance centre (Kerr, 2007) to compete with Bahrain and Malaysia. The continuing growth of Islamic banking depends greatly on its acceptability and preference by customers beyond the religiously motivated Muslims, and among all segments of Muslim and non-Muslim populations of the world. Islamic finance is expected to continue its growth, with international standard setting bodies such as the AAOIFI, IFSB and International Islamic Fiqh Academy playing a guiding role.

ISLAMIC FINANCE AND BANKING AND THE MUSLIM COMMUNITY

Islamic banks provided Muslims with the opportunity to bank and invest in accordance with their religious beliefs and without interest, while previously they had to deal with interest if they wanted to participate in the banking system. The Muslim population comprises more than a quarter of the estimated global population of 7.4 billion currently (http://www.muslimpopulation.com/World/). According to the Pew Research Center (2011), the Muslim population is expected to increase by 35%, twice the rate at which the non-Muslim population is growing, reaching 2.2 billion by 2030. Muslims inhabit all five continents, but almost 60% reside in Asia and 20% in the Middle East and North Africa (Estiri *et al.*, 2011). They constitute the majority in more than 50 countries (Damirchi & Shafai, 2011). Muslim countries generate 10% of global GDP (Karasik, Wehrey & Strom, 2007) and include 9 of the 12 members of the Organization of Petroleum Exporting Countries (OPEC) – Iran, Iraq, Kuwait, Saudi Arabia, Qatar, UAE, Indonesia, Libya and Nigeria (OPEC, 2014). The 57 member countries of the OIC have a combined GDP of nearly USD8 trillion, import about USD1 trillion and export USD1.4 trillion, creating a combined market of USD2.4 trillion. Moreover, Islam is the fastest-growing religion and some Muslim countries are the richest in the world, like Qatar, Brunei, UAE and Saudi Arabia, which are listed as having per capita GDP greater than USD50,000 (Alserhan, 2010; World Bank, 2013). The economic and political status in the Muslim world varies significantly from country to country, with the six GCC countries consisting of about 12 million high-end consumers (Marinov, 2010).

To effectively compete globally, Islamic banks need to cater not only for the Muslim population, but non-Muslims as well. Islamic banks play the same role of financial intermediation and offer products to meet the same needs as conventional banks, except that they operate within Islamic principles and regulations. As such, Islamic banks, even those operating in Islamic countries, in most instances face competition not only from other Islamic banks, but also from conventional banks.

BANKING AND ISLAMIC BANKING IN THE MIDDLE EAST AND THE GCC

Islamic finance concepts have been in existence and practiced for centuries, but have been institutionalized only in the last few decades, offering Shariah-compliant products and services. The rise of Islamic banking cannot be separated from the oil economies and the rise of the Arab Gulf countries. The GCC countries entered the global financial markets with the mid-1970s oil embargo, a dramatic increase in oil prices, huge wealth transferred to these countries with modest means, with neither the economic capacity to absorb this wealth nor the financial capacity to manage it, and a concomitant move suddenly from the fringe of the global economy to its centre (Smith, 2006). The Gulf economies were rudimentary at the beginning of the oil boom. They operated mostly with money changers and lenders, rather than banks, dealing with fees and not interest. By the 1970s they had moved to cash and credit systems based on Western interest-based banking, but the population was almost entirely Muslim, adamant about the Islamic restrictions on interest and therefore sustaining a demand for Islamic banking. Moreover, the ruling monarchies also required an acceptable financial system through which to share the oil wealth with their population (Smith, 2006).

The idea of Islamic banking began in the late 1940s; the first experiment was in Egypt with the Mit Ghamr Social Bank. Later, various Middle Eastern countries began to establish Shariah-compliant banks: Nasser Social Bank in Cairo (1972), Islamic Development Bank in Jeddah (1975), Dubai Islamic Bank (1975), Kuwait Finance House (1977), Faisal Islamic Bank in Sudan (1977), etc. Several conventional banks in the Middle East also converted partly or fully to Shariah-compliant operations (Khan & Bhatti, 2008). The world's largest Islamic banks are in the GCC, and by 2008 had captured about 35% of the banking market of those countries (Hasan & Dridi, 2010). The Middle East owns 60% of global Islamic banking assets, estimated to be about USD2 trillion, excluding Islamic windows and branches of conventional banks and Islamic insurance. At an average growth rate of 25%, it is estimated that 40–50% of the savings of the Muslim population will be acquired by Islamic banks within a decade (Al-Salem, 2008). The GCC countries operate on the dual banking system, with both conventional and Islamic banks operating side by side. The GCC banks are small, but financially strong, well-capitalized, with modern facilities (Srairi, 2009). None of the GCC Islamic banks have failed in the last few decades, partly because the governments support them and partly because they help one another (Smith, 2006). Now Islamic banks comprise 20% of the GCC's bank assets and are expected to grow, posing a serious challenge to conventional banks (Benaissa, Nordin & Stockmeier, 2003). The GCC, therefore, is a major region for innovation and growth of Islamic finance and banking, with a supportive legal system and population.

BANKING AND ISLAMIC BANKING IN SOUTH AND SOUTH-EAST ASIA AND BEYOND

The Islamic banking experiment started in around the 1960s. During the first three decades of the Islamic banks' emergence, Islamic finance development was based mainly in Bahrain and Malaysia, which appeared as the leading Islamic financial centres. In 1962, Tabung Haji Malaysia was established as an investment fund to help Malaysians save the money needed to perform Hajj, the pilgrimage to Makkah, and which provided depositors with profit rather than interest. Mit Ghamr was not very successful, as it did not get governmental support, but Tabung Haji has continued successfully to date. The inception of Islamic banking in the 21st century brought both opportunities and threats in the banking sector in other countries besides Malaysia in Asia (countries like Pakistan, Bangladesh, Indonesia, Brunei and Singapore). These Muslim-majority countries and Singapore, with its large Muslim population as well as its proximity to Malaysia, have several Shariah-compliant banks and regulatory authorities that play a significant role in providing the platform for Islamic financial institutions to operate side by side with their conventional counterparts, with regulations that allow their unique characteristics.

Islamic finance initially was concentrated in the Middle East, especially Bahrain, and South-East Asia, particularly Malaysia, but has now spread to purely Islamic Shariah-based countries like Iran and Sudan, as well as those where Islamic and conventional financial systems coexist on a dual basis (like Indonesia, Malaysia, Pakistan, the GCC) and moving beyond to the Western countries of Europe, North America and Australia.

ACHIEVEMENTS AND OPPORTUNITIES IN GLOBAL ISLAMIC FINANCE AND BANKING

The introduction of the profit and loss-based financial intermediation of Islamic banking in a world well content with the highly sophisticated conventional system was challenging. Religion was considered the main motivator of the preference for Islamic banking, but this was important only to committed believers in Islam, while to others it had little appeal. As such, it was necessary to search for another economic rationale to support the replacement of interest with the profit and loss system. By the mid-1980s, economic and financial theory demonstrated the disadvantages of interest-based contracts, which encouraged default or non-performance and suffered from adverse selection, since collateral rather than the project itself is focused on, creating conflict between the interests of the borrowers and the lenders (Iqbal & Mirakhor, 1999). According to Chapra (2007), the rationale behind the prohibition of interest is not only religious, to prevent the exploitation of the poor, but also to make the financial system more disciplined and stable, by increasing equity, offering financing linked to real assets, eliminating speculation, allocating resources efficiently and enhancing economic growth. With this view, the religious-based Islamic banks appear to achieve general economic and financial objectives better than the conventional secular banks.

The mainstream capitalist economic theory is independent of any cultural or religious influences. Islamic finance defies this, but despite this major shift it is not localized to Muslim-dominated regions only, but is spreading globally (Smith, 2006). Islam is the only religion today that requires financial activities to be carried out in accordance with its laws. Judaism and Christianity also have similar ethical standards, but the concept of interest is no longer questioned (Abdi, 2010).

Although Islamic banking is still in its infancy, it has attracted the attention of many investors and has the potential to attract new customers and grow in market share. With the development of viable Islamic alternatives to conventional finance products, Muslims, and to a certain extent non-Muslims, are seeking Shariah-based solutions to their financial needs. The world's largest Islamic banks have outpaced conventional banks with an annual asset growth of 26.7%, beating the 19.3% growth rate in conventional banks, and thus delivering a significant message that Islamic banking, while still in its infancy, is a worthwhile alternative to conventional finance (Ahmad, Rustam & Dent, 2011).

Overall, Islamic banking has been able to establish itself on the global stage, but the debate regarding its pros and cons continues. According to its supporters, Islamic banking has made many positive contributions to global banking and finance. The most impressive argument in its favour is that it integrates the financial sector with the real sector, since an existing or potential real asset needs to correspond with every financial asset, unlike in the conventional system (Siddiqi, 2006). It also focuses on the successful operations and financial viability of the projects it invests in, to be able to share in their profits (as in venture capital financing), rather than on collateral like the conventional banks do (Gupta, 2009).

Islamic finance and banking weathered the global financial crisis better than its conventional counterparts, since many of the underlying causes for the crisis were forbidden in Islam (Hassan, Kayed & Oseni, 2013). Islamic banks have shown strong performance during the global financial crisis, which has enhanced their reputation as a legitimate alternative to conventional financing and they are considered a relatively safe refuge from global financial turbulence. Unlike conventional interest-based banking, Islamic banking is more conservative, requiring real asset backing for its products. Furthermore, it does not permit short selling and is considered a legitimate alternative to conventional banking (O'Sullivan, 2009; Rammal, 2010).

CHALLENGES FACED BY ISLAMIC FINANCE AND BANKING

Overall, Islamic banking has been able to establish itself on the global stage, but the debate regarding its pros and cons continues.

Considering the significant growth of Islamic finance and banking globally, and the remarkable increase in the Muslim population, it is not wrong to expect the sector to occupy a significant position in the global finance industry. Though in reality, Islamic finance accounts for only about 1% of global financial assets (Rustam *et al.*, 2011). A major reason for this slow penetration of global Islamic finance and banking is that only a limited number of people know much about it and very few are studying or researching Islamic banking (Ahmed, 2010). As Islamic banking moves forward and aims to compete on a mass scale as a reliable alternative to the centuries-old conventional banking on the global stage of finance and banking, it faces various challenges, which are discussed below. To succeed, the industry needs to find solutions to these challenges and minimize their impact.

1. **Regulatory environment.** Ideally, the Islamic financial institutions operate best in a fully Shariah-compliant regulatory environment. Only countries like Iran and Sudan fall into this category, while most Muslim-majority countries operate under the dual banking system where mainly the conventional regulatory regime is in operation, but the Islamic financial institutions and their unique features are understood and the Shariah implications are tailored into the special regulations applying to these institutions. Non-Muslim countries operate under a fully conventional regulatory environment. The interaction between Shariah law and local law and regulation may lead to conflict and confusion, and in pure conventional environments local regulations may make it difficult to introduce Islamic financial products and services with their unique characteristics. Various adjustments to the local laws are required for Islamic finance products to be accepted, and the country in question and its regulatory regime may not be interested in this, thus making it difficult for Islamic financial institutions to operate freely. These complications are less in Muslim countries.

2. **Lack of knowledge and awareness.** A major problem faced by the global Islamic finance and banking industry is the lack of understanding of this unique finance and banking system, by stakeholders, such as customers, employees, management, regulators, investors and the public with regard to how Islamic finance and banking operates, its uniqueness and benefits, its products and services and its differences from conventional finance and banking. Muslims often patronize Islamic banks for religious reasons only, not based on reasoned choice, while non-Muslims, as well as those Muslims who do not understand Islamic banking and are not religiously motivated, are wary of banking with Islamic banks. When consumers base their decisions not on knowledge of the products, but simply on religious principles, this can lead to the risk of suppliers trying to abuse consumers and undermine the basic principle of informed consumer choice, which is the foundation of the free-market economy (Bley & Kuehn, 2004). Moreover, this lack of knowledge would be a detrimental factor in developing positive attitudes and a preference for Islamic banks, and can be a deterrent to those Muslims not religiously motivated, as well as the non-Muslim customer segment, to patronizing Islamic banks.

3. **Lack of educational initiatives.** The Islamic finance literature is critical of the future growth of Islamic finance in the 21st century (Tahir, 2009). Islamic banking and the finance industry started its operations before the development of professionals especially trained in this specialized area of banking and finance. During the early years of the Islamic finance industry, most human-resource training for professionals was met through conferences, workshops and in-house training programmes, while formal education at the tertiary level, both at the undergraduate and postgraduate level, was very little (Tahir, 2009). Moreover, neither governments nor the financial institutions have taken significant educational initiatives. In contrast, conventional banking concepts are well known to all stakeholders and are taught in educational institutions. To make rational bank selection decisions, customers rely on their pre-existing knowledge and experience, and this, for many, is

conventional banking rather than Islamic banking. A direct impact of this general lack of knowledge leads to the challenge of sourcing employees with the required training and experience for Islamic banks.

Some of the formal educational opportunities now available in the areas of Islamic finance and banking globally are at institutions like the Islamic Research and Training Institute (IRTI) of the Islamic Development Bank (IDB) in Jeddah, International Islamic Universities in Islamabad and Kuala Lumpur, the International Centre for Education in Islamic Finance (INCEIF) in Malaysia, the Qatar Foundation, the International Institute of Islamic Banking and Finance in London, the Islamic Foundation in Leicester, Al Khawarizimi Colleges and Westford School of Management in the UAE. As the growth in the industry takes place, additional institutions, as well as many mainstream universities and colleges in the Middle East and North Africa (especially the GCC), South and South-East Asia are considering offering degrees and diplomas in Islamic finance.

4. **Shortage of trained employees.** A major hurdle faced by the Islamic finance industry is shortage of human capital, with respect to employees with Islamic banking as well as conventional banking skills, and Shariah scholars, with some knowledge of banking. Training is therefore crucial for both these groups, and this would then lead to educating the customers regarding Islamic banking products. Abou-Youssef *et al.* (2012) found that consumers were generally not satisfied with the knowledge, experience and efficiency of Islamic bank employees. Some major challenges in Islamic finance education and training are knowledge of Shariah law, a shortage of well-developed curricula, teaching resources and trained teachers, as well as a knowledge of the Arabic language, since the Quran, Sunnah and Fiqh were all originally in Arabic. A pre-existing knowledge of Shariah and the Arabic language is an advantage enjoyed by the Muslim Arabic-speaking countries with regard to both employees and potential consumers.

The late start of the Islamic finance and banking industry compared with its conventional counterpart, as well as the limited number of Islamic finance educational facilities, constitute the major reason for the shortage of trained employees for this sector. Islamic banks need three types of specialists: finance professionals, familiar with both conventional and Islamic banking products; Shariah scholars and Islamic jurists, to help develop innovative Islamic products; and lawyers, who assist in structuring Islamic products, in compliance with the legal and regulatory issues, in addition to Shariah compliance (Ahmed, 2010). Most Islamic bank employees are educated and trained in conventional banking and do not have sufficient knowledge of Islamic banking; on the other hand, the Shariah scholars, learned in Islamic law and jurisprudence, are lacking in banking knowledge. Training is required for both groups (Tahir & Umar, 2008). Only about 250 to 300 Shariah scholars exist in the world (Shah, Raza & Khurshid, 2012).

Employees with an understanding of Islamic banking principles and products, its similarities and differences from conventional banking and its unique operations, can enhance awareness of Islamic banking among the stakeholders, especially customers. Though Islamic finance has developed in the global economy, at the theoretical and practical level it is still poorly understood and faces ideological and structural challenges to full integration (Karasik, Wehrey & Strom, 2007).

One attributing factor in the lack of knowledge among consumers is the shortage of employees with specific knowledge of and training in Islamic banking (Kharbari, Naser & Shahin, 2004). Islamic banks can integrate with the global financial system, coordinate with leading international Islamic organizations and penetrate the global mass market only if they can address this lack of consumer knowledge and find employees trained both in banking and in Islamic Shariah principles (Bianchi, 2007; Rammal, 2010; Shah, Raza & Khurshid, 2012).

5. **Lack of significant innovation in products.** Islamic banks are also often criticized for having products very similar to those of conventional banks. Khan (2004) contends though that the distinction between the two banking systems lies more in the operations, rather than in the product features. Considering both the supporters' and detractors' views, and the evidence available in the industry, it is evident that a growing wedge is forming between the theory and practice of modern Islamic banking, which can be a major challenge to its acceptability within its main Muslim customer segment, as well as in the global finance industry.

The more positive feelings of current users appear more allied to their religious orientation, rather than to a clear understanding of the products and operations of an Islamic bank. Most current customers of Islamic finance and banking appear to have selected Islamic banks for religious reasons more than anything else. On the other hand, Muslims not religiously motivated and non-Muslims do not feel comfortable banking with Islamic banks. Even though some Islamic finance products have been applied for centuries, the modern-day Islamic finance industry is very young and is still trying to develop a full range of products and services that meet the current needs in a Shariah-compliant manner, and these products and services can be structured quite differently depending on the geographic region or the school of thought they are associated with.

6. **Competition with conventional finance and banking.** Since Islamic banking is a new and unique system, it is less understood amongst regulators and bankers, more so in non-Muslim countries and even in countries with a dual banking system. The banking operations are designed for the conventional system and have been utilized so for a very long time. To be understood and operated, Islamic finance and banking is required to work within this environment. Additionally, the Shariah law precept within the Islamic finance and banking industry is a new paradigm interrelating finance, economy, community and society. Islamic banks are expected to carry out their operations with a combined finance and socio-economic objective, striving for economic efficiency as well as social justice (Choudhury & Hussain, 2005). This can be quite a challenge for the Islamic banks, especially in competing with the conventional banks, which only operate on profit-maximization principles and have no religious or social obligations to fulfil.

Islamic banking, being quite new in the global finance scene, on the one hand, attracts new customers, but on the other hand, also attracts increasing competition, requiring banks to design innovative marketing strategies to gain competitive advantage and a strong position (Hassan, Chachi & Latiff, 2008). By overcoming these challenges, Islamic banks will further develop as legitimate competitors to conventional banks globally, reaching out to the majority Muslim population who are not always inclined to bank on religious grounds, as well as to non-Muslims.

7. **Gap between theory and practice of Islamic finance and banking.** Since all Islamic banks are based on Shariah principles, theoretically there cannot be any differences between them, yet their practices differ significantly. Theoretically, Islamic banks are not supposed to deal with interest in any form. In practice, Islamic banks diverge in many ways from the paradigm version, and whether all Islamic banking products are fully Shariah compliant or not is an ongoing debate (Dusuki & Abdullah, 2007). Today, Islamic banks are at a crossroads, between the choice of Shariah compliance and adjusting to business and economic realities (Hasan, 2005). They are competing with conventional banks who offer fixed interest rates to customers, while Islamic banks can only offer a probable profit rate, and their profit and loss system often adds riskier projects to their portfolios (Nienhaus, 1986). Not all Islamic banks follow PLS completely, and only a small percentage of their activities are based entirely on PLS. Most Islamic bank deposits are explicitly or implicitly guaranteed, PLS principles are not applied strictly and banks are encouraged by central banks to maintain reserves to even out profits and losses (Zaher & Hassan, 2001).

The use of PLS-based products such as Mudaraba and Musharaka has declined in recent years, and more short-term financing and other debt-based contracts like Murabaha and leases are used by Islamic banks (Kuran, 2004; Zaher & Hassan, 2001). There is no theological debate about the prohibition of Riba, which is the Arabic term for interest, and it is mandatory for all Islamic banks to have Shariah Advisory Boards to ensure all products and operations of the bank are Shariah compliant. However, there is criticism of the practices of Islamic banks and suggestions are being made that they need to understand and implement Shariah law better (Dusuki & Abozaid, 2007). Many Islamic banks are diverging from their social and economic goals as well (Aggarwal & Yousef, 2000; Asutay, 2007). Often the profit rate on various Islamic banking contracts is the same, irrespective of the asset applied to, and is reminiscent of interest rates, while competitive pressure can be a reason for pegging the Islamic bank profit rates on conventional bank interest rates (Dar & Presley, 2000; Haron & Ahmad, 2000; Khan, 2004; Nienhaus, 1986). These criticisms may drive the original religiously oriented Muslims to mistrust Islamic banks and have negative attitudes about them, deterring them from banking with Islamic banks.

The emerging Islamic finance industry is promoted as an ideal alternative, away from the problems of interest-based conventional systems, where the bank shares the risk and profit with the entrepreneur. In practice, Islamic banks are executing more commercial functions rather than investing (Askari, Iqbal & Mirakhor, 2008). They are replicating conventional bank products, with Arabic names, technically complying with Shariah by mostly using markup sales of Murabaha or leasing called Ijara, rather than the equity financing of Mudaraba and Musharaka. There is little evidence that Islamic banks are significantly involved in venture capital projects, small or micro enterprises, emerging industries or agriculture; they are engaged in practices like those of conventional banks, financing well-established businesses and individuals (Kayed, 2012). Clearly, the widening gap between theory and practice could work against the Islamic finance industry in confusing stakeholders, generating negative attitudes and losing customer preference.

SOCIAL RESPONSIBILITIES OF ISLAMIC FINANCE

Shariah principles require Islamic banks to balance profit motivation with social objectives; it is considered unjust if they are unable to provide sufficient returns to depositors and shareholders who have entrusted them with their money on the one hand, but on the other hand they should not make excessive profits at the expense of their customers or by neglecting their social responsibility (Ahmad, 2000; Chapra, 2007). Dusuki (2008) found that stakeholders of Islamic banks had more favourable attitudes towards them when they served their social and ethical goals. Islamic banks are like the socially responsible and ethical investment funds that have gained popularity in Western economies (Wilson, 1997). The Turkish media report about the *Daily Vatican* newspaper, encouraging banks to study the ethical rules of Islamic finance to restore confidence among their clients, took Islamic banking to new heights (Loo, 2010). The socially responsible and interest-free operations of Islamic banking are accepted by many scholars as potential solutions to economic instability, unemployment, inflation and poverty, and can serve as a major competitive advantage among the customer group that wishes to patronize ethical banking (Ahmad, 2000; Chapra, 2007; Dar & Presley, 1999; Dusuki, 2008).

According to the International Association of Islamic Banks, the social responsibility of Islamic banks distinguishes them from conventional banks: Islamic banks have to consider the social implications of their decisions; profitability is an important priority, but is not the sole criterion in evaluating the performance of Islamic banks (Al-Omar & Abdel-Haq, 1996); they are expected to focus on the disadvantaged classes of society, aiming to make them self-reliant (Hassan, 1999), for example by offering finance to small businesses, often not served by conventional banks, without collateral on a PLS basis.

This social responsibility advocated for Islamic banks has not gone unchallenged and has generated ongoing debate. There are two dissenting views regarding the social objectives of Islamic banks. The first, called the Chapra model, says that Islamic banks should not be solely profit oriented, but have religious commitments and socio-economic objectives of social justice, equitable distribution of income, and wealth and promotion of economic development, without undermining their commercial viability.

According to the second view, called the Ismail model, Islamic banks are regular commercial entities whose only goal is to carry out business in compliance with Shariah law, and their main responsibility is towards the shareholders and depositors, while social welfare objectives should be left to other bodies such as the government (Dusuki, 2008; Satkunasegaran, 2003). Rosly and Bakar (2003) noted that payment of Zakat as a social contribution is compulsory for Islamic banks, but they should not use shareholders' or depositors' funds for any other non-compulsory social activities that may jeopardize their viability, since Islamic banks are business entities, not welfare organizations.

The world today is much more conscious of the social and ethical behaviour of business entities, and corporate social responsibility is a major competitive advantage of all businesses, including banks. Islamic banks' built-in social responsibility principle is thus an advantage for them. Ismail's model is like the Western neoclassical worldview, especially Friedman's concept of a firm's responsibility. Society is best served by individuals pursuing their own self-interest and profit maximization within the legal context (Dusuki, 2008). According to Satkunasegaran (2003), Ismail's model is more applicable in multi-religious countries like Malaysia, while Chapra's model is more practical in a primarily Muslim country.

The Islamic perspective of global business has largely been ignored by researchers, while interest in business ethics is growing. Research in Islamic finance can therefore add to this body of knowledge, as Islamic finance professes to be more just and equitable for all stakeholders, including borrowers and lenders, with its products operated in partnership and on a profit and loss-sharing basis, thus emphasizing socio-economic justice and equitable distribution of wealth (Dusuki, 2008; Saeed, Ahmed & Mukhtar, 2001; Shah, Raza & Khurshid, 2012).

GOING FORWARD

Islamic banking has grown tremendously over the last five decades, but it faces several challenges that need to be overcome for its continued growth globally as a legitimate alternative to conventional banking.

Islamic banks face competition from other Islamic banks and from global conventional banks. To survive and grow in this increasingly competitive and liberalized global banking industry, Islamic banks need to attract and retain both Muslim and non-Muslim customers. Although Islamic and conventional banks are different, they compete in the same market, offering complementary products and services (Naser & Moutinho, 1997). To effectively compete, Islamic banks need to be customer-oriented, understand well both their current and potential customers, and design marketing strategies accordingly, aiming to gain a competitive advantage and a strong competitive position. Islamic banks need to avoid over-dependence on Muslims, who prefer them primarily on religious grounds, and should find innovative ways to serve overall society, including Muslims not religiously motivated, as well as non-Muslims, but within the basic Shariah guidelines, otherwise they would lose their identity.

To establish their position in non-Muslim countries, Islamic banks need to integrate and adapt to the overall legal and regulatory frameworks of those countries, while maintaining their Shariah compliance to continue to satisfy Muslim communities. At times they may face contradictory social and legal issues, and one size may not fit all; flexibility may need to be exerted, and although Shariah is a global ideal, its interpretation varies (Balz, 2007). The social responsibilities of Islamic banks set them apart from the capitalistic and solely profit-oriented conventional banks. Islamic banks need to balance both profit as well as social objectives (Dusuki, 2008), and though the PLS basis of investment and lending of Islamic banks may disadvantage them somewhat compared with conventional banks (Gupta, 2009), the fairness of the PLS system and the social objectives allow them to be more ethical. This can be important in attracting both non-Muslims and Muslims, beyond those interested in Islamic banking solely on religious grounds.

To ensure long-term growth and prosperity, Islamic banks need to overcome general ignorance about Islamic banking, and educate all stakeholders – customers, employees, competitors, regulators and the public. Competition in Islamic banking will eventually lead to competing for the most knowledgeable and experienced professionals, who are trained in both conventional and Islamic banking, as well as in Shariah law, and such expertise is quite rare (Natt, Al Habshi & Zainal, 2009). Shortage of human capital is currently recognized as a major detriment to the global growth of Islamic finance, and expert human capital will allow banks to enhance current and potential customers' knowledge, as well as develop innovative products that meet customer needs and are comparable to conventional banking products. This is directly linked to the need to enhance educational and training facilities available for Islamic finance and banking, as well as the Shariah principles applicable to the discipline of commerce and finance.

Since Islamic banking is based on Islamic religion and Shariah principles, which are derived from the Quran and the Sunnah, written in the Arabic language, Arabic terminology cannot be completely detached from Islamic banking. On the one hand, Arabic terms reassure religiously oriented Muslims of Shariah compliance, but on the other hand, they alienate non-Muslims and non-Arab Muslims. Moreover, they complicate comprehension of Islamic banking among all customers. It is therefore recommended that Arabic be used only as and when required, and that all Arabic terminology should be appropriately translated for the general customer.

The design of effective marketing strategies is very important for Islamic banks, and they need to develop media campaigns to increase customer awareness and knowledge, build positive attitudes and trust, and reduce negativity. Islamic banks should also compete effectively in service delivery with conventional banks and focus beyond the Shariah-compliance dimension, concentrating on attributes of bank preference deemed important by current and potential customers.

KEY TERMS AND CONCEPTS

Muslim legal scholars	Global financial crisis	Regulatory environment
Muslim population	Oil boom and Oil embargo	Social responsibilities of Islamic finance

CHAPTER SUMMARY

Islamic finance was evident from the time of the Prophet and when Islam was first introduced, though modern Islamic finance and banking was reintroduced to the world in the middle of the 20th century through the efforts of Islamic economists, political activists, Shariah scholars and finance professionals and businessmen. It provides an alternative form of finance that is free of interest, the core of conventional finance, and is based on profit and loss sharing – required to follow Shariah rulings in addition to the profit objective.

Islamic finance and banking, developing over the last eight decades, has gone through early failures but over time has made its place and achieved significant success. The momentum in the Islamic finance and banking industry was majorly driven by the oil boom in the Middle East, mainly in the GCC countries, and the significant growth amongst the Muslim population and their reawakened desire to bank as per their religious beliefs. The South and South-East Asian Muslim-majority countries have also been important.

In the time it has been around, Islamic finance and banking has achieved a niche position in the global finance industry, with significant size and number of institutions operating under this alternate system, as well as several large conventional financial institutions offering Shariah-compliant products. The industry also faces several challenges, specifically regulatory challenges in non-Muslim and some Muslim countries. It also suffers from a lack of knowledge, awareness, educational initiatives, trained employees and innovation in products. Other challenges are competition from the conventional finance industry and the debate related to the gap between theory and practice in the Islamic finance and banking industry.

Islamic finance has been able to weather the global financial crisis quite well and is considered as a more conservative form of financing, with definite social responsibilities and ethical considerations making it attractive to many. The industry is expected to develop further moving forward.

END OF CHAPTER QUESTIONS AND ACTIVITIES

Discussion Questions

1. Discuss the reintroduction of modern Islamic finance and banking in the world.
2. Is interest prohibition unique to Islam? Discuss.
3. Discuss the groups of people who played an important role in reintroducing Islamic finance and banking to the world.
4. Explain the major factors contributing to the global growth in the Islamic finance and banking industry.
5. Discuss the growth of the Islamic finance and banking industry vis à vis the Muslim community.
6. Describe the Islamic finance and banking industry in the Middle East and the GCC.
7. Describe the Islamic finance and banking industry in South and South-East Asia.
8. What can be considered as the achievements and future opportunities of the Islamic finance and banking industry?
9. What are the major challenges faced by the Islamic finance and banking industry?
10. Discuss the in-built social responsibilities of Islamic finance.
11. What are the key issues to be considered in Islamic finance going forward in time?

Glossary

Adverse selection risk   Since borrowers or entrepreneurs have more information than lenders about a project, the bank could make an error in the selection of projects.

Ajr   Reward or wages for work done or services rendered.

Al Manfaah or usufruct   The right to enjoy the use and benefits of an asset belonging to someone else.

Al Masnu   The specific asset to be manufactured in the Istisna contract.

Al Musania   The seller of the Istisna contract.

Al Mustasni   The buyer of the Istisna contract.

Application of funds   An Islamic bank applies the funds it raises from depositors as well as its own funds to various financing transactions with the aim of earning a profit. The risk of loss is also there. The application of funds of an Islamic bank comprises its assets and includes a variety of products like Murabaha, Salam, Ijara, Istisna, Mudaraba and Musharaka contracts.

Aquila   The Muslims in Makkah and Medina practiced Aquila with the Prophet's approval. In this system, if anyone was killed by someone from another tribe, blood money was paid to the victim's family by the killer's tribe, who pooled together the required amount to ensure they did not suffer a loss of income from the death of the earner. Some Arab Muslim countries still use the blood money system.

Arbun   This is a non-refundable downpayment made by the buyer against the purchase price of an item in a sale contract. If the buyer finally buys the item, the downpayment would be part of the purchase price but if the buyer does not fulfil the purchase obligation, the downpayment would be lost.

Asset-backed Sukuk   Asset-backed Sukuk certificate holders rely on the underlying asset to generate yield and recover their investments, and in this case the asset is still in the ownership of the Sukuk holders and thus recourse to it is easier.

Asset-based Sukuk   Asset-based Sukuk involves purchase and sale of the asset, as in Murabaha or Ijara contracts, and in this case the asset was purchased and sold, and its deferred payments make payments to the Sukuk holders so if non-payment happens, ownership of the asset is no longer with the Sukuk holders, thus the main recourse is the creditworthiness of the customer who purchased the asset.

Bank–client relationship   In conventional banking this is a debtor–creditor relationship while in Islamic banking it varies with various contracts as seller–buyer, lessor–lessee, partners, etc.

Bedouin   Nomadic Arabs, living in the desert.

Beneficiary   Those participants who are going to benefit from the Takaful fund or else those people or institutions which have been identified or nominated by the insured to benefit from the Takaful fund in case the risky event happens.

Bilateral Mudaraba   In this type there are only two parties, one is the capital provider or Rab al Maal, while the other is the Mudarib or entrepreneur.

Binding promise In Murabaha, when the two parties contract it is morally binding on both. However, if the bank – while relying on the promise – takes the necessary steps to acquire the property, the promise becomes legally binding.

Buy-back condition In a Salam contract, the buyer cannot demand a buy-back condition from the seller that would require the seller to buy back the goods delivered. Shariah ruling does not allow the buyer to sell back the commodity to the original seller.

Capital market Most instruments in this market have a maturity of more than one year. This market is further divided into the debt market (bonds), equity markets (shares) and markets for structured or hybrid products.

Central bank The central bank is the supervisor of all banks and is involved in applying monetary policy, acts as the clearing house and is lender of last resort. Central banks are required to balance the impact of the public's preference to save or to spend.

Cheque clearing services Central banks also provide cheque clearing services to both conventional and Islamic banks.

Classic economic problem Classic economics states that wants can be unlimited while resources are limited, which leads to the classic economic problem of scarcity.

Clear financial segregation Takaful companies are not the insurer, the participants themselves insure each other and the Takaful companies are operators of the Takaful fund on behalf of the participants. As such, it is imperative to manage clear financial segregation of the Takaful fund owned by the participant and the operational funds that belong to the Takaful operator on behalf of the shareholders; as such, it is also called the shareholder fund.

Close-ended fund A close-ended unit trust or fund can issue a limited number of units only. Once the original investors have acquired these units, any subsequent buying and selling of units happens only on the secondary market, that is the stock exchange.

Commodity market This special market allows investors to trade in commodities, including precious metals. This market is utilized by traders and hedgers, and operates both via the exchanges and over-the-counter.

Constant Musharaka or permanent Musharaka In this kind of Musharaka, the partners' shares in the capital remain constant or permanent throughout the contract period. The partners can sell their shares in the Musharaka capital to a third party. Profit sharing is at a pre-agreed ratio and losses are borne in proportion to the capital contribution.

Conventional banking The standard banking activities seen the world over, based on interest-based financial intermediation.

Conventional insurance Insurance offered by the conventional insurance industry.

Conventional lease The lease of any asset in conventional finance, where the lessor rents out the asset to the lessee for the designated period for a decided rental which is like an interest rate.

Cooperative savings banking In this kind of banking, the depositors are members and together save in a cooperative society, for common good, and may borrow from the common fund.

Credit risk The risk of non-payment by its customer for the bank. To deal with this, banks can ask for security or collateral from their customers, which can be used to recover any amounts that are not paid by the customer.

Current accounts Current accounts are used by clients to pay and receive funds. Depositors can withdraw their money anytime. Islamic banks accept the funds in these accounts as Amanah or as Wadia, which involves safekeeping.

Debt-based Sukuk Debt-based Sukuks are based on receivables like those arising from Murabaha or Salam.

Declaratory rulings These are rulings that make it easy to implement the obligatory rulings by describing causes, conditions and obstacles related to the obligatory rulings.

Default after delivery In Istisna, default after delivery can be caused by the seller when they fail to meet commitments related to after-construction or after-sales service, in such a manner that the asset cannot be used by the buyer as it was intended. The buyer can then terminate the Istisna and claim return of the purchase price from the seller as well as damages for any loss incurred. Such default can also be caused by the buyer if they fail to make repayments as they fall due. The seller cannot take the asset back since title has already passed to the buyer, but can claim damages and recover its dues from the collateral or security or through a court procedure.

Default before delivery   In Istisna, default before delivery can be caused by the seller not delivering on the due date or the delivered asset not matching the specification or being damaged. The buyer can then terminate the contract and demand return of any payments already made, and even damages if – due to the default – the buyer would lose. Default before delivery can be caused by the buyer failing or refusing to take delivery of the asset when the specifications are met by the seller. The seller can then claim damages from the buyer. In case the buyer has already partially paid, and the value of the instalments paid by the buyer is greater than the damages, the seller will deduct its damages and return the excess to the buyer; but if the value is less than the damages, the buyer needs to pay the additional amount.

Economics   The discipline that deals with the production, distribution and consumption of goods or services and wealth in general.

Equity-based Sukuk   Equity-based Sukuks are those that are modelled on partnership-based Islamic instruments, like Musharaka or Mudaraba.

Family Takaful   This is a substitute for conventional life insurance. Family Takaful needs to be structured carefully to be Shariah compliant. Shariah allows savings plan-type policies which have a maturity date with specified benefits and may also be designed to help the insured's family in case of death of the insured before the maturity period by compensating financially for loss of income.

Fidya   This was a form of ransom paid to free prisoners of war amongst the Arab Muslims.

Financial intermediation   The core business of banks is financial intermediation. This is the process by which banks match surplus units or savers with deficit units or borrowers and play the role of trusted intermediary.

Financial screening   This is the second stage of the Shariah screening process to evaluate shares for Shariah compliance. There are very few companies in the global markets that are fully Shariah compliant. The majority of Islamic scholars have identified a certain level of non-compliant financial activity as acceptable, provided the income earned from these companies is purified by donating the non-compliant proportion of income to charity.

Fiqh   The knowledge of Shariah is called Fiqh.

Foreign exchange market   Foreign currency transactions are conducted in this market, both spot and forward transactions. Foreign exchange transactions are only over-the-counter, and executed in a variety of global currencies.

General Takaful   General Takaful products are offered both to individuals and to commercial entities. Most common general Takaful products are for car or motor, home and contents, health, fire, burglary, marine, education, machinery breakdown, worker compensation, employers' liability, etc.

Gharar   Gharar means taking excessive risk or having unnecessary uncertainty in the contract. Islam requires all aspects of the transaction or contract to be transparent and known to all parties, thus significantly reducing conflict.

Global financial crisis   Global financial crises are when the finance industry in most countries of the world goes through crises and assets and investments are lost and financial institutions suffer losses or go bankrupt. The last such crisis was seen in 2007–2008. Islamic finance and banking weathered this global financial crisis better than its conventional counterparts, since many of the underlying causes for the crisis were forbidden in Islam as it is more conservative, requiring real asset backing for its products, not permitting short selling, etc.

Hajj   The pilgrimage to Makkah that is compulsory for all able-bodied Muslims once in their lifetime, provided they have the financial ability.

Hawala   This exchange involves the transfer of an amount from one person to another via an intermediary. The intermediary may charge a fee, but as per Shariah ruling this cannot be a percentage of the transfer amount and the transfer should happen at the earliest without any increase to the principal amount.

Hiba   This is a gift that can be revoked before it has been handed over.

Hybrid model   Based on a combination of Mudaraba and Wakala contracts. Usually the underwriting services of the Takaful operator are compensated by a Wakala fee, while for its management of the investment services the Takaful operator shares the profit or loss with the participants on a Mudaraba basis.

Ijara   A bilateral contract involving transfer of the use of an asset from the owner to a user for an agreed period for a consideration. The owner of the object temporarily transfers its usufruct to the lessee for the agreed period and the lessee should be able to derive benefit from it without consuming it.

Ijara fund   This fund is created by investing its money in purchasing a pool of suitable physical assets that can then be leased out to a third party, who would be the ultimate user. The rentals earned from the lease or Ijara constitute the income of the fund and are distributed amongst the investors of the fund after deducting all relevant expenses.

Ijara Muntahia Bittamleek or Ijara wa Iqtina or financial lease   When the ownership of the leased asset passes to the lessee at the end of the lease period, it is called Ijara wa Iqtina or Ijara Muntahia Bittamleek and this is comparable with a conventional financial lease or hire purchase. This transfer of ownership may be with or without additional payment at the end of the lease period.

Ijara Sukuk   This is the most common type of Sukuk, and is based on the Ijara contract. Mostly used for leasing and project finance.

Ijma   The third most important source of Shariah. The jurists were required to debate and provide opinions on Shariah issues not dealt with before from the very early days of Islam.

Inan   Also called limited Musharaka, it has two or more partners who contribute capital in varying amounts, which can be cash or kind, and may or may not contribute their labour, effort, skills and enterprise. Each partner is only the agent for all the others but is not a guarantor and thus has limited liability. Profit is shared according to a pre-agreed ratio, while losses are in proportion to the capital contribution.

Indemnity   This means that the insurance or Takaful contract will compensate the insured for actual loss that has happened.

Industry screening   This is the first stage of the Shariah screening process to evaluate shares for Shariah compliance. This stage weeds out, in general, the companies that are in a Shariah non-compliant industry or that are involved in activities that are against Shariah.

Insurance claim   Upon the occurrence of the risky event that was covered under the Takaful policy, the insured or participant claims the amount of compensation from the Takaful fund.

Insurable interest   Takaful contracts, as in the case of conventional insurance, are only carried out when the event for which Takaful is executed has significant insurable interest. Insurable interest means the possibility of causing loss to the insured who is being protected by the contract arising from an uncertain future event; the insured can then be financially compensated by the Takaful fund.

Insurance premium   The premium is the consideration paid by the insured to the insurer, which in case of conventional insurance is paid by the policyholder to the insurance company while in the case of Takaful is paid into the Takaful fund as a donation.

Insured   Those participants who face the risky event and who would be compensated or helped in case they suffer from any loss from the Takaful fund into which they have also contributed.

Insurer   The insurance company that provides the risk protection in case of conventional insurance, while in Takaful the policyholders themselves are the insurer also.

Investment accounts   These are the most important source of funds for the Islamic banks. The funds are accepted on a Mudaraba basis, where the customer and the bank enter into a joint-venture agreement and are in the true sense not liability but non voting equity, where depositors are the Rab al Maal and the bank is the Mudarib, sharing profit at a pre-agreed ratio, while financial loss is that of the Rab al Maal.

Investment risk reserve   The allocation for this reserve from the Mudaraba profit is done after the share of the Mudarib has been allocated, and it aims to protect investment account holders from future losses.

Islamic asset management   The Islamic investment fund is a joint pool into which investors contribute their surplus money to be invested by professionals in accordance with Islamic Shariah guidance. The fund managers of an Islamic fund are responsible for ensuring the Shariah compliance of the instruments and processes used to build and manage the fund, avoiding non-Halal industries like alcohol, pork, gambling, uncensored media and entertainment, pornography and other things Shariah clearly forbids.

Islamic balanced fund   A mutual fund that invests its pool of money to purchase a combination of Shariah-screened shares, commodities and Islamic fixed-income instruments is called an Islamic balanced fund and provides investors – in one common fund – with the goals of both short-term income and long-term growth and capital gains.

Islamic commodity fund   In this case the fund manager uses the common pool of funds to purchase a variety of commodities that would be resold based on a deferred payment system and at a profit, which constitutes the main income of the fund and is distributed pro-rata amongst the investors after deducting all relevant expenses.

Islamic debt fund   The fund is invested in fixed-income Islamic instruments like a Murabaha, Ijara, Istisna or Salam, which are deferred payment sales contracts that yield fixed income over a given period, thus providing stability to the income generated by the fund and shared by investors of the fund after deducting all relevant expenses.

Islamic economics   Involves studying the rules provided in the Quran and the Sunnah pertaining to economic concepts, comparing and contrasting these with contemporary economics, identifying the gaps and finding ways to bridge these gaps.

Islamic equity fund   The assets of the fund are invested mostly in shares, while a small amount may be invested in cash and other fixed-income Islamic securities. The chosen shares would be Shariah screened, and this is the most common type of fund used by Islamic fund managers globally.

Islamic finance and banking   Modern Islamic finance and banking mostly follows the structure of conventional finance and banking, with the exclusion of interest-based transactions, replacing interest with a profit and loss sharing system and ensuring transactions and operations are Shariah compliant.

Islamic real estate investment trust (I-REIT)   A REIT is an investment vehicle which invests mostly in real estate. I-REITs usually use Ijara contracts or Ijara–Istisna contracts. These are often designed as equity REITs, where investors may get proportional ownership of the underlying real estate and earn stable rent income. I-REITs are structured by individual investors placing their funds into a common pool which is invested in a managed pool of real estate, generating income from renting, leasing and selling real estate.

Islamic window   When conventional banks participate in Islamic banking, they may do so through a window within their regular distribution channel for their conventional business, rather than setting up a separate subsidiary or branch network.

Istisna   This is a sales contract in which the buyer contracts with the seller to manufacture, produce, construct, fabricate, assemble or process any asset in accordance with given specifications, descriptions, quality and quantity identified, and within a specified period and at an agreed price.

Istisna Sukuk   This form of Sukuk uses the Istisna mode of Islamic finance to fund manufacturing, real estate development, large industrial projects, construction of major items like power plants, ships, aircraft, etc. To raise the requisite funds, the issuer or bank produces Sukuk certificates that provide the holders with proportional ownership in the asset to be manufactured or constructed. Once the asset is completed, its ownership may be passed on immediately to the ultimate client and the deferred payments made by the client are passed on to the Sukuk holders.

Kafalah   This is a third-party guarantee provided by a borrower against some obligation. If the borrowers fail to meet their obligations, the creditor or bank can recover their dues from the guarantor. The Arabic word means joint guarantee or guaranteeing each other in Takaful.

Lender of last resort   In case the interbank market is not able to meet the needs completely, the central bank acts as the lender of last resort and lends funds to the banks to meet their short-term needs.

Lessee or Mustajir   In a lease or Ijara, the party that uses the asset.

Lessor or Muajir   In a lease or Ijara, the party that owns the asset.

Majur   The asset involved in the Ijara contract that is given by the lessor to the lessee for use.

Markup or profit   This can be a fixed amount or a percentage of the cost of the Murabaha item. This amount will constitute the Islamic bank's profit and for the Murabaha client or buyer it is the extra cost incurred for the advantage of deferred payment. The markup or profit will be clearly stated and mutually agreed by the bank and the client, and cannot be changed later.

Maysir   This includes all kinds of games of chance or dealings where one can gain significantly or lose all depending on which way the deals moves, and are prohibited by Shariah law.

Medium of exchange   Something used as payment for buying and selling transactions, like money and in earlier times, gold, silver, animals, grains, etc.

Mismatch of quality and quantity   If the commodities specified in the Salam and parallel Salam contracts do not match completely, or the delivered goods do not match with the specifications, the supplier or manufacturer would be in default with the bank, but the bank still has to supply to the client by purchasing from the open market.

Money   The medium of exchange currently used globally.

Money market   Investors and borrowers access the money market to invest or borrow in the short term, and the period various from overnight to one year. The instruments have a maturity of one year or less.

Moral hazard risk   Only the borrower or entrepreneur has full information on the running of the business and may engage in activities that are harmful for the business, affecting the profit earned. The Islamic bank shares in the profit or loss of the business and is required to engage in thorough and careful monitoring of the business to ensure all operations are in the best interests of the enterprise.

Muamalat   Shariah or Islamic jurisprudence includes the rulings related to man-to-man relationships, called Muamalat. A major part of the Muamalat involves economic activities and commercial dealings, including Islamic finance and banking.

Muawadat   Contracts of exchange.

Mudaraba   In Mudaraba, one party provides the entire capital while the other provides the time and effort in the business venture. The capital provider is called the Rab al Maal while the entrepreneur who manages and runs the business using their time, expertise, management and entrepreneurship skills is called the Mudarib.

Mudaraba al Muqayyadah   Also called restricted Mudaraba, in this case the capital provider, the Rab al Maal, provides certain parameters or restrictions within which they would prefer the Mudarib to invest their funds. These restrictions usually relate to the type of investment, place or location of the investment, and the time of the business venture. Besides these restrictions provided at the beginning of the contract, the Rab al Maal does not interfere in the everyday operations of the business, which is completely the responsibility of the Mudarib.

Mudaraba al Mutlaqah Also called unrestricted Mudaraba, with no restrictions imposed on the Mudarib. The Mudarib has complete authority and freedom to choose any type of project, provided it is Halal, Shariah compliant and legal. The location and time of the venture is also up to the Mudarib to choose.

Mudaraba model This is based on the Mudaraba concept. The participants are the Rab al Maal, providing the capital and the Takaful operator is the Mudarib, providing the effort and skill; they share the profit in a pre-agreed ratio. In case of a loss, the participants lose their capital and the Takaful operator is not compensated for their work.

Mudaraba Sukuk Equity based where one party, the Rab al Maal, pays the entire capital while the other, the Mudarib, provides the effort and entrepreneurship. The two parties share the profit according to a pre-agreed ratio, but the entire financial loss is borne by the Rab al Maal and the Mudarib loses their effort. When the Sukuk is structured it represents undivided ownership of units of equal value in the Mudaraba equity, and these units are registered in the names of the Sukuk holders who contribute their capital to a specific project to be managed by the issuer or the Mudarib.

Mufawada In this kind of Musharaka all the partners or participants rank equally in every respect – in their initial contributions of capital, in their privileges, in their rights and liabilities. The partners have equal roles in management, and equal rights in the profits and disposition of the assets of the venture. The liabilities of all the partners are unlimited, unrestricted and equal. They are all the agent and guarantor for each other. The Mufawada form of Musharaka is not very common or popular in the Islamic banking industry.

Multilateral Mudaraba In this case there are several capital providers whose funds are collectively provided to one Mudarib or entrepreneur.

Murabaha process A client approaches the bank with a request to purchase a specific item or asset; this request could be a binding promise. The bank acquires the item and adds a markup to the costs, then sells to the client who is aware of the cost as well as the markup. The client pays the bank over the contract period either as a lump sum in the future or in instalments over the deferred period.

Murabaha or trust sale The simplest Islamic banking instrument, and a widely used product. Islam prohibits charging fixed interest on money, but permits charging fixed profit on sale of goods. Islamic banks therefore use a sale-based transaction – Murabaha – instead of a term loan for financing. Murabaha is a sales contract where profit is made by selling at a cost-plus basis. It is an agreement where the bank purchases a specified item at the request of the customer, adds a pre-agreed profit to it and sells it to them at the marked-up price.

Murabaha sale with a promise The client makes a promise to buy the item once the bank acquires it. More common than the simple Murabaha as Islamic banks want to guarantee the client buys what they asked the bank to acquire for them. In Murabaha with a promise the client has the risk of the goods not being delivered as per specification and at the contracted time, while in case of ordinary Murabaha the entire non-delivery risk is with the bank.

Murabaha Sukuk Based on the Murabaha mode of financing, where a seller interested in acquiring assets to resell using the Murabaha mode may raise the cost to acquire the assets by issuing Sukuks. The Sukuk holders would own the assets till they are resold and will be entitled to the marked-up sales price in proportion to the shares in the Sukuk issue.

Musawama This sale involves a purchase when the customer does not know the cost of the product, but is aware of the price and decides to buy or not at that price. The customer may also negotiate the price, and this includes all the purchases made at shops where customers are aware only of the price and not the cost.

Musharaka A partnership of two or more, who put together their capital and labour based on mutual trust, share in the profit and loss of the joint venture and have similar rights and liabilities. The purest form of Islamic finance instrument.

Musharaka Al Milk This is a Musharaka partnership which involves ownership of common property that the partners may have acquired through a specific contract or via inheritance.

Musharaka Mutanaqisa, Musharaka Muntahiya Bittamleek or diminishing Musharaka This type of Musharaka is a joint-ownership contract at the very onset of which it is agreed that one party has the right to purchase the shares of the other partners over a prescribed contract period at a pre-agreed price. The repurchase can be at regular intervals or could be according to the financial convenience of the purchasing partner. Commonly, in Islamic banking, the borrower or entrepreneur is the party that gradually purchases the units in the Musharaka venture owned by the Islamic bank as partner. The result is that the Islamic bank's share in the Musharaka declines, finally becoming zero, while the other partner's share increases, reaching 100%, resulting in the latter owning all units of the venture and becoming the sole proprietor.

Musharaka Sukuk Musharaka is based on an equity partnership where all parties provide the capital and the profits are shared in a pre-agreed ratio, while the losses are borne according to the capital contribution. Musharaka Sukuks are structured to raise funds for new projects, to extend an existing project or for a huge business activity based on a joint venture. The issuer or SPV are usually the active partners, while the Sukuk holders are the silent partners.

Muslam The buyer of the asset in a Salam contract.

Muslam Ileihi The seller of the asset in a Salam contract.

Muslam Fihi The purchased asset or commodity in a Salam contract.

Muslim legal scholars Scholars who are experts in Shariah law and Islamic jurisprudence.

Muslim population All the world population belonging to the Islamic faith. Currently the Muslim population comprises more than a quarter of the estimated global population of 7.4 billion currently.

Mutual insurance In both conventional mutual insurance and Takaful, the insured or policyholders create a pool of funds by contributing their premiums to it and this fund belongs to the policyholders who mutually insure each other. The fund is used to indemnify those policyholders who suffer any loss from the risks against which they have been insured.

Non-compliant stocks These are shares that do not pass the Shariah screening process or were compliant earlier but for various changes in their business or financial activities are not Shariah compliant any more.

Non-tradable Sukuk Non-tradable Sukuks are those that represent receivables such as cash or goods and hence are not tradable – for example Murabaha and Salam Sukuks.

Obligatory rulings Rulings that need to be followed and are of five types. Wajib – which needs to be followed, Mustahabb – which are recommended, Mubah – which are permissible and neither rewarded nor punished, Makruh – which are discouraged and Haram – which are forbidden.

Oil boom and oil embargo The importance of oil for the world and the economy of oil-producing countries became crucial with the formation of the OPEC and the application of the oil embargo in the mid-1970s, leading to a dramatic increase in oil prices and a sudden significant increase in the wealth of governments and the public of the OPEC countries, including the GCC countries.

Open-ended fund An open-ended unit trust is that which has the authority to issue new units and to redeem existing units at any time.

Operating lease or regular Ijara   Regular Ijara are like conventional operating leases and can also be called true leases. These are contracts of rent only and do not end in the transfer of ownership of the leased asset from lessor to lessee. Rather, the asset is returned to the lessor at the end of the Ijara period. In this kind of Ijara, the Ujrah or rentals that are charged over the Ijara period are not sufficient to recover the full value of the asset.

Ordinary Murabaha   The client asks the bank to acquire an asset that they would like to purchase without making any promise to buy it.

Parallel Istisna   The second Istisna contract is drawn up between the bank and the assigned manufacturer, the bank is the buyer and the manufacturer is the seller. The bank approaches the manufacturer with the exact same order and specifications that the customer has provided to the bank in the first Istisna. When the bank receives the quote from the manufacturer, it adds its own profit and quotes to the customer for the first Istisna. If the customer agrees, then the first Istisna is contracted. The bank then goes back to the manufacturer and enters the contract of the second Istisna agreement, the parallel Istisna. The bank makes the payment to the manufacturer either in full when signing the contract or in instalments during the manufacture, or sometimes in full at delivery. The parallel Istisna can be called a sub-contract but to be Shariah complaint, the two Istisna contracts must be completely independent of each other with respect to rights and obligations.

Parallel Salam   The Islamic bank acts as the buyer of the asset or commodity in the first Salam contract and then enters into the second Salam contract, the parallel Salam, as a seller of the acquired asset or commodity from the first Salam that it will now sell and deliver to the buyer in the parallel Salam. Shariah rules require these two Salam contracts to be completely independent of each other. Parallel Salam is allowed with a third party only.

Participants   Those individuals who contribute to the Takaful fund, as a gift or donation under the Tabarru mechanism.

Performance risk   In the parallel Istisna contract the bank is exposed to the risk of the manufacturer not delivering the asset in the required specification, quality and quantity and at the designated time and price. To manage the manufacturer's performance risk, banks may demand performance bonds and warranties after delivery.

Profit and loss sharing   A major difference of the Islamic bank from its conventional counterpart is that instead of conducting financial intermediation with the interest-based method, it shares in the profit and loss of the projects it finances and then shares its own profit and loss with the depositors.

Profit equalization reserve   The allocation for this reserve from the Mudaraba profit is made before allocating any amount to the Mudarib. This reserve aims to maintain the level of return for investment account holders.

Purification of income distribution   Some scholars do not allow investment in stocks that involves any kind of conventional debt, while others allow such stocks with the condition that the income generated needs to be cleansed or purified in proportion to the Shariah-non-compliant activities. As such, any income that is from interest or any other non-compliant source is donated to charity.

Qard Hasan   This is a benevolent loan, where the borrower is required to return only the amount of the original loan.

Qiyas   The fourth most important source of the Shariah. Qiyas involves analogical deductions. It is the process by which any original ruling, or an existing case decision, is applied to a new matter with similar characteristics on the basis that the new case has the same effective cause as the former.

Quran   The holy book of the Muslim faith. For the Muslim population it supersedes all scientific methods or human decisions.

Rahn   The security or collateral provided as a pledge or mortgage on an asset owned by the borrower. If the borrower is unable to repay, the financier can sell the asset and recover their claims from the funds generated, though if any surplus remains from the sale value it will be returned to the borrower.

Ras al Maal The payment for the asset in a Salam contract.

Regulatory environment Ideally, the Islamic financial institutions operate best in a fully Shariah-compliant regulatory environment. Only countries like Iran and Sudan fall in this category, while most Muslim-majority countries operate under the dual banking system where mainly the conventional regulatory regime is in operation, but the Islamic financial institutions and their unique features are understood and the Shariah implications are tailored into the special regulations applying to these institutions. Non-Muslim countries operate under a fully conventional regulatory environment. The interaction between Shariah law and local law and regulations may lead to conflict and confusion, and in pure conventional environments the local regulations may make it difficult to introduce Islamic financial products and services with their unique characteristics.

Reinsurance Insurance for insurance companies. Insurance companies deal with large portfolios of risk and to protect themselves they buy reinsurance from large insurance companies or companies specialized to provide reinsurance only. These companies are basically underwriting the risks of the smaller insurance companies.

Retakaful The Islamic alternative to reinsurance. In case of Retakaful, the individual Takaful operators are the participants, who contribute their agreed premiums to a common pooled underwriting fund to mutually protect each other. The operator of this underwriting fund is the Retakaful company and all Retakaful contracts are required to be Shariah compliant and devoid of Riba, Gharar and Maysir.

Riba In Islam, money is only a medium of exchange and not a commodity which can earn on its own. Riba or usury or interest is the premium paid by the borrower to the lender, it means the increase, addition, expansion or growth in the money that is owed.

Ribawi Money-like items which can be exchanged only at spot, like gold and silver.

Sadaqah Every Muslim has specified economic obligations towards society, of which Sadaqah is voluntary charity.

Salam In case of a Salam contract, the payment is made fully in advance at the time of the contract and the delivery of the asset is deferred to a specific time in the future. A Salam contract is like a forward sale contract in conventional finance, with advance payment and deferred delivery.

Salam Sukuk Based on the Salam mode of financing where the buyer pays the full price of the asset in advance on spot; usually the buyer gets a discount on the price for paying in advance. The seller would deliver at a mutually agreed future date. The contract is like a conventional forward contract. The majority of Salam Sukuks are short term.

Sarf A form of exchange where one currency is sold for an equivalent amount of another currency. Here, one currency is the asset while the other is the payment. Shariah requires the currencies to be exchanged on spot. Similarly, metals originally used as currency (like gold, silver, etc.) can only be exchanged with each other on spot also. Future trading of either currency or these metals is not permitted by Shariah law.

Savings accounts Islamic banks accept savings account funds based on Wadia (safekeeping), Wakala (agency), Mudaraba (trust financing) or Musharaka (equity financing). Banks use the funds in these accounts to finance borrowers and entrepreneurs. These accounts bear some risk and provide the depositors with some profit from the profit earned by the bank at a pre-agreed ratio.

Scarcity of resources When wants are unlimited while resources are limited, there is a scarcity of resources.

Seller's default The supplier manufacturer in the Salam contract may not deliver on the specified date and at the specified place, and this could force the bank to purchase from the market to deliver to its client in the parallel Salam contract.

Shariah compliance risk   Islamic bank operations need to follow the principles of Islamic economics and Shariah law. Any Shariah non-compliance can affect their reputation and lower the loyalty of their customers.

Shariah-compliant stocks   Equity or shares in a company is not debt and hence does not have the complication of Riba. Yet the shares of all companies are not acceptable as Shariah compliant. It is very difficult to find companies that are completely free from Shariah-non-compliant financial transactions. To deal with this significant investment challenge, the Shariah scholars and the international Islamic regulatory and standard setting bodies have developed more flexible procedures to be able to identify some companies that can be considered within reasonable Shariah compliance. This process is called the Shariah screening process for stock selection and involves a set of guidelines that are provided to select such companies and identify Shariah-compliant stocks.

Shariah governance   Corporate governance is a set of rules, laws, policies and processes by which a corporation is managed to safeguard the best interests of its stakeholders, including shareholders, creditors, customers, employees and government. The Shariah Supervisory Board is responsible for implementing Shariah governance in an Islamic financial institution.

Shariah law   Also called the Islamic law, dictates specific dos and don'ts related to all aspects of a Muslim's life, including commercial and financial transactions.

Shariah scholars or Fuqaha or Ulema   Those who are knowledgeable in Fiqh.

Shariah screening process   Not all company shares are Shariah compliant. It is very difficult to find companies that are completely free from Shariah-non-compliant financial transactions. To deal with this significant investment challenge, the Shariah scholars and the international Islamic regulatory and standard setting bodies have developed more flexible procedures to be able to identify some companies that can be considered within reasonable Shariah compliance. This process is called the Shariah screening process for stock selection.

Shariah Supervisory Board   The Shariah Supervisory Board is a body set up with a group of Islamic Shariah scholars or jurists to assist the Islamic financial institutions to operate in accordance with Shariah law.

Shirkah   Contracts of partnership.

Social responsibilities of Islamic finance   Shariah principles require Islamic banks to balance their profit motivation with social objectives; it is considered unjust if they are unable to provide sufficient returns to depositors and shareholders who have entrusted them with their money on the one hand, but on the other hand they should not make excessive profits at the expense of their customers or by neglecting their social responsibility.

Social welfare   All activities conducted by governments, other organizations or individuals to benefit society and communities within society.

Sources of funds   The sources of funds for an Islamic bank are the cash inflows and comprise the liability side of the bank. Islamic banks' liabilities or common sources of funds include current, savings and investment accounts.

Special purpose vehicle   The body set up to issue Sukuk certificates to investors and collect funds from them and distribute income to the Sukuk holders. The SPV ceases to exist after the Sukuk contract ends.

Sukuk   An Islamic alternative to a conventional bond. The AAOIFI defines Sukuks as certificates of equal value representing undivided ownership shares in tangible assets, usufructs, services, specific projects or a special investment activity.

Taawun   The mutual assistance, responsibility and protection of Takaful participants towards each other against risks from uncertain events. This is similar to conventional cooperative or mutual insurance, where participants pool their funds together to indemnify each other and share each other's risks. Policyholders or participants mutually guarantee each other; as a result, each of them is both the insured (protected against unforeseen losses) and the insurer (providing protection to others participating in the fund).

Tabarru In Takaful the participants do not just pay a premium to purchase the risk protection against any uncertain risk, rather they contribute their premium as a donation or gift into the Takaful fund. Such a donation of the premium is aimed not only at providing loss protection for the participant but for others too in the group, thus including cooperative risk protection, social responsibility and caring for others in the process.

Takaful A form of mutual help – the insured jointly guarantee each other.

Takaful model In the case of a Takaful operator, its income and profit or loss scenario can be different depending on its operational structure.

Takaful operator A registered and licensed body or corporation responsible for managing the operations of the Takaful fund on behalf of the participants.

Temporary Musharaka This kind of Musharaka involves a single transaction or short-term financing, which concludes within one year. The Musharaka could be renewed each year if required. Common uses of temporary Musharaka are working capital financing.

Tradable Sukuk Those Sukuks that represent ownership in tangible assets or in an enterprise that can be bought or sold at the Islamic capital market – for example Ijara, Mudaraba and Musharaka Sukuks.

Two-tier Mudaraba In Islamic financial intermediation, the Islamic bank executes a Mudaraba contract with the depositors, where the depositors are the Rab al Maal while the bank acts as Mudarib or entrepreneur. On the other hand, the Islamic bank enters a second Mudaraba contract with the users of the funds, the borrowers or entrepreneurs. In this Mudaraba the bank acts as the Rab al Maal and the fund user is the Mudarib. This is called the two-tier Mudaraba of Islamic financial intermediation.

Two-windows model This model is almost the same as the two-tier Mudaraba, the only difference being that it has a reserve requirement. The model divides the liability side of the bank balance sheet into two windows, one for demand deposits requiring 100% reserve and the other for investment deposits which have no reserve requirement.

Ujrah This is the consideration or rent that the lessee pays to the lessor for the right to use and derive benefit from an object owned by the lessor.

Underwriting deficit This is the shortfall of the contributions made by the participants to meet the deductions of all claims and all expenses and management fees for the Takaful operator.

Underwriting surplus This is the excess that remains from the contributions made by the participants after the deductions of all claims and all expenses and management fees for the Takaful operator.

Usufruct The right to the usefulness of an asset owned by someone else.

Utmost good faith In case of all forms of insurance, all relevant information related to the uncertain risky event and its relationship to the insured is best known to the insured rather than the Takaful operator, and due to this imbalance in available information the parties need to have trust in each other. By law the Takaful operator accepts the information from the insured on good faith and it is the responsibility of the insured to be truthful and if they are not, all liability arising from the risky event is theirs.

Wad A unilateral promise, made by one party to another, binding only on the promisor not on the promisee. According to the Islamic Fiqh Academy, promises in commercial transactions are binding even if they are one-sided and if they cause the promisee to incur some liabilities.

Wadia Islamic banks accept the funds in demand deposits as Wadia (deposit), which involves safekeeping. Legally, Wadia authorizes the Islamic bank to keep the funds of the customer in their safe custody on explicit or implicit terms. In contemporary Islamic banking, the Wadia contract is combined with the contract of guarantee or Dhaman, to provide the same functionality as conventional current and savings accounts. In this case, the bank provides a guarantee of the deposited amount.

Wakala These are agency contracts for a specific work to be done by one party on behalf of another. Examples of Wakala contracts include brokerage services, funds management, insurance underwriting, etc.

Wakala model Based on the Wakala or agency concept. The participants are the principal and the Takaful operator acts as agent or Wakeel. The Takaful operator earns an agency fee for their services and may also earn an incentive in the form of a performance fee.

Waqf This is a charitable endowment under Shariah law and involves donating an asset for the common good of Muslim society or for religious purposes, with no intention of reclaiming the asset.

Waqf model A special Takaful model developed for non-profit Takaful activities for the government or other non-profit organizations. The Takaful fund's surplus is neither distributed to the participants nor taken by the Takaful operator; instead, it is held in the fund for social welfare activities benefiting the community.

Wassiyyat The Will by which a person dictates how to distribute their assets amongst their beneficiaries.

Wujuh In this type of Musharaka one or more of the partners do not contribute financially but they contribute their goodwill, brand name or track record. Wujuh Musharaka is very suitable for financing franchising projects.

Zakat Every Muslim has specified economic obligations towards society, of which Zakat is compulsory charity imposed on Muslims who own above a certain minimum level of wealth.

References

AAOIFI (2008). *Shariah Standards for Islamic Financial Institutions*. Bahrain: AAOIFI.

Abdullah, A. A., Sidek, R. & Adnan, A. A. (2012). Perception of non-Muslim customers towards Islamic banks in Malaysia. *International Journal of Business and Social Science*, 3(11), 151–163.

Abdul-Rahman, Y. (2014). *The Art of RF (Riba-Free) Islamic Banking and Finance: Tools and Techniques for Community-Based Banking*. Hoboken, NJ: Wiley.

Abou-Youssef, M., Kortam, W., Aish, E. A. & El-Bassiouny, N. (2012). An exploratory investigation of the marketing practices conducted by Islamic banks in Egypt. *African Journal of Business and Economic Research*, 7(1), 47–63.

Aggarwal, R. K. & Yousef, T. (2000). Islamic banks and investment financing. *Journal of Money, Credit and Banking*, 32(1), 93–120.

Ahmad, K. (2000). Islamic finance and banking: The challenge and prospects. *Review of Islamic Economics*, 9, 57–82.

Ahmad, K., Rustam, G. A. & Dent, M. M. (2011). Brand preference in Islamic banking. *Journal of Islamic Marketing*, 2(1), 74–82.

Ahmad, Z. (1994). Islamic banking: State of the art. *Islamic Economic Studies*, 1(2), 1–34.

Ahmed, A. (2010). Global financial crisis: An Islamic finance perspective. *International Journal of Islamic and Middle Eastern Finance and Management*, 3(4), 306–320.

Al-Omar, F. & Abdel-Haq, M. (1996). *Islamic Banking: Theory, Practice, and Challenges*. London: Zed Books.

Al-Salem, F. (2008). The size and scope of the Islamic finance industry: An analysis. *International Journal of Management*, 25(1), 124–130.

Alserhan, B. A. (2010). Islamic branding: A conceptualization of related terms. *Journal of Brand Management*, 18(1), 34–49.

Amin, H., Hamid, M. R. A., Lada, S. & Baba, R. (2009). Cluster analysis for bank customers' selection of Islamic mortgages in Eastern Malaysia: An empirical investigation. *International Journal of Islamic and Middle Eastern Finance and Management*, 2(3), 213–234.

Ariss, R. T. (2010). Competitive conditions in Islamic and conventional banking: A global perspective. *Review of Financial Economics*, 19(3), 101–108.

Askari, H., Iqbal, Z. & Mirakhor, Z. (2008). *New Issues in Islamic Finance and Economics: Progress and Challenges*. Hoboken, NJ: Wiley.

Askari, H., Iqbal, Z. & Mirakhor, Z. (2015). *Introduction to Islamic Economics: Theory and Application*. Singapore: Wiley.

Asutay, M. (2007). A political economy approach to Islamic economics: Systemic understanding for an alternative economic system. *Kyoto Bulletin of Islamic Area Studies*, 1(2), 3–18.

Balz, K. (2007). Islamic finance for European Muslims: The diversity management of Shariah-compliant transactions. *Chicago Journal of International Law*, 7(2), 551–567.

Benaissa, N.-E., Nordin, L. & Stockmeier, H.-M. (2003). Banking in the Gulf states. *McKinsey Quarterly*, 2, 99–104.

Bianchi, R. R. (2007). The revolution in Islamic finance. *Chicago Journal of International Law*, 7(2), 569–580.

Bley, J. & Kuehn, K. (2004). Conventional versus Islamic finance: Student knowledge and perception in the United Arab Emirates. *International Journal of Islamic Financial Services*, 5(4), 17–30.

Chapra, M. U. (2007). The case against interest: Is it compelling? *Thunderbird International Business Review*, 49(2), 161–186.

Choudhury, M. A. & Hussain, M. M. (2005). A paradigm of Islamic money and banking. *International Journal of Social Economics*, 32(3), 203–217.

CIA World Factbook (2012). *CIA World Factbook*. Washington, D.C.: CIA.

CISI (2015). *Fundamentals of Islamic Banking and Finance*, 1st edn. London: Chartered Institute for Securities & Investment.

Damirchi, G. V. & Shafai, J. (2011). A guideline to Islamic marketing mix. *Interdisciplinary Journal of Contemporary Research Business*, 3(3), 1339–1347.

Dar, H. A. & Presley, J. R. (1999). Islamic finance: A Western perspective. *International Journal of Islamic Financial Services*, 1(1), 3–11.

Dar, H. A. & Presley, J. R. (2000). Lack of profit loss sharing in Islamic banking: Management and control imbalances. *International Journal of Islamic Financial Services*, 2(2), 3–18.

Duran, J.-J. & Garcia-Lopez, M.-J. (2012). The internationalization of Islamic banking and finance: The co-evolution of institutional changes and financial services integration. *International Journal of Business and Management*, 7(13), 49–74.

Dusuki, A. W. (2008). Understanding the objectives of Islamic banking: A survey of stakeholders' perspectives. *International Journal of Islamic and Middle Eastern Finance and Management*, 1(2), 132–148.

Dusuki, A. W. & Abdullah, N. I. (2007). Why do Malaysian customers patronise Islamic banks? *International Journal of Bank Marketing*, 25(3), 142–160.

Dusuki, A. W. & Abozaid, A. (2007). A critical appraisal on the challenges of realizing Maqasid Al-Shariaah in Islamic banking and finance. *International Journal of Economics, Management and Accounting*, 15(2), 143–165.

El-Gamal, M. A. (2006). *Islamic Finance: Law, Economics and Practice*. Cambridge: Cambridge University Press.

Estiri, M., Hosseini, F., Yazdani, H. & Nejad, H. J. (2011). Determinants of customer satisfaction in Islamic banking: Evidence from Iran. *International Journal of Islamic and Middle Eastern Finance and Management*, 4(4), 295–307.

Finance Forward (2016). *World Takaful Report*. Retrieved from www.takafulprimer.com/main/downloads/ms_5860.pdf [accessed 5 September 2017].

Fisher, O. C. & Taylor, D. (2000). *Prospects for the Evolution of Takaful in the 21st Century*. Proceedings of the Fifth Harvard University Forum on Islamic Finance: Dynamics and Development, Cambridge, MA. Center for Middle Eastern Studies, Harvard University, pp. 237–254.

Ginena, K. & Hamid, A. (2015). *Foundations of Shariah Governance of Islamic Banks*. Chichester: Wiley.

Global Takaful Report (2017). *Market Trends in Family and General Takaful*. Milliman Research Report, July.

Gupta, A. (2009). A talk about the Islamic banking movement in India. *Pranjana: The Journal of Management Awareness*, 12(1), 40–50.

Haron, S. & Ahmad, N. (2000). The effects of conventional interest rates and rate of profit on funds deposited with Islamic banking system in Malaysia. *International Journal of Islamic Financial Services*, 1(4), 1–7.

Hasan, M. & Dridi, J. (2010). The effects of the global crisis on Islamic and conventional banks: A comparative study. International Monetary Fund Working Paper No. 10/201, pp. 1–46.

Hasan, Z. (2005). Islamic banking at the crossroads: Theory versus practice. MPRA Paper No. 2821. Retrieved from mpra.ub.uni-muenchen.de/2821/ [posted 19 April 2007].

Hasan, Z. (2014). *Islamic Banking and Finance: An Integrative Approach*. Selangor Darul Ehsan (Malaysia): Oxford University Press.

Hassan, A., Chachi, A. & Latiff, S. A. (2008). Islamic marketing ethics and its impact on customer satisfaction in the Islamic banking industry. *JKAU: Islamic Economics*, 21(1), 23–40.

Hassan, M. K. (1999). Islamic banking in theory and practice: The experience of Bangladesh. *Managerial Finance*, 25(5), 60–113.

Hassan, M. K., Kayed, R. N. & Oseni, U. A. (2013). *Introduction to Islamic Banking & Finance: Principles and Practice*. Harlow: Pearson Educational.

Iqbal, Z. & Mirakhor, A. (1999). Progress and challenges of Islamic banking. *Thunderbird International Business Review*, 41(4/5), 381–405.

Islamic Fiqh Academy (1988). Islamic Fiqh Academy of the OIC in its fourth session in 1988.

Karasik, T., Wehrey, F. & Strom, S. (2007). Islamic finance in a global context: Opportunities and challenges. *Chicago Journal of International Law*, 7(2), 379–396.

Kayed, R. N. (2012). The entrepreneurial role of profit-and-loss sharing modes of finance: Theory and practice. *International Journal of Islamic and Middle Eastern Finance and Management*, 5(3), 203–228.

Kerr, S. (2007). DIFC raises $1.25bn via sukuk. *Financial Times*, June 8th.

Kettel, B. (2010). *Frequently Asked Questions in Islamic Finance*. Chichester: Wiley.

Kettel, B. (2011). *Introduction to Islamic Banking and Finance*. Chichester: Wiley.

Khan, A. (2004). Is Islamic banking truly Islamic or is it just cosmetically enhanced conventional banking? *Islamica Magazine*, Summer/Fall.

Khan, M. M. & Bhatti, M. I. (2008). Development in Islamic banking: A financial risk-allocation approach. *Journal of Risk Finance*, 9(1), 40–51.

Kharbari, Y., Naser, K. & Shahin, Z. (2004). Problems and challenges facing the Islamic banking system in the West: The case of the UK. *Thunderbird International Business Review*, 46(5), 521–543.

Klingmuller, E. (1969). The concept and development of insurance in Islamic countries. *Islamic Culture*, XL111, 27–38.

Kuran, T. (2004). *Islam and Mammon: The Economic Predicaments of Islamism*. Princeton, NJ: Princeton University Press.

Loo, M. (2010). Attitudes and perceptions towards Islamic banking among Muslims and non-Muslims in Malaysia: Implications for marketing to baby boomers and X-generation. *International Journal of Arts and Sciences*, 3(13), 453–485.

Marinov, M. (2010). Marketing in the emerging markets of Islamic countries. *Journal of Islamic Marketing*, 1(1), 81–83.

Mishkin, F. S. (2001). *The Economics of Money, Banking, Financial Markets*, 6th edn. Reading, MA: Addison-Wesley.

Naser, K. & Moutinho, L. (1997). Strategic marketing management: The case of Islamic banks. *International Journal of Bank Marketing*, 15(6), 187–203.

Natt, A., Al Habshi, S. O. & Zainal, M.-P. (2009). A proposed framework for human capital development in the Islamic financial services industry. *Journal of Knowledge Economy & Knowledge Management*, 1, 9–26.

Nienhaus, V. (1986). Islamic economics, finance and banking: Theory and practice. *Journal of Islamic Banking and Finance*, 3(2), 36–54.

OPEC (2014). The 165th Meeting of the Conference of the Organization of the Petroleum Exporting Countries (OPEC) convened in Vienna, Austria, June 11th.

O'Sullivan, A. (2009). Islamic banking: An asset of promise? *OECD Observer*, April, 272.

Pew Research Center (2011). *The Future of the Global Muslim Population*. Retrieved from www.pewforum.org/2011/01/27/the-future-of-the-global-muslim-population/ [accessed 27 January 2017].

Pew Research Institute (2017). www.thoughtco.com/worlds-muslim-population-2004480 [accessed 10 December 2017].

PriceWaterhouseCooper (2017). *Middle East, Financial Services, 2017*. Retrieved from www.pwc.com/m1/en/industries/islamic_finance.html [accessed 10 December 2017].

Rammal, H. G. (2010). Islamic finance: Challenges and opportunities. *Journal of Financial Services Marketing*, 15(3), 189–190.

Rehman, A. A. & Masood, O. (2012). Why do customers patronize Islamic banks? A case study of Pakistan. *Qualitative Research in Financial Markets*, 4(2/3), 130–141.

PWC REIT Report (2017). *Compare and Contrast: Worldwide Real Estate Investment Trust (REIT) Regimes*. Retrieved from www.pwc.com/gx/en/asset-management/assets/pdf/worldwide-reit-regimes-2017.pdf [accessed 10 October 2017].

Rosly, S. A. & Bakar, M. A. A. (2003). Performance of Islamic and mainstream banks in Malaysia. *International Journal of Social Economics*, 30(12), 1249–1265.

Rustam, S., Bibi, S., Zaman, K., Rustam, A. & Haq, Z.-U. (2011). Perceptions of corporate customers towards Islamic banking products and services in Pakistan. *Romanian Economic Journal*, 14(41), 107–123.

Saeed, M., Ahmed, Z. U. & Mukhtar, S.-M. (2001). International marketing ethics from an Islamic perspective: A value maximization approach. *Journal of Business Ethics*, 32(2), 127–142.

Satkunasegaran, E. (2003). Corporate governance and the protection of customers of Islamic banks. Paper presented at International Islamic Banking Conference: From Money Lenders to Bankers: Evolution of Islamic Banking in Relation to Judeo-Christian and Oriental Banking Traditions, Prato, Italy, 9–10 September 2003.

Schoon, N. (2016). *Modern Islamic banking: Products and Processes in Practice*. Chichester: Wiley.

Shah, S. F., Raza, M. W. & Khurshid, M. R. (2012). Islamic banking controversies and challenges. *Interdisciplinary Journal of Contemporary Research in Business*, 3(10), 1018–1026.

Shamma, H. M. & Maher, Y. (2012). Islamic marketing in Egypt: Evolution and implications. *African Journal of Business and Economic Research*, 7(1), 9–23.

Siddiqi, M. N. (2006). Islamic banking and finance in theory and practice: A survey of state of the art. *Islamic Economic Studies*, 13(2), 1–48.

Siddiqi, M. N. (2010). *History of Islamic Economic Thought*. Handbook of Islamic Economics, Vol. 1. Jeddah: Islamic Research and Training Institute.

Smith, A. (1776). *An Inquiry into the Nature and Causes of the Wealth of Nations*. London: W. Strahan and T. Cadell.

Smith, K. A. (2006). From petrodollars to Islamic dollars: The strategic construction of Islamic banking in the Arab Gulf (Unpublished doctoral dissertation). Harvard University, Cambridge, MA.

Srairi, S. A. (2009). Productivity growth in GCC banking industry: Conventional versus Islamic banks. *Journal of Knowledge Globalization*, 4(2), 59–90.

State Bank of Pakistan (2008). Annual Report. Retrieved from www.sbp.org.pk/reports/annual/ [accessed 10 October 2017].

Tahir, M. & Umar, M. (2008). Marketing strategy for Islamic banking sector in Pakistan (Unpublished Master's thesis). Blekinge Institute of Technology, School of Management, Ronneby, Sweden.

Tahir, S. (2009). Islamic finance: Undergraduate education. *Islamic Economic Studies*, 16(1&2), 1–29.

The Banker (2010). Top 500 Islamic institutions. Retrieved from www.thebanker.com/Markets/Islamic-Finance/Top-500-Islamic-Financial-Institutions2 [posted 24 November 2010].

Thomson Reuters (2017). Retrieved from www.thomsonreuters.com/en/press-releases/2015/05/thomson-reuters-releases-global-islamic-asset-management-outlook-report.html [accessed 15 October].

Usmani, M. T. (1999). *An Introduction to Islamic Finance*. Karachi: Idara Isha'at-e-Diniyat (P) Ltd.

Wilson, R. (1997). Islamic finance and ethical investment. *International Journal of Social Economics*, 24(11), 1325–1342.

World Bank Report (2013). Retrieved from www.cbd.int/financial/mainstream/wb-annual2013.pdf [accessed 10 October 2017].

World Islamic Banking Competitiveness Report (2016). Retrieved from www.ey.com/Publication/vwLUAssets/ey-world-islamic-banking-competitiveness-report-2016/$FILE/ey-world-islamic-banking-competitiveness-report-2016.pdf [accessed 10 December 2017].

Zaher, T. S. & Hassan, M. K. (2001). A comparative literature survey of Islamic finance and banking. *Financial Markets, Institutions & Instruments*, 10(4), 155–199.

Index